THE COMPLETE BOOK OF
DUPLICATE BRIDGE

by
NORMAN KAY,
SIDNEY SILODOR,
AND FRED KARPIN

Published by
DEVYN PRESS, INC.
Louisville, Kentucky

All score slips reprinted by permission of the
American Contract Bridge League.

Part of pages 9, 10, 11, 12 and 13
have been reprinted by permission of
Ernest W. Rovere.

Reprinted 1993 through special arrangement with
G. P. Putnam's Sons

Revised and updated by Randall Baron

Devyn Press wishes to gratefully acknowledge
the assistance of Sandi Clark, Jane Johnson,
Jim Miller and Jean Wright of the ACBL.

Printed in the United States of America.

Devyn Press, Inc.
3600 Chamberlain Lane, Ste. 230
Louisville, KY 40241

ISBN 0-910791-84-8

Contents

Foreword

BY OSWALD JACOBY
FROM THE 1965 EDITION

I don't know exactly when Sidney Silodor picked Norman Kay to be his regular partner or even if he picked him. Maybe they just gravitated together. I do know that the partnership was so good that when the committee to choose the three pairs that were to play for America in the 1961 World's Championships met, we selected Sidney and Norman and then went on to argue about the other two.

It was about that time that Sidney and Norman started to work on a complete book on duplicate bidding and tactics. The work was interrupted by Sidney's illness and untimely death but Norman, who I think looked on Sidney as a sort of older brother, wanted to complete the book more as a memorial to Sidney than anything else.

As the work progressed Norman wanted to bring the material down to where it would be enjoyed by players of all classes and he asked Fred Karpin to become a third author.

Fred is a life master and successful tournament player but primarily he is a teacher and writer who knows how to cover the entire spectrum so that this book will be interesting to top experts while easily understandable to beginners.

Sidney Silodor first appeared in tournament play around 1933 or 1934 and quickly established himself as one of the world's greatest players. We became good friends almost immediately and our friendship increased as the years went by although we never played as partners.

Sidney was just a couple of years younger than I was. On the other hand Norman Kay, who is a trifle older than my son Jim, started his tournament career around 1951. He also has been an opponent rather than a partner, although we did play together in one regional championship. It did not take Norman long to establish himself as a player of world standing. Currently Norman stands number two on the master point list. If Sidney were still alive, he would be number two and Norman number three.

I have no idea how many times I played against Sidney and Norman over the years. I do know that there was never the slightest unpleasantness between us and that, win, lose or draw, they were the toughest and nicest of opponents.

I also have had the pleasure of playing against Fred Karpin on many occasions. I don't remember him as quite as tough an opponent but he was always just as nice in addition to being tough enough so that I also knew I had been in battle.

Their book covers duplicate bidding from soup to nuts. It discusses many subjects such as part-score tactics that other authors have shied away from.

It presents practically every important modern convention and shows both how to play it and how to play against it.

The book is a must for anyone who is, or wants to be, a really successful tournament player. It is practically a must for anyone who plays duplicate and is well worth the time of anyone who only plays rubber bridge.

Introduction

Rubber bridge and duplicate bridge are not totally different games with separate laws and regulations, although the rules necessarily differ in a few particulars. Perhaps the major difference is that in duplicate bridge you play under conditions where it is completely immaterial whether you hold good or bad cards, since the holder of good cards and the holder of bad cards has an equal chance to win.

This book is written for two groups of people:

(1) For those who have never played duplicate but who wish to learn the game.

(2) For the ever-increasing number of people who have played duplicate, discovered its fascination, and are now anxious to gain greater knowledge of the special tactical and strategical factors involved.

Part I is concerned mainly with how and where duplicate bridge is played.

Part II is concerned purely with the strategy and tactics of duplicate bidding, with the emphasis on obstructionist and defensive bidding.

Part III deals with the play of the cards in duplicate, from the viewpoints of both declarer and the defenders.

CHAPTER 1

Duplicate Bridge: What, Why, Where, How?

I. What Is Duplicate Bridge?

The basic feature of duplicate bridge (also known as "tournament bridge") is that all competing players in the same position hold the identical cards throughout the duplicate game. Each player also retains the same partner during the entire game (sometimes for better, and sometimes for worse).

The winner is not the player who holds the biggest hands or who accumulates the most points but the one who obtains the best relative result with the cards which he'has at his disposal. For example, let's say that a pair bids a small slam against us and makes it. When this deal is replayed, another pair, holding the identical cards which our opponents held, bids and makes a grand slam against their adversaries (who hold the same cards we held). Quite obviously, we have done better with the same cards than the pair against whom the grand slam was bid and made. And, from the viewpoint of the slam bidders, certainly the pair that bid and made the grand slam did better than the pair who bid and made a small slam.

Obviously, in a duplicate game, a good player will show a greater profit with good cards than the poorer player holding the identical good cards; and a good player holding poor cards will show a smaller loss with bad cards than will a poorer player holding the same bad cards. It's how well you exploit the resources that were bequeathed

1

to you that serves as the criterion as to whether you end up as a winner or a loser. Being dealt good cards—or being born with a silver spoon in your mouth as is often the case in a rubber bridge game—is in itself of no significance whatsoever. The payoff is based on "to each according to his ability."

And so it might be that during an entire session of play, you and your partner hold such miserable cards that you are never able even to bid. You might still emerge as the winner, for you might do better than the other competitors who hold the identical miserable cards you hold.

In summary, a duplicate bridge game is a contest in which each hand is bid and played by four players at one table, after which the very same hand is bid and played by different sets of four players at other tables. The conditions of play are duplicated exactly at each table: the same cards in each hand, the same dealer, the same vulnerability. Your score does not depend on the luck of the deal; it is compared only with the scores made by players who hold the identical cards, and under the identical conditions.

II. Why Play Duplicate?

One reason stands head and shoulders above all others: the frequent playing of duplicate bridge is probably the best method of finding out what is wrong with your game, and of elevating your standard of bridge living. In a rubber bridge game all players make mistakes which tend to go by unnoticed or overlooked. If the identical types of errors occur in duplicate, they are exposed by comparison with the scores made by the other competitors playing the same hands, and they stand out in bold relief for you to discover.

For example, you are playing a hand at four hearts in a rubber bridge game. You go down a trick. As the cards are being dealt out for the next hand, you are trying to convince your partner that the four heart contract was unmakable; or, perhaps, you take the initiative and tell partner that he bid too much, that he should have left you in a two heart or three heart contract. But you do not sound convincing to either your partner or to yourself (for, frankly, you really haven't analyzed the deal, and are frantically seeking some justification for your failure). The next hand has, by now, been dealt out. You forget the "old world" and begin to concentrate on the challenge of the "new world." You never do find out what the cause of your failure was: overambitious bidding, bad play—or both?

If you went down at the four heart contract in a duplicate game, it is quite a simple matter in most cases to discover the reason for your defeat. If eleven other teams, holding your identical cards, arrived at the same four heart contract, and each of them fulfilled that contract, it is more than probable that the fault lay in the way you played the hand.

Quite naturally and normally, when a player's score suffers by such comparison, he—even as you and I—seeks to know the reason. By discussing the deal with the others who fulfilled the contract, you are able to find out what you did that was wrong.

Let's take another illustration. Your opponents purchase the contract for two hearts. You defeat them by one trick, and are pleased with the result. However, when all the scores have been tabulated, you observe that each of the other pairs who held your cards bid and made four spades. You realize that you have not made the best out of your cards, that something was wrong with your bidding.

Duplicate also sharpens your game by encouraging extreme accuracy in bidding and play by paying handsome dividends for achieving the optimum result. In rubber bridge, for example, you might find yourself in a three diamond contract which, if made, will give you game and rubber. What difference, really, whether you make three diamonds or four diamonds? The overtrick is an insignificant trifle. Thus, if you can see that you will easily fulfill your contract, you might tend to get sloppy and not pay strict attention to making the maximum number of tricks. In duplicate, on the other hand, the overtrick can often be worth more than the game itself.

Also, in rubber bridge, a player who bids and makes a couple of slams may often relax, knowing he can coast in a winner. In duplicate bridge, each hand is equally important. You can't relax because things went extremely well on preceding deals. Relaxing comes after, never during, the game. In these circumstances, the quality of one's game is bound to improve from week to week, for he will learn to be serious at all times and to pay close attention to "little things."

A. Duplicate Bridge: Something for All

1. A game is almost always available, afternoon or evening. (The specific details are presented in the section which follows on "Where Is Duplicate Bridge Played?") You need not make in-

numerable phone calls to assemble a game; nor do one or two last-minute "sorry-an-emergency-has-arisen" cancellations leave you feeling frustrated.

2. Anyone can play. Even a novice, having as little as two months of bridge training, is eligible.

3. The rubber-bridge player tends to be clannish. He usually plays in games with players of his own class, which may exclude you. Duplicate represents your opportunity to play against—and learn from—players who are better than you.

4. It is an inexpensive means of recreation. The cost is usually about the price of a movie.

5. Duplicate play lends itself to direct comparison. Since you will usually compete against players of all classifications, you can rate your game and easily measure the progress you are making.

6. The duplicate player learns to exercise care and concentration to a high degree. That, we think, is an asset very much worth having (in life and at the bridge table). The rubber-bridger has no time for trifles such as an overtrick at a slam contract; but an extra trick in duplicate play may well spell the difference between an excellent and a bad result.

7. Duplicate bridge is a contest. As such, it can—and often does —become exciting and exhilarating. You fight and you strive to excel and outwit. Sometimes you succeed; sometimes you fail. It is great fun; and if you become a devotee, it is even more fun— although you can't always tell it from the faces of the participants.

III. Where Is Duplicate Bridge Played?

Over 190,000 people in the United States play duplicate bridge _regularly_. There are thousands of duplicate bridge contests held _each week of the year_. Where are these contests held?

Although many country clubs, YMCA's, YWCA's, fraternal organizations and social clubs include duplicate bridge as a regular part of their social activity, the great majority of duplicate games are managed and run by many thousands of commercial clubs organized for that specific purpose.

Any bridge-playing friend will probably be able to tell you where to find a nearby game. If, however, you are unable to locate a game, drop a line to the American Contract Bridge League, 2990 Airways

Blvd., Memphis, TN 38116. The League will give you prompt assistance, since virtually all duplicate games in the United States are held under its sponsorship and jurisdiction. No matter where you live, a duplicate game will be found for you; and, if worse comes to worst, and no game exists in your area, the A.C.B.L. or Baron Barclay Bridge Supplies (1-800-274-2221) will show you how to set up a game if you have eight or more players.

Since no stakes are permitted in duplicate games, you may wonder why, with no prospects of any material gain looming on the horizon, so many of our citizens flock to these games with unfailing regularity. The following paragraphs should provide the answer.

Duplicate bridge is the only game (out of all the competitive sports) in which *all* contestants are rated competitively on a nationwide basis. This is done by the national organization, the American Contract Bridge League. As soon as a player enters into either national or local competition, his name is placed on a national ranking list; and complete, up-to-date records are kept for the 190,000 members who have participated in the various duplicate tournaments during the past six decades. In these tournaments, there is nothing awarded except the recognition of victory by the award of "master points."* Not only are no stakes permitted, but no betting is allowed either. Except for a small minority (the professionals and semiprofessionals), these duplicate tournaments hold no financial inducement or incentive, either present or future; nor does the fame achieved in winning an event extend beyond the next tournament.

And, so, again, we revert to the question: "Why, then do so many thousands upon thousands of players participate in these duplicate tournaments?"

The best answer can perhaps be found in the eighteenth-century

---

* In the section which follows, the role of the A.C.B.L. is discussed in detail, as is the subject of precisely how master points are awarded. For the moment, "master points" are points that one receives for winning, finishing second, third, etc., in duplicate tournaments. The number of points one receives varies according to a prescribed formula, and depends on the class of tournament: local, sectional, regional, or national. When one has won 300 master points, he is accorded the title of Life Master, bridgedom's equivalent of graduating *summa cum laude* from a university.

writings by Charles Lamb, who, in speaking about his famous whist-playing heroine, Sarah Battle, wrote:

> A clear fire, a clean heart, and the rigor of the game. . . . She loved a thorough-paced partner, a determined enemy. She took and gave no concessions. She hated favors. She never made a revoke, nor passed it over in her adversary without exacting the utmost forfeiture. She fought a good fight, and neither showed you her cards, nor desired to see yours. . . .

IV. What Is the American Contract Bridge League?

The American Contract Bridge League is a nonprofit organization of some 190,000 members, including the most avid and proficient duplicate and tournament players in the United States, Canada, Mexico, various islands in the hemisphere and in military and government posts throughout the world.

Affiliated with the American Contract Bridge League is a growing group of some 4000 clubs, conducting duplicate bridge activities in which a total of about 2,300,000 players take part each year.

Some of the more important functions of the A.C.B.L. are the following:

(1) Collaborates in making the rubber bridge laws for the entire world.

(2) Makes the laws for all duplicate games and tournaments.

(3) Conducts or sanctions bridge championships at all levels: NABC (North American Bridge Championships), Regional, Sectional, Local, and Club—in all some 1000 major tournaments and about 300,000 minor (club) tournaments every year!

(4) Awards master points to the winners and high finishers in all of its tournaments on a basis that provides commensurate awards according to the importance of the event and the degree of success achieved by the individual players.

(5) Records these master points for each of its members individually and grades all players according to their success in tournament play.

(6) Runs special tournaments to select the players who will represent the United States in recognized international competition and makes it possible for these players to take part in world and championship events.

A. MASTER POINTS

As was stated before, all tournament players are ranked according to their success in tournament play. The yardstick used to grade them is the *master point*.

Anybody who wins a League-sanctioned tournament is credited with a number of master points for his victory. A smaller number of points is awarded to those who finish second, third, and so on.

How many points for winning? That depends on the *class* of tournament (national championships get more than regional which in turn get more than sectional, and so on); the *size* of the field (within limits, the more contestants the higher the award); and the *quality* of the field (an event limited to high-ranking players gets a bigger award than an event limited to novices, and so on).

How many people share in the awards? Winners and second-placers always get some kind of master point award. The award may extend to third placers and even farther. This also depends on the class, size and quality of the event.

The exact amount of the award for all sizes and classes of events has been worked out into charts immediately available to the tournament director so that they can be posted on the bulletin boards shortly after the entries for each event are closed.

By way of example, the winners of the most important national championships may win 150 master points each. The same kind of event in the sectional tournament may rate only 15 to 20 points; and in a club event, the award may be only one or two points.

The clubs that are affiliated with the A.C.B.L. (at present, 4000) may issue fractional master points to the winners of their games. They may hold periodic master point games in which the award is somewhat higher. Several clubs may band together to run a special contest periodically for those who have won club contests in the previous month or so; and a master point award may be made for such a "winners' game."

B. THE RECORDS

All master point awards, whether from tournaments or League-sanctioned club games, are reported to the main A.C.B.L. office in Memphis. These awards are credited to the individual master cards of each member and then, at regular monthly intervals, all new awards during the period are reported back to the individual member on a card which confirms his total.

When a player wins his fifth master point, he becomes a Junior Master. He keeps this ranking until he acquires 20 points.

A player becomes a Club Master when he receives his 20th point. He stays with this rank until he has 50 points.

With 50 points (at least five silver won in tournaments of sectional rating), a player becomes a Sectional Master. It is theoretically possible for a player to win 100's of points in club contests, without ever earning points of sectional, regional or national rating—but this sort of thing seldom happens. People who like club duplicates will also usually play in more important tournaments and they will have reasonable success in bigger tournaments.

With his 100th point (at least 15 silver plus 5 red or gold) a player becomes a Regional Master.

With his 200th point (at least 50 pigmented), a player becomes an NABC Master. Many players pass the 200-point mark, but stay at the lower rank for lack of the pigmented points. Red and gold points are awarded in national and most regional events.

Next is the rank of Life Master, attained when a player has earned 300 points, including 25 gold, 25 red or gold and 50 silver. A Life Master is voted in as a Life Master of the league and does not have to pay membership fees. If the Life Master wishes to receive the *Bulletin* and monthly updates, the Life Master must pay a service fee.

There are additional Life Master designations, starting with the Bronze Life Master at 500 master points. The highest A.C.B.L. ranking is the Grand Life Master which requires 10,000 master points and one unlimited North American Championship.

The A.C.B.L. conducts three National Championship Meetings each year: one in spring, one in summer, and one in fall.

The Summer tournament—the oldest and invariably the largest— is usually held the last week of July extending a few days into the following month. Other major events contested are the six-session Life Masters Pairs for the Von Zedtwitz gold cup; the four-session Senior and Advanced Senior Master Pairs; and the Mixed Team Championship, with two pairs, each consisting of one man and one woman, playing together on a team. Also on the program are a national championship event for commercial and industrial teams; another team event for players holding less than 100 master points, and events for which all proceeds go into the A.C.B.L. Charity Fund; the Senior Pairs, for players 55 years of age and older (yes, women *do* play in this event); and side games every morning, afternoon, and evening.

The Fall tournament is usually held during the last week in November. Its principal events include a Team Championship; Life Master Men's Pairs and Women's Pairs; a Mixed Pair event, and a special six-session Pair Championship, limited to top-ranking Life Masters and to players who have finished high in National and Regional Championships during the preceding year.

The Spring tournament, the newest of the three Nationals, started in 1958. In addition to an Open Pair Championship, Men's Team and Women's Team, and Men's and Women's Pair events, it includes the competition for what is probably the most highly prized trophy in American bridge, the Vanderbilt Cup for the Knockout Team Championship. This event, too, confers on its winners and runners-up eligibility to compete for places in the next year's international team.

All three of these National Tournaments include single-session events, side games as they are called, providing opportunity for less experienced players to earn the red and gold points that are the most valuable in qualifying for top master ranking.

V. How Is Duplicate Bridge Played?

The fundamental difference between rubber bridge and duplicate bridge is in the mechanics of the play of the hand. In rubber bridge, when a deal has been played, it is finished and gone forever, never to return. In duplicate bridge, the deal, while being played, is kept with each hand separate and intact, so that after the play of the thirteen tricks has been completed, each player retains precisely the same thirteen cards he held at the outset. Thus, each deal can be replayed in its original form.

This is accomplished through the use of duplicate boards. A duplicate board, shown on the next page, is oblong in shape, and has an arrow pointing lengthwise. One end of the room in which the game is held is designated as "North," and all of the arrows of the boards in play—usually 20 to 32 in number—will point toward that direction. The player at each table at whom the arrow is pointing is designated as the "North" player. His partner is "South." North's left-hand opponent in "East"; and his right-hand opponent is "West." The arrangement is just as the compass says it should be.

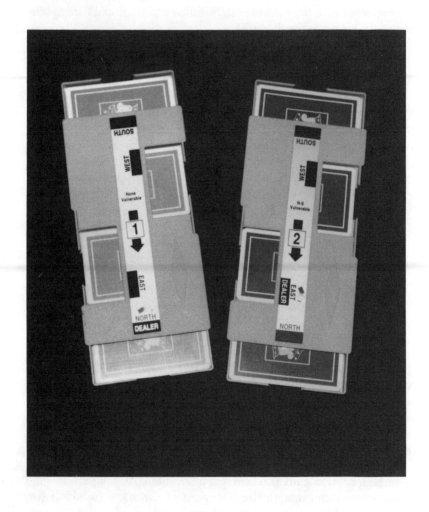

There are four pockets in each board, with thirteen cards in each pocket. These are the four hands, one belonging to North, one to East, one to South, and one to West. On each board the vulnerability is spelled out. On each board the dealer is indicated. All of these things can be observed by a casual glance at the above duplicate board. Each of the boards is also numbered, so that the result of the play on each board can be recorded and scored.

For the moment, it is sufficient to say that the cards are dealt out *just once*, at the beginning of the duplicate game. They are *never* reshuffled, and remain in their original form during the entire course of the tournament.

As in rubber bridge, the bidding begins with the dealer. When the bidding ends, the player to the left of the one who has purchased the contract makes the opening lead, just as in rubber bridge. At this point, the mechanical procedure becomes different.

As the reader knows, in rubber bridge when a trick is being played to, each player contributes a card, placing it in the center of the table when it is his turn to play. Declarer keeps the tricks his side has won, and one of the defenders becomes the custodian for the tricks his side has won.

But in duplicate bridge, to prevent mixing up the tricks so that each player can preserve his precise hand for each of the players at the other tables in the game, the method of playing to each trick takes a completely different form. Each player, when playing to a trick, merely puts his card on the table directly in front of himself. A player *never* puts cards in the center of the table, nor does any card from one hand ever join, or overlap, a card from any of the other three hands. The declarer calls the card which he wishes to play from dummy, and the dummy plays it, placing it face up in front of himself. Each of the other players, in clockwise rotation, does likewise, placing his card face up on the table, for all to see.

When each of the four players has played to the trick, the four exposed cards are then turned over (face down). Each player puts his card face down along that edge of the table which is nearest to him. The side which has won the trick will put its two cards lengthwise, toward each other. The side which has lost the trick will put its two cards widthwise, in front of each other, so that lengthwise their cards will be facing in the direction of the winners of the trick. This can be observed in the diagram which follows.

Let's say that this is your hand in front of you, at the completion of the thirteenth trick:

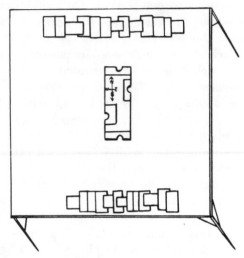

You will note that nine of your cards and nine of your partner's cards are facing lengthwise toward you and your partner. You have won nine tricks; the opponents have won four tricks. The opponents' cards, in front of each of them, will look like this:

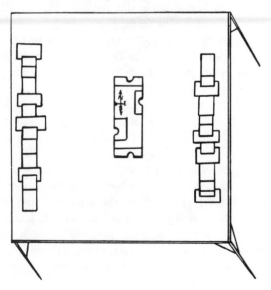

They have won four tricks, and have lost nine.

Thus, after the play of the thirteen tricks has been completed, each player will have his original thirteen cards, face down in front of him. By counting the number of cards pointing toward you and your partner and those pointing toward your opponents, it becomes a routine matter for you to determine the number of tricks you won.

The result of the deal is then posted on the "traveling" score (to be described in the next chapter). Each hand of thirteen cards is then put back into the pocket from which it was extracted originally. The deal is now ready for the next table to play. And when the foursome at the next table finishes playing the deal and recording the result, they too will put the cards back into the duplicate board exactly as the cards were when the board was received by them. It will then be replayed at the third table, the fourth, the fifth, etc.

CHAPTER 2

The Mechanics of Duplicate Bridge

I. The Entrance

Let's start at the very beginning. You have arrived at a duplicate game with your partner. If you happened to have come as a single, unattached individual, without a partner, you will go to the director of the duplicate game and tell him that you need a partner. He will usually be able to find you one whose skills are about the equivalent of yours. However, for your own benefit, it would be advisable if you made an advance date, for it might be that there will be no other unattached individual in the room, in which case you will not be able to participate in the game.

You and your partner will then sit yourselves down at a table of your choosing. Or, it might be that the director will direct you to sit at a specific table, as either a North-South pair or an East-West pair. In the center of each table you will find a card with an arrow pointing to North, with South, East and West spelled out in the proper positions around the table. Each table is numbered, beginning with "one," and running consecutively, i.e., 1, 2, 3, 4, 5, 6, etc. You (and each of the other competing pairs) will be assigned a pair number or will take your number from the position and table at which you are sitting, and you will retain that number during the entire evening. It is most important for you to remember your number, for it must always be entered on the score slip which accompanies each duplicate board. Your number and the number of the pair against whom you are playing are the means by which the director will be able to identify who made what on each deal.

II. The Deal

When all of the contestants are seated and the game is about to begin, the director will put either two or, on rare occasions, three boards at each table. Each board contains a deck of cards, distributed into the four pockets. The cards are then removed from the board by the person who is designated as "Dealer" on the duplicate board.

The designated dealer now shuffles the cards in the normal way, then offers the pack to one of the opponents to cut. He then deals them into four packets of thirteen cards each. One packet is put into the North pocket of the duplicate board, another into the East pocket, the third into the South pocket, and the fourth into the West pocket. When each board at the table has been shuffled and dealt in the above fashion, one should be placed above the other with the arrow on each board pointing in the North direction. You place the boards in numerical order, with the lowest number on top.

You will soon discover that the director has given boards to each table in progressive sets. For example, if two boards have been put at each table, Boards # 1 and # 2 will be at Table 1; Boards # 3 and # 4 will be at Table 2; Boards # 5 and # 6 will be at Table 3, etc. If three boards have been put at each table, Boards 1–3 will be at Table 1; Boards 4–6 will be at Table 2; Boards 7–9 will be at Table 3, etc.

Since the shuffling and dealing has been going on at each table prior to the outset of play, all of the boards to be used for the evening's play will usually have been dealt and shuffled before play for the first round begins. Twenty to thirty-two boards will be in circulation and use in any normal session. You *do not* shuffle or deal again during the evening.

Good bridge manners are worth cultivating. It is an impropriety to shuffle and deal the cards at the start if your opponents are not present. If you feel that you need to save time because your opponents are late in arriving at the table, shuffle the boards in the presence of the duplicate director or some other neutral witness. In actual practice, most pairs await the arrival of their opponents before shuffling.

A. THE DUPLICATE BOARD REVISITED

Let us go back, briefly, for a more intensive look at the duplicate boards which are in front of you. (P. 10.)

Each board is numbered, either on the front or on the back. Over one of the pockets, the word DEALER is clearly spelled out. On Board # 1, North is always the dealer; on Board # 2, East is the dealer; on Board # 3, South is the dealer; on Board # 4, West is the dealer; on # 5, North is the dealer; on # 6, East is the dealer; on Board # 7, South is the dealer; on Board # 8, West is the dealer, etc. Question: Who is the dealer on Board # 25? Answer: North. Each four consecutive boards, beginning with # 1, # 5, # 9, # 13, etc., constitute a series, with each of the four players, starting with North, being dealer one time in clockwise fashion. Hence, Board # 25 has the same dealer as Board # 1, since the first twenty-four boards have covered six series of four boards apiece, and Board # 25 begins the seventh series. So, on Board # 25, North is the dealer; on 26, East; on 27, South; on 28, West; on 29, North again, etc.

On some of the boards, there will be pockets marked VULNERABLE. Usually the vulnerability will be indicated not only by the written word, but by the red paint at the bottom of the pockets marked "vulnerable." The red, of course, indicates "Danger: proceed with caution." As will be discussed later on, the state of being vulnerable is a distinct handicap in a duplicate game, in contrast to rubber bridge where you can't win the rubber unless you are vulnerable.

Sometimes the board will indicate that one partnership is vulnerable; sometimes the other; sometimes neither; sometimes both. The matter of who is vulnerable is fixed and permanent, in the same general manner as the dealer is fixed and permanent according to the number of the board. If the reader is interested in the vulnerability on each board, he can glance at the diagram of the "Private Score" on page 28, where he will note how the vulnerability is related to the dealer in each series of four boards.

III. The Bidding

When the tournament director signals that all may start to play, each player extracts the packet of cards from that pocket of the duplicate board directly facing him. Each player should learn to count his cards *without looking at them* to make sure that they total thirteen. The inveterate tournament player performs this function even while sleeping. We can't recall the last time we took our cards out of a board without counting them. We are suggesting that this become a habit which you should start cultivating immediately. If there is an error in the deal, it can be corrected at once, without harm to anyone. For example, if you count your cards without looking at them, and discover that you have fourteen cards, it is a simple matter for the director to rectify the situation. But if you have looked at the fourteen cards while counting, and after the director has adjusted them properly, you find that your ace of spades has vanished into thin air, you obviously cannot play the deal, for you will know that the hand which originally had twelve cards now has the ace of spades.

You must assume the responsibility of seeing to it that each hand you pick up during the duplicate game has thirteen cards in it. If you play through a board with less or more than thirteen cards in your hand you may be subjected to penalty. Although many players also count their cards after the deal has been played and before they are returned to the proper pocket to insure that the player at the next table will receive the correct number of cards, the players at the next table are nevertheless responsible for counting their cards when they are received.

Quite obviously, if in replacement the cards are put into the wrong pocket, the next table will not be playing the same hand. The North and South hands may be transposed, or the East and West hands may be put into the wrong pockets. The next table may even wind up playing a completely different deal if each side happens to put a hand into the wrong pocket; as, for example, South puts his hand into the West pocket, while West puts his hand into the South pocket.

Improper replacement of the cards will result in much harm and much loss of time, for there will be no basis for comparison of results. Invariably, improper replacement will lead to a penalty against the wrongdoers.

IV. Differences in Rubber and Duplicate Bridge

One side, or both, may be vulnerable even on the first board you play, in contrast to rubber bridge, which starts with neither side vulnerable. There never is a part-score deal even if you have made a part-score on the previous deal. Each hand is an entity unto itself and bears no relationship whatsoever to any other hand either past or present. Neither does the fulfillment of a game contract on the preceding deal affect the vulnerability on the next deal. All sets of duplicate boards in circulation in the United States (and in the rest of the world) have the identical markings, depending on the board number, to indicate dealer and vulnerability. They are worked out to make you dealer one-fourth of the time and vulnerable half the time.

V. The Play of the Cards

When the bidding is terminated and the final contract is established, the player to the left of the declarer makes the opening lead, just as in regular rubber bridge play.

As was mentioned in passing in Chapter 1, we now come to *the distinctive difference* between duplicate and rubber bridge.

The opening lead *is not played to the center of the table.* The leader exposes it (face up), then places it on the table very near to the edge closest to himself. The dummy is then exposed on the table in front of declarer's partner, just as it is in rubber bridge. You will remember that the center of the table is occupied by the board you are now playing, and perhaps by one or two others. These should remain there throughout the play of the cards.

The declarer now takes time to look at the dummy and plan his line of play. When he is ready, he names the card from dummy that he wants to be played. He can reach over to play it himself, but it is not done. It is customary to merely call the card out. The dummy then picks up the card, removing it a bit from the remainder of the thirteen but holding it face up and touching the table for all to see. The card is now considered played.

The partner of the leader next plays to the trick in the same manner. He exposes a card and lays it on the edge of the table nearest to him. Finally, the declarer plays a card in the same way.

We now have four cards, the first complete trick, all exposed on the table. Each card is directly in front of its respective player and not piled with the others in the center of the table, as it would be in rubber bridge. A bit of practice will enable you to see at a glance who won the trick even though the winner does not gather it in. Furthermore, you can always tell who played what to each trick before it is turned over even if your attention has strayed for a moment. You may even examine the trick after it is turned over provided your side has not played to the next trick. Don't make a habit of this last privilege. Pay enough attention so that you won't have to slow up the game by inquiring, "May I look at the last trick, please?" When the trick is completed, the cards are turned face down in front of each player in the manner described in Chapter 1. The player who won the trick will lead to the next trick, as he would in rubber bridge. Each one of the thirteen tricks is played in precisely the same way as outlined above, each player exposing a card to a trick, then turning the card over after everybody has played to the trick and leaving it very near the edge of the table directly in front of himself.

At the end of the play, each player will have his original thirteen cards face down in front of him. The cards will be placed in the customary, universally adopted arrangement employed by all duplicate players except the most careless ones. Look at the diagram:

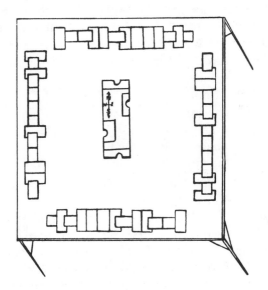

You will note that the thirteen cards which each player possesses overlap each other in an organized arrangement. You will also note that each card in each set of thirteen is facing in the same direction as each card in every other set of thirteen. The card played to the first trick is at the extreme left of each player, with each successive trick overlapping toward the right, thereby enabling all of the players to identify the card played to any specific trick. When your side wins a trick, you place your card *lengthwise* pointing toward you and your partner; when the opponents win a trick, you place your card *widthwise*, facing toward each of the oponents.

A glance at the above diagram will show that North and South have won eight tricks and lost five. Each player has eight cards facing lengthwise toward North and South; each player has five cards which are facing lengthwise toward East and West. Each player at the table agrees on which tricks each side has won and lost on this deal. You can see that this arrangement makes it easy to settle any dispute. You are able, in examination, to expose any one particular trick or even go over the play in its entirety, trick by trick, without disturbing the arrangement of the original thirteen cards.

There are players who keep their winning tricks piled together on one side, and losing tricks on the other. There are also players who keep no record at all. This can be costly to both groups in some circumstances. If you do not conform to the prescribed way of keeping your cards, no harm will come to you if no dispute arises. When, however, one does arise, then the director will tend to rule against you because you made it impossible to reconstruct the trick-by-trick order of play with certainty.

The duplicate board is placed in the center of the table. This serves as a reminder to all of the players not to play their cards in the center of the table. It also enables one to tell at a glance who was the dealer and who was vulnerable. That may, when related to the bidding, have a significant effect on your present or subsequent play. But there is one reason which is more important than any other for keeping the current board on the table: if you remove the board you may inadvertently turn the arrow in the opposite direction when replacing it. North's cards will then go into South's pocket, and South's cards will go into North's pocket. Similarly, East and West's cards will go into the wrong pockets. This will, of course, either spoil the entire game, or disrupt it.

You are not obliged to keep any board, except the one which is being played, on the table. However, as you play, you will discover that one, two, or three boards will not obstruct your vision. If there are more than that, remove them from the table.

We have now reached the point where one board has been bid and played and the cards have been returned to the duplicate board. You have achieved a result. Obviously, you and your opponents cannot carry the score in your head. You may be able to do it for one or two boards, but a lapse of memory would surely develop if you tried to remember twenty or more individual results for three hours. There is, quite naturally, an established method whereby each table's result is registered immediately following the play of each hand. Let us examine this method.

VI. The Traveling Score

Accompanying each duplicate board is a folded slip of paper carefully designed for the purpose which it fulfills, namely entering, and thereby registering, the score. It is called a traveling score slip.

Although each slip is folded inward to conceal the results that have previously been recorded when the board was played, it is easily identified from the outside because a number has been written on the outside which corresponds exactly with the number of the board in which it travels. Under no circumstances is the slip to be opened and your score recorded until *after you have played the deal*. If you open it before, you will know what the final contract and the result were at the other tables, giving you knowledge that will serve as an illegal guide to your bidding of the hand.

If the number on the outside of the slip and the number of the duplicate board are not the same, do not open the slip. In this case some error has been made and opening the slip may enable you to see a score which you are not yet entitled to see, since you might not have played that board. For example, you might be playing Board # 3, and the number on the accompanying traveling slip is numbered Board # 4. Obviously you will have an unfair advantage if you observe the results on Board # 4, which you have not as yet played. You can appreciate the importance, in the latter situation, of returning the traveling slip, unopened, to the specific board in which it belongs.

In most duplicate games, the movement is designed so that at the completion of a round of play, the sets of boards in play will be moved to the adjacent lower-numbered table (from Table 8 to Table 7, from Table 7 to Table 6, from Table 5 to Table 4, etc.), while the East–West players will move to the adjacent higher-numbered table (from Table 1 to Table 2, from Table 2 to Table 3, etc.).

As was mentioned earlier, at the outset of play each pair is given a pair number, which is retained during the entire session of play. Let's say there are thirteen tables in play, twenty-six pairs. In most types of games, the North–South pairs will remain in their original seats during the entire course of the duplicate game, while the East–West players will move to *the next higher-numbered* table at the completion of each round. Generally, the North–South pair at Table # 1 is designated as "N–S # 1"; the North–South pair at Table # 2 is designated as "N–S # 2"; the North–South pair at Table # 3 is designated as "N–S # 3," etc. Similarly, the East–West pair which started at Table # 1 is called "E–W # 1"; the East–West pair which started at Table # 2 is called "E–W # 2"; the East–West pair which started at Table # 3 is called "E–W # 3," etc.

Based on the above, if you are "E–W # 1," then at the completion of the first round of play,* during which you played Boards 1 and 2 against "N–S # 1," you move to play against "N–S # 2." (You move not when you feel like it, but rather when the director calls out, "All change for Round 2.") Boards 5 and 6 are now passed from Table # 3, where they were played on the first round, to Table 2.

On Board # 5 (North–South are vulnerable), the North–South pair arrives at a *four heart* contract against you and your partner. They make exactly four hearts. Since it is the duty of the North–South pair to do the scoring, either North or South now unfolds the traveling score slip accompanying Board # 5, and enters the score. Here is how it will look, with your score (you are "E–W # 1") having just been recorded. (The second entry will be discussed a few pages hence.)

Before we analyze the contents of the "Official A.C.B.L. Travel-

---

* If there are 13 tables in play, playing two boards to a round, then at the outset of play Boards 1 and 2 were played at Table 1; Boards 3 and 4 were played at Table 2; Boards 5 and 6 were played at Table 3, etc. . . . and Boards 25 and 26 were played at Table 13.

OFFICIAL ACBL TRAVELING SCORE

North player keeps score
Enter E-W Pair No.

Board No. 5

N-S Pair No.	CON TRACT	BY	Made	Down	SCORE		E-W Pair No.	Match Points
					N-S	E-W		
1								
2	4H	N	4		620		1	
3	4H	N	5		650		3	
4								
5								
6								
7								
8								
9								
10								
11								
12								
13								
14								
15								
16								
17								
18								
19								1
20								2
21								3
22								4
23								5
24								6
25								7
26								8
27								9
28								10
29								11
30								12
31								13
32								14
33								15
34								16
35								17
36								18

Form 234
Printed in USA by ACBL
Copyright © 1987

AMERICAN CONTRACT BRIDGE LEAGUE
2990 AIRWAYS BOULEVARD
MEMPHIS TN 38116-3847

ing Score," a brief presentation of duplicate scoring is essential.

At duplicate, each deal is an entity unto itself and is scored separately. There are never any part-scores, so that if you bid and make, let us say, two hearts, you cannot regard it as 60 toward game. Hence, each deal can be considered as an unfinished rubber, and an immediate bonus is given for a game or a part-score which is bid and made. These bonuses are as follows:

For making a vulnerable game .... 500 points
For making a non-vulnerable game .... 300 points
For making a part-score, whether
vulnerable or not .... 50 points

Honors do not count at duplicate. Almost all other items of scoring, such as penalties and slam bonuses, are the same as at rubber bridge.

Thus, if you bid and make two spades, you score: 60 + 50 = 110; if you bid and make four hearts, not vulnerable, you score: 120 + 300 = 420; if you bid four diamonds, and make an overtrick, you score: 80 + 20 + 50 = 150; if you bid four spades, vulnerable, and make two overtricks, you score: 120 + 60 + 500 = 680.

If you bid two hearts, get doubled, not vulnerable, and make exactly two hearts, you score: 120 for the trick score (60 times two); 50 points for making a (any) doubled contract; and 300 for a game bonus, for a grand total of 470 points.

Going back to Board # 5, you played this deal against "N–S # 2"; the contract was "4 H" by "N" (North); N–S "made" "4"; the North–South plus score was "620" (120 + 500); your pair number ("E–W # 1") was entered as "1."

The entry directly below yours on the traveling score slip records the result when the board was played the first time, on the previous round, at Table # 3. The North–South pair was "3"; they also bid four hearts ("4 H"); they made "5" (an overtrick); they scored "650": they played against "E–W # 3."

As of this moment—at the completion of Round 2—you have the best score on Board # 5 (or, grammatically speaking, the "better" score), since you have lost 620 points, while E–W # 3, which held your identical cards, has lost 650 points.

This is the second round and the second time the board has been played. There are two scoring entries on the traveling slip. We can tell where and by whom the board was played first: at Table # 3 by North–South pair # 3 versus East–West pair # 3. Each North (or South) player must always enter the score in the line which contains his own pair number. Therefore North entered the following information on the line which began with North–South pair # "3." From left to right, he next inserted "4 H," "N," into the first two columns, which meant that the North player played the deal at a contract of four hearts. He then inserted in the column headed "Made," the number "5," which meant that North had made an overtrick, for a total of 11 tricks. (Had North gone down one trick, there would have been no entry in the "Made" column; instead the number, "1," would have been entered in the next column, headed "Down".) In the following column, labeled "North–South, Net Plus," the figure of 650 was entered (120 trick score; 30 for the overtrick; and 500 for a vulnerable game). Whenever North–South secures a plus score, it is entered in the "Net Plus" column. If North–South obtains a minus score, it is entered in the North–South "Net Minus" column. And, finally, in the column headed "E–W Pair," the East–West pair number, "3," is entered.

It is very important for North–South and their opponents to pay close attention to the column in which the entry is made. No plus or minus signs accompany the entry. You can see, then, that if North inadvertently makes the entry in the "plus" column when he was really "minus," that particular East–West pair is scored as "minus" when they were really "plus."

Now let's revert to what happened when you played this board on the second round at Table 2 against North–South Pair # 2.

On Line "2," in the column headed "Contract," North entered "4 H"; in the next column, "By," he entered "N"; then Made "4"; then, in the "North–South Net Plus" column, 620. And the last entry was your East–West pair number, "1."

To repeat, at the end of Round 2, on Board # 5, you as East–West Pair # 1, have the best result of the East–West pairs: you are "minus 620," while East–West # 3 is "minus 650." For now it is important for you recognize only that you compete for score (on each board) *only against the other East–West pairs*, even though you will play only against North–South pairs.

Having finished with Board # 5 on the second round, we now play Board # 6, the final board of our second round. When this board has been played, the result—and all pertinent data—will be entered on the traveling score (# 6) which accompanies the board.

VII. Moving Boards and Players

You have just completed Round 2, and are now ready to make a second move to start playing Round 3. When the director sees that all of the participants are ready to move, he will call out, "All change for Round 3," thus making it possible for everybody to move simultaneously. We mentioned the move before, in passing, and are going to say a bit more about it now. However, don't be alarmed by the thought that you will have to learn a large number of complicated movements. The great majority of duplicate players, even those having many years of experience, know very little about the technical details of movements. There are very competent directors who most efficiently take care of the running of the game. You may learn if you like, but is it optional, not mandatory.

A certain minimum of knowledge, however, is essential if you are not to disrupt the duplicate game. For this reason, we repeat, in most duplicate games the North–South players remain seated at their starting tables for the entire evening. When the selection of seats is optional at the outset, almost always the North–South seats will be taken first. It is truly remarkable that so many pairs appear to be too exhausted to move even before a single card has been played.

As was mentioned, the East–West pairs move each round toward the adjacent higher-numbered table: from 3 to 4, from 5 to 6, from 9 to 10, etc. If there are thirteen tables in play, they will move from Table 13 to Table 1.

The boards move in the opposite direction, that is, to the adjacent lower-numbered table: from 6 to 5, from 3 to 2, etc. In a 13-table game, the boards go from Table 1 to Table 13.* There are other types of movements—and books and directors to explain them—which, on rare occasions, are used. But, again, you needn't worry about them, for there will always be a competent director to give instructions which will result in the game running smoothly and efficiently.

In our prime and simple movement, it is readily perceived that North–South will always play the boards in numerically ascending order. If, for example, you start at Table # 5, as North–South pair # 5, you will be given Boards 9 and 10 on the first round if two boards per round are being played. At the end of the first round, when "All change" is called, Table 6 will pass Boards 11 and 12 to you (Table 6 played them on the first round). They, in turn, will get Boards 13 and 14 from Table 7, which they will pass on to you at the conclusion of the *second* round. You can see that it doesn't require too much experience for a North–South pair to know which boards they should be playing on each round. If, by some mishap, they receive the wrong boards, they will more than likely discover it in time to rectify the error.

* If the reader recalls, Boards 1 and 2 are, at the start of the game, placed at Table 1; Boards 3 and 4 are placed at Table 2; Boards 5 and 6 at Table 3; Boards 7 and 8 at Table 4, etc.

On the other hand, the East–West pairs skip a set of boards each round (numerically, that is). For example, if you start at Table 2, as East–West pair # 2, you will play Boards 3 and 4 on the first round. On the second round, you play Boards 7 and 8, bypassing Boards 5 and 6. The reason is that Boards 5 and 6, which on the first round were played at Table 3, are now being passed on to Table 2, which you are about to leave.

If you can think of the tables as being set up in a circle, you can visualize the movement. The players (East–West) always move clockwise around the circle, while the boards move counterclockwise. Each alternate set of boards that you "skip" as you progress after each round will be encountered at a subsequent round. As you and the boards move around the circle in opposite directions, at some point you and the boards which you skipped will meet up.

VIII. The Private Score

On page 28 is a private scorecard. In most duplicate games, particularly where the more experienced players are involved, one member of a partnership keeps score, board by board. In a well-run duplicate, two such cards will be found at each table before the start of play, making one available for each competing pair. If they are not to be found at your table, they can be obtained at the director's table or at some other table used for that purpose. Occasionally, both partners would like to keep a private score. Extra cards are cheerfully supplied for the mere asking.

Why should players wish to do the work entailed in keeping a private score? There are a few good reasons. One quickly comes to mind if you realize that the only record of your accomplishments is recorded on a traveling score slip which leaves you after each round is played. It would be quite a feat to recall all the scores with all of the details for the entire evening. Even if you had a photographic memory, it wouldn't be worth the effort, since it can so easily be done otherwise.

If your partnership keeps an accurate private scorecard, you will have an exact record of what you did against each identifiable pair on every board.

You will note that there is a distinctive difference between entries on the traveling score and those made on the private scorecard.

BD # SCORE	D.F ANC VUL	BD # TEAMS	VS	CONTRACT & DECLARER	PLUS	MINUS	PTS ES'	PTS	BD # SCORE	D.F ANC VUL	BD # TEAMS	VS	CONTRACT & DECLARER	PLUS	MINUS	PTS ES'	PTS
1	N NONE								17	N NONE							
2	E N-S								18	E N-S							
3	S E-W								19	S E-W							
4	W BOTH								20	W BOTH							
5	N N-S								21	N N-S							
6	E E-W								22	E E-W							
7	S BOTH								23	S BOTH							
8	W NONE								24	W NONE							
9	N E-W								25	N E-W							
10	E BOTH								26	E BOTH							
11	S NONE								27	S NONE							
12	W N-S								28	W N-S							
13	N BOTH								29	N BOTH							
14	E NONE								30	E NONE							
15	S N-S								31	S N-S							
16	W E-W								32	W E-W							
									33	N NONE							
									34	E N-S							
									35	S E-W							
									36	W BOTH							

20-PT. VP SCALE

IMPs	VPs	IMPs	VPs	IMPs	VPs
0	10-10		14-16		16-4
1-2	11-9		17-19		17-3
	12-8		20-22		18-2
	13-7		24-27		19-1
	14-6		26+		20-0
11-15	15-5				

36-PT. VP SCALE

IMPs	VPs	IMPs	VPs	IMPs	VPs
0	15-15		9-10		24-6
1	18-12		11-13		25-5
2	19-11		14-16		26-4
3	20-10		17-19		27-3
4	21-9		20-23		28-2
5-6	22-8		21-8		29-1
7-8	23-7		28+		30-0

Always disclose,
Never Abuse,
Don't Intimidate,
Practice Active Ethics

INTERNATIONAL MATCH POINT SCALE

Diff. in Pts	IMPs	Diff. in Pts	IMPs	Diff. in Pts	IMPs	Diff. in Pts	IMPs
20— 40	1	270—310	7	750— 890	13	2000—2240	19
50— 80	2	320— 360	8	900—1090	14	2250—2490	20
90—120	3	370—420	9	1100—1290	15	2500—2990	21
130—160	4	430—490	10	1300—1490	16	3000—3490	22
170—210	5	500—590	11	1500—1740	17	3500—3990	23
220—260	6	600—740	12	1750—1990	18	4000 and up	24

Look at the above diagram depicting the scorecard, and you will perceive that you enter all scores in the line that corresponds *with the board number.* You will recall that on the traveling score entries were made in the line which corresponded with the North–South pair number. The latter was essential for correct scoring since each North–South pair would have to make an entry on the traveling score slip. If a board was played thirteen times at thirteen different tables, there would be thirteen entries on it, each made by the North–South pair.

Your private scorecard serves the same type of function—the result of each board that *you* play is recorded therein. This is, incidentally, a good time to tell you that entries on your private score should be kept in such a manner that no one but you can see what is written on it. Your opponents will not wish to see it but if they do they may inadvertently receive information about boards which they have not as yet played by seeing previously made entries on your card.

Keeping the card in accurate fashion is most simple. If you have just finished playing Board # 17, let's say, you enter the opponent's pair number in the line headed by "vs" right next to number 17. You then enter the final contract, followed by the score attained. There is a minus column and a plus column. On your private score-card, you enter in the *plus* column if *you* have scored points, and in the *minus* column if *your opponents* scored the points. Whether you are sitting East–West or North–South has no effect on your entry. When the evening is finished, you will have an entry opposite each board number which you have played with all the pertinent information relating to each board.

On each board, or on some boards, opposite the specific board number many players form the habit of entering one particular suit holding which stirs their interest, such as S–A K J 9 6 2 or D–K Q 10 9 6 4 2. Others make a check or some other mark as a reminder to bring about a discussion about the hand at the game's end. This helps them remember the cards as well as serving as a reminder that there is a need for discussion. "Post-mortem" discussions such as these are held for a variety of reasons. You may be in doubt about the bidding, the play, or the defense on some deal and wish to check to see what other people did on the board. You may wish to discuss and analyze with your partner some phase of bidding or play to smooth out some rough spots which cropped up. You may, for your own information, seek an opinion from someone you respect. If you come to him with complete and instant recall, he will be more inclined to listen and give you advice.

IX. The Final Tabulation

The results of the duplicate game are determined in either of two ways. The "match points" may be transferred from the traveling score slips to a "recapitulation sheet." In recent years many of the duplicate games are scored by a computer system. This subject of "match points" is introduced and discussed at length in the chapter that follows. For now, we would like to point out how your private score or "convention card" comes in handy. When the recap sheet is posted you will be able to check all of your scores against what others did. You will also be able to check whether the scores were entered correctly on the traveling score slips; if entered incorrectly, you can rectify the error by bringing it to the attention of the duplicate director. Also, on occasion, through your private score you will be able to catch an error in "match-pointing" made by the scorer.

In tournaments, the traveling slip is not used. Instead, an individual 2 x 3 scorecard is used each time a board is played, upon which all the relevant data pertaining to that deal are posted as soon as each deal is finished. These are picked up at each table at the completion of each round, and the scores are promptly entered on the recapitulation sheet. These scorecards look like this:

AMERICAN CONTRACT BRIDGE LEAGUE

N – S PAIR	ALL DEALS PLAYED THIS ROUND WILL BE SCORED ON THIS CARD. CIRCLE DIRECTION OF DECLARER.				E–W OK J.S.			E – W PAIR
2								2
N – S SCORE	MADE	DOWN	N – S CONTRACT	BOARD NUMBER	E – W CONTRACT	MADE	DOWN	E – W SCORE
530	3		N Ⓢ 3SX	3	E W			
100			N S	4	Ⓔ W 3NT		1	
			N S		E W			

PRINTED IN U S A   FORM 102A REV. COPYRIGHTED 1983

On Board 3, North–South Pair # 2 played East–West Pair # 2. The final contract, by South, was three spades doubled, which was fulfilled. North–South scored 530 points: 180 for three spades doubled, 300 for a nonvulnerable game and 50 points for fulfilling the doubled contract. The score was "O.K.'d" by John Smith, one of the East–West players. (The North–South pair always records the score.)

On the companion board, # 4, North–South Pair # 2 again played East–West Pair # 2. The final contract, by East, was three no-trump, which was defeated one trick, vulnerable. North–South scored 100 points.

CHAPTER 3

Scoring the Duplicate Game

We will assume that the director, a little while ago, has called, "All change for the last round." Upon completing the last round, you will have finished the entire allotment of boards to be played in this session. What happens now? How are the winners determined? The answer is simple: the little traveling score slips on which you recorded the results of each deal when it was played will determine the winner.

The duplicate director, who may have some assistance, will be found off in some corner busily working on the traveling score slips or entering the results into the computer.

It is worth mentioning again that each one of the score slips has equal importance in determining the final score of each participant. A hand on which no pair made more than two diamonds has exactly equal status with a hand on which seven spades, vulnerable, was bid and made. One or two good results will not enable you to finish first or second. You will need a consistently good performance on the majority of hands in order to emerge victorious.

It must also be emphasized again that although you, as an East–West pair, actually played every deal against some North–South pair your scores will be compared against only the East–West pairs; that is, against those who held the identical cards you held. This is manifestly the only logical way to do it. Let's assume that the East–West pairs happen to hold the good cards deal after deal, including several slam hands, while the North–South pairs hold nothing but poor cards. Obviously, the North–South players will be defeated by brute force, by East–West's overwhelming superiority of resources. There simply cannot be a way in which the East–West scores can be compared with the North–South scores. But, quite naturally, each East–West score can be compared with the other East–West scores, and the relative abilities of each can be ascertained. Conversely, the North–South scores can be compared with each other, and the relative merits of each North–South pair can be measured precisely.

The method of scoring duplicate (tournament) bridge is by means of what we call "match points."

In rubber bridge, the method of scoring is, of course, gross points —the totaling of all points that are scored, the victory going to the one who has the most. If this gross scoring were used in duplicate bridge, the result might prove absolutely nothing. For example, a pair that happened to receive a few "gifts" from inferior opponents —like those opponents being set 1400 and 1700 points on a couple of hands because they decided to go on a bidding spree—could score enough points on those two hands to win the entire duplicate game. The above "gifts" would prove nothing about the ability of the recipients; the latter might even play horrible bridge through the remainder of the deals and nevertheless finish on top.

By using match-point scoring, *the number of points that can be won on any deal is limited.* It doesn't matter whether a pair is plus 2410 or plus 50; they cannot get more than a specifically assigned number of points on any one hand. Let us now come to what match points are and how they are limited to a specified maximum on each deal.

A look at a completed traveling score slip will make match points very easy to understand. Let's use the one we introduced in the preceding chapter (p. 23). On that deal (Board # 5), we were East–West Pair # 1, playing against North–South Pair # 2. North–South bid and made four hearts, vulnerable, scoring 620 points. Before we played this board, it had been played at Table 3, where North–South also arrived at a four heart contract—against East–West Pair # 3—and had made an overtrick, scoring 650 points.

Let's assume that there were thirteen tables in play in this duplicate game; and that, therefore, each board was played thirteen times. Let's fill in the other eleven scores on Board # 5, so that the thirteen results can be observed as we "match-point" the deal.

Let us first match-point the North–South scores. Then we will match-point the East–West scores.

OFFICIAL ACBL TRAVELING SCORE

North player keeps score
Enter E-W Pair No.

Board No. ⬜ 5

N-S Pair No	CON TRACT	BY	Tricks Made	Tricks Down	SCORE N-S	SCORE E-W	E-W Pair No	Match Points
1	3NT	S	3		600		12	9
2	4H	N	4		620		1	10
3	4H	N	5		650		3	11
4	4HX	N	4		790		5	12
5	2H	N	4		170		7	4½
6	2H	N	5		200		9	6
7	3NT	S		2		200	11	1
8	4SX	E		3	500		13	8
9	2H	N	4		170		2	4½
10	4SX	E		2	300		4	7
11	6H	N		1		100	6	2
12	3NTX	N		3		500	8	0
13	2NT	N	2		120		10	3
14								
15								
16								
17								
18							E-W	
19							2	1
20							7½	2
21							1	3
22							5	4
23							0	5
24							10	6
25							7½	7
26							12	8
27							6	9
28							9	10
29							11	11
30							3	12
31							4	13
32								14
33								15
34								16
35								17
36								18

Form 234
Printed in USA by ACBL
Copyright © 1987

AMERICAN CONTRACT BRIDGE LEAGUE
2990 AIRWAYS BOULEVARD
MEMPHIS TN 38116-3847

The reader will note that there are thirteen results posted. Each pair is going to get a score which will be based on how well it did when compared to each of the other twelve pairs that played this deal.

Which pair has the best North–South result? A quick glance will inform you that it is Pair # 4. They were doubled in their four heart contract, and made it, scoring 790 points.* They will receive *12 match points.*

* 120 times two equals 240; 500 points for a vulnerable game; and 50 points for fulfilling any doubled contract.

Why 12 match points? *Because they receive one match point for each team they outscore.* And they did outscore each of the other twelve North–South teams. If, hypothetically, there had been a grand total of seven pairs sitting North–South (instead of 13), and this particular North–South pair had beaten each of the other six North–South pairs, they would have received 6 match points. Thus, no matter how many pairs are playing the same deal, you receive one match point for each team you outscore.

This method of scoring extends right down the line for each pair, thirteen in our case: *you get one match point for each team you beat in the scoring.* In addition, where two teams have each scored the identical number of points, each team receives one-half a match point for the tie. If, in a thirteen-table game, two teams had each scored 790 points—the highest of all North–South scores—each of them would obtain 11½ match points: each of them would have defeated eleven other teams (11 points), and each of them would have secured a half a match point for having tied each other.

Are you all set now to do some match-pointing? Let's continue them.

To review, North–South Pair # 4 received 12 match points for their top score of 790 points. The second-best North–South score was obtained by Pair # 3, who scored 650 points. Pair # 3 gets 11 match points for having posted a better score than the other eleven North–South pairs, one point for each pair they outscored. The third-best score was made by North–South Pair # 2, who received 620 points for bidding and making four hearts. They get 10 match points, one for each of the ten teams they defeated. The fourth-best score was made by North–South Pair # 1, who bid and made three no-trump, scoring 600 points. They defeated nine other teams—and they secure 9 match points.

The next best result was procured by North–South Pair # 8, who doubled East–West at a four spade contract, and defeated them three tricks, thus obtaining 500 points (East–West were not vulnerable). Since Pair # 8 had a better result than eight North–South teams, they receive 8 match points.

Thus far, we have assigned the proper number of match points to the five best scores: 12 match points to N–S # 4; 11 match points to N–S # 3; 10 match points to N–S # 2; 9 match points to N–S # 1; and 8 match points to N–S # 8. Let's continue.

The next highest score was obtained by North–South # 10. They also doubled East–West's four spade contract, but defeated them by only two tricks, for 300 points. They secure 7 match points.

Next we come to North–South # 6, who bid two hearts and made three overtricks, for a score of 200 points (60 points for two hearts; 90 points for three overtricks, at 30 points per trick; and a 50-point bonus for fulfilling any part-score contract). They outscored six other teams, and thus got 6 match points.

Now we come to two pairs, North–South # 5 and North–South # 9, each of whom has the identical score of 170 points: two hearts made with two overtricks. Each of these two teams outscored four other North–South pairs. So they get—each of them—one match point for each victory, a total of four. However, since they also tied each other, each of them gets another one-half match point for the tie. Thus, N–S # 5 and N–S # 9 each obtains 4½ match points.

North–South # 13 comes next. They bid and made two no-trump for a score of 120 points (70 + 50). This pair defeated three other teams, so it gets 3 match points.

Next to be tabulated are the three North–South teams who wound up with a "net minus" score because they were defeated at their contracts. Of these three minus scores, the best one was obtained by North–South # 11, who lost "only" 100 points by being defeated one trick, vulnerable, at a six heart contract. That this is a bad score is obvious, but, nevertheless, they did outscore both N–S # 12, who lost 500 points, and N–S # 7, who lost 200 points. For outscoring two teams, North–South # 11 gets two match points.

Next to be scored is North–South # 7. They arrived at a three no-trump contract, and were defeated two tricks, for a loss of 200 points. They secure one match point, for defeating one team (N–S # 12).

And last (in every respect!) comes North–South # 12, who were doubled at 3 NT and suffered a two-trick set (vulnerable), for a loss of 500 points. They beat nobody, and they got what they deserved—0 (zero) match points.

The East–West match-point scores are computed in exactly the same way. Let's do it quickly:

The best East–West score: Pair 8, plus 500 points—12 match points.
The second-best E–W score: Pair 11, plus 200 points—11 match points.

The third-best E–W score: Pair 6, plus 100 points—10 match points.
The fourth-best E–W score: Pair 10, minus 120 points—9 match points.
Tied for fifth and sixth places are Pair # 2 and Pair # 7, each of whom
  were minus 170 points. Each gets 7½ match points.
The seventh-best E–W score: Pair 9, minus 200 points—6 match points.
The eighth-best E–W score: Pair 4, minus 300 points—5 match points.
The ninth-best E–W score: Pair 13, minus 500 points—4 match points.
The tenth-best E–W score: Pair 12, minus 600 points—3 match points.
The eleventh-best E–W score: Pair 1, minus 620 points—2 match points.
The twelfth-best E–W score: Pair 3, minus 650 points—1 match point.
The worst E–W score: Pair 5, minus 790 points—0 match points.

Thus, with 13 tables in play, there will be 13 match-point scores
for each North–South pair, and 13 match-point scores for each
East–West pair. The highest match-point score, on each board, in
each direction, will always be 12 match points; the second highest
will be 11; the third highest, 10, etc., down to the lowest, which
will be zero.

If the reader will look back at the traveling score slip, at the
match points given to the North–South and East–West pairs, he
will see that *the match-point sum of each North–South and East–
West pair who played against each other, adds to exactly 12.*

Let's look at N–S # 4, which had the highest North–South score
(plus 790) and then earned 12 match points. Is it not true that the
East–West pair against whom they played (E–W # 5) had the
worst East–West score, and thus "earned" zero match points?
Twelve plus zero equals twelve.

Now let's glance at N–S # 3, which had the second-best North–
South score, for which they obtained 11 match points (for beating
the scores of 11 other teams). Did not the East–West pair against
whom they played (E–W # 3) have the next-to-worst East–West
match point score, beating just one team, thus scoring one match
point? Again, eleven plus one equals twelve.

The worst North–South score was made by N–S # 12, who were
minus 500 points. For their efforts, they received zero match points.
Does it not follow, logically, mathematically, or call it what you will,
that the East–West pair against whom they played (E–W # 8)
must have received the highest East–West score (plus 500 points),
and thereby obtained the highest East–West match-point score,
12 points?

In brief, is not the best North–South score always secured against the worst East–West score, and vice versa? And is not the second-best North–South score always secured against the team that has the second worst East–West score? Or, if a North–South score is exactly "average"—6 match points out of 12—would not the score of the East–West pair against whom they played also be exactly average: 6 match points out of 12?

The objective in presenting the above is readily apparent: once the North–South match point scores have been computed, why spend the time computing the East–West scores in the same time-consuming manner? Simply subtract the North–South match-point score from the number 12 and you will have the precise match-point score for the East–West pair against whom that North–South pair played. It will always be correct, for each time a deal is played the North–South and East–West pairs playing the deal will be sharing 12 match points between them. And if North–South obtains 7, then East–West will obtain 5, for North–South would have beaten the scores of seven North–South pairs, and East–West would have beaten the scores of five East–West teams. All the above assumes, of course, that there are thirteen tables in play, with thirteen sets of competitors in each direction.

Let's try match-pointing another board, but this time with fewer tables. There are seven full tables in play, and we are match-pointing Board # 4, on which both sides are vulnerable and West is the dealer.

On the opposite page is the traveling score slip accompanying Board # 4.

With seven tables participating, each board is played seven times, yielding seven results. So the top match-point score on each board will be 6 * (the bottom match point will, of course, be zero).

The highest North–South score was obtained by N–S # 7, who doubled their vulnerable East–West opponents (E–W # 5) at a four spade contract, defeated them one trick, and collected 200 points. N–S # 7 gets 6 match points (and does not E–W # 5 have the worst East–West score, securing zero match points?).

The second highest North–South score was secured by N–S # 6,

* "Top on the board" will always be *one less* than the number of full tables in play, with the team that outscores all of the other teams playing in the same direction securing one point for each team it has outscored.

which bid and made a two heart contract, scoring 110 points (60 + 50) against E–W # 3. N–S # 6 gets 5 match points. (E–W # 3 has the second worst East–West score, beating only E–W # 5, so E–W # 3 gets 1 match point.)

OFFICIAL ACBL TRAVELING SCORE

North player keeps score   Board No. **4**
Enter E-W Pair No.

N-S Pair No	CON TRACT	BY	Made	Down	SCORE N-S	SCORE E-W	E-W Pair No	Match Points
1	2S	E	2			110	7	3
2	2NT	W	2			120	2	2
3	4S	E		1	100		4	4
4	2S	E	3			140	6	1/2
5	2S	E	3			140	1	1/2
6	2H	N	2		110		3	5
7	4SX	E		1	200		5	6
8								
9								
10								
11								
12								
13								
14								
15								
16								
17								
18							E-W	
19							5½	1
20							4	2
21							1	3
22							2	4
23							0	5
24							5½	6
25							3	7
26								8
27								9
28								10
29								11
30								12
31								13
32								14
33								15
34								16
35								17
36								18

Form 234
Printed in USA by ACBL
Copyright 1 ACBL 1987

AMERICAN CONTRACT BRIDGE LEAGUE
2990 AIRWAYS BOULEVARD
MEMPHIS TN 38116 3847

The third-best North–South score was procured by N–S # 3, playing against E–W # 4. N–S # 3 was plus 100 points, defeating E–W # 4's four spade contract. N–S # 3 obtains 4 match points. (And E–W # 4 gets 2 match points, for they outscored two teams: East–West # 5 , and East–West # 3.) The reader might note that on each match-point result, the sum of the North–South and East–West match points is exactly 6.

The fourth highest North–South score was secured by N–S # 1, against whom their opponents (E–W # 7) bid and made two spades, scoring 110 points. N–S # 1 obtains 3 match points. (And E–W # 7 also obtains 3 match points, for they outscored the three East–West pairs [# 2, # 6, # 1] who were minus "120," "140," and "140" respectively.) Let's break off for a moment to look at the above result. Both N–S # 1 and E–W # 7 have what we call an "average" result, each team splitting the 6 match points in play on a 50-50 basis. Each team secures 3 match points, for each was exactly in the middle: North–South # 1 outscored three North–South teams, and was itself outscored by three North–South teams. East–West # 7 was in the identical position. It, too, outscored three East–West teams, while it was outscored by the three other East–West teams. Putting it another way, N–S # 1 was no better and no worse than its North–South competitors; and E–W # 7 was no better and no worse than its East–West competitors. Each team was exactly average—and they therefore split the 6 match points in average fashion, three apiece.

The fifth highest North–South score was obtained by N–S # 2, against whom their E–W # 2 opponents bid and made two no-trump, for a score of 120 points (70 + 50). N–S # 2 receives 2 match points, for beating the scores of two teams, N–S # 4 and N–S # 5. (E–W # 2 secures 4 match points, for they outscored four East–West teams, numbers 7, 4, 3, and 5.)

The sixth best North–South score is shared by N–S # 4 and N–S # 5, against whom their East–West opponents (E–W # 6 and E–W # 1) bid two spades and three spades respectively, each making nine tricks. The reader will appreciate that N–S # 4 and N–S # 5 are tied not only for sixth place, but also for seventh place. Neither of them beat any other North–South team, so they get no points for a victory. But they did tie each other, so they get ½ match point apiece. They are what is known in the trade as "tied for bottom."

The East–West pairs against whom N–S # 4 and N–S # 5 played, E–W #6 and E–W # 1, each gets 5½ match points. Each of these two East–West pairs outscored five East–West pairs—thus earning one match point for each victory—and each tied the other, getting

½ match point apiece. The total of each, quite obviously, is therefore 5½ match points. In bridge parlance, E–W # 6 and E–W # 1 have "tied for top," for they each have the best East–West score on the board.

If we were to compute the East–West match-point scores independently, we would, of course, arrive at the identical scores we obtained by subtracting any specific North–South match-point score from the number, 6, thus yielding the match-point score of that specific North–South's opponent. (If N–S # 3 scores 4 match points, then their East–West opponent scores 2 match points.)

If, for example, we look at E–W # 6 and E–W # 1, we will observe that they share the highest East–West scores, the first two places. Since first place is worth 6 points, and second place is worth 5 points, they split these 11 match points on a 50-50 basis, 5½ apiece. This is the same result we would obtain via the "shortcut": their North–South opponents, N–S # 4 and N–S # 5, each obtained ½ match point, which, subtracted from 6 for each of these North–South pairs, gave each of their East–West opponents 5½ match points. Right?

Every score slip is match-pointed in the way described and illustrated in the preceding contents of this chapter. After all of the traveling scores have been computed, each pair's scores are totaled on what we call a "recapitulation" sheet (known as a "recap" sheet), wherein are posted each score made on each board by each contestant. The pair with the highest North–South match-point score is declared the "North–South" winner. The pair with the highest East–West score is declared the "East–West" winner. And, as an aside, in what other game do you have two winners simultaneously? Of course, the North–South team which has the second highest match-point score, has finished "second"; and ditto for East–West. And so on, right down the line, with regard to "third," "fourth," etc.

Let's revert to the game in which we looked at our first traveling score slip, Board # 5 (p. 34). There were thirteen tables in play, and thirteen scores were recorded on Board # 5. Assuming that two boards were played to a round (which is always the case when there are 13 tables), all in all twenty-six boards would have been played, two boards on each of the thirteen rounds.

The top match-point score on Board # 5, and on each of the

other 25 boards in play, was 12. The total number of match points which could possibly be gained by one pair would be 26 times 12, or 312. Average, or 50 percent, would then be 156.

Since, for many reasons which will become more and more apparent as you gain experience, it is manifestly impossible (in practice) to get 100 percent of the total match points, the best percentage above 50 percent will be the winner. You usually require a percentage slightly over 62 percent to be a one-session winner.

Furthermore, a very good average compiled on many of these traveling score slips would be a good indicator of a pair's ability. Conversely, a very poor average score would likewise indicate that a pair needs more experience. However, "luck"—good or bad—may have an abnormal effect on one's score on any particular board.

The beginner should not be too discouraged by a final result which is not too high in percentage. "Good" and "bad" are terms which are more relative in bridge than in any other competitive sport we know. A very experienced player cannot be too elated with a score just a little above average. But the novice can justly be proud of a score that is average, or even a little less, especially when the class of competition is particularly good.

Now let's get to the strategy and tactics of duplicate bridge. Having learned how the game proceeds and how to score are nothing more than the essential prerequisites. The weapons and tools (the techniques) which winning players employ must now be understood. Then we will be prepared for the ultimate objective— the *mastery* of technique. When the latter is attained, a greater number of match points on each board will be your reward.

CHAPTER 4

The Approach to Duplicate Bridge

As the reader has already observed in the scoring one of the fundamental differences between rubber bridge and duplicate bridge is that each deal in duplicate bridge—no matter how low the contract—is equally crucial: the *number* of points you score is unimportant; *the number of pairs whose scores you beat is of sole importance.* For example, let's suppose that you and your partner are sitting North–South, as Pair # 1, in a five-table game. On the next page are the scores on Boards # 1 and # 2, which have been match-pointed.

On Board # 1, you bid and made one no-trump, for a score of 90 (40 + 50), thus outscoring each of the other four North–South pairs. You get a "top" on the board, 4 match points.

On Board # 2, you bid and made a vulnerable grand slam in no-trump, scoring 2220 points (1500 + 500 + 220). Unfortunately, for you, each of the other North–South pairs did likewise. You have tied with each of the other four pairs, and you get ½ match point for each tie. You score 2 match points, an average result on the board. You were no better and no worse than any of the other North–South pairs.

These two boards show the two major factors which account for most, if not all, of the strategic differences between duplicate (match-point) play and rubber-bridge play.

1. A small difference in the score of one board (say a part score of 60) has very little value at rubber bridge, but usually **great** value at match-point play. For example, a difference of 10, 20, 50,

43

or perhaps 100 points in the final result of a hand makes little difference in a session of rubber bridge. But any of these differences could be decisive in determining whether you achieve a *very good* or a *very bad* result at match points. As proof, look at Board # 1, below. And, incidentally, if you, as North–South Pair # 1, had gone down at your one no-trump contract on Board # 1, you would have been minus 50 points—and would have secured ½ match point, since you would have "tied for bottom" with N–S # 3.

OFFICIAL ACBL TRAVELING SCORE

North player keeps score
Enter E-W Pair No

Board No **1**

N-S Pair No	CON TRACT	BY	Tricks Made	Tricks Down	SCORE N-S	SCORE E-W	E-W Pair No	Match Points
1	INT	S	1		90		1	4
2	1S	N	1		80		3	2½
3	2NT	S		1		50	5	0
4	PASSED OUT						2	1
5	1S	N	1		80		4	2½
6								
7								
8								
9								
10								
11								
12								
13								
14								
15								
16								
17								
18							E-W	
19							O	1
20							3	2
21							1½	3
22							1½	4
23							4	5
24								6
25								7
26								8
27								9
28								10
29								11
30								12
31								13
32								14
33								15
34								16
35								17
36								18

Form 234
Printed in USA by ACBL
Copyright © ACBL 1967

AMERICAN CONTRACT BRIDGE LEAGUE
299K AIRWAYS BOULEVARD
MEMPHIS TN 38116 3847

OFFICIAL ACBL TRAVELING SCORE

North player keeps score
Enter E-W Pair No

Board No **2**

N-S Pair No	CON TRACT	BY	Tricks Made	Tricks Down	SCORE N-S	SCORE E-W	E-W Pair No	Match Points
1	7NT	N	7		2220		1	2
2	7NT	N	7		2220		3	2
3	7NT	N	7		2220		5	2
4	7NT	N	7		2220		2	2
5	7NT	N	7		2220		4	2
6								
7								
8								
9								
10								
11								
12								
13								
14								
15								
16								
17								
18							E-W	
19							2	1
20							2	2
21							2	3
22							2	4
23							2	5
24								6
25								7
26								8
27								9
28								10
29								11
30								12
31								13
32								14
33								15
34								16
35								17
36								18

Form 234
Printed in USA by ACBL
Copyright © ACBL 1967

AMERICAN CONTRACT BRIDGE LEAGUE
299K AIRWAYS BOULEVARD
MEMPHIS TN 38116 3847

2. Rubber bridge stresses the importance of the blue-ribbon, premium contracts—i.e., games and slams—since these involve large

numbers of points. The part-score contract, though important, is devalued, since it involves only a comparatively small number of points. In match-point play, all hands have equal importance and equal value. A one no-trump contract is just as important as a vulnerable grand slam contract—and can be even more important in determining your destiny, as a glance at Boards # 1 and # 2, above, will reveal. The maximum number of match points to be won is identical on each deal. The rubber-bridge player could relax a bit in the case of a one no-trump contract, and he will generally do so if it is obvious that the one no-trump contract is guaranteed and the only issue is whether he might be able to obtain an overtrick. The energy thus saved could be stored up to be expended when he is playing a delicate slam contract. The match-point player cannot ever relax on any deal, for each deal has equal weight in the final results.

All of the above will be brought into focus if we set it forth in numbers. Let's do it from declarer's standpoint. If declarer makes a vulnerable grand slam in rubber bridge, he earns 2100 to 2300 points on this one hand. If he goes down, he suffers only a small material penalty (plus the mental anguish for either having misplayed the hand or failing to have stopped at a small slam). If, on the next deal, he makes two diamonds, he gets a part-score of 40 points (plus the advantage of having the part-score). If, instead, he fails to make the two diamond contract, he pays a small penalty— and considers it insignificant that he has let slip an opportunity to earn a few points.

If the duplicate match-point player makes a vulnerable grand slam, in, let us say, spades, in a thirteen-table game, with 12 match points being "top" on the board, let us assume for the purpose of illustration that he gets a score of 11½ match points. (Only one other pair bid and made the grand slam, also in spades.) If he goes down at his grand slam contract, he will (let us assume) get ½ match point. A difference of 11 match points hangs in the balance.

If he fulfills his contract of two diamonds, let us assume that he will also get 11½ match points. If he goes down a trick, let's assume that he also gets ½ match point. Here, again, 11 match points hang in the balance—the difference between making one's contract and going down.

It must be understood that the above figures are theoretical and might not be true in any given case. Nevertheless the figures do illustrate that all deals have equal theoretical importance at duplicate play, but not at rubber bridge.

Sound advice on "how to win at duplicate" will, therefore, be related to the above all-important factors. For the very experienced player, if he needed it at all, it could be packaged in a few paragraphs. But for those with limited experience—or none at all—it is necessary to put each bit of knowledge to be imparted into its own topical niche, where it can be observed and analyzed in its proper perspective.

Since a very considerable proportion of the rest of this book will be devoted principally to pointing out differences between rubber bridge and duplicate bridge, it would be distorting the truth to state that the two forms of the game are not dissimilar in either theory or practice. However, it must be stated as a fact that the good performer at rubber bridge will also become a good duplicate player and vice versa, unless the bad rubber-bridge player acquires some new habits. This cannot be denied, although there are some exceptions. It has long been our contention that in order to be rated top-flight, a player must be good at both.

All this is preliminary to the statement that no vast store of knowledge applicable only to duplicate bridge is required to make a good start in the game. You need only to have made a start in bridge. If you have had extensive rubber bridge experience, so much the better.

Certainly there are many fine distinctions between rubber and duplicate bridge, or else we would not be preparing to devote a whole book to the subject. However, almost all differences between rubber bridge and duplicate will stem from some variations of the topics which are outlined below, and which are discussed at length, topic by topic, in the two following chapters.

I. The Philosophy of Duplicate Bridge

1. **Bidding for Game.** It should be done a little less often than in rubber bridge.
2. **The Bidding of Small Slams.** They should be bid as in rubber bridge.
3. **The Bidding of Grand Slams.** They should be bid a little more often than in rubber bridge.

4. Vulnerability. A most important difference which permeates all facets of duplicate bidding and play.
5. The Part-Score. Fought for much more vigorously in duplicate bridge.
6. Overcalls. Made with slightly weaker hands in duplicate.
7. The Take-out Double. Almost identical in both rubber bridge and duplicate.
8. Sacrifice Bidding. A delicate subject requiring specific detailing. It cannot be generalized upon.
9. Penalty Doubles. Greater frequency in duplicate bridge.
10. Opening Bids. Slightly dissimilar in third and fourth positions between rubber and duplicate bridge.
11. Reopening Bids. A subclassification of the topic "Part-Score." "Lighter" in duplicate bridge.
12. Attitude Toward Minor Suits. At the game level, one of contempt. At the part-score level, one of aversion.
13. Attitude Toward Major Suits vs. No-trump. No clear-cut position.
14. Differences in the Play of the Cards. Quite a difference with respect to both declarer's play and defenders' play.
15. Overtricks. Much more important in duplicate bridge.

The first 13 topics are discussed in Chapter 5. Topics 14 and 15 are discussed in Chapter 6.

It should be appreciated that the rubber-bridge player need not be apprehensive about his forthcoming transition to duplicate bridge. Most of the top-flight match-point players are also rubber-bridge players, or converts from that game. It may interest you to know that Howard Schenken, who was long considered the best player in the country, for years played strictly rubber-bridge style in duplicate tournaments. He competed against the best, and his record was outstanding. As former teammates, we can vouch for the essential truth of the above. Howard naturally made adjustments as he went along, and eventually evolved certain techniques for match-point play that were somewhat different from those he employed at rubber bridge.

Let us conclude this chapter on the "approach to duplicate bridge" by discussing the question of a theme which is voiced whenever a would-be duplicate player inquires about the "new" field he is about to enter. The theme is "free bad advice."

Much bad advice freely given to the player gaining duplicate experience will have insidious appeal merely because some modicum of logic will be inherent in it. He is certain to be assailed with maxims like this: "Stick with the field"; "Play for average"; "Never bid normally against a good pair"; "If you reach a contract of five in a minor, go on to six"; "Make fancy leads against top players," etc. You will be given reasons—by the proponents of the itemized quotations above—why each of the maxims must necessarily be winning procedure. The reasons will be persuasive, especially to a novice, but they will be unsound. Of the above, only "play for average" (that is, don't get "fancy" or "cute") comes close to being good advice.

For the graduates from the novice class, another "gem" will be offered: "Try to bid as others will bid, and pick up your points in the play." It seems to us that this is tantamount to giving up one's edge over the field, for duplicate bidding is about 75 percent of the game. It is just as logical, if not more so, to play your hands like everyone else (if only you know how they will play them!) and pick up your match points in the bidding.

Let *us* now offer some advice. It is the same old advice we have always given and followed from rubber-bridge days through duplicate: Bid well, play well, and defend well. This can be stated in another way, for college graduates: "Make the correct call and the right play." We realize, of course, that the above statements are easier said than done and as such are not followed perfectly at all times by even our best players. But it is not our present intention to immediately invest you with all knowledge and experience needed to make our advice work. That part is a job you will have to do yourself with a mere assist from us. It is your attitude toward duplicate bridge that we are trying to set right. We sincerely believe that if you start with and determinedly follow this advice, you will advance rapidly as a beginner. If you are a poor player, you will get better. If you are average, you will become better-than-average. If you are better-than-average, you will become very good. If you are near-expert, you will advance to the expert class. If you are super-expert, you need no advice—and frankly, in this case we would prefer to listen to you, to hear what you have to say on the subject. We, too, are desirous of learning.

CHAPTER 5

The Strategy of Duplicate Bridge: The Bidding

NOTE WELL: In duplicate bidding, the test to be applied is: How *often* will the bid win? The frequency of gain, not the amount of gain, is what matters, for your permanent aim is to outscore by any margin the other pairs who will be holding your cards.

I. Bidding for Game

Although a player cannot be absolutely certain of his conclusion, he should often be able to appraise (or have "a feeling" about) his chances of fulfilling a contemplated game contract before he actually bids it or while he is deliberating as to whether he should bid it. The categories of "excellent," "very good," "impossible," or "very bad" can usually be recognized quite easily by the experienced player. "Good," "fair," "possibly hazardous," and "shaky" are much harder to prognosticate. Nevertheless a player, as he is bidding, will in time develop some idea as to which of these categories fits a particular situation; and, just as important, to what extent he will be rewarded if his judgment is right and what it figures to cost him if his diagnosis of the situation turns out to be erroneous.

The *rubber-bridge* player's attitude toward bidding a game should be liberal and gambling. It will pay him to bid game, which risks the loss of a part-score contract, on much less than a 50 percent chance. The mathematics we are about to give are approximate but are nevertheless reasonably accurate as a guide:

Vulnerable game—35% $\Big\}$ Break-even point.
Nonvulnerable game—40% $\Big\}$ If less, don't bid it.

It should be noted that the rubber-bridge player assumes risks in bidding games *particularly* when vulnerable. He will be well ahead in the long run if he bids games on chances which range from 50 percent down to 35 percent. Shaky and hazardous games are not too bad a proposition for him. The reason is a purely mathematical one, or a "business" proposition, if you wish.

If, for example, you are vulnerable against non-vulnerable opponents, and you bid and make a "very bad," gambling, four spade contract, you score 700 points for the rubber, plus 120 for your trick score. If you go down a trick, you lose 100 points, plus the 90 part-score you could have had, plus whatever the "cash-surrender" value of a part-score is worth; let us say 70 or 80 points. And if you do happen to go down a trick, you and the opponents are all even going into the next deal. On a risk vs. gain basis—that is, the *amount* you stood to gain versus the *amount* you stood to lose—the gamble was worthwhile. But if you bid the very same bad game in duplicate, and go down when every other pair stopped in a part-score and made it, you will get zero match points on the board for your minus score, since every other pair holding your cards will have made a plus score.

Therefore the match-point player should not attempt any game contract which is not close to a 50 percent chance. Any *plus score*—in the form of a part-score—is too valuable to risk going minus on a chance that is less than fair or average. Bidding games at match-point play should be in the 50 percent bracket, like a finesse. As was mentioned, in rubber bridge it is the *amount* of gain that is important; in duplicate it is the frequency of gain that is important. Putting it another way, if, in a duplicate game, on one deal you win 1,000,000 points, and on the next three deals you lose 250,000 points on each, you cannot say that you have won 250,000 points all in all. On the deal where you won a million points, you have an undisputed top score, for nobody (repeat, *nobody*) scored one million points except you. And on the deals where you lost 250,000 points on each, you have an undisputed bottom—zero match points —on each. You have lost on three deals out of four—and if you don't watch out, you'll be expelled for low grades, for your 25 percent score (one victory out of four) is far below average, which is 50 percent. But in rubber bridge, the amount of your profit would have been 250,000 points, a tidy sum when exchanged for that green stuff.

In duplicate bridge, if you take, let us say, a 40 percent chance when you don't have to, you'll get a good result 40 percent of the time—and a bad result 60 percent of the time. In terms of match points, you'll wind up below average if you play "against percentage." As has been pointed out, in match-point play the number of points you score is secondary. How many teams you outscore is primary.

About 15 years ago, we didn't bid a game in duplicate unless we felt that we had about a 55 percent chance; whereas today we do it on 50 percent. The reason is that 15 years ago any plus score was worth more than it is now, for at that time people didn't bid as well and didn't reach as many games as they do today. More games are bid and made today because the average competitor bids and plays so much better than he did 15 years ago—and so we are forced to bid more close games to "keep up with the Joneses." Nevertheless, the break-even point for the match-point competitor is still 50 percent.

In conclusion, don't gamble for game in duplicate bridge as frequently as you do in rubber bridge.

About 25 years ago, in a National Tournament, a sporting wager was made in this situation: There were 38 tables in play in the National Open Pairs Championships, and 37 was top on the board —that is, each board was played 38 times (there were two sections of 19 tables each, with the boards duplicated for each section). The wager—a dinner—was made before the event started that any pair which secured a plus score on any board would never get a zero. The wager was won. On the 26 boards that were played, no plus score, no matter how low, received a zero. On one deal that we remember, North–South were able to make a small slam in either spades or no-trump, the only outstanding high card being the ace of spades. Yet one team stopped in a part-score contract of two spades, and, of course, made six, for a score of 230. They were not bottom, for two other teams, somehow or other, arrived at a grand slam in spades, missing the ace of trumps. . . . Each of the latter of course received a minus score.

II. The Bidding of Small Slams

The subject of when one should bid a small slam in duplicate bridge is easily disposed of. In both rubber and duplicate bridge, your attitude should be virtually the same: you should bid a small slam if you think fulfillment depends on nothing worse than a finesse in some suit. If it will take a finesse *plus* some other factor, such as a favorable break in a suit, then percentage is operating against you (and you are operating against percentage). A finesse is a 50 percent chance, and therefore you bid a small slam when you calculate that your chances are not worse than 50 percent. We might mention that we have been informed that in certain sections of the country you are an "underdog" if you don't bid all apparently reasonable slams because in that section everybody does. In answer, we would like to point out that mathematical percentages will still operate in the same way even under those circumstances. If one persists in bidding dubious slams, he must inevitably wind up as a loser.

On a national or international basis, if one bids a most dubious slam and goes down, he will tend to get a zero or perhaps ½ match point, for virtually everyone else will tend to stop at game and make it. When one bids a small slam on, say, a 40 percent chance, he figures to make it two times out of five (40 percent). So twice he will get a top or a tie-for-top; and three times he will get a bottom or tie-for-bottom—which will put him below average. In terms of match points, with 12 as top, he will get—let us assume— 12 match points each time he makes the slam; and zero match points each time he goes down. Thus, he will score 24 points on these five boards, an average of almost 5 per board. But "average" on each board is 6, so he will be below average—and a loser.

III. The Bidding of Grand Slams

The bidding of a grand slam in duplicate bridge requires more careful consideration and analysis. In rubber bridge, the mathematics are simple. You break even if you fulfill a grand slam contract two out of every three times you bid it (as related to having stopped at a small slam three times, and made each one). Therefore, in rubber bridge, you bid a grand slam whenever you estimate your chances of fulfillment as being very good. You can afford to bid it on no worse a hazard than a 3-2 split of the five adverse trumps, which occurs 68 percent of the time (in which case you will break even in the long run), but would not consider it if you think that fulfillment would depend on a finesse, which, of course, is only a 50 percent chance.

The match-point player's attitude toward bidding a grand slam can be more liberal. In theory, he should attempt it if he estimates that his chances are about 60 percent, possibly even a bit less, in the vicinity of 55 percent. He is compensated in match points, and not in numbers representing dollars and cents. If his chance is as good as the minimum figure recommended, he will be adequately rewarded in the long run.

In actual practice, the experienced would-be-grand-slam bidder will often content himself with a small slam, for in past performances he has learned that failure to reach a grand slam very rarely results in getting zero match points but that reaching a grand slam and going down is almost always a guaranteed way of obtaining zero match points. Hence, if the field is known to be a conservative one and not prone to bid grand slams unless a guarantee is attached, one will tend to stop at a small slam—and hope that some pairs will not reach even a small slam. But if the field is known to be of high quality, slams should be bid as recommended: on a 55 percent chance.

We would be remiss if we neglected to mention one factor at this point. The figures given are mathematical, and we vouch for their accuracy. However, where grand slam contracts are involved, a psychological factor often enters. It has to do with the personality of the partner with whom you generally play. We are not concerned with his skill but only with his attitude. Some partners cannot stand your bidding seven and going down (they just can't take it!), even when you can prove that the risk was warranted. Explaining to your partner in lucid detail the gorgeous sequence of bidding you employed to reach the grand slam that failed only because of an "unlucky" break will not placate him for the zero he just received on the board. With such a partner, you should perhaps be more careful in displaying what *he* deems to be an overly ambitious attitude on your part. With a partner who does not measure an effort merely by its result, the normal percentage *may* suffice. We say *may* because nobody really likes a loser.

IV. Vulnerability

The condition of vulnerability pervades so many facets in such an important manner that we ought not to go further without introducing it at this point. It will be discussed in more specific detail throughout the text.

Even though the rubber-bridge player assumes additional hazards when he becomes vulnerable, that condition is highly desirable to him. He cannot win the rubber, which gives him a 500 or 700 point bonus, unless he first becomes vulnerable.

In theory, the condition of being vulnerable should not affect the match-point player because he is in reality competing against players also playing under the same vulnerability conditions. In reality, such a condition is a handicap, for it restricts his maneuverability; whereas the scope and range of his non-vulnerable opponents is greatly increased.

Good players have stated, with heartfelt convictions, that they could win any tournament if only they were permitted to be non-vulnerable against vulnerable opponents. It follows, therefore, that the condition of non-vulnerability, as a prime natural resource, should be exploited to the fullest extent, within reason. A vulnerable player, conversely, will be hampered by restrictions, also within reason. As was said, we shall be going into this in more detail later.

V. The Part-Score

The good rubber-bridge player will, quite naturally, compete for a part-score but he will not usually compete vigorously. The reason is that scores involving small amounts of points have relatively little importance at rubber bridge. One will, of course, fight harder when not vulnerable, for the risk of harm is lessened: the penalties are smaller. When vulnerable, at rubber bridge, one has learned from bitter experiences to pull in one's horns and save the fighting for days when the (vulnerability) conditions will be more favorable.

The match-point player, on the other hand, fights as vigorously for a part-score as he does for a grand slam. This is quite natural, since the ultimate reward, *the identical number of match points*, is equal on each deal. Logically, therefore, the match-point player will be required to give battle much more often. Furthermore, there are many more part-score deals than there are slam deals, thus increasing the number of deals on which one must fight if he is to survive.

In match-point scoring, one cannot afford to be left out of the bidding with a fair hand. Permitting the opponents to make even a modest contract like two hearts (plus 110) when you could have made two spades, or even been down one (minus 50 or 100) may well result in a bottom score just as surely as if you had gone down 1100 points on the deal. Should your result be inferior to that of all the other teams who will be playing your cards, it is completely immaterial if the difference is 10 points or 1100 points, for the scoring is relative, not absolute.

We will not go into very great detail here, but the nonvulnerable player has a very great advantage in match-point play. He can push harder while competing because the penalties for being set are about half of those paid by his vulnerable opponents when they go set. For example, he can always afford to be down one trick, doubled, which is 100 points, to prevent the opposition from making 2 H, 2 S, 3 C, 3 D, which would net them 110 points. The vulnerable player cannot ever afford to be down one, doubled, against a part-score, for he would, in this case, lose 200 points, which is greater than the value of *any* part-score. As an aside, if one goes down three, undoubled and not vulnerable, for a loss of 150 points, he will almost always have a poor score, for the opponents' partial scores usually range from 90 to 140 (1 NT, 2 C, 2 D, 2 H, 2 S, 2 NT, 3 C, 3 D, 3 H, 3 S). Thus, when such a small difference in score has such tremendous significance, it becomes apparent that sound, delicate judgment is an essential ingredient for securing the maximum score.

To sum up: the rubber-bridge player fights for the part-score but never if he must assume a grave risk in doing so. The match-point player always fights for the part-score, regardless of vulnerability. Of course, he is much more careful when vulnerable since the penalties impose natural restrictions. Yet he cannot be ultra-conservative even when vulnerable, for his self-preservation is at stake and he cannot afford to sell out cheaply.

VI. Overcalls

Speaking very generally, our overcalls are almost the same in duplicate bridge as in rubber bridge. A good overcall at rubber bridge will be a good overcall in duplicate play. The important difference is that in match-point play, you will tend to overcall on all *borderline overcalling types of hands,* whereas in rubber bridge you would tend not to for fear of getting hurt too badly. In borderline rubber-bridge overcalling situations, especially when vulnerable, "discretion is the better part of valor." Why stick your neck out in rubber bridge when you know you figure to get, *at best,* a part-score and when you might incur an 800 or an 1100 point penalty if you run into bad distribution. But in duplicate, one's worry is not *how much* an overcall *might* go down. You are concerned with how often it will result in a bad board.

And so, in match-point play, the overcall will tend to be slightly lighter than in rubber bridge—that is, the hand will tend to be a little bit weaker. As a consequence, you will tend to make more frequent overcalls in match-point play than in rubber bridge.

There is another very sound reason for making slightly weaker overcalls in duplicate bridge. The need to indicate a good lead to partner is much more important in duplicate than it is in rubber bridge. If you can prevent the opponents from making an overtrick at their contract, you will usually gain a tremendous number of match points. In rubber bridge, of course, the overtrick is of virtually no significance.

Permit me to illustrate this point. If, for example, in a five-table game, four North–South pairs reach a four spade contract, not vulnerable, and make an overtrick, they will each score 450 points (120 plus 30 plus 300). But if, by means of your overcall, you directed your partner to a lead which resulted in preventing your opponents from making the overtrick, you would have held them to 420 points (120 plus 300). You would thus have earned a "top on the board"—4 match points—since you would have outscored each of the four other pairs who held your cards.

To summarize: overcalls at match-point play are a trifle weaker than in rubber bridge, since the major battle tends to center around part scores; and it therefore becomes more imperative to compete more vigorously—and more often—than in rubber bridge.

VII. The Take-Out Double

Our immediate take-out doubles are essentially the same in both rubber and duplicate bridge. If there is a difference, it would be that our requirements are lowered ever so slightly in duplicate bridge, especially when not vulnerable. This slight difference can be observed in the following hands:

(1)	(2)
♠ 5 2	♠ 5 2
♡ A J 6 2	♡ A J 6 2
◇ K 10 9 2	◇ K 6 4 3
♣ A J 2	♣ A J 2

Let's assume our right-hand opponent opens the bidding in first position with *one spade.*

With Hand (1), if not vulnerable, we would double in both rubber bridge and in duplicate bridge. This is a minimum doubling hand.

With Hand (2), if not vulnerable, we would double in duplicate bridge, but not in rubber bridge.

With Hand (1), if we are vulnerable, we would *tend to* double in both rubber bridge and duplicate bridge.

With Hand (2), if we are vulnerable, we would not double in either rubber bridge or in duplicate bridge, although if the opponents were also vulnerable, we would think of doubling in duplicate bridge.

As can be observed, the "take-out-double" line between rubber bridge and duplicate bridge is a pretty tough one to delineate.

VIII. Sacrifice Bidding

By definition, "sacrifice bidding" is bidding for a contract at which you know you will sustain a loss in order to prevent the opposition from acquiring a *greater* plus score at their own contract. This subject is not an easy one in which to train the beginner —or even the average player—for, to be honest, the prerequisites for its mastery are: (1) experience and (2) a sense of clairvoyance. However, let's make a beginning and let's start with this deal which, in our opinion, demonstrates an advantage of sacrifice bidding that would have remained undiscovered if people had played nothing but rubber bridge.

East dealer.
Neither side vulnerable.

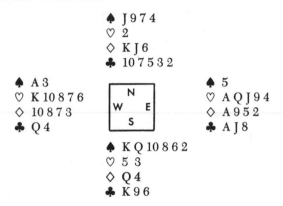

♠ J 9 7 4
♡ 2
♢ K J 6
♣ 10 7 5 3 2

♠ A 3
♡ K 10 8 7 6
♢ 10 8 7 3
♣ Q 4

♠ 5
♡ A Q J 9 4
♢ A 9 5 2
♣ A J 8

♠ K Q 10 8 6 2
♡ 5 3
♢ Q 4
♣ K 9 6

The bidding:

East	South	West	North
1 ♡	1 ♠	4 ♡	?

Playing rubber bridge, there are undoubtedly millions of bridge players who, even now, could not be convinced that it might be proper to bid four spades on the North hand. It is apparent that North–South figure to go down two tricks, doubled for a loss of 300 points, whereas East–West will score "only" 120 points by making four hearts, since the latter is not vulnerable. To most players, it will appear that North will lose 300 points if he bids and only 120 points if he chooses to pass.

We remember very vividly how we argued with such players that by bidding four spades they could prevent East–West from scoring a game worth about 300 points, in addition to the 120-point trick score. But arguments fell on deaf ears. Even some very experienced players ridiculed our position. They were unable to appreciate that *the first game of a rubber had an invisible value which, though not scored* (or, perhaps, not paid for) *immediately, was nevertheless quite real.*

But when duplicate bridge emerged as a scientific game, this theory which we had been preaching demonstrated its validity and soundness. The scoffers learned quickly that if they passed in situations analogous to the above their East–West opponents would promptly get not only the 120-point trick score but also the "invisible" 300-point value of the non-vulnerable game, resulting in an East–West score of 420 points. They also learned that by paying a penalty of 300 points at four spades doubled, East–West would get only 300 points and that the North player who passed West's four heart bid would get a bad score compared to all the other North players who bid four spades. It was also learned that on many occasions in situations such as these, either the East or West player, feeling that he was "robbed," was spurred into bidding five hearts which, as in the above deal, would go down. In this case, the North–South team invariably secured a "top" or a "tie-for-top" on the board.

Lest the reader get the impression that we are highly recommending sacrifice bidding as a good thing, let us quickly deny it. Frankly, we doubt whether sacrifice bidding ever pays off in the long run. Far too often, especially when the game bidders have aggressive personalities, they will arrive at unmakable games. If one elects to sacrifice against these overbid contracts, he will find himself minus 100, 300, 500, etc., when he could have had a plus score by simply passing. As was stated some paragraphs back, knowing when to sacrifice requires (1) experience and (2) a sense of clairvoyance. Both of these factors must take into consideration the habits of the specific opponents, in terms of whether they are overbidders, underbidders, or "down the middle" bidders.

Let us summarize in general fashion what has been presented in the preceding paragraphs:

Sacrifices in duplicate bridge, at the part-score, game, and slam levels, if *judiciously* undertaken, *may* net good results: that is, if your judgment is correct regarding *both* the impossibility of defeating the adversaries' contract *and* the number of points you are likely to go down (doubled). You know what the opponents stand to make; therefore you know what you can afford to lose. If you lose less than they could have made, you get a good match-point score. If you lose more, you get a bad match-point score. Sacrifices that result in a minus score greater than the value of the opponents' game contract will always yield a bad result.

A critical factor when considering a sacrifice bid (or a "save," as it is called) is vulnerability. In part-score bidding, for example, we have seen why one never can afford to go down even one trick, doubled, vulnerable, when the opponents can make only a part-score, for a "minus 200" result will be greater than any part-score the opponents could have made. Here are the criteria for sacrificing against the opponents' *game* contract:

1. With neither side vulnerable, you can afford to go down 300 points (down two, doubled), since their score for a game bid and made will usually range from 400 to 490 (300 plus trick score).

2. When they are vulnerable and you are not, you can afford to lose 500 points (down three, doubled), since their game will yield them 600–690 points (500 plus trick score).

3. When both sides are vulnerable, you can afford to go down 500 points (down two, doubled), since their game contract will net them 600–690.

4. When you are vulnerable and they are not, you can afford to go down 200 points (one trick, doubled) since their game contract will yield them 400–490 points. If, in this situation, you go down two tricks doubled, you will lose 500 points, more than the value of their game. Only very rarely are sacrifices undertaken in these latter circumstances (called "unfavorable" vulnerability conditions).

Generally speaking, sacrifice bids in rubber bridge, although having a sound mathematical basis, are not too often very attractive, especially since overbidding of games is much more frequent in rubber bridge than in duplicate bridge. With neither side vulnerable, if you concede 300 points by going to four spades over the opponent's four heart bid (as a "save"), you will gain 100 or so points—but you will look very foolish if it turns out on analysis that four hearts could have been beaten.

But at duplicate, the story is very different, and always most critical on each deal. Losing 300 points instead of 420 is likely being in heaven as against being in the other place—and, for the moment, in terms of match points, even better than being in heaven. As was mentioned earlier, there is also a psychological advantage in taking a materially worthwhile sacrifice: the opponents may decide that doubling your sacrificial four spade contract may produce a bad score for them and they *may* elect to try for five hearts. If you can defeat the latter contract, you will probably have the best score of all the pairs who hold your cards.

Let's look at this illustration. North–South are *vulnerable*.

North	East	South	West
2 NT	Pass	3 NT	?

You are West, holding the following hand:

♠ Q J 10 3
♡ Q J 10 9 8 6 4
♢ —
♣ 5 2

At rubber bridge, it would be a toss of a coin whether to bid four hearts or not. This bid figures to go down three tricks for a loss of 500 points. The amount of points you would gain is inconsequential because it will really not alter your material well-being one way or another. Conceivably, you may go down 800, which also will be of little import, since the opponents figure to make 800 or so points at their three no-trump contract.

But at duplicate bridge, the four heart call is a *must!* The danger of a 800-point set—a very slight danger—must be undertaken. It would be suicidal to permit the opponents to play a 600-point-plus contract when there is a very great possibility that you can lose only 500 points instead. And if they should elect to bid four no-trump over your four heart call, not only will you not have lost anything by your attempted save, but they may go down. After all, ten tricks are usually more difficult to make than nine tricks.

As a reminder, it should be mentioned again that in all sacrificing considerations, the assumption is made that the opponents can fulfill their contract. If there is any doubt about this pre-condition, any contemplated sacrifice bid becomes a pure gamble.

A. SACRIFICING AGAINST SLAM CONTRACTS

In sacrificing against opposing slam contracts, especially when the opponents are vulnerable and you are not, the outlook *appears* to be more promising than sacrificing against game contracts. At least straight arithmetic makes it appear to be that way, although, as we will show, more often than not it is an enticing delusion.

If you are not vulnerable, playing against vulnerable opponents, you can afford to go down seven tricks, doubled, for a loss of 1300 points against their small slam contract. If you permit them to play their vulnerable small slam, they will score from 1370 to 1440 points.

At the grand slam level, the height of absurdity is reached. For example, you need only two tricks in seven spades doubled, not vulnerable, if the opponents have arrived at a makable, vulnerable, seven heart contract. You will, in this case, lose "only" 2100 points, whereas they would have scored 2210 points for fulfilling their grand slam contract.

Sounds most enticing, doesn't it? But there is a rub—and it will damage you severely more often than not. Let us see why.

Surprisingly, perhaps, in the slam department sacrifice bidding will pay more handsome dividends at *rubber bridge* than it will at match-point play! In rubber bridge, if a player is beaten 700 or 900 points when the opponents could have made a small slam worth 1430 points, he has saved a substantial amount of points. His only real concern is whether the slam bidders could have made their contract. This is, of course, always a serious concern, but experienced players can usually pick the right spot for making the sacrifice bid.

But sacrifices against slam contracts in match-point play almost never pay. There are, of course, exceptions, but we know of no one smart enough to find them consistently without suffering several major calamities in the process. Here are the reasons for avoiding sacrifices against slams in match-point play.

You will discover that whenever a presumably makable slam is bid against you, you are in for a very bad match-point score, for most pairs will stop at a mere game contract. So if you lose 700, 800, 900 points to save yourself from a loss of, say, 1430 points (6 S), you will be outscored by all the other pairs holding your cards, against whom only a vulnerable game was bid and made with two overtricks. They will be minus only 680 points (500 + 180), compared to your minus 700 or more. So, one way or another, you will have a poor score. It is better, as experience has amply demonstrated, to pass and hope that by some unexpected value in partner's hand or by some unskillful play by the declarer you will be able to beat their slam, and thereby get a top on the board.

Let us illustrate this point by setting up a slam situation on a traveling score slip, assuming a nine-table game. You are East–West Pair # 1, and playing Board 2 against North–South Pair # 1. North–South are vulnerable. You are not.

OFFICIAL ACBL TRAVELING SCORE

North player keeps score
Enter E-W Pair No

Board No [2]

N-S Pair No	CON-TRACT	BY	Tr'ks made	Double	SCORE N-S	SCORE E-W	E-W Pair No	Match Points
1	6SX	E	4		800		1	7
2	6H	N	6		1430		3	8
3	4H	N	6		680		5	3
4	4H	N	6		680		7	3
5	4H	N	5		650		9	0
6	3NT	S	6		690		2	6
7	4H	N	6		680		4	3
8	4H	N	6		680		6	3
9	4H	N	6		680		8	3
10								
11								
12								
13								
14								
15								
16								
17								
18								
19							1	1
20							2	2
21							0	3
22							5	4
23							5	5
24							5	6
25							5	7
26							5	8
27							8	9
28								10
29								11
30								12
31								13
32								14
33								15
34								16
35								17
36								18

Form 234
Printed in USA by ACBL
Copyright ACBL 1987

AMERICAN CONTRACT BRIDGE LEAGUE
2990 AIRWAYS BOULEVARD
MEMPHIS TN 38116 3847

As you can observe, against N–S # 1's makable six heart contract, you sacrificed at six spades, were doubled, and went down four tricks, for a loss of 800 points. You received 1 match point, for the only East–West team whose score you beat was E–W # 3, against whom the vulnerable small slam was bid and made, for a score of 1430 points.

Had you permitted the opponents to play at six hearts, they would have scored 1430 points (assuming they didn't revoke). You and E-W #3 would have been tied for bottom, having the worst score of all East-West pairs: minus 1430. You would, in this case, have secured 1/2 match point, as against 1 match point for going down *only* 800!

Whether you went down 800, 1100 or 1400, your match-point score would have been the same, for only one other team scored more than 690 points. Was it not better, in this case, to have taken a chance and have permitted the opponents to have played their six heart contract and have hoped that, somehow, they would have gone down? Had they done so, you would have scored 7-1/2 match points, instead of the one match point which you obtained by your excellent *theoretical* sacrifice.

In rubber bridge, your sacrifice bid of six spades would have netted you a material gain: you would have made 630 points, the difference between losing 1430 and losing only 800.

On the subject of sacrifice bidding against the opponents' slam contracts on duplicate play, one additional point should be stressed. When the opponents bid a grand slam against you, two things must be appreciated. First, with the opponents holding virtually every high card in the deck most pairs will probably reach a *small* slam contract, but very few will usually reach the grand slam contract. Secondly, a grand slam contract is often a delicate one to handle and usually offers declarer no leeway. If he runs into a bad break in a suit or he makes a bad guess or he just slips once, he might go down. More often than not in our experience at match-point play, there is a chance to beat a grand slam contract no matter how weak your hand might be. Therefore, when you sacrifice against a grand slam contract, be sure that *your penalty will be less than the opponents would have scored if they had stopped at a small slam and made it.*

On the next page is a classic illustration of the above situation. The deal arose a few years ago in a duplicate game at Philadelphia's Cavendish Club. It was a 13-table game. North–South were vulnerable; East–West were not vulnerable.

As the reader will note, East–West Pair # 10 obtains zero match points for having the worst East–West score: minus 2000. They bid seven diamonds, as a sacrifice, after North–South reached a seven club contract. If North–South had fulfilled their grand slam contract, they would have scored 2140 points—and East–West would have secured the identical match-point score of zero for having the worst East–West score!

OFFICIAL ACBL TRAVELING SCORE

North player keeps score
Enter E-W Pair No

Board No [5]

N.S Pair No	CON TRACT	BY	B MADE	DWN	SCORE N.S	SCORE E-W	E-W Pair No	Match Points	
1	6C	S	6		1370		12		
2	6C	S	6		1370		1		
3	6C	S	6		1370		3		
4	6C	S	6		1370		5		
5	6C	S	6		1370		7		
6	6C	S	6		1370		9		
7	6C	S	6		1370		11		
8	6C	S	6		1370		13		
9	6NT	N	6		1440		2		
10	6C	S	6		1370		4		
11	6C	S	6		1370		6		
12	6C	S	6		1370		8		
13	7DX	W		8	2000		10		
14									
15									
16									
17									
18									
19								7	1
20								1	2
21								7	3
22								7	4
23								7	5
24								7	6
25								7	7
26								7	8
27								7	9
28								0	10
29								7	11
30								7	12
31								7	13
32									14
33									15
34									16
35									17
36									18

Form 234
Printed in USA by ACBL
Copyright ACBL 1987

AMERICAN CONTRACT BRIDGE LEAGUE
299 AIRWAYS BOULEVARD
MEMPHIS TN 38116 384?

But North–South could not have made seven clubs, as was made evident by both the post-mortem analysis and by the fact that none of the other pairs playing a club contract were able to take more than 12 tricks. So if East–West had not sacrificed, North–South would have been minus 100 points—and East–West Pair # 10 would have scored a top on the board: 12 match points.

Of course, if East–West # 10 had gone down only five tricks (minus 1100) instead of the actual eight, they would have scored 12 match points, beating each of the other East–West pairs who were minus 1370 and the one East–West pair that was minus 1440. But again, if they had passed the seven club bid, they would have hit the jackpot.

'Nuff said?

Just to make sure that the reader does not misconstrue our position regarding sacrifice bidding, permit us to restate it: Sacrifice bidding is a delicate, sensitive weapon which, to attain the sought-for result, must always be triggered by "knowing" perception (perhaps even extrasensory perception). When it is undertaken, one must accurately presuppose that the opposition can *surely* fulfill their game or slam. Since in most cases one can seldom be sure, sacrifice bidding is a hazardous venture.

Although we have the feeling that sacrifice bidding in general is a losing proposition, it must nevertheless be employed, for it involves—especially at the below-game levels—pushing the opponents one level higher than they would care to go on their own power. This is the competitive phase of sacrificing—and we are very much in favor of competing. In fact, we don't think we can survive without doing so. It is sometimes quite difficult in the early stages of bidding to separate sacrificing from legitimate competitive action, for it is not known as yet which side has the better cards. Both sacrificing and competing are inherent in the philosophy of the good duplicate player, for he has learned that quite often when he "pushes" or sacrifices, the opponents go one trick higher—and beyond their depth.

So, in conclusion, don't sell out too cheaply—but don't let your love for competition force you higher than you can afford to go.

IX. Penalty Doubles

In rubber bridge, the pitfalls of doubling game and slam contracts on high cards that may get trumped are well known. Caution is also necessary at duplicate bridge. Provided you do not consider your cards are worth a plus score on their own merit, there is seldom any need to double to get a good result. Here is an example:

North and South were vulnerable, and the bidding had proceeded:

South	West	North	East
1 ♠	Pass	2 ◊	Pass
2 ♡	Pass	4 ♠	?

East held:

♠ Q J 10
♡ K 10 7
◊ K 6 2
♣ A K 7 2

East passed!

The contract went down three tricks, and East–West scored a "top." They would have scored the same top if they had doubled. It seemed unlikely that four spades could be made, but some freakish distribution may have brought about the fulfillment of the contract. Actually, dummy did have a singleton club, which eliminated a hoped-for defensive trick. The point is this: Either the opponents were bidding too rashly or they were not. If they were, East figured to get a good score, since the other North–South pairs would have stopped in two or three spades. If they were not, East might well obtain a good score because he did not double, while other East pairs would double, unsuccessfully.

With the above as an illustration, it is apparent that there are differences in practice between penalty doubles in rubber bridge vs. those in duplicate bridge. These differences stem from the fact that in duplicate the number of points you score is not as important as the number of pairs whose scores you beat. Yet, there are not as many differences as most people think there are. But somehow restraint seems to fall by the wayside, and many players double on the slightest provocation, possibly feeling that it costs them the same card fee whether the opponents make their contracts doubled or undoubled. We often suspect that they wouldn't be so loose and carefree with their doubles if it cost them more card fee every time they made an unsuccessful double.

We can better understand the differences if we first set forth the similarities. The duplicate player goes right along with the rubber-bridge player in that he very seldom doubles a high contract which the opponents have reached voluntarily and which they clearly expect to make. In both rubber bridge and match-point play, one does not double a voluntarily assumed game contract to obtain a one-trick set. The minimum margin should be a two-trick set. In duplicate bridge, if the opponents have bid too much on their own power, the defenders will get a good score anyway—and good scores do not need to be improved, especially if in trying to improve them you stand a good chance of losing everything.

You do not ever double a voluntary and enthusiastically bid slam because you feel you can beat it. You double if you feel that you can annihilate it. In one specific situation, which will be presented later,* you may double a slam to secure a specifically directed lead which, when obtained, will give you a fighting chance to beat a slam contract which, without the lead, figures to be unbeatable.

You double all sacrifice bids by the opponents when your side does not wish to bid any higher. Another way of putting this would be that you must double for penalties or go on bidding when it is obvious by the bidding that your side has much the better of the cards.

The greatest difference in your attitude toward the penalty double will be evident in part-score situations. Once again you will be trodding on dangerous ground where good balance and keen judgment will be required. If, for example, you bid two spades, which you think you can make, and they who are *vulnerable* compete to three hearts, you may make a risky double if you suspect you can beat them one trick. If your diagnosis is proper (and your defensive play is equal to the occasion), beating them one trick doubled, for 200 points, will compensate you for the 110 your side could have scored at your two spade contract. But beating them one trick, undoubled, is almost sure to give you a bad score, for you will score but 100 points, as compared to the 110 for fulfilling your two spade contract. In cases such as this, you actually stand to lose less by an unsuccessful double than you stand to lose by not doubling if the opponents are too high.

Similarly, you may double a nonvulnerable opponent to get 100 points instead of 50 when you feel that you could have made 90 at your contract (1 NT, 2 C, 2 D). On the same reasoning, if you feel that on some hand you can make 110 or 120, then doubling a nonvulnerable opponent to set him one trick (to get 100 instead

* See page 291.

of 50) will net you very few—if any—additional match points, for plus scores of either 50 or 100 are equally inferior to the 110 or 140 you could have had. So you pass, and hope for the best.

To summarize the above, a double which, if successful, will net you a better score than the partial you could have made (and were in) warrants taking the risk. If, however, you can't reach the partial score total even if the double is successful to the extent of beating them one trick, then don't double, for the risk will not be worth it.

It should be realized that in rubber bridge a double of any part score above two diamonds (2 H, 2 S, 2 NT, etc.), if unsuccessful, will give the opponents a game; whereas a double of any contract below two hearts (2 D, 2 C, 1 NT, etc.), if unsuccessful, will give the opponents merely a larger part-score (assuming they make no overtricks). But in duplicate bridge, a double of, let us say, two clubs, if unsuccessful, will be just as costly as a double of two spades. At two clubs, doubled, they will score 180 points (40 times two = 80; 50 points for a part-score; and 50 points for fulfilling a doubled contract). This score will be greater in almost every instance than the one they could have made if left alone, and will net them a top score or near top score. An unsuccessful double of two spades will give the opponents the same top score, or near top score. And, again, it becomes apparent that the *amount* of gain or loss is not the primary consideration in duplicate bridge. The prime consideration is the number of pairs whose scores you beat, or whose scores will beat yours. Therefore it may pay, in match-point play, to risk losing a large amount of total points in order to score just a few more points.

Thus, the good duplicate player may commit what is the cardinal sin for the rubber-bridge player to commit: doubling the opponents into game. But, as is apparent, this must be chanced if one thinks that his opponents are trying to "steal" a part-score. Hence, in a part-score battle, one frequently has to be trigger-happy; and if, on occasion, one turns a low score into a zero via a double which was unsuccessful, it will be more than compensated for if the next two doubles are successful.

Frequently, some close figuring is needed to determine whether to double the opponents in a low contract at duplicate. Trying for a penalty double is often the alternative to trying for a game, and the prospects of each must be carefully assessed. Suppose that you are faced with the choice of doubling the opponents at a *one heart* contract, which is certain to be defeated, and trying for a likely three no-trump game.

The rubber-bridge player is likely to try for the guaranteed profit of the penalty in the hand to the game in the bush, but the duplicate player must study the vulnerability carefully. If he is vulnerable, and the opponents are not, his side would have to win ten tricks to make 800 points (down four) in order to outscore the 600 plus points that a game in no-trump would yield. Making ten tricks in defense can rarely be managed; if it can, the defenders will usually have a slam of their own in some other suit. So this particular kind of penalty double—against nonvulnerable opponents when you are vulnerable—rarely pays off.

But if the vulnerability is reversed, the penalty double becomes much more attractive. If the one heart overcaller is vulnerable, and the doubler is not, then a two-trick set will yield 500 points, whereas the nonvulnerable game at no-trump is worth but 400 plus points. In this case the defenders need eight tricks in defense to get an excellent score.

Doubles of one-level contracts are delicate affairs and, as often as not, one needs a crystal ball to come up with the winning solution.

X. Opening Bids

No difference exists between rubber bridge and duplicate bridge, except the opening bid in fourth position, the other three players having passed. In match-point play, we would open any 10, 11, or 12 point hand on which we felt we would have a slight advantage if we opened. We would, however, toss most of these in at the rubber-bridge table. For example, we hold each of these two hands in fourth position, playing duplicate. We are not vulnerable.

(1)	(2)
♠ A K Q 6 2	♠ 4 3
♡ 8 5 3	♡ 9 7
◇ Q 3 2	◇ A Q J 9 8 6
♣ 7 4	♣ K J 5

(1) We would open this with one spade. In rubber bridge, we would pass.

(2) We would open with three diamonds. In rubber bridge, we would pass.

On both of these hands, there is no chance of getting to a makable game, hence the pass at rubber bridge. The best you can hope for is a partial. But, again, at duplicate bridge, a partial of, let's say, three diamonds on Hand (2), for a score of plus 110, will beat the score of every pair who passed out the deal with our cards. And we think we are a favorite to make three diamonds if our partner has what he's supposed to have, mathematically speaking, namely his one-third share of the outstanding high cards.

On Hand (1), the possession of the spade suit is our primary reason for bidding. As we will illustrate by example later on, the spade suit is the loveliest of all suits to possess in competitive bidding situations, for the opponents must go to the next-higher level if they wish to compete in some other suit. Again assuming an even division of the outstanding high cards in the hands of the three other players, which means our partner has his fair share, we figure to have a respectable play for two spades. The opponents, both of whom have passed, don't figure to have much of a chance at any three-level (nine-trick) contract.

At this point, probably the most important difference in the approach to rubber bridge and duplicate bridge should be introduced. The major objective in rubber bridge is to reach game, and the opening bids are geared to this objective.* An opening bid in the responding hand facing an opening bid in the opener's hand will produce a game. In terms of the point count, an opening bid of 13 points facing a responding hand of 13 points totals to the game figure of 26 points.* * All rubber-bridge theory is designed to get a partnership to game with greater facility.

Since the objective in match-point play is to reach the best result on each deal, one would expect the requirements for an opening bid to be lowered, especially in view of the fact that more part-score hands arise than do games and slams combined. However, experience has demonstrated that partner cannot handle lighter-than-normal opening bids (less than 13 points). When each partner has, for example, 11 points, theoretically they would do well to open and reach a low makable part-score contract. But when one opens a subminimum hand, a partner who has a reasonable hand of, say,

---

* In duplicate, of course, the major objective is to outscore the opponents on any deal, whether part-score, game, or slam, *by any margin* whatsoever.

* * In the major suits or in no-trump, but not in the minor suits, where about 29 points are required.

11 points with which he intends to make two progressive bids will tend to get the bidding too high, thus going down and securing a minus score. Therefore an original pass with 11 points will produce no score (opposite a partner who also has 11 points), which is infinitely superior to a minus score.

In other words, on a board on which East–West could have made one no-trump or two spades while North–South could have made only one heart, East–West, who have a zero (neither plus nor minus) score (as do North–South), do not figure to obtain a poor match-point score because they did not make the best of their resources. If East–West had opened the bidding, they might well have reached a two no-trump or a three spade contract and would have been defeated for a minus score. Again, a zero (neither plus nor minus) score is better than a minus score.

XI. Reopening Bids

This subject deals with the situations when your opponents have opened the bidding and have then stopped at either the one-level or two-level because (presumably) they felt that they didn't have the values to go any higher. The issue then becomes whether you should sell out or whether you should reopen the bidding in the hope of either (1) driving the opponents one level higher to a possibly unmakable contract or (2) making a part-score in your best suit or perhaps in no-trump, now that you know the opponents' strength is limited.

Basically, "reopening" bids should rightfully be classified in the category of "the fight for a part-score," since they are in effect an effort in that direction. Not much need be said here, except to mention that you should reopen the bidding with fewer values and, consequently, a greater degree of risk at match-point play. The reason is that the rewards are greater if you succeed either in pushing the opponents one trick too high or in making a part-score of your own.

XII. Attitude Toward Minor Suits

The rubber-bridge player does not hesitate to play a part-score contract in a minor suit if he thinks it *equal* to any other as a good contract. The duplicate player plays a part-score in a minor suit, as opposed to a major suit or no-trump, *only* when he feels that no-trump and the major suits are *very inferior* contracts. If, at a part-score contract, the major, the minor, and the no-trump contract all turn out to be makable, the play at a minor suit will usually net him a very bad match-point result. He plays the higher-paying contract even if it is slightly more hazardous. Let us illustrate this with figures:

3 ♣ or 3 ◇ = 110	2 NT = 120
4 ♣ or 4 ◇ = 130	3 ♡ or 3 ♠ = 140

To obtain a good score in a minor suit, it may be necessary to obtain *two* extra tricks (i.e., 4 C = 130; 2 NT = 120). One therefore plays in a minor suit at match points only when it is the only possible contract which offers hope of fulfillment.

At rubber bridge, of course, the difference between a part-score of 40, 60, 70, or 90 is negligible. You would rather get 40 points below the line for score (with a probable 20 points above), than to speculate on a two no-trump partial for 70 points below the line.

At duplicate bridge, the risky part-score contract in no-trump or a major is engaged in because it will pay more; the safer minor suit contract becomes a last resort.

At the game level, there is unanimity of opinion regarding the minor suits. No-trump should properly be the final declaration about 95 percent of the time when a good minor "trump suit" is held. The main reason is not the higher payoff in the score, although that is a persuasive consideration at match-point play, but that nine tricks at no-trump will usually be easier to make than eleven tricks in a minor. Both rubber and duplicate players are well aware of that fact. Actually, when a duplicate player has a hunch that a game in a minor suit is the *only* makable contract and his hunch turns out to be correct, his reward is way out of proportion—he will usually get a top or near-top on the board, for virtually nobody else will have bid the minor suit game. Our advice is to explore every possibility for playing no-trump before settling for the minor suit game. The rubber-bridge player is also included in this advice.

In point of fact, the duplicate expert probably does not play in five clubs or five diamonds once out of twenty game contracts, exclusive of those highly competitive auctions in which either he is driven to a minor suit game or he is taking a sacrifice. If he reaches five clubs or five diamonds voluntarily (having bypassed three no-trump), the opponents not having bid, he will often continue on to an ambitious slam in the minor, for he knows from past experiences that a minor suit game contract rarely secures a good match-point result. That is, if eleven tricks are makable at the minor suit for a vulnerable score of 600 points, it is usually possible to take ten tricks at three no-trump (for a score of 630) or ten tricks at a major suit (for a score of 620).

In the slam department, the *safest* contract—whether it be in a major suit, a minor suit, or at no-trump—will pay off in the long run, for many pairs will usually wind up in a mere game contract. You may attempt no-trump instead of the minor if there is only a *slight* additional risk. Of course the difficulty here is the inability—even at the top level of play—to measure the risk, to determine whether it is slight or not. Consequently, the better players rarely get away from the safe slam unless they feel there is an extreme need for gambling.

XIII. Attitude Toward Major Suits vs. No-trump

At rubber bridge, no serious problem exists, nor could a panel of experts be found who would have divergent views. The major suit fit should be explored and if the partnership is known to have eight or more cards between them, that major suit should almost always become the trump suit. Suit contracts usually play more easily than no-trump contracts. At duplicate, when both are mak-able, the suit contract will more often produce that all-important extra trick.

We will make a forthright statement of our position at match-point play. We favor the exploration for, and playing of, the major suit contract when it is available. We tend to arrive at no-trump contracts when exploration has revealed that we do not have major suit agreement—that is, a "fit" cannot be found.

CHAPTER 6

The Strategy of Duplicate Bridge: The Play

In duplicate bridge, when your dummy comes into view, your first consideration is not the safety of your contract but how the score you will achieve is likely to compare with the scores made at the other tables. Your real opponents are not the pair sitting at the table with you but the pairs who will be holding your cards when the board will be replayed at each of the other tables. Or, if the opponents at your table have purchased the contract, your concern is not necessarily to defeat their contract but rather not to be outscored by the other pairs who will be holding your cards and defending against their opponents' identical contract.

In rubber bridge, on the other hand, the objective is always a simple, permanent, and clearly defined one: to make your contract or to defeat the contract of the opponents. In rubber bridge, one's primary concern is not whether he obtains the optimum theoretical result; or whether he is in a good or bad contract; or what the rest of the field will do on the same deal; or whether he should gamble in the play for a top or a bottom. In rubber bridge, one lives in his own little world "far from the madding crowd's ignoble strife," and there is just one enemy—at his table. His sole objective is to score as many points as he can.

In duplicate bridge, an enemy sits at each table in the room. His aim, as yours, is to outscore his competitors on every deal. In short, duplicate bridge is a game in which the continual struggle is for supremacy over *all* the competitors who will be holding your cards.

Going from the general to the specific, the rubber-bridge declarer concentrates solely on fulfilling his contract. Overtricks are considered only after the safety of the contract has become guaranteed. Likewise the defenders devote all their effort and energy toward defeating the contract. The loss of an extra trick or two which is sacrificed in such an effort is a very minor consideration.

On the other hand, a trick, practically any old trick, is a matter of utmost concern to the match-point player. The safety play which insures the contract is very rarely resorted to in duplicate play. Instead, one plays for every trick as though his life depended on it (and it generally does, too!). However, some adjustment is necessary at times. If the contract in which one finds himself is a very good one, one that few pairs figure to reach, he should play it as safely as possible. If, however, the contract will probably be reached by most, if not all, of the pairs, he will try for the maximum number of tricks consistent with reasonable play. You may even properly jeopardize a contract that is in the bag in an effort to gain an extra trick if it rates to be an odds-on chance—say 70–80 percent—in your favor.

You must sometimes graciously accept a defeat of one trick in a normally arrived-at contract if there is a probability that you will go down two or three tricks as a result of adopting a line of play that has little chance of succeeding. On the other hand, you must go all out to make any contract which is a poor one, or one which the field does not figure to reach. In these latter contracts, *any* minus score figures to give you a very bad result in match points— and whether you go down one, two, or three, there will generally be very little difference in your match-point score.

When you are vulnerable and have purchased an undoubled part-score contract after competitive bidding, you cannot ever afford to go down two tricks, for a minus score of 200. If you do, you figure to get zero match points since your loss will tend to be greater than any part score the opponents could have made. In these situations, you must exert a maximum effort to go down no more than one trick—and if, in so trying, you happen to go down five for a loss of 500 points, your match-point score will usually be the same as you would get for going down two, for a loss of 200 points— namely zero, perhaps half a match point. In bridge circles, being minus 200 on a part-score deal is known as "the death number."

The defenders' attitude must be *more cautious* than bold in match-point play. However, some blend of the two must always exist, to rise to the fore when necessity demands it. It would be unwise for a defender to go all out to defeat a perfectly normal contract by making a remote, wishful-thinking play which stands a much greater chance of losing a trick than of defeating the contract. Nevertheless, at times a defender should throw caution to the winds. This will develop if a contract is obviously an abnormal one which appears to be a "lucky," apparently makable contract, since, if it is made, the defenders figure to get a very bad match-point score.

All of the topics very lightly introduced in the preceding paragraphs of this chapter will be discussed and illustrated at greater length elsewhere in this book. However, to give some substantive evidence of the points we have made, we would like to present four deals which illustrate the major differences in play between rubber bridge and duplicate bridge. These differences pertain to: (1) the safety of the contract versus the play for overtricks as viewed by the declarer, and (2) the divergent views of the rubber-bridge defender and the duplicate defender, and (3) the effect of vulnerability on one's play.

DEAL 1:

You are sitting South, and, with no adverse bidding, have arrived at a *three no-trump* contract.

♠ 10 6 3
♡ A K Q 6 5 2
♢ 4 2
♣ 7 5

♠ Q J 8 2
♡ 4 3
♢ A K 7
♣ A K 6 4

West opens the queen of clubs, which you win with the king. In rubber bridge there is no problem whatsoever. You lead a low heart at trick two, and concede the trick to the opponents. Whether the five adverse hearts are divided 3-2 or 4-1, your nine-trick contract is now absolutely guaranteed. And if the adverse hearts are divided 5-0, your conscience is clear no matter what the ultimate result since you know that you have played the hand correctly.

But playing the hand at duplicate is another matter. You cannot abandon the 68 percent chance that the adverse hearts will divide 3-2 and play it safely to assure the three no-trump contract. If you do, you'll never be a winner, for at least 19 out of every 20 duplicate players will play for the hearts to be divided 3-2—and over two-thirds of the time they'll be right and chalk up an overtrick.

Still another factor must enter into consideration, especially for those erstwhile rubber-bridge players who find it goes against the grain to conceivably sacrifice the safety of a game contract in the quest for an overtrick. Viewing both hands, the South declarer must realize that a certain proportion of the field will be in a *four heart* contract, and if the adverse hearts break 3-2, the four heart bidders will make eleven tricks (except if a third round of spades gets trumped at trick three, after the opponents have cashed the ace and king of spades, in which case ten tricks will still be made). Should the hearts be divided 4-1, at a four heart contract, the four heart bidders will make ten tricks anyway, while the three no-trump bidders, who took the safety play of conceding the first heart trick, will make only nine tricks.

Thus, even if one makes ten tricks at three no-trump by playing "wide open" (for the hearts to be 3-2), it might well be a below-average result. But taking the safety play to guarantee nine tricks will, in all probability, bring you a nice, juicy, bottom match-point score; or perhaps, if you are lucky, a tie-for-bottom. If the latter, it will probably be with the other pair who also took the safety play, and with whom, if the trend is continued, you will eventually tie for last place when the total final scores are tabulated.

DEAL 2:

You are sitting South, *vulnerable*, and have arrived at a *three no-trump* contract via the following bidding:

South	West	North	East
1 NT	Pass	3 NT	Pass
Pass	Pass		

♠ A Q J 7
♡ K Q 2
◇ 7 5 3 2
♣ 6 3

♠ K 10 8 6
♡ A 7 4
◇ A 8 4
♣ A Q J

Let's assume you are playing rubber bridge, and West opens the king of diamonds, East following with the nine-spot. You count your tricks and perceive that you have nine, which gives you game and rubber. However, you make a "token contribution" to the hold-up play by declining to take the king of diamonds. (Hoping, perhaps, that West might pull the wrong card out of his hand at trick two, as say the king of clubs.) When West continues with the queen of diamonds, you take your ace, East discarding a low club.

As you now cash the rest of your tricks, you give at most a fleeting thought to taking the club finesse which, if it loses, will result in the defeat of your contract.

But let's say you are playing in a duplicate game, and have arrived at three no-trump via the same sequence of bidding: 1 NT by you, 3 NT by partner. Again West leads the king of diamonds, and follows up with the queen, which you take as East discards a club. Do you take the club finesse? *If you don't, you have a bottom on the board regardless of whether East or West has the club king!* Let us see why.

In this day and age, virtually every pair in the world will arrive at a *four spade* contract by employing the Stayman Convention.*
The bidding will go:

South	West	North	East
1 NT	Pass	2 ♣ *	Pass
2 ♠	Pass	4 ♠	Pass
Pass	Pass		

* This convention is presented in Chapter 22. Its purpose is to get the partnership to a major suit contract if the combined hands contain 8 or more cards in a major suit. The convention is employed after an opening bid of 1 NT and is initiated by the responder with an artificial bid of two clubs.

Upon winning the opening diamond lead with the ace, one cashes the king, queen, and ace of trumps, picking up the adverse pieces. Then the club finesse is tried. If it loses; West will cash two diamonds, and that's it. The remainder of the tricks will belong to declarer. He scores 620 points for a vulnerable four spade game. If the club finesse wins, dummy is re-entered via the king of hearts and declarer again finesses for the club king. The finesse wins again. Eventually declarer concedes two diamond tricks to West. Declarer scores up a game with an overtrick, for 650 points.

Do you see why, at a three no-trump contract, you must take the club finesse although it means jeopardizing your contract to do so? Three no-trump bid and made, for a score of 600 points, will net you no match points, for all of the spade contractors will take the club finesse and make at least ten tricks. They can afford to take the finesse, for the threat of West running the diamond suit against them is nonexistent since declarer can trump the fourth lead of diamonds.

So at three no-trump, after holding up the diamond ace at trick one, you cash four spades, ending up in dummy. You now take the club finesse. If it wins, you will re-enter dummy via a heart and finesse again. With luck on your side, you now score 660 points, for three no-trump bid and made with two overtricks. This, of course, will give you a top on the board, since the four spade contractors would score "only" 650 points for having made eleven tricks. However, if when you take the club finesse, it loses, you will be down one trick, for a score of "minus 100"—and you will secure just about the identical number of match points you would have scored had you not taken the club finesse and had settled for three no-trump bid and made for a score of 600 points.

DEAL 3:

Both sides are vulnerable, and you are sitting West. South has arrived at a *four spade* contract via the following sequence:

North	East	South	West
1 ◇	Pass	1 ♠	Pass
4 ♠	Pass	Pass	Pass

You open the king of clubs, and the dummy is put down:

♠ K Q 9 4
♡ K J
♢ A K Q J 10
♣ J 6

♠ 10 7
♡ A 5 3 2
♢ 7 6 4
♣ A K Q 2

After taking the king of clubs, you lead the ace of clubs, which also wins. What next?

At rubber bridge, your action is clear-cut. You lead a low heart hoping that (1) your partner has the queen and (2) that declarer will misguess the situation and play dummy's jack. So what if declarer diagnoses the situation and puts up dummy's king? At rubber bridge, *your sole aim is to defeat the game contract.* The overtrick is of no importance.

At duplicate bridge, if declarer has the heart queen or if he elects to put up dummy's heart king on your lead of a low heart at trick three, he will make the all-important overtrick, thereby giving you at best a tie-for-bottom on the board. As you gaze at dummy and your own hand, the only outstanding high cards are the A J of spades and the queen of hearts. Doesn't declarer, for his one spade response, figure to have all three of these cards?

So, in duplicate bridge you cash the heart ace at trick three, thus conceding the contract. You have just scored 9 out of 12 match points. The deal, which arose in the National Open Pair Championships of 1949, was:

♠ K Q 9 4
♡ K J
♢ A K Q J 10
♣ J 6

♠ 10 7   ♠ 5 2
♡ A 5 3 2   ♡ Q 9 8 7 6 4
♢ 7 6 4   ♢ 8 5
♣ A K Q 2   ♣ 10 9 7

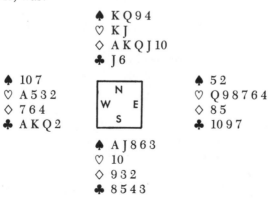

♠ A J 8 6 3
♡ 10
♢ 9 3 2
♣ 8 5 4 3

As is apparent, had you underled the ace of hearts, declarer would automatically have put up dummy's king since he himself had but a singleton heart. He would now have made eleven tricks.

DEAL 4:

You, sitting South, have reached a *one no-trump* contract on the bidding which follows:

South	West	North	East
Pass	Pass	1 ♣	1 ♠
1 NT	Pass	Pass	Pass

♠ 4 2
♡ K Q 10 7
◊ J 6
♣ K J 10 8 3

♠ K 10 3
♡ A J 6 2
◊ 5 3
♣ Q 9 7 2

Let's assume that you are *not vulnerable.*

West opens the eight of spades, East puts up the jack, and you win the trick with your king. You look the two hands over—and you like what you see: at a spade contract (or a diamond contract) East–West figure to lose just one spade, two hearts, and possibly a club (if the four adverse clubs are divided 2–2). So they figure to make a three spade contract, perhaps even four spades, for a score of 140 or 170. Or, if they play in diamonds, they will make either three diamonds, for a score of 110, or four diamonds, for a score of 130.

You cash the four hearts, lead a club—and who cares what happens? You are down two, for a loss of 100 points and an excellent score.

But suppose you were *vulnerable.* Down two, for a minus 200 score, is more than the opponents could have made at their partscore spade contract. You simply cannot afford to go down two tricks, unless you like to be a loser. How should you play the hand in this vulnerable situation?

Probably your best bet is to lead the nine of clubs at trick two.

If West plays low—which he probably will do if he has the ace, on the assumption that you will let the nine ride, finessing for the queen—your nine will win. If it wins, you breathe a sigh of relief and settle for down one for a loss of 100 points. This is less than the opponents would have made at their spade (or diamond) contract.

If East has the ace of clubs, you will go down a zillion, probably losing four spades, five diamonds, and the ace of clubs. But this we guarantee: how much you lose, if it's more than 100 points, won't make a darn bit of difference: down four, for minus 400; or down three, for minus 300; or down two, for minus 200. It's all the same, like whether you drown in 35 feet of water, 25 feet of water, or 15 feet of water. All of them spell complete annihilation—or, coming down to earth, no match points. But if you can connive to go down only one, the sun will shine again—and you will bask in it.

A stimulating game, this duplicate bridge, isn't it?

CHAPTER 7

Standard American Bidding: An Examination of the Foundation

Within this book on duplicate bridge, we have no intention of presenting *any system* of bidding, for we assume that you know your way around the rubber-bridge table for which systems were created. We are serving merely as a catalyst in effecting your transition from rubber bridge to duplicate bridge. However, since there are minor differences among the various "Standard American" bidding systems which have been put forth by our bridge authorities and since the readers of this book might not have learned their A.B.C.'s from the same authority, it becomes necessary for us to introduce, and attempt to reconcile, the areas of possible disagreement so that there will be no misunderstandings as we go along.

Our aim is to straighten out certain misconceptions—or, possibly, fill in gaps of knowledge—about how one evaluates a hand, thereby making it possible to establish a *precise* foundation of bidding upon which two partners can agree. They can then proceed confidently, as a unit, knowing that each understands what the other is doing.

I. The Point Count

Ever since about 1950, all systems of bidding have been based on the "point count." In all discussions of bridge bidding, the 4-3-2-1 point count is featured. However, there are minor differences among the various point-count systems.

First, we would like to point out that the Goren and other similar point-count systems will usually not differ greatly. When they do differ, it will almost always be only one point either way (i.e., Goren may count 26, while others may count 25 or 27). In introducing the count paragraphs which follow, we are not propagandizing in favor of any one system. Rather we are setting down the way in which we have reconciled the differences and the way in which we employ the point count in actual practice.

High Card Points
$$A = 4; K = 3; Q = 2; J = 1.$$

Singleton Honors
$$A = 4; K = 2; Q = 1; J = 0.$$

1. Add One Point for all Four Aces.

The possession of all four aces is worth at least one additional point (that is, 17 rather than 16), as all experienced players know.

2. Deduct One Point for No Aces.

This deduction applies only to the player who *opens* the bidding. It does not apply to responder or to a defensive bidder.

3. Good major suit holdings enhance the value of your hand. Length or quality in spades or hearts is a plus factor. For example, Hand (1), below, is superior to Hand (2), although each of them contains the identical number of points.

(1)	(2)
♠ A Q J x x	♠ x x
♡ A Q x	♡ x x x
◇ x x x	◇ A Q x
♣ x x	♣ A Q J x x

As has been stated, spades is the loveliest of all suits. In Hand (1), the possession of the A Q x of hearts can prove to be a greater asset if partner has hearts, than the A Q x of diamonds if partner has a diamond suit. In short, it is always an asset to have major suits rather than minor suits—and especially so in duplicate bridge where the fight for a part-score is so significant.

4. We are always mindful that picture cards in partner's suit are nice cards to possess, but we do *not* add one point for such holdings. That is, while we fully appreciate that we'd rather have, say

the K x x of hearts if partner has bid hearts than the K x x of clubs, which suit partner has not bid, we nevertheless value each holding at three points.

5. We appreciate that a 4-3-3-3 distribution is the worst possible bridge holding, but we do not deduct a point for this "bad" distribution.

Thus, while we do not make any arithmetic point-count adjustment for either (1) possession of major suits, (2) for a picture card in partner's suit, and (3) for a 4-3-3-3 distribution, we do take these points into consideration in this way: when we happen to reach the crossroads in our bidding and are faced with the choice of whether we should bid again, we tend to be a bit aggressive when we possess (1) and/or (2), which we did not count as an "extra" originally; and we tend to slow down, if not stop completely, when we possess the "minus" 4-3-3-3 distribution.

II. Assigning Points for Distribution: Long-Suit Valuation

We believe that assigning points in advance to voids, singletons, and doubletons, is unsound. For example, we know from experience that the following hand is not worth 13 points (10 in high cards and 3 for the void), some constituted authorities to the contrary:

> ♠ A J 4 3 2
> ♡ —
> ◇ A J 7 5 3
> ♣ 8 4 3

We are certain that you will agree with us, especially if you open the above hand with one spade, and you hear your partner respond with two hearts. In this case, the void is assuredly a drawback, and not an asset.

We assign points for distribution by *adding one point for every card over four in your longest suit. This applies to both opener and responder.* Do not add points for length in a second five-or-six-card suit, unless you hold *two very good* * five- or six-card suits. In this latter situation, add *two additional points to the total.*

* A "very good" suit is a suit of at least five-card length, headed by A K Q, A K J, A Q J, K Q J, A K 10 9, or K Q 10 9.

That is:

(1)			(2)		
♠ A J 9 6 2	5 + 1 = 6		♠ A Q J 9 2	7 + 1 = 8	
♡ K 2	3		♡ K 2	3	
◊ A J 9 6 2	5		◊ K Q J 10 8	6	
♣ 4	0		♣ 2	0	
Total 14			Total 17		

Add two points for two
very good five-card, or
longer, suits 2
_____
19

In (1), the value of the hand—14 points—is determined by adding the 13 high-card points plus *one* point for the fifth card in the longest suit.

In (2), the value of the hand—19 points—is secured by adding the 16 high-card points plus *one* point for the fifth card in your *longest suit, plus two points for two very good 5-card or longer suits.*

Let us look at two more illustrations:

(3)			(4)		
♠ A K Q 6 3 2	9 + 2 = 11		♠ —	0	
♡ 6	0		♡ K Q J 9 6 3	6 + 2 = 8	
◊ A 8 7 5 3	4		◊ A Q J 8 5 2	7	
♣ 7	0		♣ 5	0	
Total 15			Total 15		

Plus two points for two
very good five-card or
longer suits 2
_____
Grand Total ... 17

In (3), there are 13 high-card points, plus 2 points for the fifth and sixth spades, for a total of 15 points.

In (4), there are 13 high-card points, plus 2 points for the fifth and sixth cards of one suit (either hearts or diamonds), *plus* 2 points for two very good five-card or longer suits.

It is recognized and appreciated that the distribution, 5-3-3-2, is not as good as the 5-4-2-2, on the average. And 5-4-2-2 is not usually as good as 5-4-3-1. And 5-4-3-1 is not usually as valuable as either 5-5-3-0 or 5-4-4-0. Yet, to repeat, despite this acknowledgment, we do not take additional distributional points for the usually superior distributions. Two factors persuade us to take our position.

First, if a true mathematical valuation were to be assigned to the superior distributions, it would probably be a fractional one, like adding .63 points, etc. Certainly to do this on every deal would border on the ridiculous. Also, we have no love for too many additions and subtractions, especially when the end result is not necessarily right on any particular hand.

And secondly, partner quite often fails to fit any or either of our suits, which may then drastically reduce the value of these presumably superior-at-the-outset holdings. We have learned to take whatever distributional points may accrue *when and if a fit is found.*

III. Assigning Points for Distribution: Short-Suit Valuation

We must strongly emphasize that we never consider assigning any points for short-suit valuation either for opener or responder unless we possess trump support for partner's suit and we are anticipating the strong possibility *that we will spread our hand on the table as dummy.*

A. SHORT-SUIT VALUATION

Holding 4-card (or longer) trump support for partner, add:

Doubleton −1 point.
Singleton −3 points.
Void   −5 points.

If two short-suit values are held, take points for both.

Holding 3-card support for partner, add:

Doubleton −zero points.
Singleton −2 points.
Void   −4 points.

If two short-suit values are held, take points for both.

Note: two doubletons are worth one point.

Here are three examples. In each, partner has opened with *one spade.* You, the responder, hold:

(1)		(2)		(3)	
♠ Q x x x	2	♠ K x x	3	♠ J x x x x	1
♡ x x	1	♡ x x	{ ½	♡ Q J x x x	3
◇ A x x x x x	4	◇ x x	½ }	◇ K x	(3 + 1)
♣ x	3	♣ K x x x x x	3	♣ x	3
	10		7		11

There will be times when the opener will assign points for short
suits, but *never* for the purpose of opening the bidding. He will
assign these points when he has acquired an asset which he didn't
possess at the outset, namely trump support for partner. For example:

> ♠ K Q x x
> ♡ A x
> ◇ A K Q x x
> ♣ x x

For purposes of opening the bidding, the above hand is valued
at 19 points (18 in high cards and one for the fifth diamond). We
open with one diamond and partner responds with *one spade*. We
have just acquired four supporting trumps for partner, and we are
about to raise him. In combination with the four supporting trumps,
we have two doubletons, each of which is worth one point. But
when we count short suits, we do not count long suits. So we drop
the one point originally assigned to the fifth diamond. In support
of spades, then, our hand is revalued to 20 points: 18 in high cards,
plus one for the doubleton heart and one for the doubleton club.
Over partner's one spade response, we promptly raise to *four spades*.

It will be noted that we do *not* take credit for both long and
short suit points. To do so would be overvaluing tremendously, like
taking one piece of bread and counting it as two pieces because
you counted one side as "one" and the other side as "two." Long
suits and short suits duplicate each other, at least to a very great
extent: when you have a long suit somewhere, you've got to have
a short suit elsewhere; and if you have two long suits, you will have
either two short suits or a void (5-5-2-1; 6-5-1-1; 5-5-3-0, etc.).

A player may count:

(1) High-card points plus long-suit points.

(2) High-card points plus short-suit points.

A player may *not* count:

High-card points, plus long-suit points, plus short-suit points.

On any given hand, a player may start out counting long-suit points but can then switch to counting short-suit points when he has support for partner and is about to raise him. *One should always value his hand at the higher valuation* while staying within the counting limitations set forth above.

Let's look at two examples:

Your partner opens with *one heart*, and you hold:

(1)	(2)
♠ x	♠ x
♡ K x x x	♡ A J x
◇ K x x	◇ Q x x x x
♣ A J x x x	♣ x x x x

On (1), before partner bid, we valued our hand at 12 points: 11 in high cards plus one for the fifth club. After partner opens with *one heart*, we value our hand at 14 points: 11 in high cards, plus 3 points for the singleton spade in combination with four supporting trumps. Over his one heart opening we, as you, jump to three hearts.

On (2), before partner bids, we valued our hand at 8 points: 7 in high cards, plus one for the fifth diamond. After partner opens with *one heart*, we value our hand at 9 points: 7 in high cards plus two points for having a singleton accompanying three supporting trumps. We raise partner from one heart to two hearts.

We must take note of the subject of the fifth trump in partner's suit which plays so prominent a part in discussions of the point count. We cannot deny that we prefer holding five trumps rather than four trumps. Nevertheless, we do *not* add one point for the possession of the fifth trump. We feel that the fifth trump too often proves to be mere duplication and is a minor asset only in that we have it and not the opponents. For example:

> ♠ x x x x x
> ♡ K x
> ◇ J x x
> ♣ Q x x
>
> ♠ A K Q x x
> ♡ A x
> ◇ K Q 10 x
> ♣ x x

South bids *one spade*, which North raises to *two spades*, and South rebids *four spades*. No matter where we transpose North's fifth spade, whether it be to hearts, diamonds, or clubs, it doesn't mean a darn: South will lose one diamond trick and two club tricks. Of course, the fact that North has the fifth spade (instead of the defenders having it) eliminates the theoretical possibility that South might lose a trump trick.

IV. Rebid Valuation When Your Suit Is Supported

Our valuation in this connection is less than some systems give and more than others. Admittedly, we may in some instances be undervaluing, but other methods prescribe an unwarranted over-valuation, particularly when a very long suit is involved.

When partner supports our suit, we add just *one additional point for each card over four*. For example, we open the hand given below with *one spade*, which partner raises to *two spades*:

	Original Count	After Partner's Raise
♠ A Q J 6 4 2	9	11
♡ A Q 2	6	6
◇ K 3	3	3
♣ 7 4	0	0
Total	18 points	20 points

We would, of course, rebid *four spades*.

V. The Opening Bid

Since the opening bid is the foundation upon which the entire structure of bidding is erected, it is vital that it not be a faulty one. In bridge parlance, there is an old cliché that states that "the per-petrator of the first mistake in a bidding sequence is the more guilty party." Let us, therefore, briefly examine opening bids with a view toward eliminating "first mistakes" by establishing a mu-tually agreed upon foundation which can be used as a springboard.

We state again that our views can be characterized as Standard American, which could be Goren or any other kindred system. But there are a few misconceptions which have developed as to what constitutes Standard American or Goren. It is these that we wish to clarify and set straight.

The major "trouble area" is on the subject of what the minimum point-count requirement is for an opening bid. And, of course, if a partnership has an agreement as to precisely what constitutes an opening bid, much grief and controversy can be averted. Generally speaking, standard point-count books have this to say on the subject:

> 14 points—mandatory opening bid
> 13 points—optional opening bid
> 12 points—you may open if you have a very good rebid

Teachers and writers are, perhaps, responsible for the improper interpretation of the 13-point "optional opening." Unfortunately, most students and players holding 13 points consider that the choice between opening and passing is about 50–50. They interpret it to mean that they may, in each case, exercise their judgment or free will to do as they please. *But this is contrary to the practice of the best players and of the system makers who provided the formula.* Optional, as practiced by them, means that, holding 13 points, 95 percent of all hands are opened and only 5 percent are passed.

When do they pass with 13 points? *If they do not have two defensive tricks,** as in:

(1)	(2)	(3)
♠ Q J x	♠ K J x x x x	♠ x
♡ Q J x	♡ Q x	♡ Q J x x
◇ A J x x x x	◇ K J x	◇ A Q J x x x x
♣ x	♣ J x	♣ Q

None of the above examples qualifies as an opening bid of one in a suit.

We subscribe to the view that all 13-point hands which contain the minimum of two defensive tricks should be opened. We do not exercise any option on borderline hands—we open. We have learned, as have the proponents of other systems,** that the "lighter" opening bid prevents us from getting shut out of the auction too frequently and negates the need to back into the bidding at dangerously high levels. Further, the lighter opening bid is often in-

---

* Defensive tricks are: AK = 2; AQ = 1½; A = 1; KQ = 1; Kx = ½.
** In particular, the Roth-Stone System, which formerly advocated the super-sound opening bid (at least 14 points). They have now reduced their opening requirements considerably.

strumental in getting partner off to the right opening lead on defense and frequently prevents declarer from making that overtrick which is so vital in duplicate play. Also, we believe it most desirable to strike the first blow and thereby, in a mild way, make it a little more difficult for the opponents to compete.

Thus our position, derived from our experience, is to open the bidding lightly. But, by "lightly," we do not mean featherweight. We have our standard of 13 points, plus two defensive tricks. Where we have three defensive tricks, we will usually open on 12 points. In this latter case, the deficiency of one point is compensated for by our ability (in the form of defensive strength) to hurt the opposition if they elect to compete. We will also open 12-point hands with 2½ defensive tricks if they are rich in the major suits.

Here are some examples of our minimum opening bids, all of which we open with "one" in our longest suit, regardless of vulnerability:

(1)	(2)	(3)	(4)
♠ K x	♠ x x	♠ A K 10 x x	♠ A J 10 x x
♡ A K x x x	♡ x x	♡ K 10 x x	♡ A Q x x
◊ Q x x x	◊ A 10 x x x	◊ J x	◊ x
♣ x x	♣ A K x x	♣ x x	♣ x x x

It would take a rare hand to persuade us to waive the two-trick defensive requirement. The following example would do it. We would open it with *one spade:*

♠ K J 9 x x x
♡ A J 10 x x x
◊ x
♣ —

VI. Third-Hand Opening Bids

Through the years, the fallacy has arisen that if first and second hand pass, third hand *must open* "light" in order to protect first hand, who might have chosen to pass with 13 or 14 points. This has tended to become a custom which is slavishly—and expensively —adhered to.

Speaking subjectively, since we open with fairly light holdings, we require little or no protection by a partner sitting in third position. If he passes with a subminimum hand, much more often than not we won't be missing anything and we'll stay out of trouble. Nevertheless, we frequently open in third position with less than an opening bid, but for sound, tactical reasons and not merely because "the law permits it." The possession of 10 or 11 scattered points is no justification for a light third-hand opening bid.

Speaking objectively, we open light in third seat for either of these two reasons:

1. To direct the defense—that is, to tell partner what to lead if the opponents purchase the contract.

2. Because we feel that we have a slight advantage in that we think we have a better chance of making a part-score than do the opponents. We "feel" this way when we have a better-than-average hand—say 12 points—or we possess the major suits—even with an 11-point hand—rather than the minor suits.

Let us look at some illustrations:

We *do not* open in third position with any of the three following hands:

(1)	(2)	(3)
♠ Q x x	♠ Q J	♠ x x
♡ Q 9 x	♡ Q x x	♡ J x x x x
◇ K 10 x	◇ K 10 x x	◇ A Q x
♣ A 9 x x	♣ K 9 x x	♣ K x x

On Hands (1) and (2), a minus score will be obtained more often than not if one opens the bidding. On Hand (3), a one heart opening bid, and the "mandatory" heart lead by your partner if the opponents obtain the contract, may ruin the defense. It is much better to keep quiet and allow your partner to make his natural lead.

On each of the following hands, we would open the bidding *in third position*. Our reasons for opening are appended alongside of each hand.

1. ♠ A J 10 2
   ♡ K 9 8 2
   ◇ Q 7
   ♣ Q 10 3

We are unwilling to abandon the fight whenever we feel we have an edge. Not only do we have 12 high-card points, but also two four-card major suits, which are always highly prized possessions. We would open with *one spade*, intending to pass any response partner makes.

2. ♠ K 9 8 2
   ♡ K Q J 3
   ◇ Q 10 2
   ♣ 9 7

   We open with *one heart*. Our choice is dictated by the same reasoning as in Hand 1, above. In addition, we want the heart lead should the opponents purchase the contract.

3. ♠ Q 8 4 2
   ♡ A 9 8 2
   ◇ 9 2
   ♣ K Q 10

   One club is our choice. That is the lead we want, since neither major suit is good. Observe that a player may open a "short club" in third position. Furthermore, he may do so even if he has no intention of rebidding.

NOTE WELL: When you open in third position, you are under no obligation to rebid—and you will not rebid unless you have more than an opening bid, for partner, by passing originally, has denied an opening bid (13 points). Except in rare situations, a game cannot be made by two partners, neither of whom has 13 points.

4. ♠ K 10 9 8
   ♡ 2
   ◇ 9 8 6 5 2
   ♣ A K J

   We are willing to fight it out with this holding. Our choice would be the lead-directing bid of *one club*, and not one diamond, as an opening bid. If partner responds with one heart, we would rebid one spade—and we're through for the afternoon.

5. ♠ K J 4 2
   ♡ K J 4 2
   ◇ 7 5 3
   ♣ A 4

   We would open with *one heart*, rather than with one spade, intending to pass whatever response partner makes. If, instead, you open with one spade, you may shut out partner's heart suit, for he might be reluctant (owing to a lack of values), to bid his heart suit at the two-level. By bidding one heart, you give partner the opportunity to either raise the hearts or to bid his own spade suit (if he has one) at the one-level. In other words, you are getting "double action": if over your one heart opening partner fails to respond with one spade, it is almost certain he does not have a four-card spade suit.

6. ♠ A J 6 4
   ♡ 4 3 2
   ◇ A K 4
   ♣ 7 5 3

   We open with *one spade*, as our first and last bid. We have a reasonable hope of making a part-score. We would also open this hand in fourth position. In first or second position, however, we would pass, as we have no guaranteed rebid if partner makes either a two club or a two heart response.

7. ♠ K 4 3
   ♡ Q 5.2
   ◇ K 7 4
   ♣ K J 6 5

   We open with one club, with fond hopes of making a part-score in any suit in which partner happens to respond. We will, of course, pass any response that partner happens to make.

We have been advised by very good players that we need not take action with weak hands for the mere purpose of directing leads. They maintain that they will guess the best lead in the vast majority of cases. With all due respect to these gifted guessers, our experience persuades us to place our faith elsewhere. We therefore tend to make light opening bids in third position when we *urgently* desire to suggest some lead. Favorable vulnerability (they are, we are not) is a considerable factor, and we feel we have a slight built-in advantage because we play "weak" two-bids.*

Here are some illustrations of our lead-directing third position opening bids. Although some of them may appear to border on the "psychic" opening bid side, we would open with a one bid even if we didn't play "weak" two-bids.

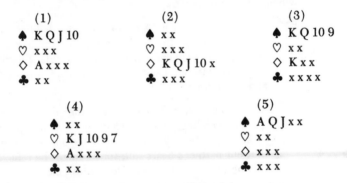

(1) One spade, regardless of vulnerability.
(2) One diamond, or a weak two diamonds, if not vulnerable.
(3) One spade if not vulnerable against vulnerable opponents.
(4) One heart, or a weak two hearts, regardless of vulnerability.
(5) One spade, or a weak two spades, if we are not vulnerable.

The reader may justifiably ask if we get into trouble by this practice. The answer is that we do occasionally. Our gains, however, have far outweighed our losses in match-point play—and we firmly believe that we have a good thing.

* The weak opening two-bid is discussed in Chapter 12.

VII. Fourth-Hand Openings

A mere statement of our policy will suffice with respect to this subject. We have very little faith in attaining a good score with a passout. We therefore tend to open the bidding on hands that are above average (over 10 points). We take action much as we would in third position, but we obviously have no need to open for the mere purpose of directing a lead. We do, nevertheless, keep the opening lead suggestion in mind when opening a light hand, the reason being that the necessity to defend is not a remote prospect. We would open a 10-point hand with a very good major, but not one with very good minors. We open any 11-point hand with length in the majors, but would toss in most 11-point hands with length in the minors. In the latter case, the opposition might too easily outbid us in the majors. We would, however, open a very good 11 or 12 point minor with a one-bid or a "weak" two-bid, depending on the holding. A key factor with minor suit holdings would be the amount of defense we possess. If we held three defensive tricks, we would surely open, as with:

♠ x x x
♡ x x
◇ A K x x
♣ A 10 x x

We would open the above hand, in fourth position, with *one diamond*.

VIII. Responses to an Opening Bid of One in a Suit

Our responses are "Standard American." We use the following as our guide in responding to partner's opening bid of one in a suit:

1. With 6–10 points:

    (a) We raise partner from one to two in his suit if we possess normal trump support.

    (b) We name a new suit at the one level.

    (c) We respond with one no-trump if we do not have support for partner and are unable to show our own suit at the one level.

    (d) In general, we intend to make just one voluntary bid.

2. With 10–12 points:

    (a) We name a new suit at the two-level with a minimum of 10 points, provided the *10 points are in high cards,* or the tenth point is derived from the fifth card in a good suit (A K J x x). Where the tenth point has been derived by adding a point for the fifth card in a poor suit (J x x x x), we prefer to respond with one no-trump.

    (b) We intend to make two voluntary bids en route to game.

3. With 13 or more points:

    (a) We intend to drive partner to a game, or higher.

IX. No-trump Opening Bids

We subscribe to the Standard American method of opening no-trump bids:

> 1 NT—16–18 high-card points
> 2 NT—22–24 high-card points
> 3 NT—25–27 high-card points

We, as you, open with no-trump whenever we have a balanced hand (4-3-3-3; 4-4-3-2; 5-3-3-2), and at least three suits fully protected, with no worse than xxx in the fourth suit.

In conjunction with one no-trump and two no-trump opening bids, we utilize the Stayman Convention.* We also employ the responses of 2 D, 2 H, and 2 S over the one no-trump opening bid as showing a poor hand, and a command to partner to pass. The type of hand with which we would bid *two spades* over one no-trump could be this:

> ♠ J x x x x x
> ♡ x x
> ◇ x x x
> ♣ x x

---

* Described in Chapter 22.

CHAPTER 8

Prologue to Obstructionist Bidding

In the preceding chapter, we said all we're going to say in this book about the opening bid of one in a suit and the various types of responses thereto. Similarly, with regard to the opening bids of one, two, and three no-trump, we're finished. We believe, from personal observation, that the vast majority of bridge players, as of the past decade, have learned to bid their *good* cards with reasonable accuracy. There may be those who will perhaps dispute this point, but not even the most stubborn die-hard will deny that the invention of the point count has improved the nation's bidding tremendously.

Top flight duplicate bridge players realize this much more than most players. Gone for the most part are the bidding "pigeons"—the sitting ducks who were just waiting to be taken—whom we so frequently encountered in the good old days. Everyone now bids games and slams with knowledge, poise, and confidence—and they fulfill their contracts.

It took a long time for this stage to be reached—contract bridge was first played in 1927. But it was not point count alone that transformed the poor bidder into a good bidder. Actually, the point count was nothing more than a refinement of the honor-trick method which it superseded. What brought about the transformation was repetition, repetition, and more repetition by constituted authority of the basic principles of constructive bidding, until they finally became ingrained in the minds of the pupils.

Historically speaking, until about 1953 in virtually every system of bidding, *all* the emphasis and stress was directed toward the attainment of as perfect a constructive partnership as is possible; that is, the attention of authorities, writers, and system makers in general was concentrated *exclusively* on devising bidding systems that would safely and accurately enable its users to reach the high, tempting contracts of game or slam when the cards held by a partnership offered a high probability of such contracts being fulfilled. How to determine correctly the precise partnership joint assets, how to find the proper trump suit, which suit to bid first, the requirements for an opening bid of one no-trump, etc., were always deemed to be the *sole* important issues.

We certainly are not minimizing or underrating the importance of constructive bidding when one has the good fortune to hold a fine hand. However, since the law of averages has made it abundantly clear (in both theory and practice) that the good hands will be held by one's opponents about half of the time, we sometimes feel rather surprised that so little attention was focused on the important matter of devising methods of *interfering* with the normal, smooth, constructive bidding of the aforementioned good-card holders.

On reflection, we realize that we really shouldn't be surprised. After all, contract bridge is a relatively young game. In its days of immaturity, it was the duty of constituted authority to establish a foundation and a superstructure for the constructive bidding of the good hands, to teach the players how to handle their big guns, and how to wend their way with accuracy and assurance to the proper final contract without any "obnoxious" interference. It was, in those days, fundamentally a matter of giving them their basic training before sending them out on the field of battle, of teaching them the basic strategy of the game before indoctrinating them with tactical maneuvers; in other words, training them to handle themselves and their weapons before teaching them how to negate or destroy the opponents' weapons and lines of communication.

From the viewpoint of good salesmanship, it was the natural and normal thing for the system makers to stress exclusively the proper methods of bidding games and slams, to illustrate how a particular system was the best—for, by using it, it was such a simple matter to arrive at a makable game or slam, and show tremendous profits as a result. What could be more appealing to the neophyte and to the bridge player who was usually a loser? Everyone loves to bid a game or a slam, and make it. As a consequence, the system makers addressed their advertising to those who wanted to know more about what to do with good cards, and offered them a self-perpetuating panacea.

And the system makers did their job well—they created a nation of "good-bidders-if-they-held-good-cards." By 1940, just about every beginner, average player, and expert employed the bidding framework of the Culbertson—to Goren—to the masses—system. American bidding, by the good-card holders, had reached the zenith.

But a pernicious side effect was developed as a result of the unilateral emphasis on what one should do with his good cards. Along about 1951–1952, revolutionary systems of bidding emerged, which were geared and dedicated to obstructing and harassing the good-card holders and making it most difficult for them to bid along indoctrinated, accustomed lines. The new systems were revolutionary in the true sense of the word; they sided with the poor card holders, the "have-nots," and introduced bids that would enable the poor-card holders to compete on more equitable terms with the "haves" for the right to survive. In these new systems, the emphasis was placed on pre-emption: depriving the good-card holders of bidding space. There were introduced more and more types of pre-emptive bids—and brought into greater prominence and usage the opening bids of three, four, and five in a suit, all of which had worth and merit in a practical sense: they often prevented the good-card holders from arriving at easily makable games or slams; or the "interferers" suffered a relatively small penalty in lieu of permitting the opponents to make a game or a slam; or the "interferers" drove the good-card holders too high, beyond their depth.

Many of these new obstructionist bids have been adopted by our better players, for they proved, in combat, to be most effective weapons. Yet the fact remains that, even as of now, the family of pre-emptive bids—and their close relations—are viewed with suspicion, as radical bids which are trying to change our way of life. Unquestionably they are trying to change our way of life, and they have made a good start. But—and here is the crux of the matter—we believe that the change is for the better, as our experiences have demonstrated to us in terms of profit and loss.

We are pragmatists. To us, any theory that has worked well over a reasonably long length of time (and especially in topflight competition) is one that should be adopted if you want to outscore your competitors. And, frankly, we want to win, whether we play duplicate bridge, rubber bridge, or pinochle. We have, for example, adopted the "weak two-bid," the "weak jump overcall," and other new bids which tend to obstruct and harass the opponents. We firmly believe that keeping the opponents out of their best contract when they have the better cards is just as essential as getting to our own best contract when our side has the better cards. We also are convinced that any bidding system or method of bidding which is not aware of this will lose to those who use a system which is aware of it. If the opponents continually obstruct you with preemptive bids when you have the good cards and you don't obstruct them when they have the good cards, you are going to lose.

Harassing, obstructing, and jamming up the opponents have become part of our way of life. We would like you to see the way we function along pre-emptive lines and to test our method in your own duplicate play. We assure you it will raise your standard of bridge living, as measured by more master points.

Although the emergence of the new pre-emptive bids started in 1951–52, they have been more or less brushed aside by the powers-that-be. Even currently, the orphan subject of all bridge writers and teachers is pre-emptive bidding. Writers skim over this subject. Teachers, for the most part, offer some vague description and a wave of the hands. Yet, like most specialized phases of contract bridge, pre-emptive bids, when handled in disciplined fashion, can become potent and highly effective weapons.

Perhaps the reason for the neglect of pre-emptive bidding, despite the realization of its efficacy, is that the rules for pre-emptive bids cannot be established through the mere presentation of numerical figures. Nor can the manner of coping with these accelerated bidding situations be outlined in one or two paragraphs. However, we are convinced that we can train you to handle pre-emptive bids adroitly, and with maximum efficiency, through the knowledge of some basic definitions and the continuing application of judgment.

And so, as was stated at the outset of this chapter, we are finished with any further discussions of opening bids of one in a suit and one no-trump and the responses thereto. Constituted authority has done that job well *—perhaps even too well, at the expense of other sub-jects. We are going to place our emphasis on the frequently occur-ring pre-emptive bids which have been neglected or pushed to the background. Of course, in the remainder of this book we are not going to forget about other basic aspects of duplicate bridge, like competitive part-score bidding, competitive defensive bidding, etc. But our emphasis is going to be on *competition,* in contrast to the presentation of unmolested, smooth, pleasurable bidding sequences by a partnership which sits in an easy chair, drinks mint juleps, and clips dividend coupons. Duplicate bridge is a struggle for sur-vival—and no participant is ever born with a silver spoon in his mouth.

One final paragraph. It may be that the whole idea of pre-emptive bids is distasteful to some readers. Such an attitude is quite under-standable if, in the past, these readers have never been obstructed and never did any obstructing, by a sort of mutual agreement, as it were ("live and let live"). But the environment has now changed drastically, and one must adapt himself to it or fall by the way-side. To bury one's head in the sand or to shout "death to the invaders" from the rooftops will not negate the proven validity and power of these bids which are—let's face it—*here to stay.* Even if one does not choose to employ any or all of the pre-emptive bids which we are going to recommend, he must, in self-defense, become familiar with their workings. Otherwise he will either perish at the table or be robbed of his rightful heritage—the right to show a reasonable or maximum profit on his good cards.

• If you feel deficient in the fundaments of basic bidding, there are many excellent books which will bring you up to date on all phases of bidding with good cards. Call Baron Barclay Bridge Supplies toll free at 1-800-274-2221 for a free 64 page catalog of bridge books, supplies and other items.

CHAPTER 9

Pre-emptive Opening Bids

An opening bid of three, four, or five in a suit (a pre-emptive bid) has a dual purpose: (1) to shut out the opponents and (2) to deprive them of bidding space, thus making it more difficult for them to reach their best contract. Generally speaking, the prime purpose of a pre-emptive bid is to prevent the opponents from reaching a game or slam. However, if by doubling your pre-emptive bid they score more than the game or slam is worth, your bid is losing strategy.

In rubber bridge, a game is worth, on the average, about 500 points. Hence, a pre-emptive bid is never made if one figures to go down more than 500 points. If one goes down 500 points, it is deemed to be a fair exchange for the game the opponents could have made. Logically, therefore, every pre-emptive bid against a game contract is geared to an expected maximum loss of 500 points.

And so, in rubber bridge, if you are not vulnerable and go down three tricks doubled, you will lose 500 points. If you are vulnerable and go down two tricks doubled, your loss is 500 points. Consequently, whenever you open with a bid of three, four, or five in a suit, you should be *two tricks short* of your contract if you are vulnerable and *three tricks short* of your contract if *not vulnerable*.

In duplicate bridge, on the other hand, we have a different set of values and different criteria. If neither side is vulnerable and you go down three doubled for a loss of 500 points, you will get zero match points, for the opponents would have scored only 300 points as a game bonus, plus their trick score—generally 100–190— for a total of 400–490.

If both sides are vulnerable, you can afford to go down two tricks doubled, losing 500 points (*if* they can make a game), for a vulnerable game is worth 500 points plus the trick score (100– 190). However, if you should go down three tricks doubled, you will lose 800 points—and get zero match points or perhaps, if it's a good day, one match point.

If you are vulnerable and they are not, a two-trick set doubled will cost you 500 points, which is more than they would have scored for their vulnerable game (300 plus trick score).

If they are vulnerable and you are not, you can afford to go down three tricks doubled for a loss of 500 points. This is a good sacrifice against the 600 plus points they would have secured for making a vulnerable game.

It should be noted that when you make a vulnerable pre-emptive bid there is always the possibility that the opponents may not have a game. And if they double you and set you *one trick,* your loss of 200 points will be greater than any part-score the opponents could have made. In experience, we have learned to make a vulnerable pre-emptive bid very rarely, especially against nonvulnerable opponents.

We have also learned, from a few bitter experiences, that when one is deliberating about whether to make a pre-emptive bid in the highest-ranking suit, spades, he should think twice about it. It may turn out, when you open with a three spade bid and go down a trick, that your side could have bought the hand for two spades. This will often be the case when the strength is evenly divided between the two sides—and the most the opponents could have made was two hearts.

To sort of sum up the preceding paragraphs, one should be a trifle more cautious in duplicate bridge than in rubber bridge about opening with a pre-emptive bid. In rubber bridge pre-emptive bids are directed exclusively against the opponents' games and slams, and if it happens that the opponents can make only a part-score and you go down 200 points, the loss is slight. But in duplicate bridge, if you go down 200 points against the opponents' part-score, you get yourself a nice, round zero—and if you contrive to get about two more such zeros, you have just about eliminated yourself from the tournament.

Lest the impression be created that we are opposed to pre-emptive bids in duplicate bridge, we vigorously deny it. Pre-emptive bids are a must if optimum results are to be attained. Keeping the opponents out of their top contract when they have the superior cards is fully as important as getting to your top contract when your side has the superior cards. Obstructing, harassing, and sniping at the opponents has become essential to one's self-preservation in this day and age. The credo "Bid your own cards and let the opponents worry about their cards" has become outmoded.

In a moment we are going to present our method of handling pre-emptive bids. By way of prologue, this point must be emphasized: If you elect to use our recommendations, *stay within the prescribed limits of the particular bid in first or second position.* Don't deviate merely because you have learned to love to plague the enemy. Pre-emptive bids can operate efficiently only if their specifically designated range is not violated. Once the range is violated, one has set forth on the route to creating three formidable enemies at the table: not only your two opponents but also your partner. In these Frankenstein circumstances, each of them is capable of inflicting a deathblow.

I. The Opening Three-Bid in First or Second Position

In our view, as well as that of most authorities, the foundation for developing a good partnership in this department starts with *disciplined* pre-emptive bids in first and second position. Only when partner has passed and you are in third or fourth position, can discipline be relaxed, thereby allowing you to bid with logical abandon, if there is such a quality.

We must strongly emphasize that the first- or second-hand pre-emptive opening is disciplined and must stay within the range agreed upon.* The limits are not as rigid on the low side as they are on the high side. That is, we do not pre-empt with a hand that is better than the upper limit of our range, but we might pre-empt with a hand that is just a shade shy of the prescribed lower limit. Why do we believe in such discipline?

* See page 127.

The non-passing partner, who might have any type of hand, must be able to make reasonable judgments about game bids, slam bids, and sacrifice bids. If we violate our agreed-upon range with a non-passing partner, it becomes impossible for him to know what the precise setup is. By being rigid in first and second position, we do relinquish some opportunities to pre-empt that the free-swinging, undisciplined bidders may have (which we do debit to the loss side), but we feel that we more than overcome the loss since we are able to deliver more accurate judgment in the interest of partnership rapport.

Let's examine a few illustrations which we think are opening three bids *in first or second position.*

1. ♠ 9   ♡ 7 6 5   ◇ K Q J 10 7 5 4   ♣ 9 3

This is a standard nonvulnerable opening three bid (3 D), which would, incidentally, be permissible in most partnerships.

2. (a) ♠ 9   ♡ 7 6   ◇ Q J 10 8 7 6 5 2   ♣ 8 4
   (b) ♠ 9   ♡ 7 6   ◇ Q 9 7 6 5 4 3 2   ♣ 8 4

If we were not vulnerable, we would open each of the above with three diamonds. Note that the length of the suit is seven cards or a bad eight. Even though a bit of boldness has always appealed to us, we cannot subscribe to a theory which permits opening with a three bid on a suit that looks like J x x x x x or Q x x x x, as some moderns do. As a matter of fact, the seven-card length is the criterion to which, for the most part, we adhere.

3. ♠ Q 9 6   ♡ 8 3   ◇ K J 9 8 7 5 3   ♣ 2

We would open, nonvulnerable, with three diamonds. Three-card support for a major, which includes an honor, is no deterrent for this opening. If partner responded in that major, we would raise to four.

4. ♠ Q 9 7 2   ♡ 8   ◇ Q J 9 7 6 4 2   ♣ 8

Though we like to pre-empt when opportunity affords, we do not pre-empt in first or second position with a three or four bid in a minor if we hold four cards in a major suit. This is not an arbitrary decision adhered to merely because the view is old and deep-rooted. We reluctantly give up the chance to pre-empt. In compensation, we have a much better chance to find the spade spot when partner has a good hand. A player usually bids three no-trump with a good hand over partner's minor suit pre-emptive. He can't afford to investigate for a major suit contract because his partner's (opener's) answer is almost always in his own suit, thus taking the partnership past the three no-trump spot. Also, if there is a sacrifice in the hand in spades, the pre-emptive call in diamonds (holding four spades) makes it impossible to find.

5. (a) ♠ 7 5   ♡ 9 3   ◇ A K Q 9 6 4 2   ♣ 7 5
   (b) ♠ A Q J 9 7 4 2   ♡ 8   ◇ K 6 3   ♣ 4 2

Informed opinion is virtually in complete agreement that pre-emptive bids, especially opening three bids, must denote *either* a good hand or a bad hand. You can't do both successfully. If you plan them to be good, as a completely solid suit, that is fine with us, but they never must be anything else. If you plan them to be bad, then they never must be too good when partner has not passed. A solid running suit, as in Example (a), would certainly be too good. ·A sound rule to serve you here is available: never pre-empt in first or second position with three or four in a minor suit headed by A K Q, since you might easily miss three no-trump.

Examples (a) and (b) are too good for the pre-empt. With Example (b), you should open the hand with a bid of one spade, or you should pass, intending to back in later.

It should be noted from the examples given that opening three-bids will not always, on an absolutely guaranteed basis, be able to take six tricks non-vulnerable or seven tricks vulnerable. Your action in responding to partner's opening pre-empt will thereby be affected, although to only a limited extent. These responses are presented later on in this chapter.

II. The Opening Three-Bid in Third Position

One circumstance exists here in contrast to first and second position which may affect materially the quality of your opening three-bids: *you have a passing partner.* The chance of your side making a game is virtually nil, and the chances of the opponents being able to fulfill a premium contract are correspondingly increased.

Your opening three-bids are not too much different on the low side but could be very different on the high side. Any holding which qualified as a three-bid in first or second position would automatically be suitable for an opening three-bid in third position. A few examples will serve to illustrate the tactical differences that do exist.

1. ♠ 7 5   ♡ 6   ◊ A K Q 9 7 4 3   ♣ 9 6 3

The objection to opening with a pre-emptive minor on a solid suit is largely eliminated. The chance of missing a game is possible, but remote. We would open as follows: nonvulnerable against vulnerable, we bid four diamonds. All other vulnerabilities, we open three diamonds.

2. ♠ Q 10 7 4   ♡ 6   ◊ Q J 8 6 4 3 2   ♣ 5

The bar against opening a pre-empt in a minor suit when holding four-card support in a major is removed when partner has passed originally. The need to pre-empt is too urgent here to give the factor of missing a spade contract too much consideration. We would consider a three opening to be correct on any vulnerability, but we would not be averse to opening with four diamonds if we were not vulnerable and the opponents were vulnerable.

3. ♠ A Q J 9 7 6 4   ♡ 2   ◊ K 10 7   ♣ 8 3

We like the three spade opening in third position for strategic reasons, particularly when vulnerable. You may miss a game on occasion, but the pre-emptive bid confers the advantage of making it pretty rough for the fourth-hand opponent to enter the bidding.

4. ♠ 3   ♡ 9 6   ◊ A Q J 9 7 6 4   ♣ A 10 4

If vulnerable against nonvulnerable opponents, we consider the three opening bid to be superior to the one opening (in third position).

5. ♠ 9   ♡ 10 6 4   ◊ A K Q 9 7 6   ♣ J 7 6

This qualifies as an opening one-bid in third position or as a "weak" two-bid if that convention is part of your system. If not vulnerable against vulnerable opponents, we favor opening with a three diamond bid. Note that the requirement of the seven-card suit is waived in third (and fourth) position. We would also open, if not vulnerable, with three diamonds on:

♠ 9 7   ♡ 8 3   ◊ A K J 9 7 4   ♣ K 10 8

III. The Opening Three-Bid in Fourth Position

On the surface, advice here would appear to be superfluous. Correct action, as viewed by most experienced players, would stick out like a sore thumb. Since there may, however, be those who can use the advice, we offer what follows.

It goes without saying that all *bad* opening three-bids are automatically passed out. Why start a fight with a terrible holding? Be thankful for the chance to pass it out. It follows that when you open with a three-bid in fourth position, you must possess a top-bracket three-bid which still doesn't contain the high cards which normally accompany a one-bid opening. The bid should inform your partner that your hand is too good to toss in, but is deficient in defensive strength. You can almost surely take seven tricks and possibly eight on a distributional basis. You don't want competition pushing you overboard, if you can eliminate or minimize that danger. Neither do you want partner to have any uncertainty about the combined defensive strength, which he might have if you opened with a one-bid. All of the following hands qualify as an opening three-bid *in fourth position:*

♠ A K Q 10 7 6 5   ♡ 7 6 3   ◇ 4 3   ♣ 8   Bid three spades.
♠ A K J 9 6 4 3   ♡ 6   ◇ Q 10 2   ♣ 7 5   Bid three spades.
♠ 8   ♡ A K J 10 9 6 3   ◇ 8 4   ♣ Q J 9   Bid three hearts.
♠ Q 10 8   ♡ 4   ◇ A K Q 9 7 6 4   ♣ 8 2   Bid three diamonds.

IV. Responses to Opening Three-Bids

To draw the student's attention to the importance of this phase of the discussion, we restate the evident truth that it takes very little knowledge, experience, or even courage to learn how and when to make a pre-emptive call. It is the partner of the pre-emptor who will have all of the problems. It is his action which usually determines the success or failure of the pre-empt.

When a pre-empt is made, it is manifestly impossible to cover every situation that might crop up. We intend merely to furnish examples which could aid you in coping with the more common situations.

We cannot launch into the subject without first outlining the ground rules which bind the respective partners. Most good partnerships the world over use this same set of rules:

1. The opening pre-emptive bidder, in first or second position, *never* bids again unless his partner enters the auction. This is a must for a smooth-working partnership, since opener has told his story and only responder is in a position to determine the joint partnership assets.

A third-hand pre-emptor is similarly bound if his opening is of the same type as would be made in first or second position. If it is very unusual, as it may be, then the opener may be permitted further action.

2. If the non-passing partner responds in a *new* suit under game, it is absolutely forcing for one round. For example:

Opener	Responder		Opener	Responder
3 ◇	3 ♠	*or*	3 ♡	4 ♣

The opener must bid again. He usually merely rebids his own suit but is permitted to raise partner if he has support. In experience, responder will very rarely prefer to play his own suit at his precise part-score bid. Even if he should so desire on occasion, the forcing feature of the new suit bid will provide greater dividends in the long run.

Opener	Responder		Opener	Responder
4 ◇	4 ♠	*or*	4 ◇	5 ♣

The responder, above, has decided where the game should be played. He asks partner not to interfere. The opener must pass.

3. Where the responder's action has been simply a raise in opener's suit, all further action can be taken *only by responder*. Proper action must necessarily depend on the combined defense; or, if you are contemplating a sacrifice, the combined trick-taking power. The responder is in the best position to know what to do.

An exception could occur when responder has raised, and the opener becomes the last to speak and must decide whether or not to sacrifice against a slam bid. We intend, elsewhere, to provide a workable formula for partnership action in these circumstances.

4. As was mentioned, the opening pre-emptive bidder in first or second position must never make a bid which figures to result in his going down more than the value of the opponents' game.

A. RESPONDING TO PARTNER'S FIRST OR SECOND POSITION OPENING THREE-BIDS WITH A GOOD HAND

1. The bidding has proceeded, with North–South not vulnerable:

North	East	South
3 ◇	Pass	?

You, South, hold:

♠ A Q 7 3   ♡ K J 9 7   ◇ 6   ♣ A J 9 7

You should *pass* as quickly as you can get the word out.

This example is given to illustrate the falsity of the theory that a responder's possession of a sound opening bid of one in a suit is sufficient justification for him to respond to the pre-emptive bidder's opening bid. Hypothetically, the only conceivable call with the above hand is three no-trump. This would not show any specific number of points, but would be a clear statement that responder believes that the combined holdings have a reasonable chance of producing nine tricks. Since an opening three-bid, especially when not vulnerable, denotes a bad hand which doesn't contain a solid suit, no reasonable chance to take nine tricks could exist here. Where could you possibly get nine tricks? As you pass, promptly, you silently hope that the opponents will enter the auction. If they do, they belong to you.

2. Partner, not vulnerable, has again opened with *three diamonds*. This time you hold:

♠ K 10 8   ♡ K 10 8   ◇ K 9 7   ♣ A 9 7 4

You should bid *three no-trump*. There is a very good chance for six or seven diamond tricks. If a major suit is opened, you may even have nine lay-down tricks at that moment. We would be inclined to think that nine tricks can be developed with this holding most of the time. The only question is whether they can be taken before the opposition gets five tricks.

3. Partner opens with three diamonds, not vulnerable. You hold:

♠ K 10 7   ♡ A 3   ◇ 6   ♣ A K Q J 6 5 4

Bid *three no-trump*. If you get a spade lead, the contract is virtually assured. If any other lead is forthcoming, then it is not unreasonable to hope that the nine-trick contract is still a good one.

The above three examples provide us with a rule. Never bid three no-trump over partner's pre-emptive opening three-bid unless you can reasonably expect to run his suit, or can take at least eight tricks in your own hand.

4. Opener again bids *three diamonds,* not vulnerable. Responder holds:

♠ A Q 10 7 5 4   ♡ K 10 7   ◇ 4   ♣ A J 7

Responder should *pass.*

Bear in mind that when responder names a new suit, opener is forced to bid again—and almost all of the time he will rebid his suit. A game in spades is most remote. Incidentally, though we would pass at both rubber bridge and duplicate bridge, the try in spades is much more attractive in rubber bridge. At match-point play, it is losing policy to jeopardize a part-score in diamonds for the slim chance of making a spade game.

5. Again partner's nonvulnerable opening bid is *three diamonds.* You hold:

(a) ♠ A Q 10 9 8 7 2   ♡ A K 2   ◇ 6   ♣ K Q

Bid *four spades.* There should be no doubt in your mind—or partner's—as to which contract you wish to play. The bid commands partner to pass. Incidentally, you may not make it.

(b) ♠ A K Q 9 6   ♡ A K Q 9 2   ◇ 7   ♣ K Q

You first respond *three spades,* which is forcing. If partner bids four diamonds—as expected—you will then bid *four hearts.* The message will be unmistakable: you wish to play the game in one of your suits. If partner prefers hearts, he passes. If he prefers spades, he returns to that suit.

(c) ♠ Q 7   ♡ A 9 4   ◇ A Q 6   ♣ A K Q 7 5

Several actions are available, but only two appeal to us:

(1) We would bid *six diamonds,* which figures to be a lay-down with any lead but spades. It may even be makable with a spade lead.

(2) A "psychic bid" of *three spades,* which is forcing since it is a new suit. Partner will probably call four diamonds, over which we will bid six diamonds. This sequence *may* prevent a spade lead. However, it may enable the left-hand opponent to double

for a spade lead. Whenever one "psyches," he is always running the risk that his bid may backfire.

6. Partner, not vulnerable, opens with *three diamonds.* You, as responder, hold:

♠ A K Q 9 2   ♡ 10 3   ◇ 7 4   ♣ 9 7 6 4

What action do you take?

Constantly bear in mind that the defensive strength of the combined hands determines, in large measure, whether and to what degree you act. Suppose we try to estimate the probabilities in this case. The three diamond bidder should be played for, at most, one trick on defense. Furthermore, he does not possess a sound suit. It is reasonable to assume that with a diamond lead *they* can make three no-trump by running the necessary tricks in hearts and clubs. They also, in all probability, can fulfill a four heart contract if no spade lead is forthcoming. They might even be able to make it with a spade lead. Should you sit idly by, permitting them to reach their premium contract—and make it with an overtrick or two? We think you must elect to strike the best logical blow to forestall it.

Bid *three spades,* with the intent of then passing regardless of what partner or the opponents do. In defending, your side will then be off on the right foot. We would take this action on any vulnerability at match-point play. At rubber bridge we would do the same in almost all situations, except perhaps if we were vulnerable and they were not.

7. Partner opens *three diamonds.* You, as responder, hold:

♠ 9 7   ♡ 8 4   ◇ K 8 7 3   ♣ A 10 8 6 5

You should recognize that the opponents have a major suit game, perhaps even a slam. If you are *not vulnerable,* and they are, do not become an ostrich by burying your head in the sand. The situation, particularly at match-point play, provides you with a choice of actions. Against very good opponents, we prefer a direct raise to five diamonds, thereby forcing them to make their decision at that high level. A response of three no-trump is a distinct possibility—and if the outstanding cards are divided evenly between the opposing hands, you might even "steal" the game. Conversely, even if the opponents take all thirteen tricks, you will be minus 450 points, which is less than the value of their certain vulnerable game.

If you get doubled at three no-trump, you will, of course, run out to diamonds, either four or five, although five is our preferred choice.

As another possibility, over partner's three diamond opening, you might make a forcing bid of either three hearts or three spades. This might work against weak opposition. If the opponents remain quiet, and partner rebids four diamonds, it would be shortsighted of you to pass. Go on with your apparent display of strength by raising to five diamonds. At this late stage, they may have a feeling that something peculiar is going on, but they won't be sure of it.

If both sides are vulnerable, with the above hand we would respond with *five diamonds* at once.

8. Opener, not vulnerable, has bid *three diamonds*. Responder holds:

♠ 6   ♡ A 7 3   ◊ K 9 6   ♣ A K Q 7 6 4

An immediate Blackwood call seems best. If the opening bidder's hand contains an ace, you ought to be willing to play for a slam in diamonds.

9. Opener bids *three diamonds*, vulnerable or not vulnerable. Responder holds:

♠ A 6   ♡ A 8   ◊ A 7   ♣ A K Q J 8 6 3

Five no-trump would be our choice here. Since a slam venture is, in our view, a must, such a try costs nothing. The five no-trump bid is a conventional one which demands that partner bid a grand slam in his suit if he holds two of the three top cards in that suit (A K, A Q, or K Q). If he does not have the king and queen (you have the ace), he will bid six diamonds. If he makes the latter response, fulfillment may be hazardous, easy, or dependent on the lead. We would let it rest in that spot. If, however, he bids seven diamonds over our five no-trump call, we will bid seven no-trump. If the diamond suit runs, we have 13 tricks. If, somehow, it does not, we can't make seven diamonds, although we might make seven no-trump.

V. Opening Four-Bids in the Minor Suits

Discipline should not be relaxed even though you are raising the level of the bidding. In first or second position, the opener adheres to the requirements. We like to describe the hand as an opening three-bid with one additional winning trick added. The addition occurs usually in the bid suit, which *more frequently is eight cards long instead of seven.* The hand is a poor one which is below the limits of an opening bid of one in a suit and which has little or no defensive strength. The suit, in first or second position, must not be headed by A K Q or A K J 10, since in this case your partnership might be missing a three no-trump contract. The following are examples of *first and second position opening bids of four in a minor suit.*

1. ♠ 7   ♡ 6 3   ◇ K Q J 10 8 7 6 4   ♣ J 5
2. ♠ 7   ♡ 5   ◇ A Q J 10 8 7 6 5   ♣ Q 10 3
3. ♠ 7   ♡ 8   ◇ A K 9 7 6 4 3 2   ♣ 9 7 3
4. ♠ 7 5   ♡ 8   ◇ K Q J 10 7 6 4   ♣ Q J 10

With 1, we open with *four diamonds* on any vulnerability at match-point play. We do the same at rubber bridge except when we are vulnerable and they are not. In this latter situation, we would open with *three diamonds.*

With 2, 3, and 4, we open with *four diamonds* regardless of the vulnerability in both duplicate and rubber bridge. Admittedly, if we are vulnerable and they are not, we are pushing a bit, but in our experience this "pushing" has paid handsome dividends.

In third position, the four of a minor opening is subject to the same changes that occur with the three opening, namely the slight relaxation of requirements. These "deviations" will almost always occur when you are not vulnerable and they are. In this favorable situation, you may push a little with a weaker suit as: S – 6 H – Q 9 8 D – K Q 10 9 7 6 5 C – 7 5, making the vulnerable opponents guess at a high level. You should also open four diamonds holding: S – 6 H – 8 3 D – A K Q J 9 6 2 C – 9 6 3. Note once again that the bar against holding A K Q in your suit can be dispensed with when partner has passed originally. Also, when you open with a four-bid, you should not possess too many winning tricks defensively or hold too much in side cards. If you do, you might well miss a game despite the fact that partner has passed.

When both sides are vulnerable or when only your side is vulnerable, we recommend that you follow the rules outlined for first and second position openings.

In fourth position, a bid of four in a minor suit should not have the high cards which normally accompany an opening bid of one in a suit but should be gilt-edged for its ability to win tricks. It should surely contain eight virtually certain taking tricks and at least a vestige of defense. In short, it should be a hand which you are reluctant to throw in.

VI. Opening Bids of Four in a Major Suit

A. IN FIRST OR SECOND POSITION

Authorities disagree more here than they do with other pre-emptive calls. We refer only to first or second position bids, since in third and fourth position there is virtual agreement. (1) A popular standard which is basic with most good players is the ability to take about eight tricks. Most, if not all, of these tricks are to be found in the main suit. No side cards of any consequence will be found in the hand unless the main suit is faulty. In no case will there be the high cards that would normally accompany an opening bid of one in a suit. (2) Simply because the call is made at the game level, some see no harm in making the bid on a long, absolutely solid seven or eight card suit, plus an outside ace or king. (3) Others diverge by nearly always making the bid on seven winning tricks when they are not vulnerable. Some use all three standards indiscriminately and promiscuously, which practice is not calculated to contribute to a life of ease for their partners.

Those who thus diverge by widening the range for an opening four-bid have the undoubted advantage of being able to pre-empt more often than players who stick with the standard "one range" requirements. They lose heavily, however, when partner misjudges by going on to slam with insufficient values or takes a sacrifice and the set is one trick too many. There is, in addition, a psychological loss: partner is always in doubt as to what he should do with a good hand.

We adhere almost rigidly to the standard four-bid in a suit. The following is the classic example found in most textbooks:

1. ♠ A K 10 7 6 5 4 2   ♡ 3   ◊ 7 5   ♣ J 7

This hand fulfills perfectly *the requirement of eight probable winning tricks* (assuming the 2-2-1 division of the five outstanding spades). Bid *four spades*.

2. ♠ A 2 ♡ K Q J 10 8 7 5 2 ◇ 6 3 ♣ 7

Open *four hearts.* You have seven solid heart tricks, plus an outside ace. Note the lack of the 2½ defensive tricks which would normally be necessary for an opening bid of one in a suit on a 12-point hand.

3. ♠ A K Q J 10 9 6 2 ♡ 3 ◇ 7 5 ♣ 9 7

Eight solid winning tricks, but still nevertheless an opening bid of four spades.

4. ♠ 7 ♡ K Q J 10 9 5 2 ◇ Q J 10 9 ♣ 3

This is not the usual type, but it does have eight winning tricks at hearts. We would open with *four hearts*.

5. ♠ K Q J 10 9 7 6 5 ♡ 6 2 ◇ 9 6 ♣ 3

We would open this hand with *four spades* if we are not vulnerable and they are. We might do it if both were vulnerable but would not if we were vulnerable and they were not. This constitutes a violation, but we like the pre-emptive nature of the holding and the total lack of defensive strength.

6. ♠ A K Q J 10 8 3 ♡ 7 5 ◇ 9 6 ♣ J 3

Some might open with four spades if not vulnerable. We would open with *one spade*. In contrast to the previous example, which also has seven winning tricks, this hand has some defense. We can stand a penalty double by partner at a very high level.

7. ♠ 2 ♡ A K Q 9 8 7 6 5 3 ◇ 5 3 ♣ 6

Despite the possession of a solid nine-card suit, we consider the *four heart* opening to be the best strategic call. This is as far as we go. The possession of a tenth heart would preclude our opening with four in a suit. In the latter situation, we would probably pass initially, and later sneak into the bidding, hoping to get doubled.

B. The Opening Bid of Four in a Major in Third or Fourth Position

Once partner has passed, the chance of missing a slam is minimized. Hence, other considerations become paramount. You may, for example, choose to avoid competition by pre-empting on holdings that would be considered unsuitable in first or second position. Thus, *pre-emptive openings of four in a major, in third and fourth position, can be psychological or tactical bids.*

Naturally, all holdings that are adequate for the four-level major suit opening in first or second position are also eminently qualified in *third* position. In addition, consider the following:

1. ♠ 6	♡ A K Q J 10 7 4	◇ A J 2	♣ J 2
2. ♠ 6	♡ A K Q J 10 9 2	◇ K Q J	♣ 7 5
3. ♠ Void	♡ K Q J 10 9 8	◇ 7 5	♣ A Q J 9 6
4. ♠ 6	♡ A K Q J 9 2	◇ K J 10 9 7	♣ 4
5. ♠ Void	♡ A K Q 10 9 7 6 4	◇ A 10 2	♣ 7 3

On each of the five above hands, we would like to avoid spade competition from the enemy. The best means available is to open with a high-level bid: *four hearts* in each case. Admittedly, in making this bid, we are giving up our chance for a slam. However, with a passing partner, a slam would be very difficult to reach even if it were there. Obviously, the bid has more appeal when *you are vulnerable and they are not* since they will tend to come into the bidding more easily in their favorable vulnerability condition. Also, there is greater reason to pre-empt if your main suit is hearts, since if you possess spades it is easier to outbid the opposition. Nevertheless, whether you hold hearts or spades, we recommend the pre-emptive call with the examples shown, *regardless of vulnerability.*

When these pre-emptive openings bring about further bidding, one might suppose that the opener has the privilege of bidding again. Such is *not* the case. A player who opens with four in a major never competes again unless his partner enters the auction. He stands or falls with the effectiveness of his pre-emptive call. This rule will also hold for a third or fourth position opening if his hand is the normal standard type. If, however, his hand is an unusual, better-than-standard one, he may compete again.

VII. Responding to Opening Bids of Four in a Major Suit

We will deal with each hand as if partner had opened *in first or second position* and we have not passed. This is our approach at the bridge table, and we strongly recommend that you adopt this approach: Always assume that your partner has the normal, eight-taking trick pre-emptive, regardless of his position at the table. He will hold that type hand much more often than any other.

Let us assume the bidding has proceeded:

North	East	South
4 ♠	Pass	?

You, sitting South, hold:

1. ♠ Q 9 5   ♡ A J 6 3   ◇ A 9 6 3   ♣ 3 2

Bear in mind that partner has promised to take only eight tricks. He should fulfill his contract comfortably and perhaps bring home 11 tricks. He may even be able to land 12 tricks, but you can't afford to risk the exploration. If you do, you may too often land at the five-level and discover to your regret that you can't make your contract (zero match points). *Pass*, and take the game that is there.

2. ♠ J 3   ♡ K Q J   ◇ K Q J 9   ♣ A K 10 2

Since partner does not have 13 points, either he does not have two aces or the spade suit has a gaping hole in it. There is no percentage in exploring for a slam via the Blackwood Slam Convention.

3. ♠ Q 3   ♡ A Q 7 2   ◇ A 2   ♣ A Q 6 3 2

There is either an excellent play for 12 tricks or they are already there for the taking. Go right to *six spades*.

4. ♠ Void   ♡ K 2   ◇ A K Q J 10 9 7 5 2   ♣ Q 3

Never take your partner out of his suit simply because you think your game spot is a better one. He will assume that your bid is forcing and will keep on bidding. Frankly, he should not be disappointed with your holding when you put it down as the dummy. Therefore *pass*.

5. ♠ 10 7   ♡ 6   ◇ A 10 6 3 2   ♣ A K Q J 3

Bid *five spades*. This call has a specialized meaning. You are commanding opener to bid six only if his suit is solid.

VIII. Opening Bids of Five in a Minor Suit

The extremely high level at which this bid is made might easily be used as an argument for the relaxation of the normal rules governing other pre-emptive bids. We do not see it that way. The bid is still pre-emptive and should, for the most part, therefore be as disciplined as any other pre-emptive bid.

In first or second position, we feel the hand should be able to deliver nine or ten tricks on a probable basis. It should not, in our view, ever have the high cards which normally accompany an opening bid of one in a suit. Major suit support should not be a deterrent. In fact, we wouldn't be averse to having four-card major support if the distribution is unbalanced enough in favor of the minor.

The following examples will illustrate. Each of them is an opening bid of five in the long minor suit:

1.	♠ 2	♡ Void	◇ K Q J 9 8 7 5 2	♣ K J 10 8
2.	♠ 3	♡ Q 10 2	◇ Void	♣ A K 10 9 8 7 5 4 2
3.	♠ Void	♡ Void	◇ K Q 10 8 7 5 4 2	♣ K J 10 4 3
4.	♠ Q 10 9 7	♡ Void	◇ 7	♣ A Q J 9 8 6 5 3

Several items should be given consideration when responder is opposite partner's opening bid of five in a suit. The opener has promised to deliver nine or ten tricks. Therefore one or two in responder's hand will just permit fulfillment of the contract. Even if responder can provide three, or even in a rare case, four tricks, they may still not be enough for a slam. Remember that the opener's hand is highly distributional, and responder's hand may not fit well. How can responder decide what is likely to fit?

There are some logical inferences about the value of certain holdings, but no guarantee goes with them. Aces are, of course, most valuable, but K Q combinations—particularly in the major suits—are not apt to be so valuable. If you have a K Q combination opposite a singleton or a void, the trick you can establish may be worthless or too late for use. High trump honors have gilt-edged values, since they are (were) a part of partner's losers going in. Similarly, aces and kings in the minors will often prove valuable.

IX. Opening Bids of Five in a Major Suit

These calls are not pre-emptive and perhaps should not be dealt with here. They describe a tremendously powerful hand and are not concerned with eliminating competition. The sole purpose for making the call is to obtain specific information from partner. To illustrate:

♠ Q J 10 9 8 7 5   ♡ Void   ◊ A   ♣ A K Q J 2

Five spades should be the opening bid with the above holding. It asks partner to raise *only* with the king or ace of spades. If he has both, he should bid seven. Notice that the bid gets the job done. If he has a spade honor or honors, he raises the required amount, which certainly puts you into the correct contract. Furthermore, it prevents his raising you with the wrong values—in the wrong places—for he knows exactly what you're looking for. He knows you have no desire to hear him speak with any part of A K Q J of hearts, or K Q J of diamonds, etc.

X. Opening Bids of Six in a Suit

The opening bid of six in a suit asks for a raise *only with either the ace or king of the trump suit.* The bidder can hardly make the call if he is missing both honors.

♠ Void   ♡ A Q J 10 9 7 3   ◊ A K Q J 9 3   ♣ Void

The opening bid of *six hearts* is a logical and appealing choice.

We occasionally open with a slam bid when we are not seeking to locate the missing trump honor. We merely have high hopes of fulfillment if we don't convey any information to the opponents. Conversely, we have very little hope of extracting from partner the specific information that is required to make a grand slam effort worthwhile. Our hand might look like this:

1. ♠ Void   ♡ A K Q J 10 7 5 3   ◊ A K 4 2   ♣ A
2. ♠ A K   ♡ Void   ◊ A K Q J 7 5 3 2   ♣ A J 10

CHAPTER **10**

Pre-emptive Bids in Action

The pre-emptive bids of three, four, and five in a suit, the pre-emptive jump overcall,* the "weak" jump overcall,* * the "weak" opening two-bid,* * etc. are all dedicated to: (1) preventing the enemy from sauntering merrily along their accustomed, unmolested paths of bidding, (2) disrupting the opponents' lines of communication, and (3) goading or taunting the adversaries into unwarranted positive action. While all the above is going on, a most practical, harmonious, and disciplined relationship with partner is being maintained, for he knows exactly what you have when you make any of the above-enumerated pre-emptive bids.

Speaking objectively, when an opponent is faced with a decision about what to do over a pre-emptive bid, he is quite frequently forced to guess—and a fair percentage of the time he will guess wrong.

Let us look at some of these obstructionist pre-emptive bids as they developed in real life. All of the deals which follow arose in topflight competition.

DEAL 1.

You are playing in the National Championships. As fourth hand, sitting South, vulnerable against non-vulnerable opponents, you pick up the following hand:

* Discussed at the end of this chapter.
** These bids are discussed in the chapters which follow.

♠ A K
♡ A K Q
◇ 6
♣ A K Q J 10 8 5

The bidding proceeds:

West	North	East	South
3 ◇	Pass	6 ◇	?

What do you bid? First, you silently curse the day pre-emptive bids were born. Then you double, and when it's all over, you collect 500 points for beating the opponents three tricks. You now have a post-mortem discussion, which reveals that you were helpless.

This was the exact setup at the Summer Nationals, held in Washington, D.C., in 1959.

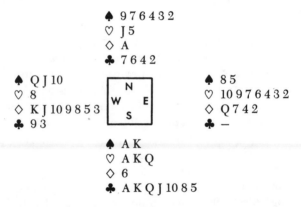

♠ 9 7 6 4 3 2
♡ J 5
◇ A
♣ 7 6 4 2

♠ Q J 10   ♠ 8 5
♡ 8   ♡ 10 9 7 6 4 3 2
◇ K J 10 9 8 5 3 ◇ Q 7 4 2
♣ 9 3   ♣ —

♠ A K
♡ A K Q
◇ 6
♣ A K Q J 10 8 5

Of course, it is rather apparent that North–South could have made a grand slam in clubs or no-trump. How can one ever get there, in view of the bidding that developed? One can't, unless he cheats.

As an aside an expert very rarely gets sympathy from a fellow expert. But when our South player on the above deal submitted "his situation" to some of the other experts, he received nothing but sincere sympathy.

DEAL 2.

This deal arose in the National Open Pair Championships of 1960. It illustrates the importance of pre-empting to the limit of one's hand.

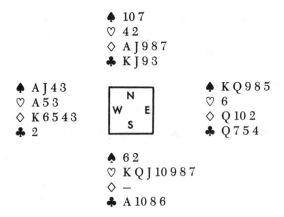

♠ 10 7
♡ 4 2
◇ A J 9 8 7
♣ K J 9 3

♠ A J 4 3
♡ A 5 3
◇ K 6 5 4 3
♣ 2

♠ K Q 9 8 5
♡ 6
◇ Q 10 2
♣ Q 7 5 4

♠ 6 2
♡ K Q J 10 9 8 7
◇ —
♣ A 10 8 6

Both sides vulnerable.
The bidding:

South	West	North	East
4 ♡	Pass	Pass	Pass

It will be noted that East–West can make plenty of spades—and
they never were able to get into the bidding because of South's
pre-emptive opening four heart bid.

Against the four heart contract, West opened the deuce of clubs,
and declarer resisted the urge to take a "free finesse." He climbed up
with dummy's king of clubs, and discarded a spade on the board's
ace of diamonds. He then led a heart, West's ace winning. West
could have defeated the contract by now underleading the ace of
spades (to get a club ruff), but he instead chose to cash the spade
ace. All declarer lost was a spade, the trump ace, and a club to
East's queen.

Actually, West should have underled the spade ace. Declarer,
for his bid, was marked with a strong heart suit. He was also known
to have the club ace, having won the opening lead with the club
king. If he had also held the spade king, he would have opened
with *one* heart, not four hearts.

DEAL 3.

This deal also serves to illustrate that when one pre-empts, he
should not attempt to "save pennies"—and wind up losing dollars.
That is, one should always pre-empt to the maximum extent con-

sistent with reasonable safety. It just happened that a couple of familiar faces were sitting North–South: Norman Kay was South and Sidney Silodor was North. The deal arose in the Philadelphia Open Pair Championships of 1953.

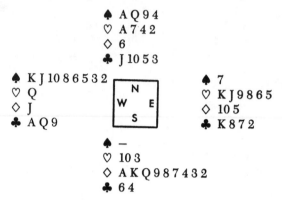

```
                    ♠ A Q 9 4
                    ♡ A 7 4 2
                    ◇ 6
                    ♣ J 10 5 3
  ♠ K J 10 8 6 5 3 2        ┌─────┐        ♠ 7
  ♡ Q                        │  N  │        ♡ K J 9 8 6 5
  ◇ J                      W │     │ E      ◇ 10 5
  ♣ A Q 9                    │  S  │        ♣ K 8 7 2
                            └─────┘
                    ♠ —
                    ♡ 10 3
                    ◇ A K Q 9 8 7 4 3 2
                    ♣ 6 4
```

Both sides vulnerable. South dealer.
The bidding:

South	West	North	East
5 ◇	5 ♠	Double	Pass
Pass	Pass		

West went down three tricks, for a loss of 800 points. If we had been permitted to play the five diamond contract, it would have been fulfilled for a score of 600 points.

Had South opened the ,bidding with an economizing four diamond bid, West would have bid four spades. If Sidney doubled this contract, North–South would have scored only 500 points, less than the 600-point value of their vulnerable game. And if South, over the double, chose to run to five diamonds (which he would *not* have done, since in our partnership the opening pre-emptive bidder is henceforth barred from using his judgment), West assuredly would not have ventured to bid five spades after having been doubled at four spades.

DEAL 4.

Here is a deal played by Bobby Jordan and Artie Robinson in the Philadelphia Open Pair Championships of 1960. Bobby and

Artie represented the United States in the International Championships of 1963 and 1964. The deal illustrates the psychological situations that can be developed out of knowing the precise meaning of partner's opening pre-emptive three-bid.

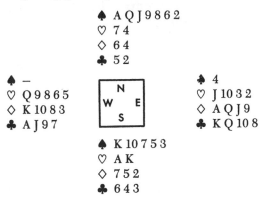

♠ A Q J 9 8 6 2
♡ 7 4
◇ 6 4
♣ 5 2

♠ —
♡ Q 9 8 6 5
◇ K 10 8 3
♣ A J 9 7

♠ 4
♡ J 10 3 2
◇ A Q J 9
♣ K Q 10 8

♠ K 10 7 5 3
♡ A K
◇ 7 5 2
♣ 6 4 3

Both sides vulnerable. North dealer.
The bidding:

North	East	South	West
3 ♠	Double	5 ♠	6 ♡
Pass	Pass	Double	Pass
Pass	Pass		

Jordan, in the South seat, knew that Robinson, for his three spade opening, had a seven-or-eight-card suit; and hence, that one of the opponents—if not both—was void of spades. He also knew that Robinson figured to have no outside strength, and that therefore the opponents had a sure game in hearts, diamonds, or clubs (if not in all three of them). His five spade bid—a pre-emptive on top of partner's pre-empt—was calculated to goad the opponent who was void of spades into bidding a slam. As can be observed, he succeeded admirably.

An interesting side note is that if North–South had been doubled at five spades, they would have gone down but two tricks, for a loss of 500 points. This would have been less than the vulnerable opponents could have made at four hearts (650), five clubs (600), or five diamonds (600).

Of such stuff are international champions made.

DEAL 5.

A situation just about identical to the one described in Deal 4 arose in a New York City tournament in 1956. Sitting East and West were Edgar Kaplan and Alfred Sheinwold, co-authors of the Kaplan-Sheinwold system of bidding.

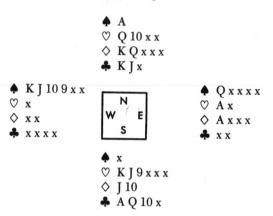

```
                    ♠ A
                    ♡ Q 10 x x
                    ◇ K Q x x x
                    ♣ K J x

    ♠ K J 10 9 x x        ┌─────────┐      ♠ Q x x x x
    ♡ x                   │    N    │      ♡ A x
    ◇ x x                 │ W     E │      ◇ A x x x
    ♣ x x x x             │    S    │      ♣ x x
                          └─────────┘
                    ♠ x
                    ♡ K J 9 x x x
                    ◇ J 10
                    ♣ A Q 10 x
```

North–South vulnerable.
The bidding:

West	North	East	South
3 ♠	Double	5 ♠	6 ♡
Pass	Pass	Pass	

South's bid was reasonable, in our opinion. He had a very strong hand opposite partner's double, and no room was available for investigation. Had East bid merely four spades, South would have checked for aces via the Blackwood Slam Convention—and would have stopped at five hearts upon learning that North held only one ace.

DEAL 6.

As was mentioned earlier, the technical requirement for an opening bid of six in a suit is that you have a solid hand which lacks only the ace or king of trumps. Partner is to bid a grand slam *only* if he has the ace or king of trumps. However, as was pointed out, many players use the six opener as a tactical bid on a hand where they figure they are a slight favorite to make a slam, at the same time hoping the opponents cannot find a fit for a sacrifice. At times, the bid is successful; at times unsuccessful. Here is a deal that arose in 1963 in New York City's Cavendish Club. The result was an unhappy one for the slam bidders.

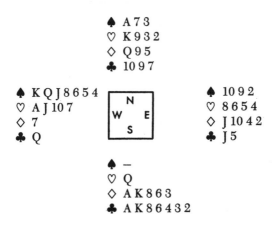

	♠ A 7 3	
	♡ K 9 3 2	
	◇ Q 9 5	
	♣ 10 9 7	

♠ K Q J 8 6 5 4		♠ 10 9 2
♡ A J 10 7		♡ 8 6 5 4
◇ 7		◇ J 10 4 2
♣ Q		♣ J 5

♠ –
♡ Q
◇ A K 8 6 3
♣ A K 8 6 4 3 2

North–South vulnerable.
The bidding:

North	East	South	West
Pass	Pass	6 ♣	6 ♠
7 ♣	Pass	Pass	Pass

West led the ace of hearts, and that was that.

It is hard to criticize North's raise to seven clubs, for he knew— by prearrangement—that his partner was not employing the classic type of six opening bid. If any blame for the result is to be assigned, it would be to the "system" which employs a hit-or-miss, undisciplined six opening.

And for those who might feel that West, holding an ace, should have doubled the seven club bid, that thought should be dismissed. West was not at all sure that he could defeat the grand slam.

DEAL 7.

This deal arose in the 1947 Lakeland Tournament held at Minocqua, Wisconsin. It features a wild hand on which part of the moral is, again, that when you pre-empt go all the way, as contrasted to trying to buy something as cheaply as possible. The bidding sequences presented occurred at two of the tables.

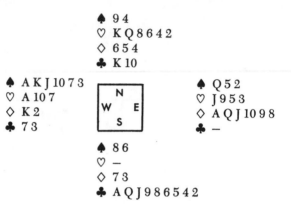

```
                    ♠ 9 4
                    ♡ K Q 8 6 4 2
                    ♢ 6 5 4
                    ♣ K 10
    ♠ A K J 10 7 3                      ♠ Q 5 2
    ♡ A 10 7          N                 ♡ J 9 5 3
    ♢ K 2        W         E            ♢ A Q J 10 9 8
    ♣ 7 3             S                 ♣ —
                    ♠ 8 6
                    ♡ —
                    ♢ 7 3
                    ♣ A Q J 9 8 6 5 4 2
```

Both sides vulnerable.
The bidding:

South	West	North	East
4 ♣	4 ♠	5 ♣	5 ♢
6 ♣	6 ♢	Pass	6 ♠
Pass	Pass	7 ♣	Pass
Pass	7 ♠	Pass	Pass
Pass			

South's four club opening enabled East–West to interchange information regarding both the spade and diamond suits. East's pass over seven clubs was the expert's conventional "forcing pass," announcing first round control of clubs (either the ace or a void). Unfortunately, instead of bidding the grand slam in diamonds, where it was unbeatable, West bid it in spades, where a heart opening would have been fatal.

However, North elected to open the king of clubs. West now had 15 tricks, if need be, and East–West scored 2210 points (honors do not count).

At the second table, the bidding went:

South	West	North	East
5 ♣	5 ♠	6 ♣	6 ♠
7 ♣	Double	Pass	Pass
Pass			

Due to South's *five* club opening, East–West never did get a chance to find out that they also had an excellent diamond suit between them. From West's point of view, he never dreamed that his side could make seven diamonds, so he doubled South's seven club bid, feeling certain that he could beat it. (Wouldn't you?)

In addition, with the grand slam in clubs having been bid by *South* at this table (in contrast to the other table where *North* had bid it), West was unable to make the forcing pass that East made at the first table, for he could not encourage a grand slam when he held two losing clubs in his hand.

If West had but known, his side could have collected the first four tricks, and 1100 points (two spades and two diamonds). But West wasn't going to risk opening his long spade suit and have it trumped, and then find North–South with a club-diamond two-suiter. So he elected to open the ace of hearts.

South trumped this, went to dummy with the ten of clubs, trumped another low heart, then went back to the board's king of trumps, and discarded all four of his losers on the established heart suit. North–South chalked up 2330 points.

It's hard to believe that on the same deal East–West scored 2210 points and North–South scored 2330 points! But it did happen exactly as described above.

A. DEALS 8 AND 9.

In these two final deals, a pre-emptive bid is introduced that has not previously been presented since it is not a pre-emptive opening bid. We refer to *the pre-emptive overcall.*＊ However, since the requirements for the pre-emptive overcall are identical to those for the pre-emptive opening bids, we feel that this is the proper place to illustrate the bid and its impact on the opposition.

By way of prologue, it should be pointed out that nothing slows down and disrupts a partnership's progressive bidding with more

＊ This subject is discussed in Chapter 15, "The Jump Overcall."

suddenness than the injection of a pre-emptive overcall by an opponent. The use of such a bid may exert great pressure on the next bidder who, in a great many cases, will have to place the final contract with his decision. The pre-emptive overcall, like the pre-emptive opening bid, is both disruptive and obstructive. Its purpose is to destroy the lines of communication, causing the opponents who have opened the bidding either to fall short of their maximum level or to end up in their least productive contract.

As was stated, the requirements for the pre-emptive overcall are the same as the requirements for the pre-emptive opening bid. The only difference is that in order to be pre-emptive, the overcall must *skip at least two levels of bidding.* That is, *three hearts over one club or one diamond,* but *four hearts over one spade.* The three heart overcall over a one spade opening bid or a two spade overcall over an opening one club bid would skip only one level, and, if vulnerable, denotes a hand of rather large proportions.*

One important note about pre-emptive overcalls: as with pre-emptive opening bids, when you make up your mind to interject a pre-emptive overcall, pre-empt to the limit of your holding and don't economize. When you have made a pre-emptive overcall, you are through for the afternoon since you will have told your complete story in one bid. Many players fail to realize that they often spoil all the good effects of their pre-emptive bid by going on with a further bid. Here is a good example of this latter point.

DEAL 8.

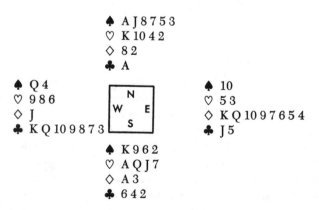

```
                    ♠ A J 8 7 5 3
                    ♡ K 10 4 2
                    ◇ 8 2
                    ♣ A
   ♠ Q 4                          ♠ 10
   ♡ 9 8 6          N             ♡ 5 3
   ◇ J          W       E         ◇ K Q 10 9 7 6 5 4
   ♣ K Q 10 9 8 7 3   S           ♣ J 5
                    ♠ K 9 6 2
                    ♡ A Q J 7
                    ◇ A 3
                    ♣ 6 4 2
```

* This subject is discussed in Chapter 15, "The Jump Overcall."

The bidding has progressed:

North	East	South	West
1 ♠	4 ◊	4 ♠	Pass
Pass	?		

Right up to the point where East has his second opportunity to bid, the pre-emptive overcall has accomplished its desired effect (and, had East passed, East–West would have scored 10 match points out of a possible 12). Two things have happened. First, North–South can make one more trick playing at hearts than at spades and they have been deprived of the opportunity to probe and arrive at the right suit. Secondly, the North–South pair has not reached the small slam that is there in either suit, with thirteen tricks being available at hearts.

But with North–South vulnerable and East–West not vulnerable, East now decided to take the "sacrifice" at five diamonds, thus allowing the opponents to re-enter the bidding to get to their slam and to their right suit. Actually, if East thought that he had sufficient values to risk five diamonds, he should have made the bid directly over one spade. Not having done so, he should have said to himself: "I did what I did because I thought it was right. I'll rest with the result."

When East, on the above hand, chose to bid five diamonds, South joyfully bid five hearts, and North was quick to grab the bait and bid six hearts. East–West scored one match point out of 12—instead of the 10 points they would have earned had East correctly passed the four spade bid.

Deal 9.

As has been stated and illustrated, the making of a pre-emptive bid poses no problem: one bids by definition. The problem usually falls on the shoulders of the partner of the pre-emptor, who must make the future decisions for his team.

Generally speaking, when a defender has made a pre-emptive jump overcall, a sacrifice bid should not be made by his partner if the latter's hand contains any reasonable prospect of defeating the adverse contract. It is wise to remember that a pre-empt places the opposition in a difficult spot, and they not only might have arrived at the wrong contract but they might have been driven too high. Here is an illustration of the latter situation:

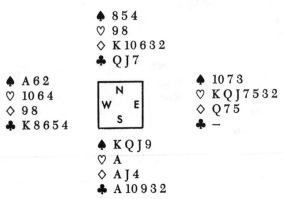

```
            ♠ 8 5 4
            ♡ 9 8
            ◊ K 10 6 3 2
            ♣ Q J 7
♠ A 6 2                        ♠ 10 7 3
♡ 10 6 4        N             ♡ K Q J 7 5 3 2
◊ 9 8       W       E          ◊ Q 7 5
♣ K 8 6 5 4     S              ♣ —
            ♠ K Q J 9
            ♡ A
            ◊ A J 4
            ♣ A 10 9 3 2
```

North–South vulnerable.
The bidding:

South	West	North	East
1 ♣	Pass	1 ◊	4 ♡
5 ◊	5 ♡	Pass	Pass
Double	Pass	Pass	Pass

The five heart contract went down three, for a loss of 500 points. Had West permitted North–South to play at five diamonds, the contract would have gone down at least one trick with the normal opening of the king of hearts. Declarer would have been unable to avoid the loss of a spade trick, a club trick, and either a heart or a diamond, if not both of the latter.

But West probably had a "hunch" to sacrifice—and it proved to be a most costly hunch.

CHAPTER 11

Counteracting the Pre-emptive Bid

The pre-emptive bid, correctly applied, can be a most devastating weapon. We know that there is not a bridge player in the world who can claim that he has never, or seldom, been greatly embarrassed—let alone seriously obstructed—by an adverse pre-emptive bid. And that includes us and all of our expert and non-expert friends.

So, having presented our usage of the opening pre-emptive bids, we would now like to introduce our counterattack, namely how we handle the pre-emptive bids which the opponents fire at us. And, as you will learn, many more pre-emptive bids are made in duplicate bridge than in rubber bridge, thus making the knowledge of counterattacking tactics most essential.

Ever since the day pre-emptive bids flashed into use at the bridge table, accelerating the bidding as they do and creating an obstructing wall, all manner of defensive measures have been erected to negate them. Only two methods, however, have withstood the test of time, and they retain a stranglehold on popular fancy.

The first defense, or counteroffense, to be described is the more efficient of the two and is employed by us, as well as by most of the bridge-playing world. The second defense, while having its virtues, also has its deficiencies; and, in our opinion, is not as affluent a weapon as the first defense.

135

I. The Optional, or Cooperative, Double

A. THE DOUBLE OF OPENING THREE-BIDS

Most players employ the use of a double in order to invite their partners into the auction after an opening bid of three in a suit. The double, which in all but one respect is identical to the take-out double as used over an opening bid of one in a suit, is classified as an optional, or cooperative, double. In other words, the responder may take it out or leave it in, whichever seems to be the wiser course.

But because the response must be made at a high level, the double of an opening three-bid should indicate more high-card strength than a double of an opening one-bid. The hand should contain at least 15 points. If it is attempted with less in high cards, the distribution should be sufficiently better to compensate for the high-card deficiency. In addition, as in the take-out double of one in a suit, the doubler must be prepared to furnish a good dummy for any suit his partner may bid and must supply *three defensive tricks* if his partner should decide to let the double stand for penalties.

Minimum-type doubles after an opening bid of *three hearts,* for instance, would resemble the following:

(1)	(2)
♠ A Q 8 4	♠ A K 8 2
♡ 7 4	♡ 8
◇ K Q 9 3	◇ A 7 5 3
♣ A 9 6	♣ Q 9 6 4

Note that the doubler can stand any suit bid by his partner. He promises excellent support in the other major suit, since the "other major" generally offers the best hope of making a game. With slightly less than the requirements for a double, one may bid a good suit over the pre-emptive call. Otherwise he passes and awaits some possible action by partner.

B. RESPONDING TO THE DOUBLE

Though the partner of the doubler will sometimes convert the optional action into a penalty pass, *he will usually comply with the request to take out.* We would estimate, from our experiences, that the responder passes for penalties about 10–15 percent of the time. With completely worthless holdings, it is extremely important that responder takes out. *With 10 or more points, responder should try for a game.*

Consider the examples that follow, with the bidding having proceeded:

West	North	East	South
3 ◇	Double	Pass	?

You are *South* and hold:

1. ♠ Q 10 6 3
   ♡ 8 6 3
   ◇ 9 5 2
   ♣ 7 6 4

   This is a case of "yours not to reason why, yours but to do or die." But your hand could be worse, with your four-card suit being in diamonds. At least you have four cards in one of the suits your partner wants to hear you bid. Bid *three spades.*

2. ♠ 8 5
   ♡ 8 6 3
   ◇ Q 10 8 6
   ♣ A 9 6 5

   Without possessing the suits your partner wants to hear you bid, without sufficient strength to expect a reasonable play for the no-trump game, and with almost 100 percent assurance of winning at least two tricks defending against a diamond contract, you should *pass*, hoping that a sure one-trick set might develop into better things but content in the knowledge that it is probably your only means to secure a plus score. Remember, your partner has promised three defensive tricks for his double.

3. ♠ 7 2
   ♡ K 9 8 6 4
   ◇ 7 6
   ♣ K 8 7 5

   There is no particular problem here. With a five-card major suit, you waste no time in bidding *three hearts.*

4. ♠ K 10 8 5
   ♡ Q J 9 4
   ◇ 7
   ♣ K 8 7 5

   This is a situation which will come up with greater frequency than you might believe. You are perfectly willing to play this hand at a game contract opposite your partner's double; your only problem is to find your best suit. You acquaint your partner with your distribution by bidding *four diamonds.* Such a "cue bid" in this sequence says: "Partner, I have enough general strength to warrant our contracting for a game. Bid your best suit. I can support it." Though it is not mandatory that you hold four cards in each of the three unbid suits, you should have an equal number of cards in the majors, which are your partner's prime interest.

5.   ♠ A J 8 7 6 3   *Four spades.* With a six-card suit and a desire to
     ♡ Q 9 6   play for a game contract, do not make the thought-
     ◇ 9   less mistake of bidding simply three spades, which
     ♣ Q 8 5   you would do without any strength and four cards
                       in the suit. Take all further problems off your part-
ner's shoulders by contracting for the game.

6.   ♠ Q 8 7   With 12 points in high cards and stoppers in the
     ♡ 9 7   diamond suit, ignore the club suit and select the
     ◇ K J 9   shorter route to game by bidding *three no-trump*.
     ♣ A Q 6 5 3   Your chances of fulfillment should be excellent.

C. DOUBLES OF FOUR IN A MINOR

Doubles of four clubs and four diamonds are still intended, primarily, to solicit a takeout by partner. While no fixed formula can
be offered, the bidding level being higher, it would be deemed
logical that the strength should be greater for the double of four
than of three. However, the handling by responder is flexible and
you must be better prepared for the double being left in. For that
reason, your high cards should be *in the vicinity of 16 points.*

D. HANDLING THE DOUBLE OF FOUR IN A MINOR

Unlike takeout doubles of suit bids at the one and three levels,
the responder to a take-out double of four clubs or four diamonds
does not feel the pressure of being forced to make a bid with a
worthless hand. After all, with the doubler holding about 16 points,
there is better than an outside chance that he can take the four
tricks necessary to defeat the contract any time the responder's hand
is evenly distributed. Thus, after partner doubles *four diamonds*,
and you hold this hand:

♠ 7 4 2
♡ 9 4 3
◇ 8 6 4
♣ Q 8 7 3

you might just as well *pass* and hope for a plus score.

However, when the responder to the double of four clubs or four
diamonds possesses a worthless hand and *unbalanced* distribution,
it is possibly better strategy to lean toward a takeout. The doubled
contract might be fulfilled if a large portion of your partner's

strength is concentrated in your longest suit, which, of course, would greatly enhance your own possibilities after bidding.

An example of an unbalanced hand with which you should respond to your partner's double of *four diamonds* with *four spades* is the following:

♠ J 10 8 7 4   ♡ 8 3 2   ◇ 8   ♣ 10 5 4 2

With a defensive trick and even distribution, the take-out double should be converted into a penalty double by the responder. With each of the following hands, you should respond to your partner's double of *four diamonds by passing:*

(1)	(2)
♠ A 9 7 5	♠ 9 7 6 2
♡ 8 7 4	♡ 8 3
◇ 8 6 3	◇ Q 10 8 5
♣ 7 4 2	♣ 7 4 2

E. DOUBLES OF FOUR HEARTS

The double of a four heart opening bid announces the ability to defeat that contract but solicits a takeout to four spades if the responder visualizes a better future with that action.

Therefore, in almost all instances where the responder is holding (1) an evenly distributed hand, (2) a worthless hand, or (3) hands containing minor suits, the double of four hearts should be allowed to stand for the penalties that will accrue. And, when holding a spade suit, the responder, whether a novice or an expert, must exercise sound judgment—or, at times, make a good guess as to whether to pass or to bid four spades.

The bidding has proceeded:

West	North	East	South
4 ♡	Double	Pass	?

You are South, holding the following:

1. ♠ 9 7 4 3   You have no reason to want to be in the auction. If
   ♡ 8 7 4   your partner says he can defeat four hearts, trust his
   ◇ 4 3 2   judgment. With no basis for speaking, *pass.*
   ♣ 8 7 3

2. ♠ A 8 6 2   Your ace of spades will assure the defeat of the con-
    ♡ 8 5   tract by one trick more than your partner was antic-
    ◇ 8 7 5 3   ipating. There is no excuse for you to venture into
    ♣ 9 7 6   an unknown world by bidding when you can be
                 assured of a certain profit by not disturbing the
status quo of the moment. If you are vulnerable and they are not, you
might elect to bid four spades for a vulnerable game—but we won't recommend it. We recommend a *pass*.

3. ♠ A 10 8 7 4   This is just like a blank check from home; you can
    ♡ 7   write your own ticket. The only consideration
    ◇ K 8 4   should be: what action will net you the greatest
    ♣ Q 9 7 2   return? In any situation where the vulnerability
                  conditions are equal, you should bid *four spades*.
You should adopt the same course if your side is vulnerable and the
opponents are not. However, if the opposition is vulnerable and you are
not, the *penalty pass* should net you more points.

4. ♠ J 10 8 7 5 4   Your length in spades materially diminishes the
    ♡ 8   defensive value of the high cards your partner holds
    ◇ 9 6 3   in that suit. For safety's sake, you should bid *four*
    ♣ 8 5 2   *spades* for which you may have a play.

5. ♠ K J 9 6   This is about the same as Example 3. You should be
    ♡ 7   able to make four spades, and you should defeat
    ◇ K 10 8 4   four hearts by at least two tricks. Leave the double
    ♣ Q J 4 2   in if the opponents are vulnerable and your side is
                 not. If the conditions are reversed, bid four spades.
If the vulnerability is equal, take the sure route by bidding four spades.
Remember that when partner doubles a four heart opening bid he can
stand your takeout to four spades.

F. Doubles of Four Spades

When the opponents open the bidding with four spades, a double
is strictly for business. The doubler says he will defeat the contract,
and he is not interested in hearing his partner bid at the five-level.
Thus, the responder should, in practically all cases, pass in such
a situation.

If, for example, the responder visualizes a slam and he knows
that the bonus points will net more revenue than the penalty points,
he may take out in his suit. And, in such cases, he usually goes all
the way to slam himself. For instance:

West	North	East	South
4 ♠	Double	Pass	?

As South, you hold:

> ♠ 4
> ♡ A Q 10 9 7 6 4
> ◇ 8 5
> ♣ K 9 6

Six hearts would appear to be a good gamble, and, in fact, should be bid. Your hand will help your partner in defending against spades only to the extent of the king of clubs and, possibly, the ace of hearts. However, many possible holdings can be laid out for North with which six hearts would be a laydown.

G. THE FOUR NO-TRUMP OVERCALL
OF A FOUR SPADE OPENING BID

By this time you should be acquainted with the sound logic behind the recommended handling of opening suit bids of four. Over clubs or diamonds, double with a good hand, hoping for a major suit game without forcing the bidding beyond the game level. Failing to find partner with a major suit, you expect to defeat the opponents. Over hearts, you hope for a game in the other major when you double, or you want the penalties. Over four spades, however, there is no place for you to go except to the five-level. Thus a double, quite logically, becomes strictly a business double.

If you were not desirous of collecting the penalties after an opening bid of four spades, there was another logical course of action which could have been selected to get your partner to bid. You could have bid *four no-trump*, a bid which, over four spades, serves the same principle as a take-out double. It expresses a wish to play the hand at the five-level (or higher) and is *a demand that partner name his longest suit*. Obviously, the four no-trump bidder must have an exceptionally powerful hand, on the order of each of the following:

(1)	(2)
♠ —	♠ 5
♡ K Q 8 7 3	♡ A K J 4
◇ A Q 10 2	◇ K Q J 4
♣ K J 10 6	♣ A Q 10 5

With your side *vulnerable* and the four spade bidder *not vulnerable*, it might be deemed more desirable for your side to play the hand. Thus, the four no-trump bid has become a powerful offensive weapon to force your partner into the bidding. Without such an instrument in your bag of tricks, you would automatically be compelled to accept the penalties which would be your reward for the double, or you would have to make a gambling overcall, in which case you will be in the right spot just about one time out of three.

H. OTHER NO-TRUMP OVERCALLS OF PRE-EMPTIVE BIDS

Overcall opening three bids with *three no-trump when you want to play the hand at that contract.* There is no set formula we can lay down as a guide. While the three no-trump overcall must have the adversely bid suit well controlled and must consist of a very fine hand, the bid merely says: "I think I can capture nine tricks at this contract." If the overcaller wanted to hear his partner bid some suit, he would have doubled. Thus, any takeout of the three no-trump venture should be resorted to only with very unusual distribution.

For example, over an opening bid of three hearts, you could bid *three no-trump* with:

(1)	(2)	(3)
♠ K 7	♠ 7 3	♠ A 2
♡ Q J 8	♡ A Q 5	♡ K J 10
◇ A K Q 8 4 3	◇ K Q J 8 2	◇ A Q J 3
♣ A 2	♣ A Q 7	♣ K Q 10 2

Your partner will know that you would have doubled if you had wanted to hear about spades. Thus, if responder to the three no-trump overcaller bids four spades, he will do it on his own.

I. WAIT FOR PARTNER'S DOUBLE

Quite frequently, the player in the embryonic stage of his bridge development asks: "But how do you double a pre-emptive bid for penalties?" And to that the answer is: "You do not." Rather, if you are especially strong in high cards in the pre-emptive opener's suit and you are the next bidder without the requirements to overcall with three no-trump, you simply pass, awaiting some action by partner. Should he be in a position to double (for takeout), you will leave the double in, for penalties. If he bids a higher-ranking suit over the pre-emptive three opening, you can try the no-trump game. And if he passes, you will obtain a plus score, although it will not be the theoretical maximum plus score you could have obtained by doubling for penalties. But, since you can't double for takeout in one tone of voice and double for penalties in another tone, you pass and employ the double in those much more frequent situations when you want your partner to take out.

With the following hands, when your right-hand opponent has opened the auction with three hearts, you should *pass*. If your partner doubles, you will pass, converting the take-out request into a penalty action:

(1)	(2)	(3)
♠ 7 6	♠ 7 5 2	♠ K 8
♡ K 10 8 4	♡ A 10 8 4 2	♡ Q J 10 4 2
◇ A J 4	◇ K 8 4	◇ 6 5 3
♣ K J 10 8	♣ 8 2	♣ K 7 4

J. OVERCALLING THE PRE-EMPTIVE BID

Overcalls of pre-emptive opening bids, as represented by the following sequences:

North	East		North	East
3 ♠	4 ♡	*or*	3 ◇	3 ♠
North	East		North	East
3 ♣	3 ♡	*or*	3 ♡	4 ◇

are executed with hands possessing a six-card, or longer, suit and a trifle in excess of the strength required for an opening one bid. With a high-card count exceeding 14–15 points, a take-out double should be the preferred call. However, a pre-emptive opening bid so accelerates the bidding that any subsequent action may be speculative.

When the overcall of a pre-emptive bid is made below the game level (e.g., 3 D . . . 3 S), it should signify less than enough to double but must denote a good place to play the hand. When the overcall must be made at the game level (e.g., 3 S . . . 4 H), the hand may be any size in excess of an opening one bid, with a really good suit.

For instance, if the bidding has been opened with *three diamonds,* consider your course of action with the following hands:

1. ♠ A Q 10 8 4 2
   ♡ K 8 7
   ◇ 3
   ♣ Q 8 2

You should overcall with *three spades.* If you pass, your partner may also pass with a fairly respectable hand—which he might well possess. If you correctly bid three spades, your partner will assume that you have just about what you

do have and will take you to four spades with something short of an opening bid, and three small spades (or K J and K x). If you should choose to double with this hand (instead of overcalling), your partner might respond with four hearts, which quite likely could be an inferior contract. However, if he makes the four heart response to your three spade overcall, you can rest assured that it is the ideal final contract.

2. ♠ K 6 4
   ♡ K J 10 8 6 5 3
   ◇ A 3
   ♣ 2

With this hand you would probably decide to overcall with *three hearts,* not wanting to be in game unless your partner has about 10 points or so. At any rate, partner will know that you have a long suit and not sufficient strength to double,

which requires about 15 points.

3. ♠ A K J
   ♡ K Q J 8 6 4 3
   ◇ 3
   ♣ K 5

You should make an immediate overcall of *four hearts,* telling partner not only that you have a good hand but that you are not worried about his having support for the trump suit.

II. The Fishbein Convention

Another counteroffensive after a pre-emptive opening bid is the convention devised by Harry Fishbein. Harry was, for many years, accepted as one of the world's greatest players. His method for combating pre-emptives languished almost to the point of extinction some years ago. But it has gained popularity lately, to such an extent that its adherents comprise approximately 10 percent of the nation's tournament and duplicate players.*

In the Fishbein Convention, *any double immediately over the pre-emptive opening bid is a business double.* The bid of the *next-ranking suit*—three diamonds over an opening three club bid; three

---

*The remaining 90 percent employ the cooperative, or optional, double, which was presented in the first section of this chapter.

hearts over three diamonds; three spades over three hearts; and four clubs over three spades—is employed as the *take-out bid*, the requirements being identical to the requirements for the take-out, or cooperative, double, as described earlier.

After responder to the "artificial" overcaller has bid, the overcaller may now name his own suit or pass.

For example, the bidding is opened with *three diamonds*, and you are the next bidder with the following hands:

1. ♠ A Q 10 9 7 5
   ♡ Q 10 9
   ◇ 9 6
   ♣ A K

   When using the Fishbein Convention, you bid *three hearts,* asking partner to name his longest suit. The odds are that he will bid four clubs or four hearts, after which you will name your suit, *spades.*

2. ♠ A 10 4 2
   ♡ A Q J 8 4 3
   ◇ 3
   ♣ K 8

   You will make the take-out overcall of the next higher-ranking suit, hearts. When your partner responds with three spades or four clubs, you rebid the hearts to show that it is your suit.

Your right-hand opponent has opened the bidding with *three spades*. With the following hand:

♠ 7
♡ A Q 8 4
◇ K 10 8 2
♣ A Q 9 3

you will overcall with four clubs, and if your partner bids four hearts, you will pass. If, over four clubs, your partner bids four diamonds, you would probably try for five diamonds.

As in the cooperative double, the *three no-trump overcall* of an opening bid of three in a suit denotes a desire to play the contract at three no-trump.

While the Fishbein Convention has certain advantages (the major one being its highly effective use against bridge players whose pre-empts are very, very weak, thus permitting the employment of an immediate double as a penalty double), we believe that the advantages are of such specialized instances that continued use will uncover more drawbacks than virtues. Where the use of the optional double will permit you to cope with any contingency, the Fishbein Convention will sometimes automatically force you to play the contract one trick too high, and will often prevent play at three no-trump when that might be the better spot. For example, if the opener bids three spades, and the next hand wants partner to take out, he must bid four clubs as the next higher-ranking suit. Thus it becomes impossible to get to three no-trump, which might well be the proper place to play the hand. With the employment of the cooperative double over the pre-emptive opening bid of three spades, a take-out double by the next hand will enable the latter's partner to bid three no-trump (if, of course, he has protection in the opener's bid suit).

Although, as we stated, we do not employ the Fishbein Convention, we are familiar with its workings since it is used against us at times. We recommend that you, too, should know the aim and the specifics of the Fishbein Convention, since it will be used against you in duplicate games and tournaments.

12

The Weak Two-Bid *

I. Its Introduction and Ultimate Acceptance

Despite the efforts of Howard Schenken to popularize the weak two-bid after he introduced it in 1940–1941, bridge players refused to accept it at that time and stuck by the "old faithful," strength-showing, game-forcing opening bid of two in a suit. It was not until the Roth-Stone system was created in 1953 that the weak two-bid found itself out of the mire and finally on the way to public acceptance.

While it is true that Roth and Stone resurrected the weak two-bid, and were a most dynamic force in bringing it into an active, fruitful life, they are entitled to but a share of the glory. As early as 1951—two years before the Roth-Stone system appeared in print —Sam Stayman had accepted the weak two-bid as an integral part of his system and had defined and explained the bid in an earlier work of his, *Expert Bidding at Contract Bridge*.

Schenken, Stayman, Roth and Stone, and other practical theoreticians were aware of the utility of the weak two-bid long before they ever dreamed of propagandizing for its employment via the written word. As of now, the weak two-bid is a component part of

---

* Either two diamonds, two hearts, or two spades. The two club opening bid is reserved for those rock-crusher types of hands with which we formerly employed the strong two-bid as a forcing-to-game bid.

not only the Schenken, Stayman, and Roth-Stone systems but also of the Kaplan-Sheinwold system. In addition, the weak two bid is employed by well over 50 percent of the 190,000 members of the American Contract Bridge League. *And we are included in this majority who use the weak two.*

II. Why the "Weak" Two-Bid?

The reason for the emergence of the "weak" two-bid is a simple and logical one: the strong, forcing-to-game type of opening two-bid arises once in a blue moon. If one accepts the obvious infrequency of hands that rate a strong two-bid opening, why waste a perfectly good type of bid on something that comes up about once a month even with those who play daily? Why not employ a better and *much more frequent use for the call?* And so, just as "the old order changeth, yielding place to the new," so the "weak" two-bid has pre-empted the strong two-bid.

III. What Is the "Weak" Two-Bid?

The reader will note that quotation marks have been put around the word "weak." That is because the weak two-bid is not as weak as a good many bridge players think it is. Speaking generally for the moment, the weak two-bid is made on a hand that is, at best, a trifle below the requirements for an opening bid of one in a suit, *plus* the requirement that the bidder have *a good six-card suit.** It denotes the type of hand that virtually everybody would have liked to open with one of a suit and probably would have done so if they were not afraid of incurring the displeasure of partner if the bid led to a disastrous result. ("You didn't have an opening bid, partner!")

Here are some illustrations:

(1)	(2)	(3)
♠ A J 10 9 x x	♠ x	♠ x x
♡ x x	♡ K Q 10 8 x x	♡ x x
◇ K 10 9 x	◇ A x x	◇ K J 10 x x x
♣ x	♣ x x x	♣ A J x
Bid 2 ♠	Bid 2 ♡	Bid 2 ◇

*The A.C.B.L. used to require that all weak two-bids must be within a 6-12 point range (high cards only). However, in recent years this regulation was relaxed considerably; currently, almost any range can be used for weak two-bids. They may also be made on any kind of five card suit (although this is definitely not recommended for non-experts).

Still speaking generally about the weak two-bid, here are some of the reasons why it is being adopted by more and more duplicate and tournament players. All of the following points will be discussed in specific detail within this chapter:

1. It gives an accurate and precise description of the opener's hand.
2. It enables its users to safely open some hands which they formerly wanted to open but had to pass because partner might get them up too high if they opened.
3. It acts as a pre-emptive bid against the opponents, thereby serving as an instrument which tends to sever or destroy the opponents' lines of communication.
4. It not only jams up or shuts out the opponents on some hands, but it also tends to get them too high on many occasions.
5. It allows the partner of the weak two-bidder great latitude and many privileges. Since the opener's rebids are forced and with rare exceptions he cannot ever bid a game, the partner can make it extremely difficult for the opponents by:

    (a) Bidding "anything" without the fear of being raised to game.
    (b) Bidding the opponents' strong suit without the fear of being passed by partner.
    (c) Taking premature sacrifices (2 D . . . 5 D) leaving each of the opponents to guess whether the bid is made with the expectation of fulfilling the contract or as a sacrifice.

Although the weak two-bid is somewhat pre-emptive in nature, it will be shown to possess *more high-card strength* and less suit length than opening bids of three and four. Where the three and four bid promises no strength outside the mentioned suit, the weak two-bid may, and usually does, include some little outside strength.

Summarizing the preceding paragraphs, the weak two-bid is a multi-pronged weapon, owing its success and acceptance to the many factors enumerated above. Its minor pre-emptive action robs the opponents of one or two rounds of constructive bidding on hands that "belong" to them. At the same time, the threat of precisely known strength in the opening bidder's hand and the uncertainty surrounding his partner's holding cause the opponents to tread with uncertainty—sometimes too cautiously, and sometimes too adventurously.

Before coming to the presentation of our requirements for the weak opening two-bid and for partner's actions with varying types of responding hands, we would like to introduce a classic deal which arose in a rubber-bridge game some years ago in New York City's Cavendish Club.

Both sides were vulnerable, and each had a part-score of 60.

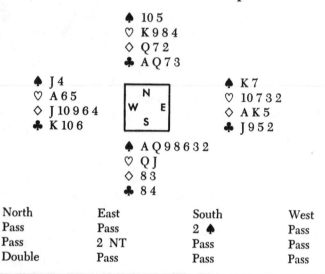

North	East	South	West
Pass	Pass	2 ♠	Pass
Pass	2 NT	Pass	Pass
Double	Pass	Pass	Pass

South chose to open the queen of hearts, which won the trick, and the continuation of the heart jack was captured by dummy's ace. Declarer elected to lead a diamond to his ace, and then a low club toward dummy. He finessed the ten-spot, North's queen winning. North–South now took the rest of the tricks. All in all they made seven spade tricks, two clubs, and two hearts, defeating declarer 1700 points. Had declarer been clairvoyant, he could have held the set to "only" 1100 points by finessing for the queen of diamonds and then cashing his four tricks.

The reader will note that the set was accomplished despite the fact that North had passed originally and that South's hand wasn't particularly robust. Had South opened with anything but two spades (either one spade or three spades), East would never have entered the auction. Probably he shouldn't have entered anyway, but we're sure he felt his side was being "robbed" by the weak two-bidder.

IV. Weak Two-Bid Openings

NOTE WELL: Our range for an opening weak two-bid is 6–12 high-card points. In addition, the suit bid will almost always be of six-card length.

We use the weak two-bid because we think it gives us advantages of the types enumerated a few pages back. It works best, as would any other gadget, against weak opponents, but it is not the devastating killer that many of its advocates claim it is. It will beat any opponent if the situation favors its use, but it may also result in otherwise avoidable losses.

Possibly the principal advantage of the weak two-bid is that it "does things" to the opponents: it takes away that first, relatively safe round of bidding. They may or may not have the superior cards, but they have to start trying to find out about it at the two or three level. The two bidder's side can better spare the loss of that round of bidding, since the opening bidder will have quite accurately portrayed his hand and his partner will safely be able to judge the potential and limitations of the combined assets.

Despite the above, the pre-emptive advantage of the weak two-bid is not as great as most of its proponents would have us believe. Of course, even casual observation will make it apparent that the opening bid of two spades has a decided advantage, the opening bid of two hearts a bit of advantage, and the opening bid of two diamonds some advantage. The first two may cause the opposition acute embarrassment when they have to compete at the three-level. Against the two diamond opening, one's opponents may more easily compete with hearts or spades. It may come as a surprise, particularly to those who are overfond of gadgeting, that the artificial two club opening ° used to describe the game-forcing "strong" two-bid type of hand is a distinct disadvantage. It may use up a valuable round of bidding in the early stages, getting you one notch higher than strong two-bidders would be. Furthermore, since the strong hand is unable to name his real suit immediately, alert nonvulnerable opponents may offer pre-emptive competition which can cause the opener painful, even unsolvable, problems.

° Discussed at the end of this chapter.

We advocate, as do most of the users of the weak two-bid, a disciplined usage of the bid in first and second position and undisciplined in third position. Possibly the most advantageous use of the bid in match-point play is in fourth position.

Disciplined though we may be, we could never permit restrictions that would deny us the opportunity to exploit a favorable situation. Neither could we sanction a degree of looseness which forces partner to make one impossibly difficult guess after another. A few examples should serve to outline the actual limitations we advocate.

In duplicate and tournament competition sanctioned by the American Contract Bridge League, weak two-bidders must state specifically what their range is for a weak two-bid opening. As mentioned previously, we have used 6-12 HCP as our range in this section. However, many other ranges are used by club and tournament players. Other popular ranges are currently 5-10, 5-11 and 6-11.

In order to keep each segment of the "weak" two-bid in its proper niche, let us head this first section:

A. First and Second Position Weak Two-Bid Openings

You only, or both sides, are *vulnerable*.

	1. (a)	(b)	(c)
♠	K Q 10 9 7 5	A Q J 9 8 6	A K J 9 8 5
♡	7	4	10 4 3
◊	A J 9 2	7 6 5	J 5
♣	6 5	Q 10 3	8 6

	(d)	(e)
♠	Q J 10 9 7 3	J 9 8 7 6 2
♡	7 5	A 7 5
◊	A Q 7	K 6 3
♣	8 4	7

It must be borne in mind that our opening bids of one in a suit are, as a minimum, 13-point hands. Weak two-bids, therefore, are some holding less than an opening one-bid. In this table position, vulnerable, the main suit will be a good six-carder. We never open a weak two-bid on a seven-card suit but a super five-carder with virtually nothing in side strength qualifies, such as A K Q J 9. The two-suiter (6-5 or 5-5) is in this position unsuitable. Partner would, if the latter were permitted, be unduly burdened in judging the offensive and defense strength of the combined holdings. In the above examples all but Example (e) qualify as an opening two bid.

Stress is placed on the possession of a good six-card suit which is playable with little or no support from partner. This circumstance minimizes the chance of partner's suit being more playable. If, in your partnership, partner's suit is always more playable, then you are most unfortunate or you are using weak two-bids incorrectly. The latter point is emphasized in Example (e), the suit, and perhaps the hand, being too weak. If two spades is incorrectly opened, you might easily find that the partnership possesses a better combined suit than spades. Furthermore, if you get to defend, you have solicited—by your two spade opening—a lead which could prove disastrous. We would not open Example (e) with two spades even if the opponents were vulnerable and we were not.

You are *not vulnerable.* They are either vulnerable or not.

2. (a)	(b)	(c)
♠ Q 10 9 8 7 2	♠ A K Q 9 2	♠ K 10 9 7 6 3
♡ 6 4	♡ 2	♡ 6 3
◇ A J 3	◇ 9 6 4 3	◇ 7 6
♣ 7 5	♣ J 7 5	♣ K J 5

Under these existing vulnerability conditions, we would open each of the above with two spades. You will recall that the ability to make the two spade call confers the greatest advantage. We would not bypass this opportunity to exploit it. We would take the same action with a heart or diamond suit, if not vulnerable, but would pass Example (c) if we were vulnerable. We would, of course, also open with two hearts or two diamonds (instead of spades) on each of the hands given in the previous set of examples, except, as was mentioned, Example 1(e).

B. Weak Two-Bids in Third Position

The principal factor which affects third position pre-emptive bids will have just about the identical effect on weak two-bids in third position. We are referring to the circumstance that *your partner has previously passed.* As a consequence, the chance for a game can, for the most part, be disregarded. *Disrupting the opposition becomes the primary objective.* A secondary objective, especially at match-point play, is to get a plus score of any size.

Although the 6-12 HCP range is still in effect, the actual use of the bid is extended in each direction. The limits are exploited to their fullest extent and can even be extended farther. You might, for example, open with a weak two-bid holding a full opening bid or on a hand valued at less than six points. Let us observe what can be done by looking at the examples which follow:

You are vulnerable. They are not. You are in third position.

1. (a)	(b)	(c)
♠ A Q J 9 6 2	♠ 7 5	♠ 7 5
♡ 7 2	♡ A K Q 8 6 3	♡ A 10 8 7 6 5 3
◇ K 9 2	◇ Q 7	◇ K 8
♣ Q 3	♣ 9 6 2	♣ 6 3

	(d)	
	♠ 7 5	
	♡ A K J 9 8	
	◇ K 7 5	
	♣ J 6 2	

A natural consequence of this unfavorable vulnerability condition is to restrict you on the low side. Unless you are more daring in your bidding habits than we are accustomed to be, a note of caution seems wise in these circumstances. Strangely enough, however, the high side in our view attains greater latitude. We would, of course, open any hand as we would in first or second position, vulnerable. But, bearing in mind that partner has passed, which reduces the chances of missing a game, we open hands with weak two-bids in third position that we would consider to be too good for the weak two-bid in first or second position. On (a), (b), and

(d), above, we open with *one* of the principal suit in *first or second* position but with a weak two-bid in third position. Note particularly the use of the five-card suit, as in Example (d).

In Example (c), if we were not vulnerable and the opponents were, we would like to get a bid in with these cards. In this unfavorable vulnerability situation, however, we can't afford the luxury. If we were both nonvulnerable, we would open with a *three heart* bid. Though we dislike opening with a two bid on a seven-card suit, we would tend to do so (as a sort of compromise) if we were both vulnerable.

You are *not vulnerable.* You are in third position.

Any hand which qualifies nonvulnerable in first or second position will automatically qualify in third position. In addition, we recommend the following positional deviations:

(1)	(2)	(3)	(4)
♠ A Q 10 9 8	♠ 8 3	♠ A Q J 10 8	♠ 8 3
♡ 7 5	♡ 9 6	♡ 7	♡ K Q J 9 8
◇ 8 6 4 2	◇ K Q 10 9 8	◇ 9 7 6 5 3	◇ Q 9 6 2
♣ 7 3	♣ J 7 5 4	♣ 6 2	♣ 7 5
Bid 2 ♠	Bid 2 ◇	Bid 2 ♠	Bid 2 ♡

It can be seen that we may open a very weak two-bid in third position when we are not vulnerable. It should be noted also that each example contains a good suit suggesting a good lead, which of course gets your side off on the right foot defensively. Partner should exercise great caution and discretion when you open with a nonvulnerable weak two-bid in third position. He should, in virtually all situations, at least investigate before undertaking any high level contract if he happens to have a good passed hand. We might add, in passing, that we would open each of the above hands, in third position, with one of a suit if we did not employ the weak two-bid.

C. Weak Two-Bids in Fourth Position

When do we make this bid? Obviously when we think we have an advantage in opening, but wish both to stifle the opponents and at the same time to warn partner to exercise some degree of restraint.

Observe the following:

(1)	(2)	(3)
♠ A K J 10 7 5	♠ A K J 10 8	♠ J 3
♡ 6 3	♡ 6 5	♡ A K 10 7 6 4
◊ Q 9 3	◊ Q 10 7 5	◊ K 2
♣ 7 2	♣ J 3	♣ 7 6 4

(4)	(5)
♠ A J 10 8 7 5	♠ K Q 10 8 7 4
♡ 5 3	♡ 4 2
◊ A 8 3	◊ A J 9
♣ 8 6	♣ 5 4

Tossing in any of the above hands at match-point play seems inconceivable to us. We feel that we possess, at the very least, a slightly better holding than either opponent. We are not, however, anxious to defend. Nor do we desire to be pushed too high either by the opponents or by our partner. If this statement of facts is concurred in, then an opening two-bid in each of the long suits above recommends itself.

V. Responding to Weak Opening Two-Bids
(FIRST AND SECOND POSITION)

The weak opening two-bid is, of course, a pre-emptive call, which circumstance places a greater burden on partner. The success or failure of the pre-emptive maneuver will depend to a great extent on him. It is not difficult to inject the weak two-bid but deciding what and whether to respond is a much more delicate matter.

Two basic methods for responding have been evolved by the various proponents of the weak two-bid. Each method will serve best when conditions favor it. Each will be discussed in turn.

The combined operations of the partnership and the obligation on each of the partners cannot be understood unless it is clearly established which responses are forcing and which are not forcing.

When responder *has not passed:*

All minimum calls in a *new suit* and also a bid of *two no-trump* are forcing for one round. Thus, the sequences that follow are forcing for one round; the opening two-bidder *must* bid again.

Opener	Responder	Opener	Responder
2 ♠	3 ♣, 3 ◇, 3 ♡	2 ♡	2 NT

The following sequences by responder are *not forcing,* and the opening two-bidder *must pass* each of them.

Opener	Responder	Opener	Responder
2 ◇	3 ◇	2 ♡	4 ♠
2 ◇	4 ♡	2 ♡	4 ♡
2 ♠	3 NT	2 ◇	5 ♣
2 ◇	5 ◇	2 ♡	3 ♡
2 ♡	3 ♠		

In the above examples, it will be noted that responder has jumped to game either in the same suit or in a new suit or in no-trump, or jumped in a new suit (but not to game), or merely confined his action to a single raise in partner's suit. *We play this single raise to be strictly pre-emptive, which bars partner from further participation in the auction.*

If you adopt this method (which we employ), it is important for you to examine closely the following illustrations.

1. | Opener | Responder |
   |--------|-----------|
   | 2 ♠ | 3 ♠ |

The single raise is pre-emptive. The opener *must pass.*

2. 2 ♡   3 ♠   This is a pre-emptive response which opener *must pass.* Responder's hand might be:
♠ Q J 10 9 6 4 3   ♡ 6 4   ◇ 8 2   ♣ 7 5. Had responder possessed a good hand, he could have bid two spades, which would be forcing.

3. | North | East | South | West |
   |-------|------|-------|------|
   | 2 ♡ | Pass | 2 ♠ | Pass |
   | 3 ♡ | Pass | 3 ♠ | Pass |
   | ? | | | |

South's three spade bid is invitational, and opener will carry on to game with a maximum two-bid. Had responder held a poor hand, with a long spade suit, he would have bid three spades directly over the opening two heart bid. For his above bidding, South might hold:
♠ A K 10 8 4 3 2   ♡ 7 2   ◇ Q 5   ♣ 9 2

4.   North   East   South   West
    2 ♠   3 ♡   3 ♠   4 ♡   *Opener must pass.* If a sacrifice bid
                                                  is in order, South should be the one
to take it. Furthermore, South should usually refrain from entering the
auction with a weak hand once East has come into the bidding. We do not
wish to push them to a game contract they might not reach under their
own power. When we do push them, as in this case, it usually signifies
that we are satisfied to let them play the game they have bid. Naturally
we have good reason to think we can beat them, doubled or undoubled.
If this is not the case, then we ought to be prepared to take that sacrifice—
and only South can estimate accurately the joint partnership assets.

5.   Action by Opener when Responder forces.

    Opener   Responder
    2 ♡   2 ♠   Since the opener has a holding which is
                                  known to be under an opening bid of one
in a suit, it follows that the responder is best able to decide how far the
partnership should venture. He may know there is a game. He may be
probing for a possible game. He may be reasonably certain that the
opposition can make a lot because he himself has a poor hand. He must,
therefore, virtually be given complete command. For these reasons, the
opener can make no rebid higher than *a single raise in his own suit.*

On this matter of making "no rebid higher than a single raise
in his own suit," let us look at these illustrations:

(a)   Opener   Responder
       2 ♡   2 ♠   Opener's three heart rebid signifies that the
       3 ♡   opener has a *minimum* weak two-bid (6–9
                                  is the minimum point range; 10–12 is the
                                  maximum).

(b)   Opener   Responder
       2 ♡   2 ♠   The 2 NT rebid signifies that the opener has
      2 NT   a maximum opening which also contains
                                  spade support, such as K x, Q x, A x, J x, or
10 x x, or better. If opener has a *minimum* opening with spade support,
he returns to his original suit at the three-level (three hearts in this illustration).

(c)   Opener   Responder   Opener   Responder
       2 ♡   2 ♠   2 ♠   3 ♣
       3 ♣ or   3 ◇ or
       3 ◇   3 ♡

In the above cases, opener names a new suit to denote a *maximum* weak two-bid and at the same time indicates the suit in which the outside value or values are held. It should be noted that opener has made no call beyond the three-level in his own suit.

(d)   Opener   Responder
        2 ♠   2 NT
        3 NT

This is the only case in which opener may make a rebid beyond the three-level in his own suit. He states that he possesses a suit which could run with reasonable breaks and no misfit in partner's hand. His suit might be: S – A K Q 7 4 2; A K J 9 7 4; or A Q J 9 8 3. Note that if responder possesses two small cards in the suit, the suit has a reasonable chance to run. If he has the missing top honor and a small card, he can be certain that the suit will run.

Opener holds S – K J 9 8 6 3   H – Q 10   D – Q 9 7   C – K 3. If opener holds a maximum two-bid (such as this is), with honors scattered throughout the three other suits, he may also rebid *three no-trump* after partner responds two no-trump. Responder should not be disappointed with opener's holding.

A. Strategic Responses

The responder has the scope and the liberty to "operate" (to indulge in shenanigans) when he knows that his partner may not rebid beyond the three-level in his own suit. If he is alert (and astute) enough to take advantage of the many opportunties that will come his way, he can create excellent results. These opportunities are also available to the rubber-bridge player, but the match-point player will more often be in a favorable position. He may, for example, be willing to suffer a multiple-trick set (like 500 points) with equanimity, even joy, when the opponents could have made a vulnerable game, while such an occurrence would be only a minor victory at rubber bridge. Let us examine some cases. You are *not vulnerable*, the opponents are *vulnerable*.

    1. Responder holds:
        ♠ 9 6 2   ♡ 4 2   ◇ J 10 7 5   ♣ Q 10 6 3

The bidding proceeds:

North	East	South
2 ◇	Pass	?

It is obvious that something drastic is in order. The opponents must have a vulnerable major suit game, if not a slam. A single raise in diamonds does not figure to hamper them sufficiently. We suggest a bid of *two hearts,* which could denote a hand of any size, good or bad. It probably will not stop the opposition completely but may jockey them out of their best spot.

2.	North	East	South
	2 ♡	Pass	?

South holds: ♠ 7 5   ♡ Q 8 5 3   ◇ K 9 6 4   ♣ K 7 2

The caliber of the opposition could determine our action with the above holding. If our opponents are known to be timid or inexperienced, we might choose to talk them out of a spot they own. We would bid *two* spades. If partner bids three hearts, we would pass. If he bids anything else, we would rebid *three hearts,* which *forces* him to pass.

More experienced opponents would double our "psychic" response of two spades for penalties, showing thereby possession of the spade suit. This is a likely occurrence with the cards they hold and would help them to find their spade spot quite easily. (This latter method—doubling—of *defending* against weak two-bid responses is most effective and is the method we employ.) Against good opposition, we would directly raise partner's two heart opening bid to *three hearts,* thus pre-empting the opponents out of a round of bidding space.

3.	North	East	South
	2 ♡	2 ♠	?

South holds: ♠ Q J 9 2   ♡ J 3   ◇ A 9 7 2   ♣ K 7 5

We would bid *three hearts,* for which contract we have reasonable support. We are hoping to push the opponents higher in spades. We could not do this if partner were permitted to compete (North, of course, is barred). We have no desire to play four hearts.

4.	North	East	South
	2 ♠	Pass	?

South holds: ♠ K 8 3 2   ♡ 7   ◇ A 9 7 6 4 2   ♣ 8 4

We would bid *four spades* promptly, for two good reasons: (1) The opponents figure to have a game at hearts and (2) we might well make four spades, especially if partner happens to have a singleton diamond. Even if we can't make it, the opponents might not double us, especially if the outstanding strength is evenly divided in the opponents' hands, for we could have a really good hand for our leap to four spades.

B. THE METHOD OF RESPONDING USING A TWO NO-TRUMP RESPONSE AS THE ONLY FORCING BID

In this method, the responder to a weak two-bid is unable to force by responding in a new suit. In fact, partner must pass any suit response. It follows, therefore, that with any distribution, or for whatever reason, the responder, in order to force opener, must bid 2 NT. That is:

Opener	Responder
2 ◇, 2 ♡, 2 ♠	2 NT

The opener must now bid again. As practiced by most pairs, the rebids have virtually the same meaning as in the method just presented. The *rebid* of the *original suit* shows *a minimum*. A *new suit* shows a *maximum* and denotes where the outside strength is held. A *three no-trump* rebid shows a suit which could easily be run barring bad breaks.

The chief advantage of this method—and we are not minimizing its efficiency—is that it permits playing in responder's suit at a lower level after partner has opened with a weak two-bid (i.e., two diamonds by opener, two spades by responder, pass by opener). A player may open with, say, a weak two-bid in hearts, but two spades, three diamonds, or three clubs may be the best part-score contract.

The disadvantage of the bid is that it takes away from the responder the numerous opportunities to outsmart the opposition. We feel that, in the long run, by using our method the responder will pick up many more match points than will be picked up by permitting the weak two-bidder's side to stop at the proper part-score at the two or three level.

C. OUR DEFENSE AGAINST WEAK TWO-BIDS

We use the same cooperative, optional double against weak two-bids that we employ against an opening bid of one or three in a suit. And, as in the latter, partner will take out unless he has good cause to pass, thereby converting the take-out double into a penalty double.

D. THE TWO CLUB OPENING BID

As was stated, only the opening bids of two diamonds, two hearts, or two spades are "weak." The two club opening bid is reserved for the rock-crusher type of game-going hands which would, in orthodox practice, be opened with a forcing two-bid in the opener's best suit. Two diamonds is used as the negative response to the artificial two club opening, showing fewer than 6 points, just as over the strong, game-forcing two-bid, the two no-trump response is used as the negative bid, showing less than 6 points. In response to the two club opening, any suit response, or two no-trump, shows positive values. The opening two club bidder reveals his real suit at his next opportunity to bid. To illustrate:

(1)	
Opener	Responder
2 ♣	2 ◇
2 NT (23–24)	

(2)	
Opener	Responder
2 ♣	2 ◇
2 ♠	2 NT
3 ♠ (not forcing)	

CHAPTER 13

The Weak Two-Bid in Action

The ten deals contained in this chapter all arose in national and local tournaments.

NOTE WELL: *While we do not subscribe to some of the "undisciplined" types of opening two-bids which will be observed,* we are presenting them to depict to the reader the devastating effect the bid can have on even topflight players who, as we, when they are forced to guess, often misguess.

DEAL 1. NATIONAL MEN'S PAIRS CHAMPIONSHIPS, 1961.

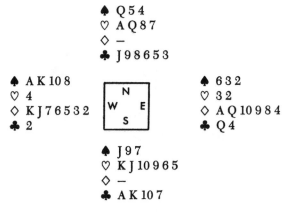

North–South vulnerable. East dealer.

The bidding:

East	South	West	North
2 ◇	3 ♡	6 ◇	6 ♡
Pass	Pass	Pass	

As is apparent, West cashed the ace and king of spades, and that was that.

From West's point of view, he knew that both North and South were void of diamonds, since East was known to have six of them and West himself had the other seven. He correctly figured that North, with his void in diamonds, would feel that West was trying to "steal," and would bid six hearts.

Actually, even if North had doubled the six diamond contract, East–West would have gone down but two tricks for an excellent sacrifice against North–South's vulnerable heart game. It was a nice team effort by East–West, especially by West.

DEAL 2.

On this deal, a third-position weak opening two-bid not only succeeded in getting the opponents to an inferior contract but also caused them to misplay the hand. The deal arose in the Masters' Pairs Championships of 1961.

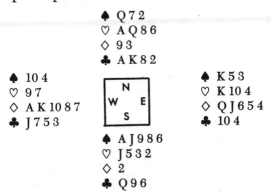

```
                  ♠ Q 7 2
                  ♡ A Q 8 6
                  ◇ 9 3
                  ♣ A K 8 2
  ♠ 10 4                         ♠ K 5 3
  ♡ 9 7            N             ♡ K 10 4
  ◇ A K 10 8 7   W   E           ◇ Q J 6 5 4
  ♣ J 7 5 3         S            ♣ 10 4
                  ♠ A J 9 8 6
                  ♡ J 5 3 2
                  ◇ 2
                  ♣ Q 9 6
```

Neither side vulnerable. East dealer.
The bidding:

East	South	West	North
Pass	Pass	2 ◇	Double
4 ◇	4 ♠	Pass	Pass
Pass			

West's two diamond opening on a five-card suit was completely justified in third position (in first and second position, a six-card suit is necessary). East's four diamond bid, over the double, was a fine pre-emptive call, aimed at depriving North–South of bidding space. At four diamonds, doubled, East–West would have been down but two tricks.

The king of diamonds was led, after which the diamond ace was ruffed by declarer. A club was played to dummy's king, and the queen of trumps was led, covered by the king, and taken by South's ace.

Assuming that West had six diamonds, and hence, probably a shortage of spades, declarer went back to dummy via the club ace, and played the deuce of trumps. When East followed with the three-spot, declarer finessed his nine-spot. West took this with his ten, and returned a club, which East ruffed. Eventually South also lost a heart to East's king, and went down a trick.

Of course, four hearts is an easily makable contract even if one misguesses the spade situation, since at the heart contract no club plays are necessary and East never gets in a ruff. But it would have been rather unreasonable for South to have bid hearts, don't you think?

DEAL 3.

This deal arose in the All-Western Pairs Championships held in Los Angeles in 1954. East–West were a very strong pair, but they missed a lay-down game in spades because of a weak opening two-bid.

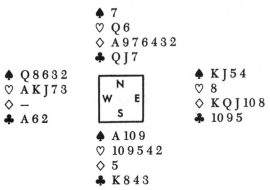

```
                    ♠ 7
                    ♡ Q 6
                    ◇ A 9 7 6 4 3 2
                    ♣ Q J 7
    ♠ Q 8 6 3 2        ┌─────────┐      ♠ K J 5 4
    ♡ A K J 7 3        │    N    │      ♡ 8
    ◇ —                │ W     E │      ◇ K Q J 10 8
    ♣ A 6 2            │    S    │      ♣ 10 9 5
                       └─────────┘
                    ♠ A 10 9
                    ♡ 10 9 5 4 2
                    ◇ 5
                    ♣ K 8 4 3
```

East–West vulnerable. North dealer.

The bidding:

North	East	South	West
2 ◇	Pass	Pass	Double
Pass	Pass	Pass	

East–West took four diamond tricks, two hearts, and one club, inflicting a two-trick set on declarer. The 300 points they received did not compensate them for the vulnerable game they would have made at four spades.

Had West gambled with a "cue bid" of three diamonds, instead of doubling, the four spade contract would, of course, have been reached. And if North had not made the pre-emptive two diamond call, the four spade contract would also undoubtedly have been reached.

DEAL 4.

As was mentioned, there are times when the weak two-bidder loses out because his artificial two club opening (to denote a game-going hand) enables the opponents to jam him up before he can show his real suit. Here is one example, although in all fairness the same result would probably have been obtained even if his opening two club bid had denoted a real club suit.

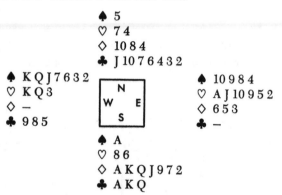

```
                    ♠ 5
                    ♡ 7 4
                    ◇ 10 8 4
                    ♣ J 10 7 6 4 3 2
  ♠ K Q J 7 6 3 2        ┌─────┐        ♠ 10 9 8 4
  ♡ K Q 3                │  N  │        ♡ A J 10 9 5 2
  ◇ —              W     │     │    E   ◇ 6 5 3
  ♣ 9 8 5               │  S  │        ♣ —
                         └─────┘
                    ♠ A
                    ♡ 8 6
                    ◇ A K Q J 9 7 2
                    ♣ A K Q
```

North–South vulnerable. South dealer.
The bidding:

South	West	North	East
2 ♣	2 ♠	Pass	4 ♠
5 ◇	5 ♠	6 ◇	6 ♠
Double	Pass	Pass	Pass

It was not South's day, for East–West made six spades! Their only loser was the ace of trumps.

DEAL 5.

On this deal, East's bidding needled North–South into a precarious game contract which went down two tricks for a loss of 500 points.˙ The hand was played in a Philadelphia duplicate game in 1956.

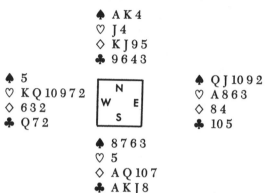

```
                  ♠ A K 4
                  ♡ J 4
                  ◇ K J 9 5
                  ♣ 9 6 4 3
  ♠ 5                              ♠ Q J 10 9 2
  ♡ K Q 10 9 7 2        N         ♡ A 8 6 3
  ◇ 6 3 2            W     E       ◇ 8 4
  ♣ Q 7 2               S         ♣ 10 5
                  ♠ 8 7 6 3
                  ♡ 5
                  ◇ A Q 10 7
                  ♣ A K J 8
```

North–South vulnerable. West dealer.

West	North	East	South
2 ♡	Pass	3 ♣	Double
Pass	Pass	3 ◇	Double
Pass	Pass	3 ♡	3 ♠
Pass	4 ♠	Double	Pass
Pass	Pass		

The reader will note that East had "values" for his psychic bidding: he knew also that he had a haven in the heart suit, with West holding six cards in that suit. Certainly, from East's seat, North–South figured to make a game somewhere.

DEAL 6.

When this deal was played in a duplicate game in 1959, seven out of the twelve North–South pairs arrived at a good six diamond contract which was defeated only because West happened to hold the four outstanding trumps: the Q J 10 9. At one table, the West defender decided to indulge in some horseplay—and it got him a bottom on the board.

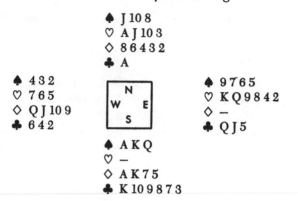

Neither side vulnerable. West dealer.
The bidding:

West	North	East	South
Pass	Pass	2 ♡	Double
2 ♠	Double (a)	Pass	Pass
3 ♡	Double (b)	Pass	Pass (c)
Pass			

- (a) North had met West before.
- (b) Dollars from Heaven.
- (c) Nervous but game.

East–West went down four tricks, for a loss of 800 points.

DEAL 7.

This is a once-in-a-lifetime deal. It arose in a Washington tournament in 1956.

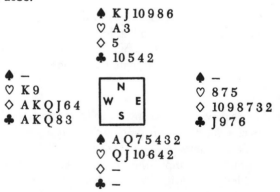

Neither side vulnerable. North dealer.

North	East	South	West
2 ♠	Pass	4 NT (a)	5 ♠ (b)
Pass	Pass	Pass	

(a) South wanted to gamble playing the hand at six spades, so he made the psychological bid of four no-trump (Blackwood) as a display of strength.

(b) West wanted his partner to bid, so he made the cue bid of five spades (why we don't know; his partner might well, in theory, have bid six *hearts*).

This is the only hand we've ever seen where the final contract was in a suit that both declarer and dummy were void of.

North opened his singleton diamond—and South trumped. Down eleven tricks, for a loss of 550 points. At all the other tables, the North–South pairs bid either six or seven spades, and thirteen tricks were made via the successful heart finesse.

Thus, as happens on occasion, a player (West) made a bad bid, but came out smelling like a rose.

DEAL 8.

Two of the proponents of the weak two-bid are Alvin Roth and Tobias Stone. This pair is one of the strongest in the world. This deal and the one which follows illustrate their handling of the weak two-bid.

The deal below arose in the 1951 National Championships. Roth was South and Stone was North.

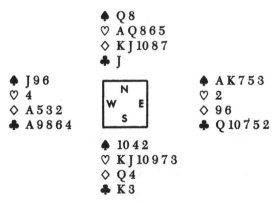

```
                    ♠ Q 8
                    ♡ A Q 8 6 5
                    ◇ K J 10 8 7
                    ♣ J
      ♠ J 9 6                        ♠ A K 7 5 3
      ♡ 4              N             ♡ 2
      ◇ A 5 3 2    W       E         ◇ 9 6
      ♣ A 9 8 6 4      S             ♣ Q 10 7 5 2
                    ♠ 10 4 2
                    ♡ K J 10 9 7 3
                    ◇ Q 4
                    ♣ K 3
```

Both sides vulnerable. South dealer.

South	West	North	East
2 ♡	Pass	2 ♠	Pass
2 NT	Pass	4 ♡	Pass
Pass	Pass		

Stone indulged in shenanigans, and his "operations" kept the opponents out of a makable spade game. North–South went down one. There was no chance for the two spade bid to go wrong, since opener is not allowed to make any embarrassing rebid (he could rebid no higher than three hearts).

DEAL 9.

This deal arose in the Vanderbilt Championships of 1959.

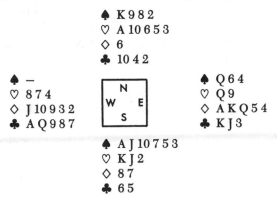

```
                    ♠ K 9 8 2
                    ♡ A 10 6 5 3
                    ◊ 6
                    ♣ 10 4 2
        ♠ —                         ♠ Q 6 4
        ♡ 8 7 4          N          ♡ Q 9
        ◊ J 10 9 3 2   W   E        ◊ A K Q 5 4
        ♣ A Q 9 8 7      S          ♣ K J 3
                    ♠ A J 10 7 5 3
                    ♡ K J 2
                    ◊ 8 7
                    ♣ 6 5
```

Both sides vulnerable. South dealer.
The bidding:

South (Roth)	West	North (Stone)	East
2 ♠	Pass	4 ♠	Pass
Pass	Pass		

Four spades was made via a successful heart finesse. When the board was replayed, South passed originally, and East–West arrived at a five diamond contract which was fulfilled with two overtricks when South opened the ace of spades. (A heart lead would have held East to eleven tricks.)

DEAL 10.

One of the advantages of the weak two-bid which has not been illustrated previously is the lead-directing aspect. Here is a good example, as demonstrated by one of the foremost practitioners of the weak two-bid, Samuel Stayman.

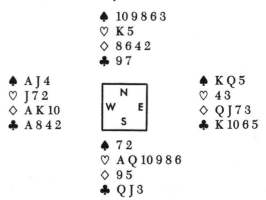

Neither side vulnerable. The bidding:

South	West	North	East
2 ♡	Double	Pass	3 ♡
Pass	4 ♣	Pass	5 ♣
Pass	Pass	Pass	

The five club contract was defeated one trick. Had South passed originally (as standard practice adherents would have done), West would unquestionably have opened the bidding with one no-trump, which East would have raised to three no-trump. Unless North were clairvoyant, and had opened the king of hearts, West would have taken the first nine tricks at three no-trump.

14

The Overcall

Silence may be considered an excellent virtue in a woman, but it is not a desirable trait in a bridge player, especially in a duplicate bridge player. If you sit quietly by with your thirteen cards clutched tightly in your hot little hands, be resigned to having the opponents bid around you, over you, and through you; and, in the end, you'll be a loser. In short, silence breeds defeat. You haven't a ghost of a chance. The modern-day players—in both duplicate and rubber bridge—bid much too well for you to grow fat on their errors.

While it is true that your bids sometimes aid the opposition, they more often tend to hurt the opponents. The failure to make a sound overcall when you possess the requirements can be just as costly (and just as reprehensible) as the failure to bring home a lay-down game contract when you are the declarer. If maximum results are to be obtained, one must inject himself into the auction whenever his holdings warrant it. Good theorists are always devising means to enable players to enter the auction with greater frequency. We are members of this "bid more" congregation.

The following fundamental cannot be overstressed:

> You must overcall if you possess a holding which warrants an overcall. The failure to overcall is an error of omission which, in our view, is as serious as any at the bridge table.

However, even though you may possess the points, the length of suit, or both, you may not have an overcall. You may, instead, have a holding with which you should properly double or pass. Every overcall must have a sound reason which motivates it and a card holding to substantiate that reason. When you have both, sound off with an overcall.

A sound overcall must fulfill at least one of the following purposes:

1. To bring forth a good lead from partner in defense of a contract played by the opposition. This first reason outweighs the next two combined.
2. To contest the auction in an effort to purchase the contract at a part-score or a game, with the idea of fulfillment.
3. To suggest a suit for a profitable sacrifice bid.

While we have seen various attempts to classify overcalls in terms of point count, we are morally convinced that the subject does not lend itself to such precise treatment. However, in response to the clamor of the multitudes seeking such packaged guidance, we will, with some misgivings, comply.

The length and strength of the suit you contemplate bidding is most important in determining whether to make an overcall. Of equal importance, though, is your motivation for bidding. If you want a point-count guide, it is safe to assume that overcalls begin with 9-point hands and range up to about 16 points. (In fact, there are cases where even stronger hands do not lend themselves to any satisfactory treatment except with an overcall.) However, for the most part, you should consider an overcalling hand as possessing—in addition to a good suit—from about 9 points up to the strength of a sound opening bid.

I. Overcalls at the Level of One

Let us examine some examples. East has opened the bidding with *one diamond,* and you, South, hold the following hands. *You are vulnerable.*

1. ♠ J 10 8 6 5 4
   ♡ 8 6
   ◇ 9 3
   ♣ K 8 2

If you are considering an overcall because the level is cheap, and you possess a six-card suit, ask yourself this question: What purpose will be served by the overcall? You can have no desire to call for the spade lead, especially against a suit contract, nor can you have any real hope of purchasing the contract profitably, since even a cheap save seems remote unless your partner is in a position to take some strong action voluntarily. The usual result of an overcall such as this finds partner doubling the opposition for penalty, which they either fulfill—possibly with overtricks—or you refuse to stand for the double, with equally painful results. A *pass* is the only proper action—and better days will come.

2. ♠ A 7 4   An overcall solicits a lead of that suit from partner,
   ♡ J 8 7 5 3   and with a jack-high suit it is a good bet that
   ◇ 8 2   *any uninvited* lead would have more merit. Only
   ♣ A 10 9   if you number yourself among the habitually care-

less will you overcall with suits of such texture, unless, of course, the general strength of your hand demands that some action be taken. Under such circumstances, you have some justification for the alibi: "But I did have compensating values!" If your partner can take no independent action, your side should not be in the contest. *Pass!*

3. ♠ A 10 8 5   Although you hold 11 points in high cards, you do
   ♡ 7 5   not have any suit which is designed for an over-
   ◇ K 9 6   call, and the last fact is the prime consideration.
   ♣ A 8 6 3   If you happen to be one who has been getting

away with overcalls on such a flimsy excuse as "I had 11 points," either mend your ways or prepare yourself for some extreme shocks. Actually, the suit in which you overcall should be of such texture that you do not normally expect to lose more than two tricks in the suit itself. Do not be overly impressed by your 11 points. *Pass.*

4. ♠ K Q J 8 4   This example is the perfect overcalling type of
   ♡ 6 5   hand. The level is cheap and your spade suit has
   ◇ 8 7 2   body. You surely want your partner to lead spades
   ♣ K 9 5   in defense. This is a sound overcall, regardless of
               vulnerability. Bid *one spade*.

5. ♠ 9 7 6   While it is true that an overcall should always
   ♡ A K Q 10   show a good five-card suit (or longer), you should
   ◇ 8 6   bear in mind that the difference between medi-
   ♣ 8 7 5 3   ocrity and expertness at the bridge table is meas-
               ured by the interpretation of rules containing the

words "always" and "never." Such rules should be correctly stated "almost always" and "almost never." So it is with a hand of this type. It would not meet the requirements of slogan writers for a vulnerable overcall. How-ever, based on our experiences, *we advocate such an overcall regardless of vulnerability*. For one thing, it is extremely unlikely that an opponent can have sufficient values in the heart suit to venture a double at this low level. (One virtually never doubles a one-level overcall without at least two trump tricks.) And we not only want to be assured of a heart lead should we become the defenders but we want to keep any "hope and a prayer" opponents honest—those speculative characters who delight in stealing a no-trump game without a stopper in some suit. While it is true that this overcall may occasionally cause you some embarrassment, the prospective dividends far outnumber the potential liabilities.

6. ♠ 4
   ♡ A 10 9 7 6 3
   ◇ 6 4
   ♣ K 7 6 2

This is the normal type of hand for a sound over-call at the level of one. There should be a spon-taneous one heart overcall after the opponent's one diamond opening bid. Any six-card suit headed by the ace is a good suit. You want the lead of a heart if your side defends, and you do not appear to be putting your head on the block for a death-dealing blow.

7. ♠ A Q 10 9 7 2
   ♡ 6 5
   ◇ 7 4
   ♣ J 9 7

You would overcall with this hand for the same reasons as in Hand 6. The suit is very good; you want the spade lead in defense; and you are will-ing to play the hand at the contract you name without any fear of severe damage. Overcall with *one spade* by all means. Failure to take advantage of a bidding oppor-tunity when such action is cheap will leave you forever wondering what better result might have been yours if you had made the call.

8. ♠ 9
   ♡ A Q J 9 6
   ◇ 8 6
   ♣ A K 10 8 4

This type of example should be given serious at-tention. Many players would deem this holding to be too powerful for a simple overcall. Since neither suit is solid and the general strength is not quite sufficient for a strong jump overcall (to be dis-cussed in the next chapter), they would make a take-out double (to be discussed two chapters hence). If it were only a question of points, we would concur in the latter bid. But your first concern should be this: What course of action will afford me the opportunity of best describing my hand to partner? If you double and the bidding then proceeds in a mild and easy fashion, you will have no difficulty in showing your suits; and, in this case, the double would turn out to be the best bid.

The bidding, however, seldom proceeds in that manner. Partner bids, and the opponents get into the act, leaving you unable to show both of your suits without courting disaster at dangerously high levels. If, instead, you make a simple overcall of *one heart*, the bidding is less likely to accelerate. You intend, of course, to re-enter the auction with your second suit at the level of three. Partner will, by then, appreciate the fact that you have a good hand, for no player of sound mind would contest un-assisted for nine or ten tricks without an adequate array of cards to warrant it. The one risk you must accept in pursuing the course of making a simple overcall is that you may be passed out. The chance of that occurring is relatively slight, since the opponents' hands figure to be as unbalanced as your own and there are plenty of high cards outstanding.

There is still another argument in favor of the simple overcall in lieu of the take-out double: it keeps your partner from becoming too excited should he possess a reasonably good six-card spade suit.

9. ♠ J 9 6 5   This hand is too good for a mere overcall in hearts.
   ♡ A K 10 9 2   It is tailor-made for a take-out double (two chap-
   ◇ 8   ters hence), inviting a response in spades, which
   ♣ A 6 3   suit might be shut out with an overcall. This situ-
                ation bears no comparison to the previous illustra-
tion. This is not a two-suited hand, in that both suits will not stand on their own. Here you welcome partner's assistance in placing the final contract if your side is destined to play it.

II. Overcalls at the Level of Two

While considerable freedom should be exercised in overcalling at the level of one, safety is the prime consideration for overcalls at the range of two. You must always bow to the possibility of being doubled for business. Consequently, overcalls at this level must be stepped up in quality. *Vulnerability conditions are much more important than at the range of one,* and the suit you intend to name should be a healthy one—at least five cards in length and blessed with greater solidity than would be necessary with overcalls at the one-level. For those who prefer a point count guide, let us say that the hand should be, as a minimum, the equivalent of an opening bid, as low as 12 points if not vulnerable and between 13 and 17 when vulnerable. The suit should be headed by at least two of the three top cards (A K x x x, A Q x x x, or K Q x x x).

If the bidding is opened to your right with *one spade,* what action should you take with the following hands?

1. ♠ 8   While you might get by with a nonvulnerable
   ♡ J 10 8 4 3 2 overcall of two hearts holding such a hand as
   ◇ A 9 4   this, the chance of accomplishing anything worth-
   ♣ K 7 6   while is negligible. You might, unfortunately, so-
              licit the lead of the king of hearts if partner holds
the K x, which is not a healthy prospect to contemplate. Furthermore, you might suffer damages sufficient to break your partner's morale—to say nothing of your own (and his) checking account. *Pass!*

2. ♠ 6 3
    ♡ A Q 7 6 2
    ◊ 8 7 3
    ♣ A Q 4

After weighing prospective gain against possible loss, you should conclude that the heart suit is too weak to warrant an overcall of two hearts. We strongly recommend that you *pass* and await developments. This holding is better suited to a take-out double than an overcall, but even that meditated action appears too risky. However, if your partner is able to inject himself into the auction voluntarily, be prepared to toss your weight around a bit.

3. ♠ 8 7
    ♡ 7 2
    ◊ A 6 3
    ♣ K Q J 9 6 5

The club suit is good, and the hand should produce six tricks without any assistance from partner. This is worth an overcall of *two clubs*. Such an overcall directs the lead and indicates a spot for a possible sacrifice if the opponents arrive at a game contract in a major suit.

4. ♠ 4 2
    ♡ 6 5
    ◊ A 7 6
    ♣ A K J 9 8 2

For the same reason as in the previous example, an overcall of *two clubs* is indicated. While this is a good hand, it does not fulfill the requisites for a take-out double. If your partner cannot bid over your overcall, your side is not likely to be in any position to make a game.

5. ♠ 8 5
    ♡ 7
    ◊ A K 10 5
    ♣ Q J 10 8 7 4

An overcall of *two clubs* will adequately describe your hand. This and the two preceding examples differ in general strength ·but tend to serve as demonstrative proof that overcalls have a wide range.

6. ♠ K 7 6
    ♡ 4
    ◊ A K J 9 5
    ♣ K 9 5 4

While two diamonds does not seem to do justice to your more-than-adequate possessions, it is the only reasonable action that can be ventured over an opening bid of one spade. A take-out double instead would probably solicit a heart response from partner and would serve no useful purpose. Overcall with *two diamonds* and hope it offers sufficient encouragement to induce partner to continue.

7. ♠ K 10 7 5 3
    ♡ 8
    ◊ A K J 9 5
    ♣ Q 7

The correct manner of handling combinations of this type is, to say the least, debatable. A good many players would choose to pass rather quickly because they are so well fortified in the opponent's spade suit. However, we differ in theory about hands of this kind, and we find that the maximum benefits will be returned if an immediate overcall—*two diamonds*, in this case—is inserted.

With the bidding thus accelerated, the "interference" will tend to disturb an easy flow of information between the opponents. It has been our experience, in analogous situations, that when the opposition is left alone, they rarely remain in the spade suit and instead find a satisfactory fit elsewhere. While it is conceded that the opener's partner is bound to be short in spades and therefore is more likely to be harboring thoughts of a penalty double, your partner is just as certain to be short in spades and his diamond holding will be lying over the doubler's. Furthermore, who can say that this hand should be played by the enemy? It can just as easily be your hand, and the immediate overcall is the most practical method of investigating any such eventuality. The latter factor alone outweighs the risk of a severe penalty double.

III. Overcalls at the Level of Three

The footing of the overcaller is even more treacherous at this altitude, and the player with designs on entering the auction at such a level should adopt stringent safety precautions. Such opportunities to overcall usually present themselves after both opponents have bid and your partner has passed. Therefore, your overcall should be supported by well-founded reasons for inserting the call, in addition to having a high degree of safety.

If the bidding has proceeded:

West	North	East	South
1 ♠	Pass	2 ♡	?

and you, South, hold:

(1)	(2)	(3)
♠ 7 5	♠ 9	♠ 5 4
♡ 9 6	♡ 7 3	♡ 7
◇ A K Q J 8 2	◇ K Q J 10 7 6 4	◇ K Q 10 9 8 7 4
♣ K 5 3	♣ A 9 8	♣ A Q 9

With vulnerability conditions equal or in your favor, you have valid reasons for bidding *three diamonds* on each of the above hands. However, we would be inclined to forego the dubious pleasure with Hand (1) if we were vulnerable and the opponents were not. There is hardly enough to be gained under these conditions. The bidding indicates that your partner holds little, if anything. Therefore, you cannot seriously entertain thoughts of purchasing the contract profitably. Your one aim must be to secure the diamond lead. But the opponents are not likely to contract for three no-trump without anything in diamonds. Against a suit contract, partner will almost surely lead a club or a diamond, which gives you an even chance without running a needless risk. Bear this in mind: if the opponents decide to double you for penalties (*you* are vulnerable, they are not), your loss figures to exceed the value of the game they could make. With neither side vulnerable, or if the opponents were vulnerable and we were not, we would risk the three diamond bid to make sure of getting the diamond lead.

With Hands (2) and (3), we would make the overcall regardless of vulnerability. We do not figure to be mutilated by a double and if the opponents have any leanings toward a no-trump contract, we would want to insure getting the diamond lead from partner while we still have a sure entry in the ace of clubs.

IV. Responding to Overcalls

Point count must give way to common sense in determining a procedure after partner has made an overcall. Any attempt at strict classification of procedure must, of necessity, bog down in a morass of contradiction. Nevertheless, some general rules can be adhered to with profitable results.

From earliest days, we have believed that an overcall even at the one level should show a reasonably good five-card suit (or longer). This was a view subscribed to by virtually all top performers. It was the neophyte who continually overcalled on four-card suits simply because he held some points. However, the impact of match-point play has, through the years, wrought some changes. In this game, the part-score fight is more intense, and the opening lead is very important because one trick can be of such consequence. Strangely enough, the neophyte has, in this case, proved to be more right than the expert. Nevertheless, it should be borne in mind that, when overcalling, you will possess a five-card, or longer, suit far more often than a four-card suit. Your partner should, for best results, *always* play you to possess at least a five-card suit. If he labors under the mental stress that your overcalling suit is only four cards long, your partnership will falter.

Years ago it was accepted doctrine that the overcaller's partner should not name a new suit of his own merely because he disliked the suit partner had named. Furthermore, if he did, he should have:

(1) A suit worth bidding twice;
(2) The hand should be of such quality that more than one bid is warranted.

Even though the above advice was formerly offered by us, we now deem another tactic much more preferable, especially at match-point play:

> In neither game (rubber bridge or duplicate) is the naming of a new suit in response to an overcall a forcing bid.

West	North	East	South
1 ♣	1 ♢	Pass	*1* ♠

The *one spade* bid in the above sequence is *not forcing*. Only two bids are forcing on an overcaller: (1) cue-bidding the opponent's suit, or (2) a jump-shift by a non-passed hand (2 S by South in the above sequence, in lieu of one spade). Since such is the case, we feel that the partner of the overcaller should be permitted to name a new suit of his own without it being construed as encouraging. As a matter of fact, it should be viewed as mildly discouraging insofar as the *overcaller's suit* is concerned.

The type of hand that South might have held for his one spade bid in the above sequence might have been any of the following:

(1)	(2)	(3)
♠ K Q 10 9 6 4	♠ A Q J 7 5	♠ Q J 9 8 6 2
♡ 8 3	♡ 9 4 3	♡ A 4
♢ 7 5	♢ 6	♢ 6 3 2
♣ 9 4 2	♣ J 8 6 2	♣ 7 5

A. No-trump Shows Strength

Do not respond to your partner's overcall with a one no-trump bid merely for the purpose of showing a stopper in the adversely bid suit. A no-trump takeout is a forward-going bid and must be predicated upon sound and substantial values, although some slight relaxation of the rule is permitted in certain match-point situations where greater stress is placed on arriving at the most lucrative part-score contract. In duplicate, you should have 9–10 points to respond with one no-trump to your partner's overcall. In rubber bridge, we are of the opinion that this bid should show 10–11 points.

If the bidding has proceeded:

West	North	East	South
1 ♡	1 ♠	Pass	?

and you, South, hold:

(1)	(2)
♠ 7 6	♠ J 8
♡ K 10 8 2	♡ K 10 9 5
◊ A 7 6 4	◊ A 7 6 4
♣ J 8 2	♣ Q 10 6

With Hand (1), you should simply *pass* your partner's overcall.

With Hand (2), you would be justified in making the progressive bid of *one no-trump*. You have a fairly good hand with all suits stopped and a sufficient fit in partner's suit to encourage the belief that the suit can be brought home without too much trouble. You have no reason to feel panicky about a rebid of spades, should partner choose to rebid that suit.

B. When to Show the "Other Major"

When your partner has overcalled an opening bid of a major suit, you should not take out to the other major without well-founded reasons. It is extremely likely that partner has chosen to overcall, rather than make a take-out double, because he did not want to hear you bid the other major.

The bidding has proceeded:

West	North	East	South
1 ♠	2 ◊	Pass	?

You, South, hold the following hands:

1. ♠ 8 6 5
   ♡ A J 9 8 6
   ◊ 7
   ♣ K 8 4 3

   Pass. There are no possibilities for a game contract in view of your partner's action in making a mere overcall. If he had the values that would provide even a fair play for game, he would have made a stronger effort. Without prospects for a better future, bow out now.

2. ♠ 9 7 2 With this holding, you should bid *two hearts* in an
   ♡ A J 10 9 5 attempt to improve the contract. You are well-
   ◇ K 6 2 cushioned in support of diamonds if your partner
   ♣ 8 5 returns to that suit. With this hand, in contrast to
   Hand 1, above, you have a haven in diamonds if your
partner can't stand hearts.

3. ♠ 8 2 Bid *two hearts* with confidence. You can stand a rebid
   ♡ A J 10 8 3 of diamonds, and there are distinct game possibilities.
   ◇ Q 9 You should welcome the opportunity to try for the
   ♣ K J 9 2 ten-trick·game in hearts if partner comes up with a
   heart raise. If partner shows control of the spade
suit by rebidding no-trump, you should try for the nine-trick route to
game.

C. RAISING AN OVERCALL

Single raises of partner's overcall should be the adopted procedure on hands of moderate strength and support of his suit. With
four cards in support of the suit, you may raise with 8–9 points.
With but three cards to support the suit, you should have additional
values (about 10–11 points). Such raises cannot be construed as
anything more than a mild try for game in the hope that the overcaller's hand was really good. If it serves no other purpose, the
raise will act as a barricade against the opponents' free flow of
information.

On either of the following bidding sequences:

West	North	East	South
1 ♡	1 ♠	Pass	?

or

West	North	East	South
1 ♡	1 ♠	2 ♡	?

if you, South, hold any of these types of hands:

(1)	(2)	(3)
♠ A 7 6 2	♠ Q 7 6	♠ J 9 2
♡ 9 5	♡ 8 2	♡ 8 7
◇ K 10 8 7	◇ A J 9 5	◇ K Q 8 2
♣ J 8 6	♣ K 7 6 2	♣ A 10 5 3

you should make *the single raise* of your partner's spade overcall,
with each of the above hands, even though in each instance there
is not likely to be a real play for game unless partner is able to

make a further move over your raise. The suit in which partner overcalled will almost always be at least five cards long. Therefore, even three-card support is ample. This precludes the possibility of any serious damage to your side and paves the way for any eventuality. You may purchase the contract, at part-score or game, and fulfill it. You may be able to push the opponents beyond their depth. You may suffer a loss which will be less than the opponents could earn by playing the contract.

D. With 13–16 Points Opposite Partner's Overcall

With a sound opening bid opposite your partner's overcall, you should make some strong show of strength. With 13–14 points, a non-forcing jump response in partner's suit or in no-trump will adequately advertise your values. With 15 or more points, you should immediately raise to game in either partner's suit or in no-trump, or make a jump bid in some new suit, which is forcing on the overcaller if you have not passed previously.

Assume the following bidding sequence:

West	North	East	South
1 ♡	1 ♠	Pass	?

As South, what would you do with the following:

1. ♠ Q 7 6
   ♡ 8 2
   ◇ A Q 9 6
   ♣ K J 6 5

Your hand amounts to a good opening bid once you have heard a spade bid from your partner. You should invite a game by jumping to *three spades*. The overcaller will carry it to four if his initial effort was predicated on maximum values (an opening bid, or better). Otherwise, he will pass since *the double raise of an overcall is not forcing*.

2. ♠ A 8 7 6
   ♡ 5
   ◇ K 8 4 3
   ♣ K 7 6 4

For about the same reasons as in the preceding example, you should bid *three spades*, acquainting your partner with the fact that your hand approximates an opening bid when evaluated in support of his suit. Again, this jump raise is not forcing.

3. ♠ 7 6
   ♡ K J 6
   ◇ K 9 5 3
   ♣ A Q 9 8

With values equivalent to an opening bid, all unbid suits protected, and lacking normal support for partner's spade suit, you provide partner with an excellent picture of your hand by *jumping to two no-trump*. The overcaller may pass, but with a sound overcall he will try for the game in spades or no-trump.

4. ♠ J 9
   ♡ K J 7 6
   ◇ K Q 9
   ♣ A J 4 3

With 15 points, you should be willing to gamble this hand out at game. Bear in mind that no-trump jump responses to overcalls are not forcing, and if you want to be in game, you must take the full leap yourself. Bid *three no-trump.*

5. ♠ Q 8 7 6
   ♡ 10
   ◇ A Q 8 6
   ♣ K Q 10 7

Holding more than 14 points and excellent support for the spade suit, you should jump to game with this hand. *Bid four spades.*

6. ♠ K 9
   ♡ 7
   ◇ A Q J 7 5 3
   ♣ K J 10 7

A jump response in a new suit following partner's overcall is forcing and should be resorted to in situations such as this. *Bid three diamonds.* Partner may not be able to do anything more than rebid three spades; and, if he does, then his spade suit should prove to be an adequate vehicle for a game venture at spades. At any rate, once the overcaller has acted, your holding is much too good to contemplate anything less than a game contract somewhere.

7. ♠ J 8
   ♡ Q 6
   ◇ A K J 6 4
   ♣ K Q 8 5

For the same reasons as in the previous example, you should make *a jump takeout to three diamonds.* You will, in this case, be a little more receptive to three no-trump than in Hand 6, above, and, of course, will pass should partner make the latter bid.

Some readers may be slightly concerned with the fact that we advocate being in game with 15–16 points opposite partner's one-level overcall. It may well be that, in many situations, your partnership will be in a game with less than 26 points, the latter being the yardstick usually prescribed for a game. But several things should be borne in mind:

1. When you raise the suit in which your partner has overcalled, his suit becomes stronger by the consolidation, making his hand surpass his original estimation.
2. A good fit in the combined hands of the partnership actually makes the joint assets a couple of points better in the play.
3. More important than either of the first two reasons is the fact that the known good hand of the opponents (the opener) is sandwiched between your two good hands. But opener's partner's hand is worthless, which means that the opening bidder will be saddled with the entire burden of defense.

Under these conditions, locating key cards for the purpose of finessing offers no problem. By the same token, end plays, throw-ins, and squeezes can be executed with more ease and confidence. To repeat: when two good hands surround one known good hand, the two become stronger, and the single hand weaker; and the deficiency of a point or two in the two strong hands will be more than compensated for by the knowledge of where the missing high cards are located.

V. Overcalling with No-trump

When the opponents have opened the auction with a suit, an overcall of one no-trump shows the same value as an original one no-trump opening bid (16–18 points). The only restraining requisite, founded upon sheer logic, is that the no-trump overcaller *must have* the opponent's suit well protected. Without the bid suit covered, you would have a very sound take-out double and no reason to make the no-trump overcall.

Following are some typical examples of hands which might be held after the opposition has opened the bidding with a call of *one spade*. What action would you take?

1. ♠ K J 6   Since you would have opened the auction with one
   ♡ Q 10 2   no-trump, your fine protection against the adversely
   ◊ A Q 7 6 bid spades should hasten your adoption of a like
   ♣ A J 5   measure as a competitive action against the attack
   launched by the enemy. Your partner will respond to your efforts in the same manner as if you had opened the bidding with one no-trump.

2. ♠ A Q 8   Since the purpose of our effort is to acquaint you with
   ♡ 10 9   the bidding and thinking mechanisms of the players
   ◊ A Q 6 4 who have emerged from the "average" class, this par-
   ♣ A J 9 7 ticular type of situation warrants special attention.
   While it is true that this hand would not have met the requirements for an opening one no-trump bid, it is one of the exceptions sanctioned by expert practice. *A no-trump overcall made in the face of an opening bid in one major suit may denote a weakness in the other major.* The shortcoming may be of such proportions as to bar the no-trump bid as an opening maneuver, as the weak doubleton in the heart suit of this example. The partner of the no-trump overcaller should bear this in

mind and tend to refrain from showing a heart suit unless his holding is such that he is convinced that a heart contract would be best. If partner had more than a passing interest in the heart suit, he would have doubled rather than made a one no-trump overcall.

3. ♠ K J 7   You must encourage a heart response whenever your
   ♡ A J 8 5   hand warrants it. With four-card support for hearts, it
   ◇ K 6 4 3   is considered better tactics to fall back on a take-out
   ♣ A Q   double with the intention of bidding two no-trump if
                 your partner responds in anything but hearts. You may,
of course, get one level higher by adopting this procedure, but it greatly enhances your chances of finding the heart spot if there is one. That is considered to be the more important practical consideration.

4. ♠ K 7 6   Even with only a single stopper in the adversely bid
   ♡ A Q 9   suit, the no-trump overcall is considered a better
   ◇ A 10 9 2   strategem than a take-out double or a "trap pass"
   ♣ K 7 2   (creating the impression, by passing, that you have a
                 poor hand and hoping that the opponents keep on
bidding). The double would elicit a response which would leave you in the position of still having to guess the best final contract. The trap pass should be rejected because of your strength in high cards outside the spade suit, making it distinctly possible that such action would be followed by two more passes, terminating the auction. The *one no-trump overcall* adequately and aptly describes your hand.

5. ♠ K 7 6 2   Everything we said in the preceding example is mag-
   ♡ A Q   nified in this hand. You do not want to encourage your
   ◇ K J 7 5   partner to bid hearts—which a take-out double would
   ♣ A 4 3   do—and you have to be starved for a possible killing
                 even to consider a trap pass. *One no-trump* is the
                 perfect call.

VI. The Two No-trump Overcall

It is not sufficient to dismiss two no-trump overcalls with the all-encompassing statement that these bids show the same requirements as needed for a two no-trump opening bid. While such is the case technically, there is the added proviso that *the two no-trump overcaller promises a double stopper in the suit bid by the opponents.* The two no-trump overcaller, like the two no-trump opening bidder, shows 22–24 high-card points. However, you should lean toward such an action with 20–21 points when you think this would be favorable to your interests. In addition, an excellent result might be achieved on a different-type hand which, technically, does not conform to the requirements for a two no-trump bid.

For example, if the bidding had proceeded:

West	North	East	South
1 ♠	Pass	2 ♠	?

and you, South, hold something like this:

♠ A Q
♡ 7 5
◊ A K Q J 8 6
♣ K 10 7

the two no-trump overcall would portray the trick-taking power of your hand. At the same time, it serves as a warning that you have no interest in a heart takeout. If you had such an interest, you would have chosen to double for takeout.

VII. The Three No-trump Overcall

An overcall of three no-trump after an opening bid by the opponents expresses a desire to play that contract and no other. Since the overcaller will just about *never* possess 25–27 points (as in an *opening* three no-trump bid), it would be losing tactics to wait for a 25–27 point hand to make the three no-trump overcall. The partner of the three no-trump overcaller should entertain no thoughts of proceeding to a suit of his own unless he possesses some extremely unbalanced distribution, like 6-6-1, 7-5-1, 8-3-2, etc. The three no-trump bidder will usually have a long, solid suit of his own, in which he expects to capture six or seven of his tricks; and his other suits will, more often than not, prove more valuable if led up to, rather than through. For example, the bidding has gone:

West	North	East	South
Pass	Pass	1 ♡	3 NT

South's hand would, conceivably, look something like this:

♠ A 7
♡ K 8
◊ A K Q 9 8 5 2
♣ K 6

CHAPTER 15

The Jump Overcall

Since we use both the strong and the weak jump overcall, it must be made clear when each applies. A jump overcall (1 D ... 2 S) made when *we are not vulnerable* is *weak*. The opposition's vulnerability does not matter, although it may affect the extent and degree of our maneuverings. *If we are vulnerable,* our jump overcalls (1 D ... 2 S) are *strong*.

Before discussing the specifics of our strong and weak jump overcalls, we would like to present our reasons for incorporating the weak jump overcall into our method of bidding.

A marked tendency toward weak bids of all types—i.e., the weak two-bid, the weak no-trump opening, etc.—can be noted in all American bidding systems. Of course, each of us has seen cases where our bids gave declarer the precise information he needed to fulfill his contract. Nevertheless, authorities agree that "weakness" bidding tends to hurt the opposition more than it helps.

Howard Schenken conceived the weak two-bid simply because he felt that it was advantageous to bid more often. The same considerations must have motivated the weak no-trump opening (12–14 points), the foundation of the Kaplan-Sheinwold System of bidding. The Roth-Stone System has several features which could be placed in this "bid more" category, but even their first- and second-hand super-sound opening bids have undergone a revision downward. This last was for them a must; they needed to bid more since they were getting shut out of the auction too often. Even Goren capitulated to a degree with the adoption of the weak jump overcall. His revision is not as weak as the weak jump overcall others use, yet it is still a radical departure from the strong jump overcall. It shows less than an opening bid.

We were a holdout. We countered the argument that the strong jump overcall didn't arise often enough to warrant its use with the obvious rejoinder: the strong jump overcall is most precise in the more important situations, namely those involving the possibility of games and slams. In rubber bridge, we thought our position was correct. But in duplicate bridge, where the *amount* of gain or loss is not important but the *frequency* of gain or loss is the major consideration, we appreciated that our position might be wrong.

So we effected a compromise and put it to the test. It worked well, and we enacted our compromise into "law." Here it is:

The need for a strong jump overcall is less in nonvulnerable situations, while the opportunity to use a weak jump overcall doesn't arise too often in vulnerable situations. *We therefore advocate the use of strong jump overcalls when we are vulnerable, and weak jump overcalls when we are not vulnerable.*

We do not feel, however, that digesting a few paragraphs and memorizing two or three examples will provide sufficient knowledge for the handling of the "weak jump" overcalls. A comprehensive and disciplined usage is required for success. In the succeeding pages, we will attempt to outline such a course. But, first, let's discuss the time-honored, strength-showing, strong jump overcall, which we employ *whenever we are vulnerable.*

I. The Strong Jump Overcall

Just as the golfer has a club available for each situation, so the bridge player has a bid available for any occasion that may arise.

When an opponent opens the bidding ahead of you, there is a precise bid available that will adequately paint a picture of your holdings. When you feel your hand is as good as, or better, than the opening bidder's, you may so indicate with a take-out double or an overcall in no-trump. Sometimes, however, you have a trump suit which requires little or no support from partner, and you feel pretty certain that the suit should be the final trump suit. *When vulnerable,* you transmit such a picture by bidding exactly one more than necessary in that suit. For instance:

East opens *one heart,* South overcalls with *two spades;*
or East opens *one heart,* South overcalls with *three diamonds;*
or East opens *one club,* South overcalls with *two hearts;*
or East opens *one diamond,* South overcalls with *two spades.*

In each of the above illustrations, South's bid indicates a hand above the specifications for an opening bid, and one which will, on a reasonable basis, probably take about as many tricks as called for in the contract named. Examples of sound jump overcalls would be:

1. ♠ 8   Bid *two hearts* over an opening bid of one club
   ♡ A K Q 9 4 3   or one diamond.
   ◇ 6 5 3
   ♣ A Q 10

2. ♠ A Q   Bid *three clubs* over one diamond or one heart,
   ♡ 6 2   suggesting a continuance to three no-trump if
   ◇ 8 7   partner has a stopper in the adversely bid suit
   ♣ A K Q J 9 5 2   *and* one other card of value.

3. ♠ A Q J 10 6 5 4   Bid *two spades* over one club, one diamond, or
   ♡ 8 4   one heart.
   ◇ A
   ♣ K 5 2

A jump overcall is sometimes used to describe a strong two-suited hand, such as:

♠ 8 6
♡ A K Q 10 6
◇ A Q 10 9 5
♣ 7

With the above hand, over an opening bid of one club, overcall with *two hearts,* with the intention of showing your diamond suit at the next opportunity.

A. GAME WITH MODERATE VALUES

A jump overcall alerts partner to the possibility of fulfilling a game contract if he is possessed with but moderate values or favorable distribution. *The jump overcall is not forcing.* It *is* strongly

* The only forcing bid by the opponents of the opening bidder is the cue bid in one of the suits bid by the opening side. For example, 1 S by opener, 2 S by second hand.

invitational to partner, who is at liberty to pass without any trick-taking possibilities. With one sure trick-taking card (e.g., A, K Q, etc.), and any one possible trick-taker (K x, Q J x, etc.), the responder should make a bid. It will be observed from the examples just given, that normal trump support is unnecessary. Therefore, the responder should give definite value (a trick) to three small trumps and a singleton and about a half trick to three small trumps and a doubleton.

It should be noted, however, that complete lack of a fit, such as a singleton or a void in partner's suit, should be viewed as a definite flaw in the combined trick-taking potential. Such a lack of support will usually cause a downward revision of your partner's trick-taking estimate in his own suit. While two small cards are considered adequate support for a suit in which a jump overcall is attempted, tend to underbid your hand with any lesser support in response.

The responder to a jump overcall must evaluate his assets on a commonsense basis. He need only exercise reasonably good judgment to determine whether or not he can provide one sure winner and one possible winner.

Assume the bidding has proceeded:

West	North	East	South
1 ♡	2 ♠	Pass	?

You, South, hold:

♠ 7 6 2
♡ 6 4
◇ K 7 3 2
♣ K 10 6 5

If partner's two spade jump overcall was proper, one of your two kings must be a sure winner and the other can be rated as a possible winner. If either of your kings were to be exchanged for the king of hearts (West's bid suit), which would be practically worthless, we would tend to pass. As the hand now stands, we would raise to *three spades*.

B. Do Not Pass a Raise

Though you may jump to four spades—assuming the jump overcall was to two spades—when your holding warrants it, you need not fear that your partner will pass your milder raise to three. *He should never hang below game* but should accept any game invitation. You, as responder, might have a strategic reason for raising to only three of his suit. Assume, for example, that on the previous bidding you have:

♠ Q 7 6
♥ 4 3
♦ A 10 9 2
♣ K J 8 7

A raise to four spades would not do full justice to your hand. Yet, to bid six spades is overambitious, while a bid of five spades might cause partner to worry about controls (like the diamond ace). You might, therefore, simply raise to three spades, so that when partner bids four spades, you can bid five diamonds. He cannot fail to interpret your action to mean that you possess the ace of diamonds and sufficient values to warrant taking the contract beyond the game level.

When the jump overcall is made in a major suit, the bidder is usually seeking a game in that denomination. When, however, the jump is made in a minor suit, the bidder will normally be happy to accept a contract of three no-trump. In that case, the responder to the jump overcall should view stoppers in the opening bidder's suit with optimism.

If the bidding has proceeded:

West	North	East	South
1 ♠	3 ♣	Pass	?

South should bid *three no-trump* with either of the following hands:

(1)	(2)
♠ K 8 7	♠ Q J 6
♥ 10 9 6 3	♥ K 8 7 4
♦ A 5 4	♦ J 8 7
♣ 7 4 2	♣ 5 3 2

II. The Weak Jump Overcall

Regarding the strength, or weakness, of the weak jump overcall, there is a wide difference in practice. The range is from Goren's "just under an opening bid with a six-card suit" to a hand containing practically nothing.

We feel that rigid requirements are highly desirable, if not absolutely essential. This is particularly true *if the bid is made in second position when partner has not passed.* Our two rigid requirements are: (1) a fair six-card suit, and (2) no more than one ace or king within the hand.

Here are some illustrations of our second position weak jump overcalls made *only when not vulnerable,* when partner has not as yet passed.

A. At the Two-Level (In Second Position)

1. West (opener)
   1 ◇

   North
   ♠ K J 10 9 6 2
   ♡ 4
   ◇ 8 6 3
   ♣ Q 7 2

   Bid 2 ♠. At the two-level the bid should describe a hand containing a fair six-card suit and *one ace or one king*, but not more.

2. West (opener)
   1 ◇

   North
   ♠ Q J 9 7 5 3
   ♡ 6 4
   ◇ 5 3
   ♣ A 8 6

   Bid 2 ♠. The one high-card requirement (either an ace or a king) need not be in the suit itself, but the suit should have some substance. J 10 8 x x x should be the weakest holding permissible.

3. West (opener)
   1 ◇

   North
   ♠ K Q 10 7 3 2
   ♡ 8 4
   ◇ 9 6 3
   ♣ 6 5

   Bid 2 ♠.

4. West (opener)
   1 ◇

   North
   ♠ K Q J 9 5 3
   ♡ 7 5
   ◇ 8
   ♣ J 7 5 4

   Bid 2 ♠.

5. West (opener)
   1 ◇

   North
   ♠ K 8 7 5 4 2
   ♡ 8 6
   ◇ 5 3
   ♣ K J 9

   Bid 2 ♠. When the six-card suit is weak—even though it is headed by an ace or a king—the restriction concerning only one ace or one king in the hand may be waived.

Safety should *not* be the most important consideration when contemplating making a pre-emptive call. A player should pre-empt to the full extent of his values. Do not fall into the error of jumping to two spades on the following type of hand because it is safer:

♠ K J 10 9 8 6 3
♡ 8 5
◇ 4
♣ Q 9 6

Over an opening bid of one diamond, *bid three spades* on the above hand.

Similarly, with the following two hands, do not jump to two spades merely because you like to employ a gadget. These two hands are too good for a weak jump overcall in second position:

(1)	(2)
♠ A J 10 8 5 2	♠ K Q J 9 6 2
♡ 7 5	♡ K 4
◇ 6 5	◇ 8 4
♣ K 5 2	♣ 9 7 5

On both of the above hands, simply overcall with *one spade*.

B. THE JUMP OVERCALL AT THE THREE-LEVEL
(IN SECOND POSITION)

West opens the bidding with *one heart*. Sitting North, not vulnerable, bid *three clubs* on each of the following hands.

(1)	(2)	(3)
♠ 5 3	♠ 6	♠ 8
♡ 7	♡ 8 5	♡ 4 2
◇ 8 6 3	◇ K 9 2	◇ Q 10 5 2
♣ K Q 10 9 7 4 2	♣ Q J 10 8 7 4 2	♣ A J 10 9 7 6

From the three above illustrations, it can be observed that the jump overcall to the three-level describes a hand containing either a six- or seven-card suit, and the high cards do not include more than an ace and a king. It is the type of hand that you would have opened with a pre-emptive three-bid (nonvulnerable) if your opponent had passed originally.

C. THE JUMP OVERCALL IN THIRD OR FOURTH POSITION

In second position, we strongly advise you to stay within the strength limitations set forth in the preceding paragraphs. If you do, your partner will be able to judge accurately whether, and how far, to compete.

But such self-discipline is not required—or even desirable—if your partner has passed originally and you are in third or fourth position. The main concern then becomes to disrupt the communication of the opponents. You may thus employ the weak jump overcall with any holding short of an opening bid of one in a suit, with hands either better or worse than the previous examples given.

If second or third hand opened with *one diamond,* and you were next hand holding any of the previous or the following hands:

(1)	(2)	(3)
♠ K Q J 9 8 2	♠ A K J 9 8 6	♠ J 10 9 8 6 3
♡ K 6	♡ 4	♡ 7 5
◇ 7 5	◇ Q 2	◇ 4
♣ 8 6 4	♣ 8 6 4 3	♣ Q 7 5 2

(4)	(5)
♠ A J 10 7 4 3	♠ Q J 10 8 6 3
♡ 6 4	♡ 7 3
◇ 9 4	◇ 3
♣ K 6 2	♣ J 9 8 5

You should overcall with *two spades* on each of the above. You have a passing partner and a bidding opponent, which makes game for your side virtually impossible—and a disruptive call most attractive.

In some of the five above examples, a higher pre-empt is not an implausible action if the opponents are vulnerable (and you are not). In match-point play, in Hands (1), (2), (3), and (5), a bid of *three spades* is a reasonable gamble. We appreciate that this higher pre-empt may go against the grain—but certainly no one using weak jump overcalls could seriously quarrel with a jump to *two spades* on any of the above five illustrations. Hand (4), in our opinion, is too good defensively for a pre-emptive jump to three spades.

III. Responding to Weak Jump Overcalls

As always in pre-emptive situations, the player who makes the pre-emptive bid is not usually confronted with very difficult decisions. He merely learns the holdings on which the pre-empt should be made, then inserts the call when the proper situation arises. It is his partner who has all the difficult problems. He must judge where, and how far, to go in each instance.

One constant exists: the jump overcaller's hand is reasonably restricted as to both the length of the suit and the high cards held. Discipline will pay dividends here. The responder knows almost the precise value of the pre-emptor's hand, but the pre-emptor knows nothing of partner's hand. Only the latter knows the approximate joint assets of the combined hands. Surely then, the captaincy of the team should be awarded to the responder; and it becomes proper to impose some further discipline on the pre-emptive overcaller by relegating him to a subordinate role.

Let us see what this role should be and how it should be handled by viewing the following situations:

If the bidding proceeds:

	West	North	East	South
1.	1 ♡	2 ♠	Pass	3 ♠
	Pass	?		
2.	1 ♡	2 ♠	3 ♡	3 ♠
	Pass	?		
3.	1 ♡	2 ♠	3 ♡	3 ♠
	4 ♡	Pass	Pass	4 ♠
	5 ♡	?		

In each of the three above bidding sequences, North has made a pre-emptive jump overcall, and South merely raised his suit one or more times. *North, the pre-emptive jump overcaller, must pass!* South is the only one in a position to know whether to go on or not.

The proposition may be better stated as a rule. If the responder's action to the weak jump overcall is merely a raise, or raises, of the bid suit, *the overcaller is barred from further participation in the auction.* All decisions must be left to his partner.

One possible, remote exception might occur in the following situation. North and South are not vulnerable, East and West are vulnerable, and the bidding has proceeded:

West	North	East	South
1 ♡	2 ♠	3 ♡	3 ♠
4 ♡	Pass	5 ♡	5 ♠
Pass	Pass	6 ♡	Pass
Pass	?		

We would presume that *South* has one sure defensive trick—but not two. If South had no defense, he would have sacrificed at six spades since North is presumed to have, at most, one defensive trick. If South had two defensive tricks, he probably would have doubled the six heart contract. North, in this situation, is being asked to double or pass with any holding on which he feels reasonably certain that he can produce a trick. If he can't, he should take the sacrifice at six spades. Any side suit ace or the trump king behind the bidder will be satisfactory for the purpose of making a penalty double. Of course, North might well pass with a possible trump trick, not being certain whether the trick will actually become a trick. But the point is that in this one situation, he *is* being given the option of bidding or passing.

A. Responder Raises the Suit of the Pre-emptive Overcaller

West	North	East	South
1 ◇	2 ♠	Pass	?

East–West vulnerable; North–South not vulnerable. South holds:

(1)	(2)	(3)	(4)
♠ A 8 7 4	♠ Q 8 6 5	♠ K 10 6	♠ K 8 6 5
♡ 8 6	♡ Q 9 3	♡ A 8	♡ 7 2
◇ 10 9 6	◇ 5	◇ 9 6 5 3	◇ 5 3
♣ A J 8 5	♣ K 10 8 4 2	♣ Q 8 7 4	♣ Q 10 8 5 3

Three spades would be our choice on (1), (2), and (3) above. There is a fit, and we cannot be hurt too much at this level. A quick count of our defensive values reveals that our opponents most likely have a game somewhere. We do not intend to sit by and let them saunter unmolested to their spot. You are bidding because *they* can make something. On (4), we would jump to 4 S, as a premature sacrifice.

In all situations of a pre-emptive nature, when the opponents have not as yet got together, the maximum possible, logical, concerted action is desirable. Therefore, a good rule to remember is:

Bid with all *bad hands* that fit;

Bid with all *good hands* that fit.

(5)	(6)	(7)	(8)
♠ 9 8 6 5	♠ A 8 6	♠ K 7	♠ J 10 7
♡ K Q 7	♡ 7	♡ K Q 10 9 5	♡ A 9 4 3
◇ 8	◇ 10 9 6 3	◇ A 8 7	◇ A 9
♣ A Q J 8 6	♣ A K J 10 7	♣ A 9 3	♣ K Q 7 6

We bid *four spades* on each of the above hands. It is our expectation to have a good play for that contract. In this instance, you are bidding because you feel *you can make* something substantial.

B. RESPONDER NAMES A NEW SUIT

It must be borne in mind that the nonvulnerable jump overcall reflects a weak hand which probably contains a suit with very little defensive potential. In many cases, the responder should guide the defense even before the actual need for such action arises. With North–South *not vulnerable,* and East–West vulnerable, let us assume the bidding has proceeded:

West	North	East	South
1 ◇	2 ♠	Pass	?

South holds:

1. ♠ 8 6
   ♡ A J 8 5
   ◇ 7 2
   ♣ K Q J 10 5

South should bid *three clubs* even though there appears to be no great future for his partnership. The bidding of a new suit by South is not forcing upon North. Why, then, has South made this bid? The answer is obvious. A club lead is certainly the best lead against any contract, and will be particularly effective against three no-trump. Opposite partner's weak hand, the opponents may easily gather in nine tricks if a club is not led.

2. ♠ 8 7
   ♡ A Q J 8 5
   ◇ A 10
   ♣ 7 6 3 2

Three hearts should be bid for the same reason outlined in Hand (1) above. If matters get out of hand, how badly can you be hurt at three spades?

3. ♠ J 9 6 4
   ♡ 6 5 3
   ◇ 9 5
   ♣ A K Q 10

Even in the light of the risk of being left in the contract, we would bid *three clubs* with this hand. We are so anxious for a club lead that we are willing to take the risk.

C. The Pre-emptive Overcaller Has a Fit in Partner's Suit

Close analysis of the subsequent situation will be rewarding. The bidding has proceeded, with North–South not vulnerable:

West	North	East	South
1 ♡	2 ♠	Pass	3 ◊
3 ♡	?		

And North holds:

♠ Q J 9 8 6 5
♡ 8
◊ K 10 9 5
♣ 9 2

North should bid *four diamonds*. A raise in partner's suit figures to be the proper action regardless of the type of hand South holds. Admittedly, if you make the raise, the top result may not be attained. However, a big swing against your side must certainly be avoided. If you have either a premium contract or a profitable sacrifice, you reach it. If it turns out that you could have defeated the opponents, your loss figures to be a small one and less than they could have made at a three heart contract (down one trick, doubled for a minus 100 score as contrasted to 140 that the opponents would get for making three hearts).

We strongly believe that the raise of the above type should be given at practically any level. For example, if the bidding has proceeded:

West	North	East	South
1 ♡	2 ♠	Pass	3 ◊
4 ♡	?		

We would bid *five diamonds* with the same North hand.

We repeat—a jump overcaller must give a raise if he has a good fit in the suit bid by partner.

D. Action by the Responder When Both of the Opponents Have Bid

Some change in tactics is logically advantageous when the opponents are aware that each possesses merchandise. For example, if the bidding has proceeded (North–South *not vulnerable;* East–West vulnerable):

West	North	East	South
1 ♡	2 ♠	3 ♡	?

or

West	North	East	South
1 ♡	2 ♠	3 ♣	?

South holds:

1. ♠ K 8 6 5　In this type of situation, it is our belief that the best
   ♡ 7 5　action is to *pass*. We do not wish to push our opponents
   ◇ A 8 4 2　into some premium contract which they might not arrive
   ♣ 8 7 5　at on their own steam. If it is reached, then we can use
   our discretion as to whether or not to sacrifice.

2. ♠ Q 8　We recommend a raise to *three spades*. Although your
   ♡ Q J 9 5　trump holding is only a doubleton, it is adequate, since
   ◇ A 10 8 4　your partner is marked with a six-card suit. We want the
   ♣ K 10 9　opponents to bid more, and we are speeding up the
   process. Our bid crowds the bidding, and less bidding
space is afforded them for interchanging information.

From the above examples, it can be seen that we don't believe
in prodding the opposition when uncertainty exists as to whether
they'll land in their best contract, but we do push them when we
are desirous of their going forward.

E. THE PRE-EMPTIVE SAVE

If the bidding has proceeded, with East–West vulnerable, and
North–South not vulnerable:

West	North	East	South
1 ◇	2 ♠	3 ♡	?

and South holds:

(1)	(2)	(3)
♠ K 7 6 4	♠ K 10 6 4 3	♠ K 7 5 4
♡ 9	♡ 7 5	♡ Q 10 5
◇ Q 10 7	◇ 3 2	◇ 8
♣ A J 9 5 2	♣ A Q 9 5	♣ K J 6 4 3

An immediate jump to *four spades* is our choice on the three
above hands. When East bids at the three-level in a new, higher-
ranking suit, the opposition will certainly contract for a makable
game. Based on our holdings, a sacrifice seems wise. Therefore we
sacrifice promptly and put the pressure on the opposition. Now they
must guess whether to double us or bid five in one of their suits.

CHAPTER 16

The Take-Out Double

Although the subject of the take-out double has been covered most capably and exhaustively by many writers, it has been our observation that a large segment of the bridge-playing public uses this most potent weapon with a great deal of indiscretion. Especially in duplicate bridge is the take-out double misused, or misapplied. The aim of our contribution is to amplify and clarify in this important field where help is sorely needed.

With the advent of the point count, an old take-out double disease has taken on a new name. Where formerly we heard: "I had an opening bid behind his opening bid," the present refrain is: "He opened, but I also had a 13-point hand." Both statements were offered as complete justification for making the take-out double. But they have not made a case. They are merely half-truths.

A take-out double immediately over an opening bid says: "If my right-hand opponent had not opened the bidding, I probably would have—though not necessarily so. In addition to the possession of at least 2½ defensive tricks, my holding will serve as a good dummy in support of any suit you may be forced to name. If my hand does not provide a good dummy for the suit you mention, I have an excellent suit of my own, or I can take care of myself in any subsequent bidding sequence that progresses normally."

There are several points to absorb from the above:

First: You promise to provide a good dummy for the suit your partner names.

Second: You promise to provide 2½ defensive tricks in case partner should subsequently decide to make a penalty double.

Third: You do not actually promise to produce 13 or more points. You only hint that your hand is the equal of an opening bid.

Should you not meet all the requirements, your match-point results will be more gratifying if you refrain from doubling for a takeout. Having erred in your ways, however, be gracious enough to admit your own shortcomings if an unproductive end results.

Suppose you held this hand:

> ♠ A 8 6 3
> ♡ 4
> ♢ A 10 7 2
> ♣ A K 5 4

Surely you would be planning to open the bidding. But before it is your turn, your right-hand opponent opens with *one spade*. Would you now double merely because you have better than an opening bid?

Without any doubt, you should *pass*. Your hand does not meet all the essentials of a take-out double. If you double, and your partner bids two hearts, which you have every right to expect he will, you will find yourself in a most unhappy position. You cannot relish the thought of playing the hand at two hearts, and to consider any further action is courting disaster. Remember: your partner has spoken at your insistence, and he may have no values whatsoever.

To return for a moment to the point where your right-hand opponent has opened the bidding with a suit you would like to bid, why disturb a situation which will probably terminate profitably? Is it not better to pass and await developments? If the opponents go too far in the suit, you are sure to show a profit. If your partner takes some independent action, you can emerge from the bushes and show the true worth of your hand. If it happens that the hand is passed out at the one level, we feel that you will get better than an average score more often than not.

A different situation, with far less high-card count, is the following hand:

♠ 2
♡ A 9 6 2
◇ A 10 5 3
♣ K 10 7 4

If your right-hand opponent opens the bidding with *one spade*, you should double with this hand, even though you possess but 11 points in high cards and *would not* have opened the bidding had you had the initial opportunity. However, you have the required three defensive tricks (the club king behind the opening bidder is almost sure to produce a trick). Your hand will become a good dummy, regardless of which unbid suit your partner names. In fact, your hand will grow in stature. In support for any suit your partner names, you have 14 points. You do not figure to be badly off at the two-level, no matter how meager your partner's possessions are.

To sum up: you may have a take-out double with as few as 11 high-card points; but you do not necessarily have a take-out double even though you possess as many as 16 high-card points.

I. Inviting the Other Major

Since the ability to spread a good dummy is one of the distinguishing features of most take-out doubles, it quite logically follows that when you double one major suit, you usually will be able to furnish fine support for the other major suit.

When an opponent has opened the auction with *one spade*, and you hold this hand:

♠ 2
♡ A 6 5 3
◇ A K 9 5 2
♣ Q 8 5

you should *double*.

No matter which suit your partner mentions, you will not be embarrassed. If your partner bids the other major suit—hearts—you will be delighted. If he should respond with clubs, you are still in the position to show the diamond suit at the level of two.

On the other hand, if you were dealt these cards:

♠ 7 5
♡ 6 2
◇ A K J 8 3
♣ A Q 9 4

and the right-hand opponent starts the auction with *one spade*, you should content yourself with a mere overcall of *two diamonds*. If you prefer to double to show your opening bid, notice that you will not provide a good dummy should your partner respond in hearts. If, in that event, you try to rectify the situation by proceeding to three diamonds, you are treading on dangerous ground.

With the first of these two preceding hands, the double invited a heart response, and if it were not forthcoming, you could content yourself with the knowledge that hearts was not the spot to play the hand. In the situation that followed, if you invite a heart response by doubling, you are almost a sure bet to be wrong. But if your partner can respond to your diamond overcall with a free bid in hearts, you can now expect to be in the right spot.

II. More Than a Double

In some instances, where your hand is of sufficient strength to warrant exploration of that power at higher levels, you may reveal that great power by first making a take-out double and subsequently showing your suit. For example, if your right-hand adversary bids *one spade,* and you hold either of these hands:

(1)	(2)
♠ 6 3	♠ 6
♡ Q 2	♡ 9 6 3
◇ A K Q 6 3	◇ A K Q 10 5 4
♣ A Q J 9	♣ A Q 10

you would be perfectly justified in *doubling*, with the intention of bidding diamonds at the three-level after your partner responds. Such a procedure announces a powerful take-out double, because you have pushed the bidding to the range of three without any definite knowledge of your partner's strength (he could have zero points!).

With both of these hands, you have partial support for the other major, support which would be considered adequate if partner is able to rebid the suit.

III. Responding to the Double

More often than not, you will have a poor hand when called upon to respond to partner's take-out double. As depressed as you might be, however, at the prospect of entering the auction, you should bear in mind that partner doesn't expect you to have a robust holding. The equivalent of two opening bids has already been announced by the opening bidder and the doubler. What little there is remaining is divided between you and the opening bidder's partner. Adopt an optimistic viewpoint if you possess even a smattering of strength.

When responding to a take-out double:

> 6, 7 points give you a *fair* hand.
> 8, 9 points give you a *good* hand.
> 10 or more points give you a hand with which you will usually have a good play for game. With 10 or more points, you will make a jump response to partner's take-out double.

A. PREFER TO SHOW MAJOR SUITS

Holding a five-card minor suit and a four-card major suit after your partner has made a take-out double, you should prefer to respond with the four-card major suit, as against the minor suit. When your partner has doubled the opening bid of *one heart,* and you hold:

♠ Q 10 7 2
♡ 6 3
◇ K 10 7 3 2
♣ J 4

you should bid *one spade,* for which suit your partner will undoubtedly have very good support. If you are presented with a second opportunity, you may elect to show the diamonds.

B. WITH TWO FOUR-CARD MAJORS

Consider the situations where your partner has made a take-out double over an opening one diamond bid, and you hold the following hands:

(1)	(2)
♠ Q 10 6 2	♠ Q 10 6 2
♡ 10 8 7 5	♡ A J 7 4
◇ 8 4 3	◇ 10 8 2
♣ 5 2	♣ J 4

The modest holding in Hand (1) will not give you any grand ideas, but you cannot pass. Simply bid *one heart.* Since you do not intend to bid again (unless forced) you should name the lower of your two four-card major suits. This will give your partner the opportunity to bid a spade at the one-level with some holding such as this:

♠ A J 9 8 3
♡ A Q 9
◊ 7 2
♣ Q 9 7

Suppose, however, that you had responded with your spade suit, merely because it was stronger than the hearts, and your doubling partner held this hand:

♠ A J 9
♡ A Q 9 6 2
◊ 7 5
♣ K 9 3

He would not feel justified in bidding two hearts over your spade response, and, in fact, he would have no reason to do so. It simply boils down to the proposition that if you bid correctly, you will end in the most profitable contract with greater frequency.

Conversely, with Hand (2), you should mention the spades first. You intend to make a free bid later on (you did not have enough to make a jump response at your first opportunity), and at that point you will bid the suit (hearts) that ranks directly below the suit you named first, thereby giving your partner a choice of either of your suits, at the same level.

C. NO-TRUMP OR A SUIT

Following are two distinctly different types of hands held after partner has doubled for a take-out:

(1)	(2)
♠ K 10 6 3	♠ J 5
♡ Q 10 9 4	♡ Q 10 9 4
◊ J 9 3	◊ Q J 9 6 3
♣ K 4	♣ K 4

In both situations, your partner has doubled the opening bid of *one heart*. What should you do?

With Hand (1), you should waste no time in bidding your "other major." Your partner has doubled hearts. He would love to hear that you have four spades. Give him the good news without delay. The point to remember in such a situation is that you should not become enamored with the stoppers you hold in hearts, and fall into the bad habit of bidding no-trump. Your partner, by doubling, has told you that his hand will provide a good dummy if you bid a suit. When you have the other major suit, tell him what he wants to know.

With Hand (2), however, the situation is altered slightly. Here you do not have the unbid major suit. It is obvious that your partner is well-prepared in spades and clubs. There is little to be gained by naming the diamond suit. Your most profitable course would be to try for a no-trump contract, by bidding one no-trump. However, if your two clubs were both small cards, your hand would hardly be worth the no-trump call. It would then be of the suit type, and a two diamond response would be in order.

D. DON'T PASS

It is important to remember that not knowing exactly what to do in no way justifies a pass after your partner has doubled for a takeout. As a matter of fact, the less attractive your hand seems to be, the more important it is that you make a bid. Consider this hand, for instance:

♠ 7 5
♡ Q 10 9 4
◇ 10 8 6 3
♣ 7 5 4

If your partner has doubled *one heart*, comply with his request that you tell him which is your longest suit. Your suit is *diamonds*. Bid it! You do not have anything resembling the requirements for bidding one no-trump.* A possible pass should not even be accorded the courtesy of contemplation.

Change the above hand so that the three of diamonds becomes the three of spades, and you have the stock question put to all bridge teachers: What do I do if my only four-card suit is the suit bid by the opponents? We would like to remind you that when these

---

* A one no-trump response to partner's double shows 9–11 points, with a sure stopper in the opponent's suit. For example, if partner doubles an opening one heart bid, one no-trump would be bid with: ♠ A 4 ♡ K 9 6 ◇ Q 8 3 2 ♣ J 7 6 3

things happen, you should want to make the cheapest response you can. The cheapest response is the suit that ranks just above the doubled suit. Bid *one spade,* and relax.

Likewise, with this hand:

> ♠ 10 5 2
> ♡ 10 6 3
> ◇ 9 7 5 4
> ♣ 6 3 2

If partner has doubled one diamond, you should bid *one heart.*

E. Bid Four-Card Suit

The following is debatable, but here is our view on it.

Your partner doubles an opening bid of one heart, the next hand passes, and you hold:

> ♠ 9 5 2
> ♡ 6 4 3
> ◇ 6 5 2
> ♣ 9 7 5 3

You may respond with *one spade* or *two clubs.* Those who champion the one spade response contend, with reason, that partner figures to be prepared for that response, and, furthermore, that there is less chance of your being doubled for penalty at the level of one. We believe, however, that there is greater safety in numbers. We would not consider a response in a three-card suit when a four-card suit is available, even if it necessitates bidding at a higher level. The very fact partner may have a fit in spades may be used as an argument against that response. When he thinks that your side holds the top suit, he may be encouraged to compete and may do so at a level that is disastrous.

F. The Penalty Pass

The examples cited above emphasize the point that a player may not pass out his partner's take-out double merely because he doesn't have anything to bid. But the question that naturally arises and plagues many players is: What kind of holding would permit me to convert my partner's take-out double into a pass for penalties? You may do so only when you are *absolutely certain* in feeling that the contract will be defeated.

Naturally, you will not accept any small penalty whenever you have better prospects through bidding. Your partner, the take-out doubler, promises to provide three tricks defensively. Therefore, *as a minimum*, you must be able to contribute four tricks in defense. Of these, *at least three tricks must be in the trump suit itself.* You must, however, consider that your trump holding lies under the declarer, which is a distinct disadvantage.

You must be prepared for an opening trump lead from partner, which is certain to be made if he has a trump. One of the few rules considered to be close to an "always" rule is that the opening leader invariably leads a trump when a take-out double is left in for penalty. The reason for the rule is apparent. You are saying: "They shouldn't be playing the contract in this suit. We should." What do you usually do first when you play a hand? You extract trumps. Your side, when defending, will hasten to do this so that the declarer will be unable to make any small trumps by ruffing.

In illustration, observe the following:

West	North	East	South
1 ◇	Double	Pass	?

You, South, hold:

(1)	(2)
♠ 5 3 2	♠ 6
♡ 7 5 4	♡ 8 5
◇ K 10 9 6 3	◇ J 9 6 4 2
♣ 4 3	♣ Q 8 6 4 3
Bid 1 ♡	Bid 2 ♣

Do not leave either of the above in (at 1 D doubled) on the theory that you would rather settle for a small loss, which the fulfilled contract nets the enemy, than face the trouble that a bid may bring. Suffer a loss if you must, but don't give up without putting up a struggle. The effect on your partnership morale will be devastating if they fulfill the contract, which they certainly figure to do.

(3)	(4)
♠ 7 6	♠ K 5
♡ A 4 2	♡ 7 5
◇ Q J 10 9 8	◇ Q J 10 8 6 5
♣ 8 7 4	♣ 6 3 2

With the two above hands, we would pass partner's take-out double of the opening one diamond bid, but they are minimum holdings for the action.

Common sense may permit you to pass with far less in certain situations. If, for example, the bidding has proceeded:

East	South	West	North
(Vul.)	(Not vul.)		
1 ◇	Pass	1 ♡	Double
2 ◇	Pass	Pass	Double
Pass	?		

You, South, hold:

♠ K 5 2
♡ 9 6 3
◇ Q 10 9 7
♣ J 6 3

You should *pass*. In your position *behind* the two diamond bidder, you figure to take three tricks with your holding. When your partner repeated his take-out double, he advertised a very strong hand. You may now count on him for four tricks. It adds to a 500-point set, and even if you have miscalculated slightly, you will surely beat the contract one trick, for a plus score of 200.

G. WE MAY HAVE A GAME

A more comfortable situation would be one where your partner doubled *one club* and you held this hand:

♠ A J 3
♡ Q J 7 4
◇ K J 9
♣ 8 6 3

With *10 or more points* opposite your partner's take-out double, you should always expect to have a good play for game. You can convey this message to your partner by bidding one more than necessary. In this case, *bid two hearts.* You will observe that you do not need a five-card suit to jump the bidding after your partner has doubled. Your response shows the general strength of your hand, and only the most naïve partner would expect you to have more than a four-card suit before it is rebid.

In the same vein, but by a different route, is the following:

♠ Q 8 4
♡ Q 10 9
◇ K Q 8 5
♣ K J 7

When your partner has doubled the opening club bid, you should in this situation ignore your four-card diamond suit and prefer instead to give your partner a good general picture of your hand by responding with *two no-trump*.

One does not always ignore the minor suits, however. With this hand:

♠ Q J 10
♡ 7 3
◇ K Q J 8 4
♣ K J 4

you should respond to your partner's double of one heart with three diamonds—an invitation for your partner to bid three no-trump if he can assume responsibility for the heart suit. If, on the other hand, partner has doubled an opening spade bid, you should give but casual thought to the diamond suit, and respond with *two no-trump*. Your partner, having doubled spades, can take care of the heart suit.

At times, when your partner doubles, say an opening bid of one club, you will have a hand with which you feel your side can make a game, but you have no adequate bid available. For example:

♠ K 10 8 4
♡ K 10 7 3
◇ K Q 3 2
♣ 6

With this type of hand, the proper action is to bid *two clubs,* a cue bid of the opponent's suit. If your partner now bids a major suit, you will raise him to game in his suit. If instead, he bids no-trump or diamonds, you will raise his bid.

Generally speaking, the cue bid of 'the opponent's suit shows first round control of their suit, either the ace or a void. The above type of situation is the exception, and is used to denote a good hand with support for the unbid suits.

IV. When Partner's Opening Bid Is Doubled for Takeout

The tempo of modern bidding has been so accelerated that you will find yourself shut out of many an auction if you do not take advantage of every reasonable opportunity to make your presence felt. When your partner's opening bid has been doubled for takeout, you should have some very definite thoughts on what course of action you should take under various standard circumstances.

It should be noted that vulnerability does not influence the doubler's partner.

A. To Bid or to Pass?

There is an apparent misconception that a bid over a take-out double is a sign of weakness. The only way to describe a weak hand is to *pass*. The only reason you should ever want to bid is to convey some message to your partner about either your distribution or your strength.

When your partner's opening bid has been doubled and you hold a worthless or near worthless hand, without any features worth talking about, you should gladly pass, pleased not to be embroiled in the auction and welcoming the opportunity of allowing the battle to be waged without your contribution. Consider the following examples, after your partner's opening *one club* bid has been doubled:

1. ♠ 7 4 3   *Pass.* You have neither high cards nor a good suit
    ♡ J 9 7 6 3   worth mentioning. Dispel any fear you might have
    ◇ 9 8 6   that the hand will be played at one club doubled.
    ♣ 5 3   If partner has opened on a three-card suit, or a
weak four-card suit, he should be the best judge of the manner of extricating himself from the mess. If he wants to hear about your anemic suit, he will let you know. The chances are better than 100-to-1, however, that doubler's partner will bid before your partner has to make such a decision. A bid by you will serve no useful purpose, and might lead to a lack of trust in your bids in similar situations.

2. ♠ Q J 8 6 5   *Pass.* Though this hand is slightly better than the
    ♡ 8 6 3   one in the previous illustration, there is still no
    ◇ J 7 5   merit to any plan for inserting a bid. To name a
    ♣ 8 6   suit in this sequence should show *about six points,*
                   which might be shaded to five in an emergency.
You have no reason to be panicky—this is not an emergency.

3. ♠ Q J 10 8 6 5   *Bid one spade.* In addition to having a perfectly
    ♡ 8 7 4   good six-card spade suit, which length you do not
    ◇ J 9 8 5   hold on every hand, there is an emergency. You are
    ♣ —   void in partner's bid suit! It is easy enough to arrive
                         at six points for your holdings, either by counting
your long cards in spades or your void in clubs.

B. SIX TO TEN POINTS

With a good many hands that fall into the six- to ten-point
category—hands with which you intended to make but one bid if
the double had not been inserted—you will obtain the best results
by bidding directly over the double. Should you choose to wait instead, you may find yourself in the position of having the urge to
take some action while at the same time dreading the punishment
which might result from such action.

To illustrate, let us suppose the bidding has proceeded:

North	East	South	West
1 ◇	Double	Pass	1 ♠
Pass	3 ♠	?	

You, South, hold the following hand:

♠ 7 5
♡ A J 9 4 2
◇ 10 4 2
♣ K 7 5

You must admit that you have permitted yourself to be ma-
neuvered into the inglorious position of being slightly "fixed." If
you had shown your smattering of strength by bidding hearts on
the previous round, your partner may have helped in providing
guidance.

Since many similar bidding sequences will readily suggest themselves and you can conjure up many others, we again suggest that
with hands containing moderate values you should make yourself
heard at once if you think you have anything worth talking about.
You may not have an opportunity to do so later.

Consider a few situations where your partner has opened the
auction with *one diamond,* and the next hand has doubled. You
hold:

1. ♠ A 8 6 5   Your seven points in high cards do little to overcome
   ♡ K 9 3   the otherwise flat distribution. Without either a suit
   ◇ 8 7 2   or short suit values you should not need any en-
   ♣ 9 7 4   couragement to *pass*. In fact, you should make up
                      your mind to stay out of the auction entirely unless
   your partner offers some very strong encouragement.

2. ♠ K 8 7   This holding is slightly stronger than the previous
   ♡ Q 7 4   hand, with eight points and the same flat distribution.
   ◇ 9 8 6   You should welcome the opportunity to announce
   ♣ K 10 8 3   your moderate values at this comparatively safe level,
                      by bidding *one no-trump*. Your partner may be suffi-
   ciently influenced to take aggressive action of one kind or another. Over
   an opponent's double, the one no-trump response shows 8–9 points.

3. ♠ A 10 8 7 4   A bid of *one spade* immediately will make your part-
   ♡ 6 4   ner aware of the fact that you have a spade suit and
   ◇ 10 8 7   moderate strength. Failure to inject your bid at this
   ♣ K 9 5   point may well cause you severe embarrassment later,
                      when you have to decide whether you should venture
   in at the three, or even four, level.

4. ♠ 3   For somewhat the same reasons as in the previous
   ♡ K J 10 8 4   hand, you should bid *one heart* now. Moreover, you
   ◇ Q 8 2   may find it expedient to raise your partner's diamond
   ♣ 10 8 7 6   bid later in the auction, providing partner with an
                      even better picture of your hand.

C. The Redouble

When your partner's opening bid has been doubled, you should redouble with (1) *10 or more points in high cards* or (2) with no less than eleven points in support of partner's opening suit (counting short-suit values). However, even with the support for partner's suit you should possess a minimum of 8 points in high cards. With exactly 11 points, including a void or singleton and strong support (at least four cards) for partner's suit, a jump bid in the suit—probably to game—would be better action. Such a procedure is not only relatively safe, but it serves to keep the opponents out of the auction, unless, of course, they have the tickets and the nerve to risk a high-level bid.

With 10 points or more in high cards and less than normal support for partner's suit, do not fret and squirm. *The redouble is called for* and such action by you *emphatically does not promise trump support*. You may, in fact, be void in partner's suit. Your high cards will provide partner with safety to spare if the opponents risk the ill-conceived decision to pass for penalties. The most lucrative penalty premiums are usually returned on such hands where you do not fit your partner's suit, which is a pleasant thing to contemplate, particularly when your side has no game.

The redouble is, conventionally, a request that your partner permit any bid by the opponents to return to you, the redoubler, unless he chooses to double for business before you have the opportunity. While your partner will usually comply with your wish, it is not compulsory that he do so, and he should not if there is some feature of his hand about which you should be warned.

Your partner has opened the bidding with *one spade*, the next hand has doubled, and you hold:

1. ♠ 6
   ♡ A J 8 2
   ◇ K 9 8 4
   ♣ K 10 5 3

This should be a particularly delectable result. You redouble temporarily and sit back, comfortable in the knowledge that you will subsequently double any bid the opponents make. The spoils will be even sweeter to contemplate if the opponents are vulnerable.

Notice that your side may not have a game.

2. ♠ A 9 7 6
   ♡ 7
   ◇ K J 8 3
   ♣ 10 8 7 5

With 11 points in support of spades, 8 of which are in high cards, you should redouble initially, intending to raise the spades at your next turn. Such a course will accurately describe your high-card strength and distributional values to your partner.

3. ♠ 8 4 2
   ♡ 9 6
   ◇ A K J 8 3
   ♣ K 9 8

Holding the same high-card strength as in the first example, you redouble, but with an entirely different plan for future action. At your next opportunity you intend to show your diamond suit. *When the redoubler names a new suit, it is forcing for one round.*

The final contract will depend upon how the auction progresses.

4. ♠ A 9 7 6 4
   ♡ 5
   ◇ K J 8 5 2
   ♣ 7 3

While you have sufficient values to redouble, you should forego such action. Even if you do redouble, as your next step you most certainly intend to support your partner's suit with. vigor. Then make your robust bid now, before the enemy has had an opportunity to do any communicating. A direct leap to *four spades* is called for.

5. ♠ K 9 7 5   Now is the time to show that you have some support
   ♡ 8 5   for your partner's suit. Bid *two spades* immediately
   ◊ Q 8 7 4   over the take-out double, which indicates that you
   ♣ 10 3 2   hold the requirements for a light raise if the double
                    had not been interjected. (A double raise of partner's
suit immediately over the take-out double shows that you hold the where-
withal for a solid raise if the double had not intervened.)

6. ♠ Q 10 8 5 4   This hand is at least one playing trick better than the
   ♡ 7 3   hand above. It would be considered a good raise
   ◊ K J 7 2   without the double. You should jump to *three spades*,
   ♣ 9 6   which cannot be construed as showing anything
                    better than you have (you didn't redouble), and it
will present an irritating obstacle to the opponents.

7. ♠ A 9 8 7   This is a good hand. You do not have to worry about
   ♡ 8   the opponents making any bid that will cause you
   ◊ K J 5 3   distress, since there isn't much question about your
   ♣ Q 10 7 2   satisfaction with a four spade contract. You *redouble*
                    first, and *jump in spades* at your next opportunity,
showing 13–15 points. A check back to Hand 2 will recall that to redouble
and simply raise the suit later shows 8 points in high cards, and 11 or 12
points counting your distributional values. Going further, to redouble and
then leap to four spades would show a hand just short of jump shift
proportions—16–18 points and strong trump support. In the latter sequence, your partner will try for a slam with any tangible excess values
beyond those needed for a minimum opening bid.

8. ♠ K J 8   With this hand you have redoubled after your part-
   ♡ 10 7   ner's opening *one heart bid* has been doubled. Your
   ◊ A 9 8 5   left-hand opponent follows with a one spade bid,
   ♣ Q 6 5 3   your partner and right-hand opponent pass. Your side
                    is vulnerable, the opponents are not. What action
should you take? Just bid *one no-trump*. Your partner will then know that
you have but a minimum redouble—about 10 or 11 points—because you
did not take more vigorous action. With a better redouble, you would
have bid two no-trump. The one no-trump bid by the redoubler, unlike
a simple bid of a new suit, is not forcing.

You will find it particularly remunerative to vary your tactics
once in a while when you hold a hand which warrants a minimum
redouble but lacks support for partner's suit. In some cases, partic-

ularly when the opponents are vulnerable and you are not, you may be presented with an opportunity to double a higher contract for penalties if you lie dormant after the opponent's take-out double. As an example, you hold this hand:

♠ 10 8 4
♡ 7 6
◇ A Q 3 2
♣ K J 9 5

and the bidding proceeds:

North	East	South	West
1 ♡	Double	Pass	1 ♠
Pass	2 ♠	?	

You are sitting South. Without the fit in partner's suit, and with the 10 points in high cards needed for a redouble, you decide to play "injun," hoping to lure the opposition one step higher than they would venture if you had redoubled.

It is quite conceivable that East, with little more than a minimum take-out double, will raise his partner's takeout, since he is not entirely sure whether South or West holds the balance of power. In the situation we show above, it is clear to you that West is "broke," and you pounce for the kill by *doubling for penalties*. We hasten to caution you that such waiting tactics seldom work if you hold more than the bare minimum requirements for a redouble, since, in that case, East will probably make no forward move.

V. When There Has Been Action Over Partner's Take-out Double

If, following a take-out double by your partner, the partner of the opening bidder makes some bid, you should consider your hand from the standpoint of being able to make a free bid. Remember, you are now relieved of your obligation to bid. You will bid only because you want to, not because you have to. The requirements for a free bid are approximately the same as in responding to your partner's opening bid.

A. AFTER AN INTERVENING BID

Your partner has *doubled one diamond,* the next opponent has bid *one heart,* and you hold:

1. ♠ J 8 4 3 2
    ♡ 7 2
    ◇ J 8 5
    ♣ 9 7 6

    While it is true that your partner would be pleased to hear you bid spades, a free bid by you would advertise more values than you possess. If you *pass,* as you should, your partner will double again if he is desirous of hearing you speak.

2. ♠ K J 9 7 4 2
    ♡ 7 2
    ◇ 8 5
    ♣ J 10 5

    You have a perfectly respectable free bid of *one spade.* In fact, replace the jack of clubs with the king (a total of 7 points), and you should respond freely even if your spade suit were only four cards in length.

Do not have any fears that your partner will play you for more strength than you have when making the free bid. The requirements for jump bids In response to partner's take-out doubles are just the same after an intervening bid as without the bid (10 or more points). Thus, your simple free bid has a floor and a ceiling.

We should not leave this phase of our subject without calling attention to some common chicanery. The bidding has gone:

North	East	South	West
1 ♡	Double	1 ♠	?

and you, West, hold something like this:

    ♠ A 10 9 6 3
    ♡ 7 4
    ◇ Q 8 3
    ♣ K 10 7

Your partner, in doubling hearts, expressed a desire that you bid spades. Thus, when the opponent named that suit, he was trying to muddy the water. After you *double,* they will undoubtedly seek a safer haven, probably at two hearts. South has probably bid the spades with a singleton or a doubleton. He hopes to entice you into falling into the rhythm of doubling, subsequently taking a shot at him in a contract where his loss will not be damaging.

While a double by you is for business after your partner has made an earlier take-out double, the original doubler must remain on the alert to assure a maximum contract for his side. If he, East, held these cards:

♠ K J 8 4
♡ 9 6
◇ A K J 2
♣ Q 9 8

and the bidding continued:

North	East	South	West
1 ♡	Double	1 ♠	Double
Pass	Pass	2 ♡	Pass
Pass	?		

he should do a little serious thinking. Something is happening! He should inform his partner that the spade suit is theirs by now bidding *two spades*. West thus far in the auction has held South in suspicion, but could not be certain. But East has been armed with the knowledge that West probably held five spades and a fair hand. When East bids *two spades*, the cat is out of the bag.

B. AFTER A REDOUBLE

The intervening redouble, like its brother the intervening bid, relieves the doubler's partner of bidding. A pass in this sequence does not show a desire to play the redoubled contract for penalties. On the contrary, the pass tells partner that you have no reason for saying anything. The original doubler is "on his own" about selecting a course of action.

Nevertheless, a bid over a redouble does not necessarily show the strength for a free bid. It may, in fact, be injected merely for the purpose of showing a suit, if no bidding space is consumed by the effort. Theoretically, the bidding has advertised the presence of three strong hands, and little or nothing remains for the fourth player.

The proposition is best illustrated by example. Therefore, examine the following hand:

♠ 8 7 5
♡ J 5 2
◇ 9 5 4 3
♣ Q 8 4

The bidding has proceeded:

North	East	South	West
1 ♡	Double	Redouble	?

You have nothing to gain by bidding two diamonds, and you will have prevented partner from bidding either one spade or two clubs, both of which are cheaper bids, in that they consume less space. If your diamond bid happens to be doubled, and partner does not care for it, he will be obligated to rescue at a higher level.

If, however, on the same sequence, you hold:

♠ 10 8 7 5 2	♠ Q 10 7 5
♡ 8 3	♡ 8 5 4
♢ 9 7 6 or	♢ 9 7 6
♣ 8 6 5	♣ 8 5 2

there can be no objection to a bid of *one spade* directly over South's redouble. In each case, even though you have nothing in the way of strength, you can announce your suit without consuming any bidding space.

If the bidding had followed the same course, however, and you held this hand:

♠ 8 7
♡ J 5 2
♢ 10 9 7 5 3 2
♣ 7 5

you do want to tell your partner something. You want to tell him that you have a place to play the hand. The place is *diamonds*. Make the bid with alacrity; it guarantees no offensive or defensive strength.

With strength over a redouble, you have to decide from the vulnerability conditions whether to make an immediate strength-showing response or to wait until the psychic bidder has been smoked out. There can be but three opening bids in one deal; so if you have strength, someone at the table is "horsing around."

This is a ticklish situation, and one which will require that you exercise sound judgment. You should make a jump bid with any holding on which you would have jumped without the intervention of the redouble. With more moderate hands, a pass is probably the better course of action. If you choose to bid, the opener will probably pass, as will your partner, who can only infer that you are merely showing a suit without high-card strength. In the latter case, if the redouble is psychic, the hand may be passed out.

CHAPTER 17

The Penalty Double

In a game where a small difference is usually all-important, the use of the penalty double would naturally be expanded. Differences such as 100 rather than 50, or 100 rather than 200, or 100 as against 90 have little significance at rubber bridge, but could easily mean the difference between a bad score and a good score at match-point play.

Let no one assume that we advocate a general policy of doubling at the drop of a hat when playing at match points. In most situations, your attitude toward the penalty double should be the same as it is in rubber bridge: you double when you can visualize a set of more than one trick. There are, however, many recurring match-point situations where a very close double is virtually a must. Since the margin for error will be small, good judgment and experience will be even more valuable than in normal circumstances.

These dangerous situations will engage our closest attention. We do, however, deem it necessary to review more or less comprehensively the entire subject of the penalty double for a clear understanding of the match-point approach.

Rather naïvely, perhaps, we would like to emphasize the obvious: Penalty doubles are based on the number of tricks the partnership estimates it can take on defense. A commonsense, natural approach will serve best in estimating your own trick-taking power on any given hand. But a chart which presents a reasonable degree of accuracy is available for estimating the number of tricks your partner can be expected to produce. If your partner has:

Made an opening bid	3 tricks
Made a take-out double	2½ tricks
Opened with 1 NT	4 tricks
Overcalled at the one-level	1 trick
Overcalled at the two-level	2 tricks
Opened with a pre-emptive bid	½ trick

it follows logically that if, on any of the above, partner has taken additional action indicating more than minimum-expected strength, it is proper to revise your estimate upward.

Your own hand, to repeat, is estimated in a commonsense, arithmetic manner. The high cards are easily totaled, but keep in mind the hints that follow.

In the trump suit, be realistic. If you hold the K J 9 x *behind* the bidder, it is worth three defensive tricks if his partner has not raised. The same holding is not worth more than one trick if it is *in front of* the bidder. If the opposition shows unmistakable signs of a misfit—where dummy cannot lead through you more than once—then revise upward again, to two defensive tricks.

Honor holdings in short suits can be counted at full value in normal circumstances, but you should *never* rely on taking more than *2 tricks* in a side suit.

Here is the way you count defensive tricks in a side suit:

A K Q	2 tricks
A K	2 tricks
A Q	1½ tricks
A	1 trick
K Q	1 trick
K x	½ trick

Odd jacks, tens, and even queens, are only "plus" values, having no numerical trick-taking value. However, when grouped with higher honors in the same suit, a queen, jack, or ten will usually produce at least one defensive trick, and should be computed as such (A Q J, A Q 10, K Q J, K Q 10, etc.).

The possession of four of the enemy's trumps is a valuable asset, and will usually produce a trick except where the opponents have shown extreme length or unusual strength.

The length of a suit, especially the combined length, that is yours and partner's, has great effect on the defensive strength in that suit. For example:

A K x is obviously better defensively than A K x x x, for the opponents are less likely to trump the second round of the suit. Similarly, A K x x x is not worth as much defensively when partner supports you as when he evidences a dislike for your suit. Logically, therefore, you should double more quickly when you are short in partner's suit; and double less quickly when you are long in his suit.

In order to clear the way for a discussion of those penalty doubles that demand a high degree of delicacy, we must first dispose of some doubles that are absolutely mandatory in any trained partnership. The "mandatory" feature means that you cannot permit the opponents to play their contract undoubled. You may, of course, take any one of dozens of other conceivable actions. Here are the situations where the opponents must not be permitted to play an undoubled contract.

1. If you or your partner has opened with a strong two demand bid (or an artificial strong two club bid), either your side will purchase the contract, or the opponents *will be doubled* at their contract. They cannot be permitted to play the hand undoubled.

2. If either you or partner has opened the bidding with a standard two no-trump bid (22–24 points) or a three no-trump bid, either your side purchases the contract, or the opponents will be doubled at their contract.

3. If the bidding clearly indicates that your side figures to have much the better of the cards, your side must either buy the contract, or the opponents will be doubled at their contract. For example, when either you or your partner opens the bidding and the other makes a strong response:

	(a)		(b)
You	Partner	You	Partner
1 ♠	2 NT	1 ♠	3 ♠

An entire sequence might proceed:

(1) North	East	South	West
1 ♡	1 ♠	2 NT	3 ♠
Pass	Pass	?	

or

(2) North	East	South	West
1 ♡	1 ♠	3 ♡	3 ♠
Pass	Pass	?	

On the two above illustrations, *South must either make a bid or double.* He cannot elect to pass.

(3) South	West	North	East
1 ♡	1 ♠	3 ♡	3 ♠
4 ♡	4 ♠	Pass	Pass
?			

On the above three sequences, the passes by North came after strong bidding by the North–South partnership. It was thus established in the minds of each partner that their side possessed much the better of the cards in the particular deal. North's pass in each case is described as a *forcing pass,* shifting the final decision to South, who must either double or bid. He is not allowed to pass.

In (3), note that the bidding might have proceeded so that South passed to North, thus forcing the final decision on the latter. That is, if South had passed instead of bidding four hearts and if West had then passed, North would have been compelled either to bid four hearts or to double three spades. In this case, a pass by South (in lieu of bidding four hearts) would not necessarily have been a confession of weakness; rather it would have been a confession of indecision, a statement that he was uncertain what to do. If his holding indicated some positive action, he would have taken it. If he didn't wish to go on, he would have doubled. Nor does South guarantee to abide with North's decision to double after the latter makes that bid. An opportunity for crafty maneuvering is presented in these types of situations. South may pass, knowing that North's probable action will be to double. He may want the opponents to hear that double, after which he will proceed to four hearts, which he was aiming for all along. He hopes thereby to eliminate further competition by the opposition.

Partnerships should not guess in these situations in respect to the pass or penalty double, even if occasionally an opponent succeeds in fulfilling his doubled contract. The partner who is last to speak must accept the responsibility, and he must either bid or double. He cannot pass.

I. Penalty Doubles at the Level of One or Two

The juiciest penalties are obtained at the level of one or two. This circumstance develops because some player has ventured into the bidding, perhaps even rightfully, before it is revealed which partnership holds the better cards—and he gets ambushed in between two strong hands. But when a good pair ventures a voluntary game or slam contract, they will rarely be beaten a sizable amount, for they will usually have the tickets to justify their co-operative venture.

Therefore a player must be ready to seize the opportunities for low-level penalty doubles as they present themselves. A word of caution is necessary. Almost all of these penalty doubles come after partner has taken some positive action in the auction. Thus the doubler is expecting his partner to provide certain assistance in defeating the contract. If such assistance will not be forthcoming, then a withdrawal may be in order. What we are trying to say is that in order to achieve maximum results, low-level penalty doubles must be cooperative and not single-handed, binding decisions made by the doubler. You will, of course, lose some lucrative doubles when your partner fails to sit for them and "takes out." However, in the long run, you will be better off if each partner is permitted his say in the final decision.

Suppose the bidding proceeds (regardless as to vulnerability):

North	East	South
1 ♡	1 ♠	?

and South holds:

1. ♠ K 10 8 7 6 5
   ♡ 6 2
   ◊ 9 7 5
   ♣ 8 6

   South should *pass*. A low-level double should not be made unless the doubler can contribute substantially toward the defeat of some other contract.

2. ♠ A J 9 7 2
   ♡ 9 2
   ◊ K 10 7 4
   ♣ J 2

   South should double, for this is a hand in which the penalty may be juicy but, as yet, no premium contract is available to your side. Generally speaking, in this type of situation, *double* if the overcalling opponent has bid what you were *very desirous* of bidding.

When the bidding proceeds:

North	East	South
1 ♠	2 ♡ or	?
	2 ♢ or	
	2 ♣	

the match-point player is usually confronted with different and more perplexing problems than his rubber-bridge counterpart. At rubber bridge if you double a part-score contract such as two hearts or two spades and they make it, you have doubled them into a game, which is a major catastrophe. On the other hand, if the over-calling opponents succeed in fulfilling a doubled contract of two clubs or two diamonds, it is only a minor setback, since the total point loss is slight. But at duplicate play, the fulfillment of any doubled contract—2 S, 2 H, 2 D, 2 C—will probably prove to be equally fatal. Furthermore, the rubber-bridge player can proceed to the next deal with unruffled calm if he is forced to accept a penalty which is a little less than he would have obtained if his side had kept bidding instead of doubling the opponents. On the other hand, if the match-point player collects 300 points when he could have fulfilled, say, a nonvulnerable game (worth 400 points), the match-point difference can be considerable. How is one to judge in these treacherous match-point situations? The vulnerability conditions, the fit or lack of a fit with partner, the size of the holding, etc., all of which enter into the determination of whether the chances of making a game are good or bad, will have a great effect on rendering each decision.

Let us examine a few cases:

North	East	South
1 ♠	2 ♡	?

(1)	(2)	(3)
♠ 8 4	♠ 7 5	♠ 5 4
♡ K J 9 6	♡ 10 7 5 2	♡ J 9 3
♢ A J 10 9	♢ A Q 10 3	♢ A K 7 5
♣ 10 8 2	♣ A J 10	♣ A Q 9 2

Holding Hand (1), you have a routine double of two hearts on any vulnerability. You figure to beat two hearts at least two tricks if partner leaves it in, and no game is as yet in sight. If partner takes out your double, you will be forced to make another decision.

Holding Hands (2) and (3), you must take action since you have far too much to sit passively and await further opportunities. If *they are vulnerable* and you are not, we recommend that you double. They do not figure to take more than six tricks, which will net you a penalty of 500 points to offset the loss of your game. Note that the penalty double is permissible in favorable vulnerability circumstances without the possession of a single trump trick. (Many authorities insist that the possession of at least one *sure* trump trick is a requisite for a penalty double.)

With Hand (2), we would double under any vulnerability conditions, even though such action might at times turn out to be costly. No other action is appealing and without flaws. Bear in mind that you have only 11 points, and in doubling, you deny a good spade fit. Naming your diamond suit at the three-level will automatically lead to a game contract, which you might well not make. By doubling, you inform your partner that you have some assets other than hearts. A bid of two no-trump without a heart stopper is left to souls more intrepid than we are.

With Hand (3), if *we were vulnerable* and they were not, we would bid three diamonds in the hope that we would land successfully on our feet in a game contract. We cannot accept a 300 or 500 point penalty when it is likely that we have a game in hand.

North	East	South
1 ♠	2 ◇	?

(4)	(5)
♠ 7 3	♠ 9 6
♡ K 9 6	♡ J 7 5 2
◇ K 10 8 4	◇ A J 9
♣ A 9 7 5	♣ K Q 9 5

On Hands (4) and (5), in *rubber bridge*, a penalty double by South would be appealing on any vulnerability. You figure to get a profit, whereas a bid *may* net you a loss.

At match-point play, we would double if *they were vulnerable* and we were not. If both sides are vulnerable, we still like the double, since even a one-trick set gets you 200 points to offset the part-score you figure to have. If you have a game or more, partner is privileged to go on after you double. If neither side is vulnerable, it is a very close choice between the double and the free bid of two no-trump. The latter bid would denote a good 10 points, or 11, or just possibly 12. *The two no-trump response is not forcing*, and opener can pass if he opened a hand which is a bit on the light side. If *we were vulnerable* and they were not, we would respond with two no-trump.

The student should note that whenever he is considering a call of two no-trump over the opponents' overcall, he should always give at least some consideration to the possibility of making a penalty double.

II. Opener's Action When Partner Doubles for Penalties

We would like to state that we dislike any rubber-stamp arrangement where partner never takes out his partner's double for penalties. If he will provide much less defensively than could be expected from his prior participation in the auction, then he will usually be better off "running out" instead of "sitting for" the double. We have seen partnerships gloat over the success of such a leave-in with subminimum assets. Success lingers on in the memory, blotting out the bitter failures of similar ventures as though they had never occurred.

Let us assume the bidding has proceeded:

South	West	North	East
1 ♠	2 ◇	Double	Pass
?			

If South holds any of the following hands:

(1)	(2)	(3)
♠ A K 6 4 2	♠ A K 7 4 3	♠ K Q J 9
♡ Q 7 3	♡ K J 9 6	♡ A K J 5
◇ 10 2	◇ 3	◇ 7 5 3
♣ A 6 2	♣ K 8 2	♣ J 6

He should leave the penalty double in. He has a perfectly normal opening bid and possesses the usual, expected, defensive characteristics. Furthermore, he has no assurance that any run-out would provide better results.

If, however, South held these hands:

(4)	(5)	(6)
♠ K Q 10 9 7 5	♠ A Q 10 7 5 4 3	♠ K Q 10 8 5
♡ J 2	♡ 9 6	♡ A J 10 8 4
◇ 7	◇ 5	◇ —
♣ A J 9 5	♣ K J 4	♣ Q 9 5

With Hands (4) and (5), South's opening bid is predicated on distributional values and lacks the three defensive tricks which an opening bidder is supposed to contribute toward the defeat of any low-level contract. He should, therefore, take out to *two spades*.

With Hand (6), South's holding might easily produce three tricks in defense. We would, nevertheless, take out to *two hearts*. We require more than three defensive tricks if we possess a void in the doubled suit. Moreover, we may have a part-score or game in hearts if partner has a fit there and is short in spades, the latter being quite likely.

Sometimes it becomes necessary to take a calculated risk and pass a penalty double even though you have grave doubts about defeating the contract. This is the case when you have reason to believe that a bid by you will result in disaster.

For example, you, sitting South, hold:

♠ A K 7 5 4 3
♡ Q J 3
◇ —
♣ Q J 6 4

The bidding has proceeded:

South	West	North	East
1 ♠	2 ◇	Double	Pass
2 ♠	Pass	Pass	Double
Pass	3 ◇	Double	Pass
?			

It is quite possible that the three diamond contract will not be defeated. However, three spades almost certainly will be unmakable. Therefore a *pass by South* is in order on the basis that "hope is better than no hope."

III. When Your Side Is Doubled for Penalties

The bidding has proceeded:

West	North	East	South
1 ♠	2 ◇	Double	?

You, South, hold:

(1)	(2)
♠ 6 3 2	♠ 5 3
♡ Q 10 9 7 5	♡ A J 7 5 2
◇ —	◇ 4
♣ K 10 9 7 5	♣ Q J 8 5 2

The issues are: Should South rescue? If he does, in which suit?

For some years now, many topflight players have embraced a foreign import to take care of the type of situation depicted above. An analysis of the dilemma which confronts us may point out a reasonably good solution.

It certainly seems probable that partner will be beaten, and perhaps badly, at two diamonds doubled, since that suit is stacked behind him. It is also probable that North holds something in one of your suits, but North can hardly be expected to rescue himself if he possesses but three cards in either hearts or clubs. A run-out by you is also not too appealing, since you don't know which suit to choose. If you choose one and that gets doubled, you may run to the other, but if they keep doubling, you may possibly be running out of your best contract even after you have found it. What, then, is the solution?

If you are willing to concede that South should always be content in match-point play to fulfill *any doubled contract*, then it will be easy to convince you that *a redouble* at this point should not indicate satisfaction with the contract of two diamonds doubled. On the contrary, *it should scream for takeout in one of the two unmentioned suits, hearts and clubs* in this case. We have found this to be a highly effective procedure, and we heartily endorse it.

Several notes of caution should be inserted before you decide to employ this gadget. First and foremost, your partner must agree, by prearrangement, *to use the redouble for a rescue.* If the over-caller leaves it in when he should not, you will probably suffer a real disaster. And secondly, *the redouble for takeout applies only when your partner has overcalled at the level of one or two* and has been doubled for penalty. It does *not apply* to doubles of any higher-level contract.

For safety at rubber bridge, we advocate that the redoubler must hold at least 5-5 in the unbid suits. It must be borne in mind that your partner may be forced to bail out in a two-card suit. At match-point play, a 4-5 distribution in the unbid suits will suffice if you are void in your partner's doubled suit. The overcaller must run, after your redouble, to the unbid suit for which he has a preference. He may stay at his redoubled contract only if he is very confident that he can fulfill it despite the circumstances of the suit being stacked behind him and your evident dislike of his suit. If the bidding proceeds:

West	North	East	South
1 ♠	2 ◇	Double	Redouble
Pass	?		

and North holds:

♠ A 2
♡ J 9 7
◇ K Q 9 8 7 5
♣ K 2

North must bid two hearts.

In the more normal and more frequently recurring types of situation when your partner's overcall has been doubled, you will not have a 5-5 (or a 5-4) distribution in the unbid suits. Thus the "conventional" redouble for rescue—presented above—cannot come into play. Under these circumstances, when should you sit for the double and when should you "rescue"?

Speaking generally, both the player who "always" and the player who "never" rescues his partner from a business double are equally guilty of lacking imagination.

When your partner is doubled and your hand will provide a better dummy than he might reasonably expect, you should probably not interfere with the doubled contract. He cannot be hurt too badly unless he has made a bad overcall, in which case he may have a sheltering run-out of his own.

If, however, your holding will serve as a poor dummy at the doubled bid but you have reasonable prospects as declarer in a suit of your own, you should make the rescue. Should the character of your hand be such as to render it worthless for either purpose, you sit quietly by as a nonchalant, uninterested spectator. Any move you might make in this latter situation might aggravate and intensify your position.

Consider the following hands, after the bidding has proceeded as indicated:

West	North	East	South
1 ♠	2 ◇	Double	?

You are South, holding each of the following hands:

1. ♠ 6 4 3
   ♡ 10 9 7 4 3
   ◇ 8 6
   ♣ 10 7 3

   With absolutely no assets to benefit your partner in his unfortunate plight, you must also realize that you have no port of rescue. Sit tight with the situation—and hope.

2. ♠ 9 7 6
   ♡ J 10 9 8 3 2
   ◇ —
   ♣ 7 6 3 2

   Your hand will produce absolutely no tricks for partner at the diamond contract. With hearts as trumps, you should be able to win three tricks in your own hand—and partner does have some winning high cards in his hand. In addition, by bidding *two hearts*, there is the possibility that the opponents will not double the heart contract. They may pass or continue the bidding in their own suits. Bid *two hearts*—it should be the superior contract.

3. ♠ 8 6 3
   ♡ A K 8 7 3
   ◇ 5
   ♣ Q 10 5 4

   The ace and king of hearts will furnish two unexpected tricks for partner. Further, the clubs should be of benefit to him. While your partner may not turn any handsprings in glee when he sees your hand, he will not be unhappy with it. *Pass* the doubled two diamond contract.

4. ♠ A 7 4 3
   ♡ K 10 9 7
   ◇ 6
   ♣ K 10 8 7

   With three potential trick-taking cards, you should not consider running out. If you are flirting with thoughts of running to two no-trump or three clubs, the result could be disastrous. *Pass*. Things may not be too bad.

IV. Doubles of Opening One No-trump Bids

The incidence of a one no-trump opening bid has increased tremendously in recent years. Not only do we have the standard 16–18 point opening, but also we now have the 15–17 point no-trump, and the weak 12–14 point no-trump opening. Furthermore, where, in ideal form, one should have each of the four suits protected, this requirement has been lowered and lowered throughout the years. Once upon a time, it was all right to open with one no-trump if three suits were fully protected and in the fourth suit you had no worse than Q x, J x x, or x x x x ("partial protection," as it was called). Later this requirement was reduced to no worse than x x x in the fourth suit. And currently, many of the better players are convinced that if the points are there and the hand is a balanced one, the possession of a worthless doubleton in the fourth suit should not militate against an opening bid of one no-trump.

It is quite apparent, therefore, why many more hands are being opened with one no-trump—the range for the bid has been expanded and a much greater number of hands are now acceptable as a one no-trump opening.

What does a double of one no-trump mean? Is it for penalty or for takeout? The standard approach, in both expert and non-expert circles, is embodied in one line: "A double of one no-trump is for penalty." However, no one-line explanation can adequately cover any phase of bridge bidding, especially a phase which is a most important, recurring one. We feel, therefore, that the subject deserves some special consideration.

In the following sequence:

West	North	East	South
1 NT	Double	Pass	?

must South automatically pass, regardless of what his holding might be? If the double is strictly for penalty, as some would have you believe, then perhaps he should. Since most authorities state that a double of a strong one no-trump opening bid (16–18) should be at least the equal of that bid, it follows that the standard for doubling is the same when the opening no-trump bid is weak (that is, if the opening no-trump bid shows 12–14 points, the double should show at least 12–14 points). With holdings less than the equivalent of the opening no-trump bid, it is deemed advisable to pass or to take some other action.

Fifteen points *behind* the opener is considered to be equal to sixteen points in front of the opener. Therefore, the player who directly doubles a strong one no-trump opener will possess 15 or more high-card points. If, then, the doubler possesses 15–18 points, and his partner has little or nothing, will the pass for penalty by the latter succeed? It is obvious that *it will not*. Furthermore, the defenders usually require a decisive edge to offset the playing advantage normally enjoyed by declarer.

It surely follows, except in the extreme cases where the doubler has 20 or more points, that the balance of power will be decided between the holdings of the partner of the one no-trump opener and the partner of the doubler. If it is conceded that such is the case, then the double should be treated as a cooperative venture. The possession by the doubler's partner of *six or more points* should confer the balance of power to the defensive side. With such a holding, the partner of the doubler should *pass for penalty* unless the expected opening lead might be ruinous to the defenders.

In the sequence:

West	North	East	South
1 NT	Double	Pass	?

and South holds:

1. ♠ Q 9 2   The pass for penalty is automatic.
   ♡ 9 6 4
   ◇ K 9 7 3
   ♣ J 7 5

2. ♠ —   This hand is worth 6 points, counting two points for
   ♡ J 9 7 6 5 2 the length in hearts. We would, nevertheless, take out
   ◇ K 7 5   to *two hearts* because the expected spade lead could
   ♣ 9 7 6 2   prove to be too treacherous for handling.

3. ♠ J 9 7 6 5 2 Vulnerability is a condition that must be considered
   ♡ J   seriously both on this hand and the preceding one.
   ◇ K 7 5   If they are not vulnerable and you beat them just
   ♣ 8 6 3   one trick, you will secure a bad result. You will, in
               this case, be plus 100 points, whereas if you take out
in your suit, you figure to be plus 110 or more. We, naturally, recommend that you take out in these circumstances.

The no-trump doubler must always be very much aware of vulnerability and what his partner is apt to do in a given situation. Assume that *East and West are vulnerable,* and North–South are not. In this sequence:

West	North	East	South
1 NT	?		

North holds:

♠ A J
♡ A Q 9 3
◇ K J 3
♣ K Q 10 4

North can safely predict that South will take out if North doubles, simply because South can hardly have enough count (6 points) for the penalty pass. If he does take out—particularly to two spades—North–South may suffer a loss. If South has a little something, you figure to beat the hand two tricks, for plus 200 points. We recommend that you, sitting North, *pass* West's one no-trump opening bid. If vulnerability conditions were reversed, then we would double, hoping that we could produce a profit at a part-score large enough to surpass the plus 100 that we might net if we chose to pass and beat them two tricks.

The no-trump *opener* and his partner may encounter trouble in deciding whether subsequent doubles are to be construed as penalty or for takeout. The rubber-bridge player will also profit by examining the basic situations which follow:

South	West	North	East
1 NT	2 ♠	Pass	Pass
Double	Pass	?	

This should logically be played 90 percent for takeout—that is, North will take out probably 9 out of 10 times. After all, the opener can hardly be expected to take six or seven tricks at spades when he is in front of the bidder. He has a good opening no-trump, but his strength is concentrated in the other suits. Partner will take out unless he can take one plus spade tricks (Q 10 x x, K 9 x x, J x x x x) or one long card spade trick plus some other good value.

South	West	North	East
1 NT	Pass	Pass	2 ♠
Double	Pass	?	

This double should be 90 percent for penalty. The opener is well prepared for spades, and he is behind the overcaller. Partner should pass with any balanced or near-balanced hand containing two or more points. If he holds nothing but two's, three's, four's, and five's, he should take out to two no-trump as a confession of weakness, even though partner doubled for penalties. If responder should pass with zero points, the single-handed defense which opener will be forced to conduct will probably wind up one or two tricks short of expectations.

The following situation is discussed here simply because it probably could not fittingly be discussed elsewhere.

South	West	North	East
1 NT	2 ♠	Pass	Pass
2 NT			

This action by South is possible, and even logical, with certain type holdings where a double is impractical and a pass seems undesirable.

If South holds:

♠ K J 2
♡ A 2
◇ 9 6 3
♣ A K Q 9 4

this is not too good a defensive hand against spades because of the position of the spade holding and the heavy concentration of honors in the club suit. A double will be construed as takeout, and if partner takes you out to three of a red suit (as is probable), you will probably suffer a loss. Since there is a good chance that you can run seven or eight tricks with a spade lead, we would compete with *two no-trump*. Partner should not think that you have found an ace previously overlooked but should recognize the bid for what it is. In most cases, he should pass. If he has the exact cards needed, such as an ace and a side queen, he can consider risking a three no-trump bid.

CHAPTER 18

Competitive Part-Score Bidding: The Fight for the Partial

NOTE WELL: In both rubber and duplicate bridge, more than 50 percent of all deals are properly played at a part-score contract.

I. From the Opener's Seat

Without a doubt, the most important difference between rubber and duplicate bridge lies in the life-or-death struggle for the part-score. In duplicate play, one must be much more aggressive for the simple reason that he is confronted with many more crucial decisions in which experience has demonstrated that aggressive action is called for if optimum results are to be attained. The more frequent crucial decisions arise because each deal is equal in importance to every other. And, of course, in duplicate play success is measured not by the amount of gain, but by the *frequency* of gain. That is, if one sticks his neck out three times and "steals" a part-score twice for a top on the board and the third time he gets doubled and goes down 1100 points, he has won two out of three boards, for a 66.67 percent score, enough to win just about any duplicate game. In rubber bridge, he would go bankrupt in short order if he out-scored the opponents in two part-score hands and on the third hand he lost 1100 points fighting to win another part-score.

As an illustration of match-point vs. rubber-bridge tactics at part-score contracts, let us look at the following hand which points out why there is no percentage in waging a vigorous fight for at best a part-score contract in rubber bridge but why percentage is in favor of not selling out in match-point play.

You are *vulnerable,* and are sitting South holding this hand:

♠ K Q 10 3 2
♡ 8 5
◇ K 6
♣ A 9 4 2

South	West	North	East
1 ♠	2 ♡	Pass	Pass
?			

Playing rubber bridge, you pass as quickly as you can get the word out. What is the percentage in bidding opposite a partner who couldn't make a free bid? If it's a good day, your side might make a part-score in spades, or perhaps clubs. How much can you lose by passing in rubber bridge? Only an insignificant part-score if the opponents fulfill their contract. How much can you lose by bidding two spades? Perhaps 800 or 1100 points if East happens to be well stacked in spades, in which case a reverberating double will echo throughout the room. It surely must be considered horrible rubber-bridge tactics to reopen the bidding with two spades.

But duplicate play is a horse of another color. You cannot permit West to purchase the contract for two hearts. With tongue in cheek, perhaps, you rebid two spades. Admittedly, you may go down 500, 800, or 1100 points on rare occasions, but it is most unlikely. Your partner figures to have a little something, perhaps like:

♠ J x x
♡ J x x x
◇ Q x x
♣ Q J x

If he happens to have a reasonable facsimile of the above—which isn't too much to expect—you will probably fulfill your contract. And if you happen to go down one trick, undoubled, it will cost you 100 points, as against the 110 or 140 the opponents would surely have made at their two heart contract.

Of course, there is also the enticing possibility that the opponents will refuse to sell out at two spades and bid three hearts, at which contract they might well go down a trick, giving you a plus score as a reward for your tactical aggressiveness.

Another example of a situation where an opener wouldn't dream of reopening the bidding at rubber bridge but would consider it to be a mandatory reopening at duplicate bridge is the following:

Both sides vulnerable. North holds:

♠ x x
♡ K x
♢ A J x x x
♣ A Q x x

The bidding:

East	South	West	North
Pass	Pass	Pass	1 ◇
1 ♠	Pass	Pass	?

In rubber bridge, a pass would be the only acceptable call. In duplicate bridge, a pass by North would be the mark of a loser; a bid of *two clubs* would be the proper call.

Admittedly, South has a very poor hand; he has twice had the opportunity to bid and has passed each time. Nevertheless, there exists the distinct possibility that he may have club support and that two, or perhaps even three, clubs can be made. Surely, if North passes, East–West figure to score a plus score by making some number of spades, and North–South figure to get few match points for permitting East–West to purchase the contract at one spade. Of course when North reopens with a two club call, there is always the possibility that he may go down one or two tricks, doubled, at his contract. But this is a risk that must be taken in order to secure a plus score, even if it is only 90 points for bidding and making two clubs. Getting zero match points for going down 500 points is very little worse than getting ½ match point for letting the opponents play at one spade and making their contract.

The major point of this deal is that where you have a second suit to bid at a low level, in addition to the suit you showed originally, you should just about always bid it. In so doing, you will offer partner a choice of the two suits and thereby increase your chances of striking a playable trump suit.

In rubber bridge, to reopen the above hand with a two club bid would be foolish, for you stand to gain very little while standing to lose a lot.

One of the few times when, having opened, you should decline to reopen the bidding after an opponent has overcalled is when your judgment indicates that the opponents probably have a better contract and will tend to find it if they obtain another chance to bid. Here is an illustration of this point.

North	East	South	West
Pass	Pass	Pass	1 ♣
1 ◇	Pass	Pass	?

West holds:

♠ A x
♡ x x
◇ K Q 10
♣ K 10 x x x x

West realizes that his partner, East, after having passed originally, could not even stick in a bid of one heart or one spade at his second opportunity to bid. Undoubtedly, East has a pretty miserable hand. Technically speaking, West could not be condemned for reopening with a two club bid. Almost surely, though, if he reopened, North–South would re-enter with either spades or hearts. From the bidding to date, North–South assuredly have at least half of the high-card strength in the deck; and they certainly figure to outbid East–West in the major suits. At one diamond, North–South will score but 20 points per trick; in spades or hearts, it will be 30 points per trick. Also, in view of West's diamond strength, North–South aren't going to make many overtricks. In spades or hearts, they might make nine or ten tricks with ease.

West should, in our opinion, therefore *pass* North's one diamond overcall.

Another type of reopening bid available to the opening bidder after his partner has failed to respond initially and the opposition has reopened is the "double." In match-point play, especially if not vulnerable, this take-out double is employed much more frequently than in rubber bridge. In the latter game, the emphasis is, of course, on making a game, hence the opener does not strain himself too much when contesting a part-score. In match-point play, on the other hand, the emphasis is on getting any plus score.

An example:

Neither side vulnerable. North holds:

- ♠ K x x x
- ♡ x
- ◇ A J 10 x
- ♣ K J 9 x

The bidding has proceeded:

North	East	South	West
1 ◇	1 ♡	Pass	Pass
?			

North should double for a takeout in match-point play, hoping to get together with South in spades, clubs or, perhaps, diamonds. In rubber bridge, North should pass and save his fighting for some other day when he will possess more resources to fight with.

The final type of reopening bid available to the opening bidder after his partner has failed to respond, is the *one no-trump rebid*. This bid shows 18–19 points and denotes the type of hand that was a little too good for an original opening of one no-trump and the type where a reopening double might land the partnership in an inferior contract. Here is such a situation:

Neither side vulnerable. North dealer.

North	East	South	West
1 ◇	Pass	Pass	1 ♠
?			

North holds:

- ♠ A K x
- ♡ Q x
- ◇ K Q x x
- ♣ A J 9 x

If North reopens by doubling, South might be compelled to bid two hearts, on a broken-down four-card suit. The two heart contract, in these circumstances, figures to yield a worse result than one no-trump. (And if responder happens to have a long heart suit, he can always bid it over the one no-trump rebid.)

Of course, when the reopening bidder bids one no-trump—as recommended above—partner knows exactly what the joint assets are. The opener is now through for the afternoon and if any future captain becomes necessary, the responder will assume command.

II. Reopening Bids: From the Defender's Seat

The most difficult segment of defensive bidding is the subject of reopening the bidding when the opening bidder or his partner have passed the hand out at the one or two level. This subject has always been more or less ignored or treated very superficially in most bridge books for the logical reason that virtually every bridge book that has ever been written has dealt with rubber bridge, in which the *amount* of points scored is all that matters. In these circumstances, when responder has passed the opening bid, or where both the opener and the responder have bid but have stopped at the one or two level, it usually does not pay to enter the bidding just to compete for a part score at the risk of incurring a big set.

A corollary reason contributing to the lack of published data on the question of "reopening the bidding" is the following. Systems of bidding, in the past, have been designed exclusively for rubber bridge. In rubber bridge, of course, the primary consideration is the safety factor. The system makers calculated how much one might lose by bidding in different situations and how much one might lose by passing and concluded that, generally, one would tend to lose more by bidding in delicate situations than by passing. Thus was evolved the natural position that it was usually unsafe—on a risk vs. gain basis with total points as the consideration—to compete vigorously against the opening side's passed-out part-score.

But in duplicate bridge, where all deals are "born free and equal," the safety factor becomes subordinated to a secondary role and the frequency of gain (or loss) replaces the amount of gain (or loss) as the primary consideration. Thus, in duplicate bridge, one tends to bid more than in rubber bridge. This does not imply that one gambles more in duplicate bridge, but rather that one is thrust into many more gambling situations and must, accordingly, take many more "gambles" than he does in rubber bridge.

It is quite natural, therefore, since keen competition is the way of life in duplicate bridge, that the requirements for practically every type of bid are lowered from the rubber-bridge requirements. This is true with respect to opening bids (though ever so slightly), with responses, with overcalls and take-out doubles, with pre-emptive bids, and with sacrifice bids. It is especially true with respect to virtually all bids made to reopen the bidding when the opponents have stopped at a low-level contract.

A final reason for the past lack of emphasis on the subject of reopening the bidding is that the requirements are flexible and not easy either to define in point count or to establish principles that can be applied to apparently similar recurring types of situations. When to reopen the bidding—and with what—when the opening side has passed out at a low-level part-score contract is frequently a judgment situation rather than a clearly defined one, in which the bidder is always treading on dangerous ground since he is bidding in the face of displayed strength.

Let's now go from the approach to competitive part-score bidding to the application, from the general to the specific, using as our guiding philosophy the principle that when the opening side stops at a low-level part-score contract, self-preservation dictates that you or your partner must make every effort to get into the auction, even with a poorish hand; or at least pause for consideration if you are in the position of making the final pass and deciding whether or not to reopen the bidding. It will be observed, incidentally, that in most cases *the last man to speak will reopen the bidding.* In so doing, he will sometimes find himself out on a limb. But, in the long run, the adoption of this course of action will result either in finding a good part-score contract for his side or in pushing the opponents one trick higher, giving his team a plus score instead of a minus score.

The theory under which the defensive side reopens the bidding is known as *The Balance of Power Principle.* This is the principle:

> When the opening side has stopped at a low-level part-score contract, the assumption is made that their combined values are limited. Therefore the balance of power may well be against them. Usually, they will have 18–22 points, and the defensive side will have 18–22 points. Should the hand be passed out at the opening side's contract, their result figures to be either a plus score or a relatively insignificant minus score. Since experience has demonstrated that poor match-point scores are generally obtained by allowing the opening side to purchase low-level contracts without competition, "protective" bidding becomes essential to the defending side's welfare.

In applying this balance of power (protection) principle, the player in the "pass-out" (last) position is bidding not only on the values in his hand alone *but on the combined values he and his partner are presumed to hold.* If the potential reopener has a poor hand, his partner figures to have a good hand. That is, if East–West, for example, open the bidding and stop at the one or two level, they are presumed to have (as was mentioned) in the area of 18–22 points; and, of course, North–South is presumed to have 18–22 points. It doesn't matter much how North–South's 18–22 points are divided, so long as both North and South are each aware of the situation. The one who reopens the bidding isn't bidding on the values in his own hand; he is bidding on the presumed 18–22 strength in the combined partnership hands. In other words, he is bidding his partner's hand as well as his own.

If the reopener's bid results in pushing the opening side to come in again at a higher level, the "balancing" partnership has increased its chances of obtaining a plus score—or a lower minus score—if they are set at their protective bid.

Let us now look at the more frequent types of "protection" situations:

1. When the opening side has stopped at a *seven-trick contract.*
2. When the opening side has stopped at an *eight-trick contract.*

In each of the illustrations presented below, the man in the "pass-out" position has three possible courses of action. He either: (1) passes; (2) bids, or (3) doubles. Let us see if we can establish some guiding principles or at least a pattern of behavior about when he should (2) bid or (3) double. Once the latter two have been determined, the reader will then recognize when he should sell out by passing.

I. When the Opening Side Has Stopped at a Seven-Trick Contract

	North	East	South	West
A.	1 ♡	Pass	Pass	?
B.	1 ♡	Pass	1 NT	Pass
	Pass	?		
C.	1 ◇	Pass	1 ♠	Pass
	1 NT	Pass	Pass	?
D.	1 ◇	Pass	1 ♡	Pass
	1 ♠	Pass	Pass	?

	North	East	South	West
E.	Pass	Pass	1 ♣	Pass
	1 ♡	Pass	Pass	?
F.	Pass	Pass	1 ♡	Pass
	1 NT	Pass	Pass	?
G.	Pass	Pass	1 ◇	Pass
	1 ♠	Pass	1 NT	Pass
	Pass	?		
H.	Pass	Pass	1 ♣	Pass
	1 ◇	Pass	Pass	?
I.	Pass	Pass	1 ♡	Pass
	Pass	?		

II. When the Opening Side Has Stopped at a Two-Level Contract

	North	East	South	West
A.	1 ♡	Pass	2 ♡	Pass
	Pass	?		
B.	1 ◇	Pass	1 NT	Pass
	2 ◇	Pass	Pass	?
C.	1 ♡	Pass	1 NT	Pass
	2 ♡	Pass	Pass	?
D.	1 ♣	Pass	1 ♠	Pass
	2 ♣	Pass	Pass	?
E.	1 ♠	Pass	1 NT	Pass
	2 ◇	Pass	Pass	?
F.	1 ♠	Pass	1 NT	Pass
	2 ♡	Pass	Pass	?
G.	1 ♡	Pass	1 ♠	Pass
	2 ♡	Pass	2 ♠	Pass
	Pass	?		
H.	1 ◇	Pass	1 ♡	Pass
	2 ♡	Pass	Pass	?
I.	Pass	Pass	1 ♡	Pass
	2 ♡	Pass	Pass	?

	North	East	South	West
J.	Pass	Pass	1 ♡	Pass
	2 ♣	Pass	Pass	?
K.	Pass	Pass	1 ◇	Pass
	2 ♣	Pass	Pass	?
L.	Pass	Pass	1 ♡	Pass
	1 ♠	Pass	2 ♠	Pass
	Pass	?		
M.	Pass	Pass	1 ♠	Pass
	1 NT	Pass	2 ♡	Pass
	Pass	?		
N.	Pass	Pass	1 ♡	Pass
	1 NT	Pass	2 ♣	Pass
	Pass	?		
O.	Pass	1 ♡	Pass	1 NT
	Pass	2 ♣	Pass	2 ♡
	Pass	Pass	?	
P.	Pass	Pass	1 ◇	Pass
	2 ◇	Pass	Pass	?
Q.	Pass	1 ◇	Pass	1 ♠
	Pass	2 ◇	Pass	Pass
	?			

All of the above situations are illustrated and analyzed in the chapter which follows, "Reopening Bids by the Defensive Side."

CHAPTER 19

Reopening Bids by the Defensive Side

Prologue

At the part-score level, duplicate bridge and rubber bridge can be as different as night and day. This can be evidenced in the bidding sequence that follows:

North	East	South	West
Pass	1 ♣	Pass	1 ♡
Pass	2 ♣	Pass	Pass
2 ♠!			

In rubber bridge, North's two spade reopening bid would be the height of folly. He didn't have sufficient values to open the bidding, he didn't have even enough to make a one spade overcall; and now, when all he has to do is to say, "Pass," to terminate the auction, he sticks his neck out with a two spade bid! What is the sense of it, you ask? Is it to prevent East from making a trivial, insignificant part-score of two clubs? In rubber bridge, to repeat, North's bid would be absurd. But in duplicate bridge, it is a perfectly normal bid—and, more important, it is motivated, and usually vindicated, by sound logic.

As was stated, in duplicate bridge it is most important to strive for a plus score, especially at the part-score level, for experience has amply demonstrated that a minus score—at a low part-score contract—almost invariably gives one a very poor match-point result. Surely, on the given bidding, East–West figure to secure a plus score at their two club contract. In terms of match points, it can be just as costly for North to pass two clubs as it can be for him to bid two spades, get doubled, and go down 500 points. But if he can (1) make his two spade contract or (2) go down only 50 points—against the 90 that East–West would figure to score at their two club contract—or (3) push the opponents to an unmakable three club contract, then North–South will obtain an excellent match-point result.

As to the danger that East–West might be pushed to a game, that thought must be eliminated. In this day and age, no person stops at two clubs if he is even close to a makable game. In this situation, East–West obviously have limited values.

North's justification for reopening with a two spade call is the following. Over East's opening bid, South may not have desired to overcall on a split suit, not knowing whether West had a good hand or a bad hand and not wishing to run into a penalty double by West. When East rebid two clubs, South might still have been in the same position, not knowing whether West had a good hand or a bad hand. Since South, up to now, was never in the position where he could bid safely, he might well have a respectable hand despite his silence.

But when West passed East's two club rebid, the picture became clarified: West was now known to have a poor hand, certainly no more than 9 points, and possibly as few as 6. And East didn't even have an interest in improving the minor-suit contract. East also figured to have a minimum-type holding, with no interest in either no-trump or in partner's suit, hearts. Almost certainly, North–South figure to have as much high-card strength as East–West, somewhere in the area of 18–22 points. If North–South can find agreement in spades, they figure to make that contract and thereby secure a plus score; or possibly, by bidding spades, they can drive East–West to an unmakable three club contract, also giving North–South a plus score. There can be no doubt but that the incentive for North to reopen the bidding exists at match-point play whereas in rubber bridge it would be losing policy to fight against a measly two club contract.

This is not to imply that North is not taking a risk by bidding two spades with a poorish hand at duplicate bridge. He is definitely taking a risk, but one which is warranted in view of the prime importance of obtaining a plus score. In our opinion, it is less of a risk to bid two spades than to allow the opponents to play in their uncontested two club contract.

Here is the actual deal, which arose in the National Men's Pair Championships of 1947. Neither side was vulnerable.

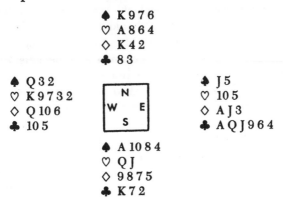

♠ K 9 7 6
♡ A 8 6 4
◇ K 4 2
♣ 8 3

♠ Q 3 2   ♠ J 5
♡ K 9 7 3 2   ♡ 10 5
◇ Q 10 6   ◇ A J 3
♣ 10 5   ♣ A Q J 9 6 4

♠ A 10 8 4
♡ Q J
◇ 9 8 7 5
♣ K 7 2

The bidding:

North	East	South	West
Pass	1 ♣	Pass	1 ♡
Pass	2 ♣	Pass	Pass
2 ♠	3 ♣	Pass	Pass
Pass			

Looking at all four hands, the reader will perceive that North–South, at the two spade contract, will lose three diamonds, one spade and one club. In the actual bidding, East elected to bid three clubs over North's two spade call—and went down a trick, losing two spades, two hearts, and one club. North–South secured 8½ match points out of 12 for this result. Had North–South been permitted to purchase the contract for two spades, they would have obtained 10½ match points out of 12. And—this is the crux of the subject—had East–West been permitted to play at two clubs, North–South would have scored 2 match points out of 12!

The above deal is an introduction to the contents of this chapter. It is typical of the fierce competitive part-score struggle that is inherent in duplicate bridge bidding. Various recurring types of sequences will be presented and analyzed to give the reader further insight into the logic that motivates a would-be reopening bidder to stick his neck out. Of course, we give no guarantees on any specific deal. However, we firmly believe that the tactics which we will be recommending will, in the long run, gain many more match points than they will lose.

As was stated earlier, when the opening side has passed the hand out at the one or two level, the player in the protective (re-opening, or pass-out) position should always consider reopening the bidding. He usually has very little to lose by stepping in, even if it turns out disastrously on occasion and he gets zero match points, since the opponents were probably in a position to score most of the match points if allowed to play their low-level contract. Thus, if one steps from the frying pan into the fire, he is hurt no more than if he remained in the frying pan. His only hope of a beneficial result is to emerge unscathed—and to achieve this end, positive movement becomes essential.

Generally speaking, if the principal strength of the would-be protective bidder lies in the opponents' suit, he should tend to pass, especially if the opponents are vulnerable. In the latter circumstance, the possibility exists that the opponents might suffer a two-trick set for a loss of 200 points, which will almost always net the defensive side a top, or near-top, on the board.

Where the would-be reopening bidder is vulnerable, great caution must always be exercised when considering reopening the bidding, for if a two-trick set is incurred by the reopening side, *they* will usually get zero match points, or thereabouts.

Also to be considered seriously is the character of the opposition. Are they timid?—in which case reopening bids can be on the lighter side, since timid opponents will not double reopening one or two bids too often. Or are they aggressive (trigger-happy, if you will)?—in which case one must not stretch reopening bids lest he get doubled and go down a trick if vulnerable (minus 200), or two tricks if not vulnerable.

The following are our general recommendations for protective-position action when the opening side has passed out a hand at the one or two level. We believe, from experience, that the adherence to these recommendations will bring winning results in the long run, although on any particular deal a loss might occur.

1. *Double* with 10 or more high-card points *and* either fair support for each of the unbid suits *or* a good suit of your own.

2. *Bid one no-trump* with 8–11 high-card points and a balanced hand (one of the unbid suits might not be protected).
3. *Bid a new suit:*
   (a) At the one-level, a probable range of 6–10 high-card points.
   (b) At the two-level, the same 6–10 point range, based on the assumption that the reopening side has about 20 high-card points and that even if you have a poorish hand your partner figures to have a good hand.

In addition to the above, there are other actions that the reopening bidder might take in the protective position. These "specialized" actions will be introduced as we go along in this chapter.

Let us now get to the specifics.

I. When the Opening Side Has Stopped at a Seven-Trick Contract

A. Let us consider the easiest, and most frequent type of situation first:

North	East	South	West
1 ♡	Pass	Pass	?

With the following hands, West should reopen by *doubling*:

(1)	(2)	(3)	(4)
♠ K Q 6	♠ K J 3	♠ Q 9 3 2	♠ J 10 8 3
♡ 8 4	♡ 8 4	♡ 5	♡ 2
◇ J 9 3 2	◇ A 10 6 3 2	◇ Q J 8 4	◇ A K 6 3 2
♣ A J 7 5	♣ Q 10 4	♣ A J 4 2	♣ Q 7 5

With the following hands, West should reopen with a *one no-trump* call:

(5)	(6)	(7)	(8)
♠ Q 7 2	♠ A Q	♠ Q 5 2	♠ K J 6
♡ K 3	♡ Q 8 4	♡ A J 10	♡ A Q 2
◇ A 8 3 2	◇ 10 8 4 3	◇ J 10 9 3	◇ 7 5 3
♣ Q 9 4 3	♣ Q J 3 2	♣ Q 10 9	♣ J 9 7 3

With the following hands, West should reopen by naming his *longest suit*:

(9)	(10)	(11)	(12)
♠ A J 6 4 3	♠ K 10 8 3 2	♠ K 6	♠ K Q 10
♡ 8 2	♡ 6 3 2	♡ 4 3 2	♡ 7 5 3
◇ Q 7 5	◇ A Q 4	◇ J 6 5	◇ A J 9 6 2
♣ 8 4 3	♣ 8 5	♣ K Q 10 8 3	♣ 7 3

With the following hand, West should pass *if North–South are vulnerable:*

(13)

♠ A K 10 4
♡ K Q J 9 8
◇ 4 2
♣ 7 5

On the above hand, if neither side is vulnerable, a bid of *one spade* is recommended. True, you figure to beat one heart, but if they are not vulnerable, and you defeat them a trick (50 points), your score will not compensate you for the part-score you could in all probability make. Even a mere one spade contract will net you 80 points.

B. This situation is also a most frequent one:

North	East	South	West
1 ♡	Pass	1 NT	Pass
Pass	?		

In this type of situation, East must tread with caution, for South *may have* a nine- or ten-point hand. Also, South may have a long suit, which he was unwilling to show at the two level since the overall high-card strength of his hand was limited. It might well be, in this latter case, that North–South are not in their best contract at one no-trump. However, any immediate thoughts that East might have of passing promptly should be eliminated and serious consideration must always be given to reopening the bidding.

With the following hands, East should *double:*

(1)	(2)	(3)
♠ K 6 4	♠ A Q 2	♠ J 10 3 2
♡ 7 2	♡ 6 5	♡ 6 5 3
◇ A J 3 2	◇ J 9 8 6 3	◇ A J 3
♣ K 7 6 4	♣ K J 7	♣ A J 7

With the following hands, East should bid his *longest suit* at the two level:

(4)	(5)	(6)
♠ K Q 10 8 4 2	♠ Q 6	♠ J 5
♡ 6 5	♡ 8 4 3	♡ A 8
◊ J 9 4	◊ K 9 5	◊ Q J 10 6 4 3
♣ 8 4	♣ A J 10 8 4	♣ 7 3 2

With the following hands, East should *pass:*

(7)	(8)	(9)
♠ J 7 6	♠ 6	♠ 7 2
♡ K J 10 9	♡ Q J 8	♡ K 10 8 7 5
◊ Q 8 2	◊ Q 9 8 4 3	◊ A K 9
♣ K 7 5	♣ A 7 5 2	♣ J 7 6

On (8), the anticipation that partner's long suit figures to be spades militates against a two diamond overcall.

C. Another recurring type of situation is the following:

North	East	South	West
1 ◊	Pass	1 ♠	Pass
1 NT	Pass	Pass	?

With the following hands, West should *double:*

(1)	(2)	(3)
♠ 7 3	♠ A 8 3 2	♠ A 5
♡ A J 9 2	♡ Q 10 8 3	♡ K J 8 4
◊ 9 4 2	◊ 7 5	◊ 3 2
♣ A Q 7 3	♣ K Q 5	♣ Q J 8 4 2

With the following hands, West should name his *longest* (or *best*) suit:

(4)	(5)	(6)
♠ A 5 2	♠ A K	♠ 8 4
♡ Q 6	♡ Q 10 8 6 3	♡ J 7 6 5 3
◊ 8 4	◊ 8 4 3	◊ 2
♣ K J 10 8 6 3	♣ J 10 2	♣ A K 8 6 3

In (6), the "double" may well turn out to be the better bid, leaving the avenue open for partner to bid hearts. The two club bid is recommended, however, for if the opponents purchase the contract, you want your partner to lead clubs, not hearts.

With the following hands, West should *pass:*

(7)	(8)	(9)
♠ A 9 5	♠ —	♠ 3
♡ Q 10 4	♡ J 8 4 3	♡ 8 5
♢ A K 6 2	♢ Q J 9 6 2	♢ A Q 6 4 2
♣ J 8 4	♣ A 9 8 3	♣ K 9 8 7 3

On (8), partner's longest suit is probably spades (South's suit), and your side figures to get into trouble if you bid since your hands figure to be misfit.

On (9), the same reasoning applies as in (8). Your partner's length is probably in spades and hearts.

D.

North	East	South	West
1 ♢	Pass	1 ♡	Pass
1 ♠	Pass	Pass	?

This is a delicate situation. South is known to have a very poor hand. North, however, may have as much as 17–18 points. Usually West will tend to pass; for *when the opponents have bid three suits, it is most difficult for your side to find your best contract.* Nevertheless, there are times when West should not sell out.

In the following situation, West should bid *one no-trump:*

(1)	(2)	(3)
♠ Q 9 5	♠ A Q 4	♠ Q 10 8
♡ A 6 2	♡ A Q 8 2	♡ K Q J
♢ K 10 8 2	♢ J 10 6 2	♢ A J 7 5 3
♣ K 10 3	♣ 7 5	♣ 3 2

In the following situations, West should *double:*

(4)	(5)
♠ K J 3	♠ 3 2
♡ 9 6 2	♡ K 7 5
♢ A 7 5	♢ A K Q 6
♣ Q J 6 2	♣ J 8 3 2

In (4), East will know that West does not have a really good hand, for if he did, he would have doubled at his first opportunity to bid. One no-trump, instead of the double, is also an acceptable bid.

In (5), on the same reasoning as in (4), partner will appreciate that you are "protecting."

With the following hands, West should bid *two clubs*, the unbid suit:

(6)	(7)
♠ A 8 4 3	♠ 7 5 4
♡ 9	♡ 9 5
◇ 6 2	◇ 7 6
♣ Q 10 9 8 7 4	♣ A J 10 8 6 3

With the following hands, West should *pass*:

(8)	(9)
♠ K J 8 4	♠ Q J 10 9 3
♡ K 8 3	♡ 6
◇ Q J 10 6	◇ 5 3
♣ 7 5	♣ A Q 8 4 3

In (9), partner figures to be "loaded" in hearts and diamonds. The opponents' one spade contract certainly figures to be *your* best parking place.

Let us now view some situations where the dealer (your opponent) has passed originally and his partner has opened the bidding in third seat and then dropped his partner's response at the one-level.

E.

North	East	South	West
Pass	Pass	1 ♣	Pass
1 ♡	Pass	Pass	?

With the following hands, you should *double*:

(1)	(2)	(3)
♠ Q 10 6 2	♠ 7 5 3 2	♠ A Q 9 4
♡ A 3	♡ A K	♡ 7 5
◇ K J 8 4	◇ 7 5 4 2	◇ J 8 6 5 3
♣ 9 5 4	♣ A 8 6	♣ K 4

With the following hands, you should bid *one no-trump*:

(4)	(5)	(6)
♠ J 6 2	♠ 7 5 4	♠ 8 2
♡ A J 9	♡ A K	♡ K Q 3
◇ 8 7 4 3	◇ J 7 6 4	◇ A 8 6 4 2
♣ A Q 3	♣ K 10 6 2	♣ Q J 10

With the following hands, you should bid *one spade:*

(7)	(8)	(9)
♠ A Q 8 4 2	♠ K J 8 3	♠ J 7 5 4 2
♡ 5 4 2	♡ A K	♡ K Q
◊ 7 5	◊ 7 5 2	◊ K 10 5
♣ 6 5 3	♣ 9 7 5 3	♣ 8 6 5

On (7), we would pass if vulnerable.
With the following hands, you should bid *two diamonds:*

(10)	(11)
♠ A 8	♠ A 5
♡ 7 6 2	♡ A 6
◊ K 10 8 6 5 3	◊ J 10 9 7 5 3
♣ 9 5	♣ 8 6 4

With the following hands, you should *pass:*

(12)	(13)	(14)
♠ 7	♠ 7	♠ K J 8 3
♡ A Q 4	♡ A Q 4	♡ 6
◊ 9 7 5 3	◊ A 10 9 5 2	◊ 10 5
♣ A J 9 5 2	♣ 9 7 5 3	♣ A J 9 4 3 2

On (14), a one spade reopening bid has merit. The danger is that partner may be loaded in hearts and diamonds, and one spade may suffer an unhappy fate. We feel that the bid will gain more often than not—which is sufficient justification for refusing to sell out at the one-level.

F.

North	East	South	West
Pass	Pass	1 ♡	Pass
1 NT	Pass	Pass	?

With the following hands, West should *double:*

(1)	(2)	(3)
♠ Q J 8 3	♠ A 6 4 2	♠ A K 7
♡ 6	♡ 7 5	♡ 9 4
◊ K J 8 4	◊ A 9 8 2	◊ Q 10 8 6
♣ K 7 5 2	♣ K J 10	♣ Q 10 8 6

With the following hands, West should name *his longest suit:*

(4)	(5)	(6)
♠ Q 10 9 8 5 2	♠ 7	♠ 9 7 6 5 3·2
♡ 7 5	♡ Q J 6	♡ A 8
◇ A J 3	◇ A K 8 5 2	◇ A Q 6
♣ 6 2	♣ 9 6 4 3	♣ 7 4

With the following hands, West should *pass:*

(7)	(8)	(9)
♠ K 6 5	♠ 7	♠ —
♡ A K Q	♡ J 9 7 3 2	♡ A Q J 8 4
◇ Q 9 3 2	◇ A 10 6 4	◇ A J 6
♣ 8 5 4	♣ K Q J	♣ 9 7 6 3 2

On (8) and (9), your partner figures to have "millions" of spades (neither opponent has bid spades), and any action you take may well result in partner coming in with his spade suit.

G.

North	East	South	West
Pass	Pass	1 ◇	Pass
1 ♠	Pass	1 NT	Pass
Pass	?		

This is a highly precarious type of situation. South may well have 14 or 15 points, and North might have 9, or even 10, points. If you bid on the "balance of power" principle, you might get hurt. Remember that the opponents know you have passed twice previously.

With the following hands, you should *pass:*

(1)	(2)	(3)
♠ Q 7 5	♠ A 8 3	♠ 7 5 2
♡ K J 6	♡ A Q 8 4 2	♡ A K 8 4
◇ 9 5 2	◇ 7 5 3	◇ 9 6 5
♣ A Q 8 4	♣ J 7	♣ A 7 3

With the following hands, you should *double:*

(4)	(5)	(6)
♠ 6 4	♠ 8 6 3	♠ Q J 10 9
♡ A J 7 3	♡ K J 9 8	♡ Q 10 9 8
◇ 6 3	◇ 4	◇ 7
♣ A J 8 4 2	♣ A J 5 4 2	♣ A J 6 3

With the following hands, you should name your *longest suit:*

(7)	(8)	(9)
♠ 7 5 4	♠ A K J	♠ A Q
♡ Q 10 9 6 4 3	♡ 7 3	♡ J 9 8 6 4 3 2
◇ 6 2	◇ 8 2	◇ 7 3
♣ A K	♣ Q J 9 7 4 2	♣ 6 4

H.

North	East	South	West
Pass	Pass	1 ♣	Pass
1 ◇	Pass	Pass	?

Here more freedom of action is available than on the previous bidding sequence. The opponents have not even tried to get into a major suit, being content to play the contract at a minor suit.

West should *double* with:

(1)	(2)	(3)
♠ K J 8 4	♠ 9 6 3 2	♠ Q J 6 3
♡ K J 8 4	♡ 9 6 3 2	♡ K Q 4
◇ 7 5 2	◇ A 3	◇ 6 4 3 2
♣ K 6	♣ A Q 4	♣ K 2

West should bid his *major suit* with:

(4)	(5)	(6)
♠ K Q 7 5 2	♠ A Q	♠ K 10 9 5
♡ 6 3	♡ Q J 9 3 2	♡ 7 3
◇ 8 4 2	◇ 6 4 3	◇ A K 4
♣ Q 7 5	♣ 9 5 2	♣ 9 8 6 2

West should bid *one no-trump* with:

(7)	(8)	(9)
♠ 10 6 2	♠ J 7 2	♠ J 5
♡ Q 7 3	♡ J 8 4	♡ A 7 2
◇ A J 7	◇ K Q 6	◇ Q 6 5 3
♣ A J 6 4	♣ K Q 7 5	♣ Q J 7 5

West should *pass* with:

(10)	(11)	(12)
♠ 6 3	♠ 6 3	♠ 2
♡ 8 4 2	♡ 7 5	♡ A K Q
◇ K J 8 4	◇ A 10 4	◇ J 10 9 8 6 4
♣ A J 9 3	♣ K Q 7 5 3 2	♣ Q 5 3

On (10), you hate to sell out (as a principle!), but there is simply nothing that you can bid, except perhaps one no-trump.

On (11), if you and your partner treat a two club bid by you as showing a club suit (and not as a cue bid of the opponents' suit), then two clubs would be the acceptable reopening bid if not vulnerable.

On (12), you might have a heart suit between you, but partner is almost certain to have a long spade holding. If you either double or bid one no-trump, partner is quite likely to bid spades. Surely your best chance for a plus score is to let the opponents play the contract at one diamond.

I.

North	East	South	West
Pass	Pass	1 ♡	Pass
Pass	?		

In the above sequence, North is known to have a truly miserable hand and unless East is absolutely "broke," he should not sell out. East should *double* with:

(1)	(2)	(3)
♠ 9 6 4 2	♠ A Q 6	♠ Q J 8 5
♡ A 5	♡ 8 4 3	♡ 5
◇ K 9 4 2	◇ K 7 5	◇ Q J 10 6
♣ Q J 3	♣ J 8 4 2	♣ Q J 8 2

East should bid *one no-trump* with:

(4)	(5)	(6)
♠ 7 2	♠ 7 5 3	♠ Q 3
♡ A Q 10	♡ K Q 6	♡ A 10 2
◇ J 8 4 3	◇ A 6 3 2	◇ J 10 8 6
♣ J 7 5 2	♣ J 9 5	♣ J 10 7 5

East should bid his *longest suit* with:

(7)	(8)	(9)
♠ Q 10 5 3 2	♠ 5 2	♠ 3
♡ 8 4	♡ Q 7 5	♡ A 8 2
◇ K 9 7	◇ J 8 3	◇ 9 7 6 4 3 2
♣ 7 4 2	♣ A J 10 8 4	♣ J 10 4

East should *pass* with:

(10)	(11)	(12)
♠ 5 4 3	♠ 6	♠ 8
♡ 5 4 3 2	♡ J 10 9 7 5	♡ K Q J 9 8 4
◇ 4 3 2	◇ A 9 4	◇ 6 4 3
♣ 4 3 2	♣ 8 6 3 2	♣ K J 2

On (12), it is a close question whether to pass if you are *vulnerable*, and the opponents are not. The alternative to passing would be to bid one no-trump, and try to make eight tricks for a score of 120 points, instead of attempting to beat them three tricks for a score of 150 points. However, we would pass, since there is no assurance that partner will permit us to play a one no-trump contract. If *they are vulnerable*, you should pass automatically, and try to beat them two tricks, for the magic 200 number.

II. When the Opening Side Has Stopped at an Eight-Trick Contract

There are two major situations where the would-be reopening bidder possessing a rather poor hand knows that his partner has a good hand, even though the latter has never bid:

1. The opening side has passed out the hand at the two-level.
2. The opening side has found a suit fit, which means that in all probability the defensive side also has a suit fit which they undertake to locate.

And so, although the level of bidding is now at eight tricks (rather than seven), the defensive side will not be less aggressive in its efforts to prevent the opening side from purchasing the contract cheaply. A good match-point score is rarely obtained by selling out at the two-level, and quite often a minus score of 500 points will yield no fewer match points than will a minus score of 110.

Let's start off with the simplest and most frequent type of situation, where a defensive player will tend to compete with marginal, or even submarginal, values.

A.

North	East	South	West
1 ♡	Pass	2 ♡	Pass
Pass	?		

In this position, East will tend to reopen more often than not when not vulnerable, regardless of how good or how bad his hand is. Here is the logic that underlies his position:

North figures to have perhaps 13 or 14 *high-card* points. If he had 15 high-card points (plus distributional points, plus the asset of agreement in a suit), he would tend to make a move toward game. If South had more than 8 high-card points (plus the distributional values for a void, singleton, or doubleton in combination with supporting trumps for partner), he would have found a stronger bid than a mere "weakness" single raise to two hearts. And, of course, both North and South might each have a minimum hand. Thus North and South figure to possess somewhere in the area of 18–22 high-card points—and East–West figure to have the same amount. And further, since North–South have found a fit in hearts, *East–West figure to have a fit also*, in either spades, diamonds, or clubs. Hence the incentive for East to bid is apparent.

The guide for the defensive side for reopening the bidding when it has died at the two-level is about the same as at the one-level:

1. *Double with 10 or more high-card points,* and fair support for each of the unbid suits.
2. Bid a *new suit* with 6–11 points.
3. Make the artificial call of 2 NT to command partner to name a minor suit. This bid will be discussed in a moment.

Over South's two heart response in the above bidding sequence, East should take the following actions:

He should *double* with:

(1)	(2)
♠ A 10 3 2	♠ A Q 9
♡ 7 5	♡ 5 2
◇ Q 9 7 5	◇ Q J 8 3
♣ K Q 4	♣ K 7 6 4

He should bid his *longest suit* with:

(3)	(4)	(5)
♠ Q 10 9 4 3	♠ 7 5	♠ A
♡ 4 2	♡ 8 4 3	♡ 6 4 3
◇ A J 4	◇ K 7 5	◇ Q J 8 7 5 3
♣ Q 6 2	♣ A Q J 8 2	♣ J 6 4

He should *pass* with:

(6)	(7)	(8)
♠ 5 3	♠ 7 6 3	♠ A K
♡ K 10 8 7	♡ 9 5 2	♡ Q J 10
◇ 9 4	◇ K 9 2	◇ 7 5 3 2
♣ A J 6 3 2	♣ A Q 7 3	♣ 8 4 3 2

He should *bid two no-trump* with:

(9)	(10)	(11)
♠ 6	♠ 8 3 2	♠ 7
♡ 8 5	♡ —	♡ 5 2
◇ K Q 8 4 2	◇ K J 10 8 4	◇ J 10 8 5 4 2
♣ K Q 7 3 2	♣ A Q 8 6 4	♣ A K J 10

This "two no-trump" bid, *as a command to partner to bid a minor suit,* is a creation of the Roth-Stone System and is known as the "unusual no-trump." It is a logical, and most useful, type of bid. Here are the details.

When a player bids two no-trump when it is perfectly obvious that he cannot desire to play the hand at that contract because of (1) the bidding of the opponents or (2) his own previous bidding, he shows an abnormally distributional hand loaded with *the minor suits.* This bid of two no-trump is forcing upon partner, who must name his *longest minor suit.* The requirements for the bid are:

1. A probable nine (or more) high-card points.
2. The minor suit holding must be either 5-4, 5-5, or better.
3. Negatively speaking, a warning that the bidder has no support for the unbid major suit and that the latter should not be bid unless partner has a self-sufficient suit.

B.

North	East	South	West
1 ◇	Pass	1 NT	Pass
2 ◇	Pass	Pass	?

West should *double* with:

(1)	(2)	(3)
♠ Q J 6 2	♠ 9 7 5 2	♠ K J 8
♡ Q J 5 3	♡ A Q 8 3	♡ Q 10 5 2
◇ 3 2	◇ 7 5	◇ 6 3
♣ K Q 3	♣ A J 4	♣ A 10 8 2

West should bid his *longest suit* with:

(4)	(5)	(6)
♠ K J 10 6 3	♠ 6 2	♠ 7
♡ A 8 2	♡ 10 8 6 3	♡ J 10 9 8 4 3
◇ 7	◇ A 5	◇ A 6
♣ J 10 4 2	♣ K Q 10 8 7	♣ Q 10 6 2

West should *pass* with:

(7)	(8)	(9)
♠ K J 8 3	♠ A 8 4	♠ 6 3
♡ A 4	♡ 7 5 3	♡ A Q 8
◇ 9 7 5 2	◇ K 8 6	◇ Q J 10 9
♣ Q 8 3	♣ A 9 3 2	♣ J 6 3 2

In situations such as (7) and (8), beware of bidding when you have length in the opener's suit when responder has not supported that suit, for it will usually turn out that these cards will all be losers. Responder may well have a singleton, and he will trump partner's leads of that suit. In (8), your diamond king figures to be under North's ace, and it will be trapped.

C.

North	East	South	West
1 ♡	Pass	1 NT	Pass
2 ♡	Pass	Pass	?

West should *double* with:

(1)	(2)
♠ J 6 3 2	♠ A K 7
♡ 8	♡ 4 2
◇ A J 3 2	◇ Q 9 4 3
♣ A J 5 3	♣ Q 8 7 2

West should bid his *longest suit* with:

(3)	(4)
♠ Q J 8 4 3	♠ 7 5
♡ 9 2	♡ 6 2
◇ K J 7	◇ A 9 3
♣ Q J 2	♣ K 10 9 7 5 3

West should *pass* with:

	(5)		(6)
♠	K J 8 4	♠	3
♡	8 7 6 2	♡	J 8 5 3
◇	A Q 6	◇	K 7 2
♣	8 4	♣	A J 8 5 3

West should bid *two no-trump* (the "unusual") with:

	(7)		(8)
♠	6	♠	5
♡	8 4	♡	A 6
◇	A J 7 5 3	◇	Q J 9 8 4
♣	K J 8 5 3	♣	Q J 7 6 2

On (8) a pass might well be the winning bid, for East figures to have length in the major suits.

D.

North	East	South	West
1 ♣	Pass	1 ♠	Pass
2 ♣	Pass	Pass	?

In this situation, there is less freedom of movement, since the opponents have bid *two* suits. Nevertheless you should make every effort not to sell out, for you and your partner figure to have about half of the high-card strength in the deck.

West should *double* with:

	(1)		(2)
♠	Q 6	♠	A 8 4
♡	Q 10 8 4	♡	J 9 6 2
◇	A K 8 5 2	◇	K Q 8 4 2
♣	5 2	♣	5

West should bid his *longest suit* with:

	(3)		(4)
♠	8 4 3	♠	A 5 3
♡	Q 9 7 5 3	♡	7 4
◇	A K 7	◇	K J 9 6 4 3
♣	5 2	♣	6 3

On (3), we would tend to pass if vulnerable.

West should *pass* with:

	(5)		(6)
♠	K Q 9 4	♠	3 2
♡	A 7	♡	A K 8 3
◊	9 4 3	◊	8 6
♣	J 8 5 3	♣	Q 9 7 5 4

E.

North	East	South	West
1 ♠	Pass	1 NT	Pass
2 ◊	Pass	Pass	?

The reader, as he views the illustrations covering West's different actions in the above sequence, should realize that South, by passing, denotes a minimum responding hand with a preference for North's diamond suit.

West should *double* with:

	(1)		(2)		(3)
♠	6 3	♠	A 9 4	♠	7 5
♡	K Q 8 4	♡	J 8 5 3	♡	Q J 8 3
◊	8 5 4	◊	A 3	◊	A 7
♣	K Q 5 2	♣	Q 7 6 4	♣	Q J 8 6 5

West should bid his *longest suit* with:

	(4)		(5)		(6)
♠	6	♠	A 5 3	♠	A 4 3
♡	K Q 9 7 4	♡	7 2	♡	K 7 6 5 3 2
◊	8 7 4 2	◊	7 6 3	◊	9 7 5
♣	A 5 4	♣	K J 10 7 5	♣	4

West should *pass* with:

	(7)		(8)		(9)
♠	K 8 4	♠	8 7 2	♠	8 5 4
♡	A Q 8 2	♡	K Q 8 6 3	♡	Q 6
◊	K 7 5	◊	9 8	◊	Q 9 2
♣	6 4 3	♣	K 5 2	♣	A Q 10 8 7

F.

North	East	South	West
1 ♠	Pass	1 NT	Pass
2 ♡	Pass	Pass	?

This could be a treacherous situation, for West must venture into the three-level or force his partner to bid at the three-level. Yet West should never pass automatically, regardless of vulnerability.

West should *double* with:

(1)	(2)	(3)
♠ A 4	♠ A 3	♠ A Q 6
♡ 3 2	♡ A 2	♡ 5 2
◇ Q 10 9 4 2	◇ J 10 8 6 2	◇ Q 9 8 4
♣ A K J 3	♣ K Q 7 3	♣ K 9 8 4

In (1) and (2) above, although West has the high-card strength required to double *originally*, to do so would be ill-advised, since he is not prepared for East's probable heart response. In (3), not only is West ill-prepared for hearts but his hand is too weak in high-card strength for a take-out double.

West should bid his *longest suit* with:

(4)	(5)	(6)
♠ 3 2	♠ A 7 5	♠ 6 3
♡ A 8 4	♡ 8 6 4	♡ 4 3
◇ A 6	◇ K J 8 6 4 3	◇ A J 9 5 4 2
♣ Q 10 7 6 4 3	♣ 5	♣ K Q 3

West should *pass* with:

(7)	(8)	(9)
♠ 8 3	♠ 6	♠ 5 2
♡ 9 7 5	♡ 9 5 3	♡ Q J 10 7
◇ A K J 6	◇ K J 8 4 3	◇ A J 8 3
♣ K 8 4 3	♣ A J 7 5	♣ Q J 7

In (7) and (8), East's long suit figures to be spades, and the chances of getting together with East in clubs or diamonds is remote. In (9), West's best chance for a plus score lies in the hope that the two heart contract will be defeated.

West should bid the "unusual" *two no-trump* with:

(10)	(11)	(12)
♠ 8 5	♠ 6 3 2	♠ 5
♡ 6	♡ 7	♡ 4
◇ Q J 8 6 3	◇ A J 8 5 2	◇ Q 10 8 6 5 3
♣ K J 7 5 2	♣ A 10 9 6	♣ Q 10 7 6 3

On (12), West could easily be wrong: East *may have* a spade-heart hand.

G.

North	East	South	West
1 ♡	Pass	1 ♠	Pass
2 ♡	Pass	2 ♠	Pass
Pass	?		

This is a most dangerous position in which to reopen, for *whenever the opening side has not found a fit in a suit, the chances are that the defensive side will not find a fit either.* The tendency (as per principle) in these situations should be for East to stay out of the bidding. However, the following actions are recommended as winning bids *in the long run.*

East should *double* with:

(1)	(2)	(3)
♠ 3	♠ A 8 4	♠ A 2
♡ A 7 4 2	♡ 6	♡ K Q 7
◇ K J 6 3	◇ Q 10 9 6 3	◇ Q J 3 2
♣ K Q 8 4	♣ K J 10 2	♣ Q J 5 3

East might bid the "unusual" two no-trump with:

(4)	(5)	(6)
♠ 6	♠ 2	♠ —
♡ A 5	♡ 7 5	♡ 6
◇ K 10 8 6 4	◇ Q J 10 9 4	◇ J 10 8 4 3 2
♣ K 10 7 5 2	♣ Q J 10 8 4	♣ J 10 8 4 3 2

There are few hands with which East should bid three clubs or three diamonds, for if East had a good minor suit, he should have overcalled immediately after North's one heart opening bid.

H.

North	East	South	West
1 ◇	Pass	1 ♡	Pass
2 ♡	Pass	Pass	?

In this sequence, North may well have nine cards in the red suits, which seems to give East–West a good opportunity of finding a fit in the black suits. However, North may have a pretty decent hand and South may have as many as 9 high-card points. Thus, it could be costly for West to step in—but it could be equally costly for West to stay out of the auction by permitting North–South to play the contract at two hearts. In our experience, West, by bidding on borderline reopening hands, will tend to gain match points more often than not—in the long run.

West should *double* with:

(1)	(2)	(3)
♠ Q 6 3 2	♠ K J 3 2	♠ Q 8 6 4
♡ 9 4 3	♡ 5	♡ 8 6 5
◇ A 3	◇ K 6 4 3	◇ 5
♣ K J 7 5	♣ K 8 7 2	♣ A J 10 8 6

On (2), we would pass if vulnerable.

West should bid his *longest suit* with:

(4)	(5)	(6)
♠ Q J 7 5 2	♠ A 3 2	♠ A K
♡ 7 5	♡ 6 4 3	♡ 8 6 5
◇ 6 3	◇ 5	◇ J 7 5
♣ A Q 4 3	♣ K 10 8 6 4 3	♣ Q J 10 3 2

West should *pass* with:

(7)	(8)	(9)
♠ K 9 5	♠ K 8 6 3	♠ A 10 6 4 3
♡ 8 4 3	♡ Q J 10	♡ Q 3 2
◇ K 8	◇ 7 5	◇ Q 9 5
♣ K 8 6 4 3	♣ Q 9 4 2	♣ 6 5

I.

North	East	South	West
Pass	Pass	1 ♡	Pass
2 ♡	Pass	Pass	?

It should be pointed out that North's two heart response, in the above sequence, might show a respectable hand, a hand with which he might have been tempted, after passing, to jump to three hearts, but, instead, chose to take the underbid of two hearts. However, he might also have a poor hand. In the above type of sequence, after having passed, the upper limit of the single raise often becomes higher than the upper limit of the single raise by an unpassed hand. For West to bid might result in his side getting hurt; but for him to pass might yield the same bad result.

West should *double* with:

(1)	(2)	(3)
♠ K 6 3 2	♠ K Q 5	♠ 7 5 4 3
♡ 4	♡ 7 2	♡ A
◇ K 8 6 2	◇ Q 10 7 2	◇ K 9 6 3
♣ K J 5 3	♣ K 8 5 3	♣ Q J 8 3

West should bid his *longest suit* with:

(4)	(5)	(6)
♠ Q J 10 9 2	♠ 4 2	♠ 3
♡ A 5 2	♡ 5 3	♡ 8 5 4
◇ 7 4	◇ K J 10	◇ J 10 9 6 3 2
♣ 6 3 2	♣ Q 10 9 8 4 2	♣ A K 10

West should *pass* with:

(7)	(8)	(9)
♠ A J 8 4	♠ K J 8 3 2	♠ 6 3
♡ K J 10 6	♡ Q J 10 2	♡ A 4
◇ A 6	◇ 4 2	◇ 8 5 3 2
♣ 7 5 4	♣ 5 3	♣ A Q 7 3 2

West *might* bid 2 NT (the "unusual") with:

(10)	(11)	(12)
♠ 5 2	♠ 4	♠ 6
♡ 6	♡ 6 3 2	♡ 8 5
◇ Q J 6 5 3	◇ A J 9 3	◇ A Q 9 5 3
♣ Q J 7 5 3	♣ K 10 5 3 2	♣ K J 10 8 5

With (10) and (11), one is taking his life and (partner's) in his hands. The hope is that partner's suit is either clubs or diamonds. With (12), the hand is perfectly suited for the unusual no-trump; and, further, partner will know that you can't stand spades, for if you could you would either have doubled or bid that suit.

J.

North	East	South	West
Pass	Pass	1 ♡	Pass
2 ♣	Pass	Pass	?

In the above type of sequence, West will *pass* more often than not. North's naming of a new suit at the two-level indicates a 10 high-card point hand, and North–South figure to have the better cards. Further, the opponents are playing in a lowly minor suit; also, their hands might be misfit and therefore yours might be misfit also. But, again, this does not mean that you will automatically sell out.

West should *double* with:

(1)	(2)
♠ A Q 6 2	♠ A K J 3
♡ 8 4	♡ 6 3
◊ K Q 8 4	◊ K J 8 6 4
♣ 9 4 3	♣ 6 2

West should bid his *longest suit* with:

(3)	(4)
♠ K 10 8 5 3	♠ A 5
♡ A 8 4 2	♡ 8 6 3
◊ Q 6	◊ A J 10 8 4
♣ 5 2	♣ 9 6 4

West should *pass* with:

(5)	(6)
♠ A Q 6 3	♠ K 10 6 2
♡ 5 2	♡ J 4
◊ 7 4	◊ K 10 8 6
♣ J 10 9 6 4	♣ K 8 4

K.

North	East	South	West
Pass	Pass	1 ◊	Pass
2 ♣	Pass	Pass	?

In this situation, North has bypassed the major suits, and it may well be that your side can find agreement in hearts or spades. However, as in the previous sequence, North's venture into the two-level in a new suit shows 10 or more points and the opponents figure to have the greater high-card strength. You must tread with extreme caution.

West should *double* with:

(1)	(2)	(3)
♠ K Q 8 4	♠ J 8 6 2	♠ K 10 8 4 2
♡ K Q 7 4	♡ A K Q 3	♡ A Q J 4
◊ 9 4 2	◊ 6 4	◊ 5 3
♣ 6 3	♣ 7 5 2	♣ 5 3

West should bid his *longest suit* with:

(4)	(5)	(6)
♠ 10 4 3	♠ Q J 8 3 2	♠ Q 7 6 4 3 2
♡ K J 10 6 4	♡ K 6 3	♡ A K
◊ A Q 6	◊ A 4	◊ 6 4
♣ 8 2	♣ 10 4 2	♣ 9 5 2

West should *pass* with:

(7)	(8)	(9)
♠ J 6	♠ Q J 9 5	♠ A 10 6 4
♡ A 7 5	♡ A 7 5	♡ Q 6
◊ Q J 9 5	◊ J 6	◊ 8 6 5
♣ Q J 8 6	♣ Q J 8 6	♣ K J 9 6

L.

North	East	South	West
Pass	Pass	1 ♡	Pass
1 ♠	Pass	2 ♠	Pass
Pass	?		

In the above sequence, it is dangerous for East to step in. South may have quite a respectable hand.

East *might* double with:

(1)	(2)
♠ 8 4	♠ A 4 3
♡ A K 6	♡ A 5
◊ Q J 8 4	◊ Q 8 7 6
♣ Q 10 7 5	♣ Q 10 6 2

M.

North	East	South	West
Pass	Pass	1 ♠	Pass
1 NT	Pass	2 ♡	Pass
Pass	?		

Although North and South may have limited hands, South might have a pretty fair hand. Any hand in which East has length in spades should be passed, for North figures to be short of spades, and East might well be stuck with his spade losers. Yet, although it is dangerous to bid (speaking generally), it could prove to be just as costly to pass.

East should *double* with:

(1)	(2)	(3)
♠ A 8 4	♠ A 2	♠ A K
♡ 6 2	♡ A 2	♡ 6 5
◇ Q J 6 3	◇ Q 10 4 3 2	◇ J 8 7 5 3
♣ K J 4 2	♣ J 10 9 3	♣ Q J 6 2

East should bid his *longest suit* with:

(4)	(5)
♠ 6	♠ 6 2
♡ A 8 2	♡ 5 3
◇ K J 9 8 3 2	◇ A J 6
♣ J 10 5	♣ Q J 9 8 4 2

East should *pass* with:

(6)	(7)
♠ 7 5 3 2	♠ 8 4 2
♡ 8 4	♡ 5 3
◇ K 7	◇ A J 8 3
♣ A Q 8 4 2	♣ K Q 8 3

East should bid the "unusual" two no-trump with:

(8)	(9)
♠ 6 5	♠ 7
♡ A	♡ 4 2
◇ Q J 8 4 3	◇ K 10 8 7 5
♣ Q J 7 5 2	♣ A K J 3 2

N.

North	East	South	West
Pass	Pass	1 ♡	Pass
1 NT	Pass	2 ♣	Pass
Pass	?		

The above is a delicate situation: North–South have gotten out of both the high-ranking no-trump contract and the major heart suit into the lowly minor suit of two clubs. Certainly, every incentive for "balance of power" bidding exists. However, caution should be exercised by East when possessing length in hearts, for North figures to have at most two hearts (with three he would have given a preference bid to two hearts instead of having passed two clubs).

East should *double* with:

(1)	(2)
♠ Q J 6 2	♠ A K J 6
♡ 4 2	♡ 7
◇ A Q J 4	◇ K 7 5 3 2
♣ 7 5 3	♣ 8 4 3

East should bid his *longest suit* with:

(3)	(4)
♠ Q J 5	♠ K J 9 6 2
♡ 3 2	♡ 6 5
◇ K 10 8 3 2	◇ A 8 7
♣ A 6 2	♣ 5 4 2

East should *pass* with:

(5)	(6)
♠ K J 8 4	♠ Q 10 6 2
♡ 9 6 3 2	♡ 7 5 3
◇ 10 4 3	◇ A 8 4
♣ A 5	♣ K Q 10

O.

North	East	South	West
Pass	1 ♡	Pass	1 NT
Pass	2 ♣	Pass	2 ♡
Pass	Pass	?	

In this sequence, South should give every consideration to reopening the bidding, for both East and West have indicated "weakness." South should *double* with:

(1)	(2)
♠ Q J 9 4	♠ 7 5 3 2
♡ 5	♡ A 4 2
◇ K J 8 6 2	◇ A Q 7 5
♣ Q J 3	♣ 9 3

South should bid *his longest suit* with:

(3)	(4)
♠ Q 9 7 5 2	♠ A J 6
♡ A 8 4	♡ 7 5
◇ K 9 3	◇ J 10 9 6 3 2
♣ 6 4	♣ K 4

South should *pass* with:

(5)	(6)
♠ A Q 4 2	♠ 7 5
♡ J 9 6 3	♡ A J 6
◇ Q 8 3	◇ J 10 9 6 3 2
♣ 7 5	♣ K 4

P.

North	East	South	West
Pass	Pass	1 ◇	Pass
2 ◇	Pass	Pass	?

It is rather apparent that East–West have the major suits. West should go out of his way to reopen the bidding.

West should *double* with:

(1)	(2)	(3)
♠ Q J 6 2	♠ 8 5 3 2	♠ A K 7
♡ Q J 5 3	♡ 7 6 4 2	♡ Q 10 8 3
◇ A 5 2	◇ A K 5	◇ 6 4 2
♣ 6 4	♣ K 6	♣ J 10 5

West should bid his *major suit* with:

(4)	(5)	(6)
♠ A 8 4 3 2	♠ 9 5 4	♠ K 10 8 3 2
♡ K 8 3	♡ Q J 8 3 2	♡ 7
◇ 9 4	◇ A 7	◇ K Q 7
♣ 7 5 3	♣ 8 4 3	♣ 6 4 3 2

West should *pass* with:

(7)	(8)	(9)
♠ 6 3	♠ 7 5	♠ K J 5 3
♡ 9 5	♡ Q 8 6 2	♡ K 9 8 2
◇ A 4 2	◇ Q J 10 6	◇ —
♣ K J 9 7 5 2	♣ A 8 4	♣ 8 6 5 3 2

On (7), a three club reopening bid could be costly, for partner figures to be loaded in spades and hearts and your combined hands are probably misfit.

On (8), although you and your partner might have a respectable trump suit in hearts, it appears to us that the best chance of obtaining a plus score is to let the opponents play their two diamond contract.

On (9), partner may have four, or even five, diamonds and even if you have a good trump suit between you, you have to be a good guesser to find it.

Q.

North	East	South	West
Pass	1 ◇	Pass	1 ♠
Pass	2 ◇	Pass	Pass
?			

Assuredly, East–West have limited values, and North should strain not to sell out.

North should *double* with:

(1)	(2)	(3)
♠ J 7 2	♠ A 3	♠ 5 2
♡ A J 10	♡ A K 4	♡ K 7 5 3
◇ 7 5 4	◇ 8 4 2	◇ A 6 3
♣ A J 10 3	♣ 9 7 5 3 2	♣ A 9 4 2

North should bid his *longest suit* with:

(4)	(5)	(6)
♠ A J 6	♠ A K 7	♠ 5 3
♡ Q 10 7 5 3	♡ 4 2	♡ 8 7 4 3 2
◇ 8 5 2	◇ 5 3	◇ 6 2
♣ 4 3	♣ J 9 7 6 4 2	♣ A K 7 5

North should *pass* with:

(7)	(8)	(9)
♠ Q J 8 4	♠ 8 7 5	♠ 5 2
♡ A 6 4 2	♡ Q 10 6 2	♡ 6 3
◇ 9 7 5	◇ K Q J	◇ Q J 8 6
♣ 5 4	♣ A 3 2	♣ K J 9 6 2

CHAPTER 20

The Position of the Partner of the Reopening Bidder

It must always be borne in mind that the reopening bidder has bid *both* of the partnership hands. That is, if the opening side has passed out a hand at the one or two level, they are presumed to have in the area of 18–22 high-card points. Consequently the reopening side also has in the area of 18–22 high-card points. So if your partner reopens the bidding and you have 8 high-card points, he is presumed to have about 12; if you have 10 points he figures to have about 10; and if you happen to have 13 points, he is assumed to have about 7 points.

If the bidding goes:

North	East	South	West
1 ♡	Pass	2 ♡	Pass
Pass	2 ♠	Pass	?

And you are sitting West, holding:

♠ K Q J
♡ 10 5 3
♢ A Q 8 4
♣ J 6 4

don't bid three spades! Your partner has already bid your thirteen points once. If you bid, your partner will be furious—and rightfully so—especially if he holds:

♠ A 10 6 5 3
♡ 8 4
◇ K 5 2
♣ 9 7 5

Two spades figures to make just two, with two heart losers and three club losers. The opponents' two heart bid also figures to make eight tricks, and possibly nine depending on how the six diamonds are divided. Be grateful that your partner reopened the bidding with a rather "trashy" hand.

If the bidding should continue:

North	East	South	West
1 ♡	Pass	2 ♡	Pass
Pass	2 ♠	Pass	Pass
3 ♡	Pass	Pass	?

Now you may have a problem as to whether to bid three spades. If not vulnerable, there is justification for bidding three spades hoping for a set of no more than one trick, doubled, for a score of minus 100. If vulnerable, a pass is recommended since a minus 200 score (down one doubled) will give you approximately zero match points.

In situations such as the above, and *especially when your side is vulnerable*, always remember that where you, the partner of the reopening bidder, have a good hand, your partner has a bad one. And, in all probability, at most of the other tables East (your partner's position) did not reopen. Thus at the other tables, North–South were permitted to play at *two hearts*. The fact that your partner reopened, and in so doing drove the opponents to the three-level, gives you a tremendous edge. If you beat three hearts one trick, you will get an excellent score since all the two heart bidders will have fulfilled their contract. And if the opponents happen to make three hearts, you will get the same score as all the other defenders who played against a *two heart* contract—which contract, in this latter case, would be made with an overtrick.

When one reopens the bidding when the opening side has passed out the hand at either the one or two level, he does so because experience has demonstrated that if he "sells out," his side will obtain a very poor score. In reopening, one has two objectives in mind:

1. The outside hope that his side will be able to make a part-score.
2. Pushing the opponents one trick higher and hope that they have been driven beyond their depth.

If either of the above objectives is accomplished, the reopening side will obtain a good match-point score.

Logically, therefore, the partner of the reopening bidder should appreciate and respect the dual purpose of the latter's bid. The reopening bidder is usually sticking his neck out hoping it won't get chopped off by the opponents. If he also has you to be concerned with as his potential executioner, your partnership has collapsed. As a parting thought on this point remember that it is much nicer (and much more rewarding) to defend at the three-level than at the two-level.

Let us now look at some examples of what the partner of the reopening bidder should do in different types of competitive reopening situations.

You are sittting West, and the bidding has proceeded as follows:

North	East	South	West
1 ♡	Pass	2 ♡	Pass
Pass	2 ♠	3 ♡	?

You hold:

(1)	(2)	(3)
♠ K J 8 5 2	♠ K J 8 5 2	♠ J 8 3
♡ 7 3	♡ 6	♡ Q J 10 6
◇ A 8 4	◇ A 8 4 3	◇ A 7 4
♣ 9 6 2	♣ 9 6 2	♣ K 8 2

(1) Pass—and be thankful that your partner pushed them up to the three-level. The combined partnership hands might be:

West	East
♠ K J 8 5 2	♠ A Q 7 4
♡ 7 3	♡ 10 5 4
◇ A 8 4	◇ K Q 2
♣ 9 6 2	♣ 7 4 3

(2) *Bid three spades* because of your favorable distribution. The hands might be:

West	East
♠ K J 8 5 2	♠ A Q 7 4
♡ 6	♡ 10 5 4
◇ A 8 4 3	◇ K Q 2
♣ 9 6 2	♣ 7 4 3

(3) *Pass*—and don't give even a passing thought to doubling. If your partner had not been enterprising enough to bid two spades, the opponents would be playing a *two heart* contract. If you beat them at three hearts, you're a cinch to obtain an excellent match-point score. And if they happen to make three hearts, you're no worse off than if they had played at two hearts and made an overtrick. But if you double and they happen to make it, you have just secured zero match points—and have convinced partner that you are a menace in reopening situations. The actual hands, taken from a duplicate game some years back, were (East-West vulnerable):

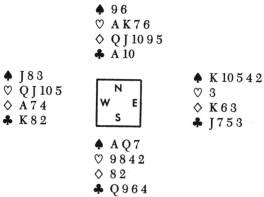

North hand:
♠ 9 6
♡ A K 7 6
◇ Q J 10 9 5
♣ A 10

West hand:
♠ J 8 3
♡ Q J 10 5
◇ A 7 4
♣ K 8 2

East hand:
♠ K 10 5 4 2
♡ 3
◇ K 6 3
♣ J 7 5 3

South hand:
♠ A Q 7
♡ 9 8 4 2
◇ 8 2
♣ Q 9 6 4

The three spade contract, doubled, will go down at least one, for a loss of 200 points. In all probability, it will go down two or three for a loss of 500 or 800 points. The three heart contract by North–South is a difficult one to play and may well go down a trick.

Here is a case where the partner of the reopening bidder obtained a zero because he failed to realize that his partner's reopening bid figured to be light.

This deal arose in the National Open Pair Championships of 1954. For being overtly aggressive West received only one-half of a match point out of 12.

Both sides vulnerable. South dealer.

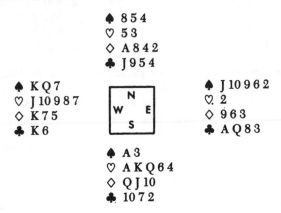

```
                    ♠ 8 5 4
                    ♡ 5 3
                    ◇ A 8 4 2
                    ♣ J 9 5 4
   ♠ K Q 7                        ♠ J 10 9 6 2
   ♡ J 10 9 8 7      N            ♡ 2
   ◇ K 7 5       W       E        ◇ 9 6 3
   ♣ K 6            S             ♣ A Q 8 3
                    ♠ A 3
                    ♡ A K Q 6 4
                    ◇ Q J 10
                    ♣ 10 7 2
```

The bidding:

South	West	North	East
1 ♡	Pass	Pass	1 ♠
Pass	3 ♠	Pass	Pass
Pass			

South opened the king of hearts and then shifted to the queen of diamonds, the defenders rattling off three diamond tricks. Eventually South took the spade ace for the setting trick.

Certainly West should have bid no more than two spades (and a pass by him was a conceivable action). When East reopened with one spade he was doing so in the knowledge that East–West had twenty or so points between them—and he was bidding West's hand as well as his own. Had East had enough to make a game, surely he would have *doubled*—to show at least 10 points—and would not have made a mere overcall.

Had East not reopened the bidding South would have made one heart, for a score of 80. By going down one trick vulnerable, East–West were minus 100. Of course, by stopping at either one spade or two spades, East–West would have scored 110 for making eight tricks.

When partner reopens the bidding with a double, one must also tread cautiously, for his hand may contain no more than 10 high-card points. Don't go leaping all over the place opposite partner's reopening double. Tend to make a minimum, non-jump response. If he happens to have a sound, any-position double, he will bid again—and *then* you can carry the ball and look for a game. For example, suppose the bidding has gone:

North	East	South	West
1 ♡	Pass	Pass	Double
Pass	?		

Sitting East, you hold the following hands:

(1)	(2)	(3)
♠ A J 8 2	♠ K 9	♠ K 2
♡ K 8 4	♡ Q J 10 8 4	♡ K Q 10
◇ K 10 7 3	◇ A 6 3 2	◇ J 10 8 3
♣ 7 2	♣ Q 7	♣ A J 7 4

(1) Bid only *one spade,* resisting the urge to jump to two spades. Had partner doubled directly over the opening bid your proper bid would be to jump to two spades. If partner fails to bid over your one spade call, the great odds are that your side cannot make a game.

(2) *Pass for penalties.* Your profits should be king-sized.

(3) Jump to *three no-trump.* Even if partner has only a 10-point hand, a game should be easy, for the opening bidder is marked with all the outstanding strength and the play should be greatly facilitated by your knowledge of where the missing high cards are.

As was mentioned, when partner reopens the bidding, he is bidding not only his hand, but also yours. If the bidding then becomes competitive (the opening side re-entering the auction), tend to be conservative when determining whether you should compete further. Remember that many pairs sitting in your direction may never have entered the bidding—and your partner, by reopening, has pushed them one trick higher than they would have gone without the push. For example:

North	East	South	West
1 ♣	Pass	1 ◇	Pass
2 ◇	Pass	Pass	2 ♡
3 ◇	?		

You, sitting East, hold:

(1)	(2)	(3)
♠ K 8 3	♠ A 8 4 3 2	♠ A Q 10 8 3
♡ K Q 6 2	♡ K 10 6 2	♡ A 10 6 2
◇ A 5 2	◇ 6 5	◇ 9 5 4
♣ 9 5 4	♣ 9 3	♣ 7

(1) *Pass.* Your partner has a really poor hand, with perhaps 8 points. If he had a respectable hand, surely he would have overcalled with one heart immediately.

(2) You have just about enough to gamble out a *three heart* bid if not vulnerable. If vulnerable, it's a guess what to do, for if they double and beat you one trick (200), you get zero match points.

(3) *Four hearts,* because of your highly favorable distribution and the bidding of the opponents. Your partner has, at most, a doubleton diamond, and may even have a singleton. If the latter, four hearts should be a cinch. If not, success will depend on a finesse (or finesses) in the spade suit. But if the queen of spades had been a low spade, you would have bid only three hearts.

Now let us look at various types of recurring situations in which the partner of the reopening bidder has the problem of whether "to bid or not to bid"; and if "to bid," then the question is "what to bid?"

1. ♠ A 9 8 4 2	North	East	South	West
♡ 7 5 3	Pass	Pass	1 ♡	Pass
◇ K 10 6	1 NT	Pass	2 ♡	Pass
♣ J 5	Pass	2 NT	Pass	?

No choice but to bid *three diamonds.* Partner, in employing the "unusual" two no-trump bid, has commanded you to name your longest minor suit. His hand might be:

> ♠ 6   ♡ 4 2   ◇ A J 8 4 2   ♣ K Q 6 3 2.

2. ♠ K J 10 8 4 2	North	East	South	West
♡ 7 3	1 ♡	Pass	1 NT	Pass
◇ 6 2	Pass	Double	Pass	?
♣ K 9 3				

Bid *two spades.* Do not jump to three spades, and do not pass for penalties. If your partner had a good hand, he would have doubled directly over one heart.

3. ♠ Q 10 7 5

	North	East	South	West
♡ A 8 4	1 ♡	Pass	1 NT	Pass
◇ K Q 7	Pass	Double	Pass	?
♣ K 6 2				

Pass, as you figuratively lick your chops in glee. Partner has at least 10 high-card points, which, combined with your 14, should yield a handsome profit.

4. ♠ A 9 7 3

	North	East	South	West
♡ K 4	1 ♡	Pass	1 NT	Pass
◇ J 7 5 3	2 ♡	Pass	Pass	2 ♠
♣ K 8 6	Pass	Pass	3 ♡	Pass
	Pass	?		

Pass. Partner has pushed the opponents to the three-level with a courageous bid. Don't punish him by bidding three spades. Is it not better to defend against three hearts than against two hearts? Are you not in the position of "heads, we win; tails, we break even"?

5. ♠ K J 6 3

	North	East	South	West
♡ K J 8 4	Pass	1 ♣	Pass	1 ♠
◇ 7 5	Pass	2 ♣	Pass	Pass
♣ Q 10 9	2 ♡	Pass	Pass	3 ♣
	Pass	Pass	?	

Pass. This is a very close situation, and a pass might turn out to be the losing bid on any particular deal. However, in the long run it will be the winning bid in terms of both match points and partnership morale. If you bid three hearts or double three clubs, you are penalizing a partner who may have made a desperation bid of two hearts in order to try to push the opponents one trick higher. Do not destroy partnership confidence in this delicate situation.

6. ♠ A 10 6 5

	West	North	East	South
♡ 8 4 3	1 ♣	Pass	1 ♡	Pass
◇ A J 10 8 4	2 ♡	Pass	Pass	2 ♠
♣ 5	3 ♡	?		

North should bid *four spades*, since a raise to three spades would correctly be interpreted as a competitive raise. On the bidding, South has at most a doubleton heart and possibly only a singleton. North's singleton club should give South an excellent play for his four spade contract. Had North held:

♠ Q 10 6 5   ♡ 8 4 3   ♢ A J 10 8 4   ♣ 5,

he should bid only three spades. Had North held:

♠ Q 10 6 5   ♡ 8 4   ♢ A J 10 8 4   ♣ 5 3,

he should pass, being thankful that South pushed the opponents to three hearts.

Again, bear in mind that when the decision as to whether to bid or pass is close, lean to the conservative side since many pairs sitting in your direction probably never entered the bidding, thus permitting the opponents to purchase the contract at a lower level.

The opponents are vulnerable; you are not.

7.	♠ Q 10 4	West	North	East	South
	♡ A Q 9 5	1 ♡	Pass	1 NT	Pass
	♢ 7 6 2	2 ♡	Pass	Pass	2 ♠
	♣ A 10 4	3 ♡	?		

Double! You have four tricks in your own hand, and partner figures to have one trick. A one-trick set—200 points—will net you more than you could have scored at two or three spades (110 or 140).

Neither side is vulnerable.

8.	♠ K J 7 5	West	North	East	South
	♡ A J 2	1 ♡	Pass	1 NT	Pass
	♢ J 6 3	2 ♣	Pass	Pass	2 ♠
	♣ Q 10 9	Pass	Pass	3 ♣	Pass
		Pass	?		

A *pass* is recommended, although it could turn out to be wrong. Three options are available: pass, double, or three spades. We believe there is a reasonable chance of defeating the three club contract, while our own three spade contract figures to go down. The double is a poor gamble, since a one-trick set will then give us 100 rather than 50—and if the opponents happen to make three clubs, partnership confidence will be shattered. Again, is it not better to be defending against three clubs than against two clubs?

In summary, it is most important that you understand the objective of reopening the bidding when the opening side has passed the hand out at the one or two level: it is to push the opening side to the next higher level, where you have a fighting chance to defeat them. Thus if the auction has proceeded along the following lines:

Opponent	Partner	Opponent	You
1 ♡	Pass	2 ♡	Pass
Pass	3 ♣	3 ♡	?

The only option you have—with possibly an exception once in a blue moon—is whether to say, "No Bid," or to say, "Pass." Partner has accomplished the desired objective—he has pushed the adversaries one trick higher. And, in so doing, he was bidding not only his hand but also yours. If you bid in this position, you are punishing your partner for having protected your interests; and next time, in an analogous situation, he will probably "sell out" at two hearts. In conclusion, don't make an enemy of your partner.

CHAPTER 21

Conventional Doubles

Some doubles are penalty or "business" doubles; some are take-out or "informative" doubles; and some are neither. In this latter category fall the doubles which have a specialized, precise, artificial significance.

The penalty and take-out doubles have been presented in the preceding chapters. In this chapter there will be introduced those specialized types of doubles that are employed by our nation's most efficient players.

I. The Responsive Double

This is a useful bidding tactic which is employed by many match-point players. It has had printed exposure in bridge periodicals, but not too much elsewhere. It is designed to enable you to say you have a little something when the nature and texture of your holding would otherwise forbid it. If, for example, the bidding proceeds:

West	North	East	South
1 ♠	Double	2 ♠ or 3 ♠	?

and South holds:

♠ A 3
♡ 9 7 6 2
◇ K 7 5
♣ Q 9 6 3

South should *double* if his partnership is playing *responsive doubles*. It is not for penalty, but shows instead a smattering of strength (8–11 points) and no suit worth bidding at this level. Had South held a good suit, he would have bid it instead of employing the double.

Here are a few more illustrations.

1. South holds:

> ♠ Q 10 6 2
> ♡ Q 9 6 2
> ◇ A 6 5
> ♣ 8 2

The bidding has proceeded:

West	North	East	South
1 ♣	Double	2 ♣	?

South should *double*.

2. South holds:

(a)	(b)
♠ 8 3	♠ A
♡ K J 9 4 2	♡ K 10 6 2
◇ A 10 7 5	◇ Q 7 4 3 2
♣ 7 3	♣ J 5 3

The bidding has proceeded:

West	North	East	South
1 ♠	Double	3 ♠	?

South should *double*.

Partner—who doubled *originally* for takeout—always has the option of converting to penalty (by passing) if his holding is suitable, since he knows you have some defensive values. Note that you, South in the above holdings, will rarely ever have the desire to double for penalty yourself. Most pairs who play responsive doubles use it up to and including three spades by East. They play doubles of higher pre-empts by East to be penalty doubles.

The responsive double, by the way, is used only when opener's partner, after an intervening take-out double, has raised opener's suit to the two or three level. In this case, fourth hand employs the responsive double.

II. Negative Doubles

Devotees of the Roth-Stone and the Kaplan-Sheinwold systems are the principal users of this bidding device. Since it has undeniable merit, it is slowly gaining adherents—although we think it has an undeniable lack of merit as well. As always with such devices, infinite variations and partial usages abound. It is a cousin—or an outgrowth—of the responsive double which preceded it by several years. As can be observed in the following illustrations, it is different because the cast of characters (the bids) changes, and the field of operations becomes broader. South's doubles, below, are *negative* doubles.

	North	East	South
1.	1 ◇	1 ♠	Double
2.	1 ◇	2 ♣	Double
3.	1 ♣	2 ♡ (weak)	Double

The negative double comes into play when partner opens the bidding and the next opponent overcalls. A double by the responder announces 8–11 points, little or no support for opener's suit, and values in the suits other than the one in which the opponent has made his overcall. At the same time, the negative doubler indicates that he has not enough of a hand to make a free bid in a new suit.

Here are two illustrations of the negative double:

The bidding has proceeded:

North	East	South
1 ◇	1 ♡	Double

South might hold:

(1)	(2)	(3)
♠ K J 7 2	♠ Q 8 6 4 2	♠ Q 7
♡ 7 5 3	♡ 8 5 3 2	♡ 9 6 4
◇ 8 4 2	◇ 9 4	◇ 5 3 2
♣ A J 7	♣ A Q	♣ A K 8 6 3

The bidding has proceeded:

North	East	South
1 ♡	2 ♣	Double

South might hold:

(4)	(5)	(6)
♠ A 9 4 2	♠ A Q 7 4	♠ 9 7 5 3 2
♡ 3 2	♡ 8 2	♡ 6 4
◇ K J 9 4	◇ Q 10 8 3 2	◇ A K J 4
♣ 7 5 4	♣ 10 7	♣ 5 3

The negative double obviously enables the player to announce meager values when he might otherwise have been forced to keep silent. An obvious and most important disadvantage is that no penalty double by the responder at the level of one or two is possible, and those have always proven to be the most lucrative penalty doubles.

The element of surprise is probably the major virtue of the negative double. Many opponents are caught off guard before they discover the double is not for penalty. To negate this unfair advantage that the users of negative doubles would otherwise have, the latter are required to have this convention listed on their private scorecards and must also explain its nature to their opponents at the time the negative double is made. As of this writing, that is the law in competition sanctioned by the American Contract Bridge League.

III. Lead-Directing Doubles

We are reminded of an old story about a bridge game that had been going on for 20 consecutive hours, during which there had been much eating and imbibing but no sleeping. At the very end, a player reached a contract of seven hearts, which was doubled and promptly redoubled. When the opening lead had been made and the dummy came into view, declarer perceived that he was off the ace of trumps. He won the first trick, and played the king of trumps, upon which a defender played the ace. No one reached to clear the trick from the center of the table, so declarer kept on playing high cards to which everyone followed as long as they were able to for the next four or five tricks. Now, with all the preceding tricks still lying in the center of the table, declarer showed his hand and claimed the balance of the tricks. The defense conceded, whereupon declarer raked in all the tricks and proceeded to score the hand as seven hearts, doubled and redoubled and fulfilled. The defender who had held the ace of trumps scratched his head and muttered sleepily: "I know I had this hand beaten, but I'm darned if I can remember how."

The above is the type of game in which we would like to double voluntarily bid slams. But, at either rubber bridge or match-point play, the mere defeat of a slam automatically nets a very good result even without doubling. Bear in mind that you will seldom defeat a voluntarily bid slam (bid by a reasonable pair) more than one or two tricks. If, by doubling, you present declarer with the key to fulfillment (by pinpointing the outstanding high cards), you will regret it deeply. Furthermore, he may be able to run out to a contract he can make. Here is a classic illustration of this latter point. The deal arose in a National Championship event many years ago.

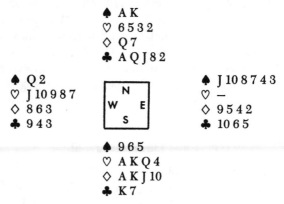

```
                    ♠ A K
                    ♡ 6 5 3 2
                    ◊ Q 7
                    ♣ A Q J 8 2
  ♠ Q 2                               ♠ J 10 8 7 4 3
  ♡ J 10 9 8 7         N              ♡ —
  ◊ 8 6 3         W         E         ◊ 9 5 4 2
  ♣ 9 4 3             S               ♣ 10 6 5
                    ♠ 9 6 5
                    ♡ A K Q 4
                    ◊ A K J 10
                    ♣ K 7
```

Both sides vulnerable. South dealer.
The bidding:

South	West	North	East
1 ♡	Pass	3 ♣	Pass
3 ◊	Pass	4 ♡	Pass
4 NT	Pass	5 ♡	Pass
5 NT	Pass	6 ◊	Pass
7 ♡	Double	Pass	Pass
7 NT	Pass	Pass	Pass

As is apparent, South's seven heart contract would have suffered a two-trick set. But when West doubled, South, knowing that his side had all the aces and kings, realized that West had to be doubling on trump length. Thus, having been forewarned, South ran out to seven no-trump, at which contract 14 tricks were available. He graciously settled for only 13 tricks.

A. When to Double Slam Contracts

Some holdings that ordinarily precipitate thoughts of doubling slam contracts but that should not elicit more than fleeting contemplation are these:

> Two aces.
> An ace and a side K Q combination.
> An ace and two kings.

If you possess any of these combinations, you should pass quietly and hope the opponents have erred.

What then, you might ask, is a good penalty double of a slam? Well, the holding of the ace and king of trumps would comprise a sound double; but the ace, king, and queen would be better. We would double with either of these combinations because no runout figures to be successful. However, we would not consider doubling a slam with the Q J 10 9 of trumps (or, as evidenced a few paragraphs back, with the J 10 9 8 7 of trumps) because we could be left holding an empty bag if the opponents, having been forewarned, ran out to six no-trump.

We have tried to make it apparent that doubles of slams are not considered winning tactics unless you have the opposition inescapably trapped. However, some risky doubles are advocated when the double enhances your chances of defeating the contract.

B. Conventional Meaning of Slam Doubles

All slam doubles, except when the opponents are obviously sacrificing, *have a conventional meaning* and call for a *specific lead* from partner. If you have the contract defeated in any event, the lead will have no bearing on the result. If, however, a specific lead which you would have no reason to expect provides you with a good opportunity to procure the two tricks necessary to defeat the contract, you should double to insure the lead.

> The double of a slam contract calls for the lead of the *first side suit* (other than trumps) bid by the dummy. If the dummy has not mentioned any suit but the trump suit, the double demands the lead of the first side suit bid by the declarer.

As examples of the double calling for the lead of the *first suit bid* by dummy, observe the following:

The bidding has proceeded:

South	West	North	East
1 ♡	Pass	2 ◇	Pass
3 ◇	Pass	4 ♡	Pass
6 ♡	Pass	Pass	?

East, holding any of the following hands, should double:

(1)	(2)
♠ A 9 7 6 2	♠ A 9 7 4 2
♡ 8 6 3	♡ 7 4
◇ —	◇ K J 4
♣ Q 9 6 5 3	♣ 8 7 3

The double calls for a diamond lead, the *first suit* bid by dummy. Without the double, partner figures to lead a spade or club, neither of which rates to be of any material benefit. In Hand (1), above, the diamond lead permits you to trump the opening trick, and you hope the ace of spades will be cashable. In Hand (2), you hope to establish a diamond trick before the ace of spades is removed from your hand.

As examples of the double calling for the lead of the first side suit bid by declarer (in the absence of a side suit bid by dummy), observe the following illustrations.

If the bidding has proceeded:

South	West	North	East
1 ♡	Pass	3 ♡	Pass
4 ◇	Pass	4 ♡	Pass
6 ♡	Pass	Pass	?

East, holding either of the following hands, should double:

(1)	(2)
♠ A 9 6 5 3	♠ 8 6 4 2
♡ 9 7 2	♡ 7 4 3
◇ —	◇ A K 2
♣ Q 9 7 5 3	♣ 7 6 4

Since dummy has not mentioned a side suit, the double calls for the lead of the *first side suit bid by declarer,* namely diamonds.

When East trumps the opening diamond lead (on Hand (1)), the ace of spades figures to set the contract. On Hand (2), when the diamond lead is forthcoming, East figures to take two diamond tricks.

When a member of the defensive side has bid a suit, the significance behind his double of a slam is unchanged. The double, in this case, demands that you *do not* lead the suit bid by your partner and that you again adhere to the conventional meaning behind the double.

When the bidding proceeds:

South	West	North	East
1 ♡	Pass	2 ♣	2 ♠
3 ♡	Pass	4 NT	Pass
5 ♡	Pass	6 ♡	Double
Pass	Pass	Pass	

If East had not doubled, the lead of a spade would have been the normal lead. However, with the double, West is commanded to lead a club, dummy's first-bid suit. East's hand might have been:

♠ A Q 10 9 6 4 2
♡ 7 5 3
◊ Q J 10
♣ —

If neither the declarer nor dummy has mentioned a suit other than the trump suit, the double commands the lead of one of the unbid suits. This is especially applicable when the defensive side has bid a suit. The double forbids the lead of the suit bid by the defense. For instance, with this bidding:

South	West	North	East
1 ♡	Pass	3 ♡	3 ♠
6 ♡	Pass	Pass	Double
Pass	Pass	Pass	

East demands, by his double, that West select either a diamond or a club as the opening lead. Had East desired a spade lead, he would not have doubled.

Many players, holding five or six cards (or even four) of dummy's first bid suit, automatically lead that suit against a slam contract in the hope that partner will be able to ruff. Almost always, they find that declarer is the one who is short in that suit and that some other lead would have been more effective.

In these situations, we have a set policy that has paid handsome dividends. When we are void in dummy's first bid suit and the opponents bid a small slam in some other suit, we *automatically* double to make sure of securing the lead of dummy's first bid suit even if we have no idea of where the setting trick is coming from. Thus, our failure to double indicates that we are not void in dummy's first bid suit—and in these circumstances partner finds some other lead.

Our hope that the setting trick will come from somewhere does not always materialize, but our experience has indicated that it is a good gamble to double when void of dummy's first bid suit. In so doing, we have gained many more match points than we have lost.

C. Doubles of Game Bids

As players became familiar with the conventional meanings of slam doubles, they sought to extend such meanings to doubles of game bids. This attempt proved impractical. Doubles of all game bids *except three no-trump* have no conventional meaning. You make that lead which, in your judgment, seems best.

D. Doubles of Three No-trump

Careful observation over a long period of time has convinced us that a common theory about what a double of three no-trump calls for is, in part, fallacious. We refer to the theory that states that when a contract of three no-trump has been doubled and either defender has bid, the doubler demands the lead of the suit bid. Such practice will be effective whenever the doubler is the partner of the bidder and has a few meager possessions plus a key card in the suit bid. It will also be effective if the doubler has bid a suit that is reasonably solid and holds an entry card to cash the suit after it has become established.

However, if the doubler is the partner of the player who has bid the suit, he more often holds strength in all departments except the suit partner has bid. We suggest that the leader be permitted to exercise his judgment in this case.

We believe the rule should be that if only one defender has bid and then doubled, if his partner has the lead, the lead of the doubler's suit is mandatory. If only the opening leader has bid and his partner has doubled, then judgment should prevail. If both the opening leader and his partner have bid a suit, then again judgment should prevail, with one of their suits being a likely candidate but neither being mandatory.

Let us illustrate the above through various bidding sequences.

West	North	East	South
1 ◇	1 ♡	Pass	2 NT
Pass	3 NT	Double	Pass
Pass	Pass		

As was stated, it has been accepted theory (unfortunately) that when one player bids and his partner doubles three no-trump, the bidder is compelled to lead his suit regardless of his own holding. In the above sequence, West, holding the following hand:

♠ 6
♡ A 9 5
◇ K J 7 4 3
♣ K Q J 2

would be compelled to lead a diamond rather than the more attractive lead of the king of clubs. We deem this "accepted theory" to be at least slightly on the absurd side because East will more often than not have values in the opponents' suit (or suits), rather than specifically one stopper in their suits and a high honor in his partner's suit. Therefore, in the above case, we lead the king of clubs which in our judgment is the more practical lead. We state our rule as:

> When the partner of the bidder doubles, the bidder (and leader) will use his judgment about what to lead. But when the partner who has bid doubles and is not on lead, the lead of his suit is absolutely demanded.

For example:

North	East	South	West
1 ◇	1 ♡	1 NT	Pass
2 NT	Pass	3 NT	Pass
Pass	Double	Pass	Pass
Pass			

West *must* lead a heart.

However, in this case:

North	East	South	West
1 ♡	1 ♠	Pass	1 NT
Pass	2 NT	Pass	3 NT
Pass	Pass	Double	Pass
Pass	Pass		

The double does not call for a mandatory heart lead. North should be permitted to exercise his judgment.

It is accepted practice that when neither partner has bid, and the opposition has arrived at a three no-trump contract, a double strongly suggests (in some circles, "commands") that partner lead the first suit bid by dummy.

We would be remiss in our duty if we failed to caution that this double of three no-trump contracts has led to widespread abuse. The mere possession of a few cards in dummy's first bid suit is not enough reason to double. Sometimes the opposition retaliates with a resounding redouble. At match-point play, such a contract fulfilled (doubled *or* redoubled) is bound to result in a bottom score. You must possess enough assets so that you can reasonably expect to defeat the contract if the lead you seek is forthcoming. Admittedly, by not doubling in dubious cases, you will sometimes relinquish the opportunity to beat a few hands you could have beaten by doubling. In compensation, however, you will salvage many an average score which the double would have converted into a bottom score.

To repeat, and to conclude. In the following sequence, West has no alternative:

West	North	East	South
Pass	1 ◇	1 ♡	2 NT
Pass	3 NT	Double	Pass
Pass	Pass		

West's hand is:

♠ K Q J 7 5
♡ 6
◇ 9 8 5
♣ 9 5 4 2

He must lead the singleton heart in compliance with his partner's demand. Actually, without East's double, West would probably have selected the king of spades as his opening lead. The lead of singletons is usually unattractive at three no-trump contracts because the opening leader will not be able to lead that suit again should he subsequently be in the lead. However, the double demands a specific lead regardless of your own holding. You must comply.

E. Lead Opponents' Suit

As was stated a few paragraphs back, when a three no-trump contract has been doubled and neither defender has bid during the auction, the double suggests that, lacking a really attractive lead of one's own, the contract can probably be defeated through the lead of the first suit bid by dummy. When that suit has been rebid by dummy, it is practically certain that such an offense should not be originated. Also, when the suit has not been rebid, the opening leader should open any *good* suit of his own (e.g., K Q J 8 5, Q J 10 9 3, etc.), thus permitting the doubler to retain his stoppers in the opponent's bid suit.

When the bidding has proceeded:

South	West	North	East
1 ◇	Pass	1 ♡	Pass
2 NT	Pass	3 NT	Double
Pass	Pass	Pass	

West, holding:

♠ 8 7 5 3
♡ 9 3
♢ 7 5 4
♣ 8 7 5 3

should lead the nine of hearts. Not having an attractive lead of his own, he accepts his partner's suggestion that the contract can probably be defeated with the lead of the dummy's first bid suit, hearts. With two cards in the suit, West leads the higher.

On the same sequence, if West held:

♠ 9 4
♡ 7 4 3
♢ Q J 10 8 6
♣ Q 5 2

he should forego the lead of the heart in deference to his own good suit, diamonds. The doubler probably has something in the diamond suit. It is expedient to get started along that line of defense while East still has the heart suit well bottled up. Lead the queen of diamonds, ignoring the double.

F. DOUBLES OF CONVENTIONAL BIDS

Many opportunities to strike a telling blow for their side are lost by players lulled into a somnolent state because the opposition is holding all the cards and is doing all the bidding. In many cases, the failure is not always due to a lack of either wit or alertness. Often these players have not been apprised that such opportunities exist. Most competent pairs of our acquaintance treat *doubles of all artificial conventional bids as penalty doubles,* and, consequently, lead-directing.

The most frequent type of situation occurs when the opposition is indulging in a Blackwood sequence:

West	North	East	South
1 ♡	Pass	3 ♡	Pass
4 NT	Pass	5 ◇	Double

South is asking North to lead diamonds against the eventual heart contract. It is vital for South to have the kind of diamond holding which would render that lead an inviting prospect. He should hold an A J or K J combination or better. He must not double simply because he is long in diamonds (as with J 9 8 7 5 3), since a lead by partner to that holding will hardly prove damaging to a slam contract, except to the player making the lead.

Valid inferences may logically be drawn from the failure to double. If, on the above sequence, South has failed to double, North, with the following holding:

♠ J 6 2
♡ 9 6 4
◇ J 8 7 5
♣ J 7 6

should choose to lead either clubs or spades because partner had a chance to solicit the diamond lead (by doubling) but passed it by.

Where the opponents are employing the Stayman Convention, as in:

West	North	East	South
1 NT	Pass	2 ♣	Double

South should have a good club holding which he wants led, such as K Q 10 7 5 or Q J 9 8 3, plus other values.

South should be very careful in the above situation because he may be subjected to a redouble, showing a desire to play two clubs redoubled.

West	North	East	South
1 NT	Pass	2 ♣	Pass
2 ◇	Double		

North, in the above sequence, should have a good diamond holding, and he is urgently soliciting that lead.

G. WHERE THE OPPONENTS' SUIT BIDS ARE STRONG BUT ARTIFICIAL

West	North	East	South
2 ♣	Double		

West's two club opening is the strong, artificial, two club opening. Very little use will be found for a take-out double in these cases; therefore this double should always indicate a good club suit. Thus the doubler points the way either to the correct defense or to a successful sacrifice in the club suit. Similarly:

West	North	East	South
2 ♣	Pass	2 ◇	Double

East's two diamond response is the negative response to the strong, artificial, two club opening. South's double is not asking for a takeout but is showing a good diamond holding.

We distinctly recall one case that had an all-star cast in a national tournament. East–West were vulnerable, North–South were not. The bidding proceeded:

North	East	South	West
Pass	Pass	Pass	2 ♣
Double	Pass	5 ♣	?

West held:

♠ A K Q 10 2
♡ A K J 7 2
◇ Q
♣ A 2

West now elected to bid five spades, which purchased the contract. It was defeated one trick, but a five heart contract would have been there for the taking. It could be argued—with justification—that West's final action was ill-advised. Nevertheless, it must be conceded that the alert North–South partnership deprived West of bidding space and made his task much more difficult.

Where no suits have been bid and the opponents reach a three no-trump contract, we employ a double to *demand* a spade lead. For example:

South	West	North	East
1 NT	Pass	3 NT	Double
Pass	Pass	Pass	

East might have:

♠ A K Q J 2
♡ 7 5 3
◇ 8 4
♣ 9 3 2

Admittedly, this type of situation will come up rather infrequently but it gives up nothing and enables us to have a bid "on the house."

22

Conventional Bids

This chapter is devoted to acquainting the uninitiated players with the major conventional (artificial) bids which are used by many of our duplicate and tournament players. It is not required that the reader employ all or any of these conventional bids. They are presented as an aid to all would-be duplicate players so that they can cope with those who do employ these conventions. Thus, intimidation and bewilderment when these conventional bids are made by one's adversaries will be avoided.

Some of these conventions are undoubtedly already known to the rubber-bridge reader, as, for example, the Blackwood Slam Convention, which, universally, has always been utilized in all types of bridge games. Many of the conventional bids, however, are unfamiliar to the "rubber-bridge-only" player.

Within this chapter, these conventional bids are divided into two types: (1) Offensive Conventions designed to get the "good-card" holders to the optimum contract and (2) Defensive Conventions designed to allow the opponents of the opening bidder to get into the bidding more often than in the past.

Some of the conventional bids that are employed by most of our nation's duplicate players have already been introduced in the preceding pages of this text, such as the Fishbein Convention, the Negative Double, the Responsive Double, the Unusual No-trump, and the Weak Two-Bid. These conventions, naturally, will not be discussed within this chapter.

I. Offensive Conventions:

    A. Aces Over Strong Two-bids.

    B. The Blackwood Slam Convention.

    C. The Roman Blackwood Slam Convention.

    D. The Culbertson Four–Five No-trump Convention.

    E. The Gerber Four Club Convention.

    F. The Stayman Convention.

    G. The Drury Convention.

    H. Jacoby Transfer Bids.

    I. The Texas Transfer Convention.

    J. The Flint Convention.

    K. The Weak No-trump—the transition between an offensive and a defensive convention, since it is, in a sense, a pre-emptive type of bid.

II. Defensive Conventions:

    A. Landy Over No-trump.

    B. Ripstra Over No-trump.

    C. The Michaels Cue Bid Convention.

I. Offensive Conventions

A. ACES OVER STRONG TWO-BIDS

In response to a strong opening bid of two in a suit, these are the artificial responses which are made:

    1. No aces and no kings—*two no-trump.*

    2. One ace—bid *the suit* in which the ace is possessed.

    3. Two aces—jump to *four no-trump.*

    4. Two kings—jump to *three no-trump.*

    5. No aces, one king—bid *two no-trump*, then if partner rebids below game, bid *the suit* in which you have the king.

    6. One ace, one king—bid *the suit* in which you have the ace (as in 2), then bid the suit in which you possess the king on the next round.

Here is a typical illustration:

	North		South
♠	K Q J 10 9 6 4	♠	A 5
♡	—	♡	10 7 6 3 2
◇	A Q 6	◇	K 8 4 2
♣	A K Q	♣	7 6

North	South
2 ♠	3 ♠ (a)
4 ♣	4 ◇ (b)
7 ♠ (c)	

(a) Showing the ace of spades.
(b) Showing the king of diamonds.
(c) South can count 13 winners with spades as trumps.

B. THE BLACKWOOD SLAM CONVENTION

This convention is initiated by the artificial bid of *four no-trump*. It asks partner: "How many aces do you have?" The responses are as follow:

No ace or all four aces	5 Clubs
One ace	5 Diamonds
Two aces	5 Hearts
Three aces	5 Spades

If all four aces are possessed by the partnership, and the initiator of the convention wants to know how many kings his partner has, he now bids *five no-trump*. Partner responds thusly:

No king	6 Clubs
One king	6 Diamonds
Two kings	6 Hearts
Three kings	6 Spades
All four kings	6 No-trump

When an opponent interferes with the normal response to the Blackwood Four No-trump bid, the responder takes this position:

1. With no aces . . . . pass.
2. With one or more aces, he begins his count with the suit bid by the opponents. If, over partner's Blackwood four no-trump bid, an opponent bids five diamonds, you bid five hearts to show one ace, five spades to show two aces, etc.
3. A double of the opponent's bid informs partner that you think you can score more points than you would score if your side continues to bid.

Occasional situations will arise where judgment must replace strict adherence to the Blackwood Convention. For example, you are sitting South, holding the following hand, and the bidding has proceeded as indicated:

♠ K 8 3
♡ 7 5
◇ J 2
♣ A K Q J 9 4

North	East	South	West
1 ♠	Pass	2 ♣	Pass
3 ♠	Pass	4 ♠	Pass
4 NT	Pass	5 ◇	Pass
5 NT	Pass	?	

With the partnership known to possess all four aces, surely a six heart bid by South would not do justice to his hand. South can almost surely take six club tricks, which combined with a solid spade suit and the two red aces, figures to produce a grand slam. South should bid *seven no-trump*.

C. THE ROMAN BLACKWOOD CONVENTION

This variation of the Blackwood Convention was developed by the top Italian teams and has been widely adopted as an improvement over the original Blackwood Convention.

In response to the Blackwood Four No-trump bid asking for aces, here is the schedule:

1. No aces or three aces .... 5 Clubs
2. One ace or four aces .... 5 Diamonds
3. Two aces, both the same color (both red or both black), or both the same rank (both major suit aces or both minor suit aces) .... 5 Hearts
4. Two aces, different both in color and in suit rank (spades and diamonds or hearts and clubs) .... 5 Spades

For example:

If partner bids four no-trump, you respond *five hearts* with each of the following hands:

(1)	(2)	(3)	(4)
♠ A 10 4	♠ K 7 3	♠ A 8 4	♠ 9 4
♡ A 8 3 2	♡ Q 9 4 2	♡ 8 4 3	♡ A Q 10 6
◇ 5 4	◇ A Q 8 3	◇ Q 7 2	◇ A Q 8 4
♣ Q J 9 2	♣ A 5	♣ A Q 9 2	♣ J 7 3

The *five heart* response, showing two aces, is made on four different patterns:

    (1) Both aces in the *major* suits.
    (2) Both aces in the *minor* suits.
    (3) Both aces in the *black* suits.
    (4) Both aces in the *red* suits.

D. THE CULBERTSON FOUR–FIVE NO-TRUMP CONVENTION

When either partner wishes to investigate for a slam, a bid of *four no-trump* indicates that the initiator holds either three aces or two aces and the king of a suit previously bid by either partner. Responder bids as follows:

1. Five No-trump shows two aces, or one ace and the kings of all bid suits.
2. Holding an ace or a void in a suit of lower rank than the agreed-upon trump suit, the responder to the four no-trump bids five in the suit of the ace or void. Otherwise he bids five in the agreed-upon trump suit.
3. Having an ace of a bid suit or the kings of all bid suits and added values, he bids six in the agreed-upon trump suit.
4. If responder has neither an ace nor the kings of all bid suits, he must sign off by bidding five in the lower-ranking of the suits bid by the partnership.

To illustrate:

South	West	North	East
1 ♡	Pass	3 ♣	Pass
3 ♡	Pass	4 NT	Pass
?			

South holds:

    ♠ Q J 10   ♡ A K 10 8 4   ◇ Q 7 3 2   ♣ 5

South must bid *five clubs*, the lower-ranking suit bid, not five hearts. For all South knows, North may have a solid club suit, with no support in hearts.

E. THE GERBER FOUR CLUB CONVENTION

Where the partnership has agreed upon a trump suit, or when there has been an unusual jump to four clubs, or when the immediately preceding bid has been any number of no-trump, and when one of the partners wishes to ask for aces and/or kings, the *four club* bid demands these responses:

No aces	....	4 Diamonds
One ace	....	4 Hearts
Two aces	....	4 Spades
Three aces	....	4 No-trump
Four aces	....	5 Clubs

To ask for the number of kings, the original four club bidder now bids the next higher-ranking suit over his partner's response and partner begins his king-showing at that point. For example:

North	East	South	West
1 NT	Pass	4 ♣	Pass
4 ♡ (a)	Pass	4 ♠ (b)	Pass
5 ♡ (c)			

(a) Showing one ace.
(b) The "automatic" next-ranking suit, asking for kings.
(c) Showing three kings.

If the bid asking for kings happens to be the agreed-upon trump suit, skip that suit and make the bid asking for kings in the next higher-ranking suit. A bid in the trump suit asks partner to pass. For example:

1. North	South		2. North	South
1 ♠	3 ♠		1 ♠	3 ♠
4 ♣ (a)	4 ♡ (b)		4 ♣ (a)	4 ♡ (b)
4 ♠ (c)			4 NT (c)	5 ♡ (d)

(a) Asking for aces.
(b) Showing one ace.
(c) The sign-off. South must pass.

(a) Asking for aces.
(b) Showing one ace.
(c) Asking for kings, and bypassing the agreed-upon trump suit.
(d) Showing two kings.

Many players currently use a variation in asking for kings in which the original four club bidder (after his partner has shown the number of aces) always bid five clubs, asking for kings. This is, of course, similar to the Blackwood 4 NT–5 NT convention: just as 4 NT asks for aces and 5 NT asks for kings, so 4 C asks for aces, and 5 C asks for kings.

F. THE STAYMAN CONVENTION

Experience has demonstrated that when a partnership possesses eight cards in a major suit, the final contract will usually play best in that major suit. The Stayman Convention was devised to uncover this major suit fit—if one exists—over an opening bid of either one no-trump or two no-trump.

After an opening bid of one no-trump, the response of *two clubs* is artificial. It asks opener if the latter has a major suit of four or more cards. If he doesn't, he responds artificially with a *two diamond* bid regardless of the strength of the opening one no-trump bid. If opener has a major suit of four or more cards, he bids that suit.

(1)	(2)	(3)
♠ K x x	♠ K x x	♠ Q J x x
♡ A Q x x	♡ A Q x	♡ K J x
◇ K x	◇ K Q x	◇ K x x
♣ A x x x	♣ A x x x	♣ A Q x

Each of the above hands is opened with one no-trump (16–18 points), and responder bids two clubs. With Hand (1), opener rebids two hearts; with Hand (2), opener rebids two diamonds; with Hand (3), opener rebids 2 spades.

(4)	(5)	(6)
♠ Q x x x	♠ K x x x	♠ Q x x x
♡ Q J x x	♡ A K x	♡ Q x
◇ A Q x	◇ Q x x x	◇ x x
♣ x x	♣ x x	♣ A Q x x x

If partner opens with one no-trump, with Hands (4), (5), and (6), responder bids two clubs. With each of them, if opener rebids two diamonds (denying a major suit of four or more cards), responder rebids 3 NT.

With Hand (4), if opener rebids two hearts or two spades, responder will bid game in opener's suit.

With Hand (5), if opener rebids two spades, responder will raise to four spades; if opener rebids two hearts instead, responder will bid three no-trump. (Opener knows that since responder, by his

two club bid, expressed an interest in spades or hearts and since
responder doesn't like hearts, he therefore must have four spades.
For responder to bid two spades over two hearts is, therefore, unnecessary.)

With Hand (6), if opener rebids two spades, responder bids
four spades; if opener rebids either two diamonds or two hearts,
responder jumps to three no-trump.

If opener has both major suits, he bids the higher-ranking spade
suit first; and if responder does not support it opener will bid the
heart suit at his next opportunity to bid. For example:

North	South
♠ A K 8 3	♠ Q J
♡ A J 10 5	♡ Q 9 4 2
◇ Q 7 2	◇ A J 10 9 3
♣ K 9	♣ 6 4
1 NT	2 ♣
2 ♠ (a)	3 NT (b)
4 ♡ (c)	

(a) Showing a spade suit of four or more cards.

(b) Showing no interest in spades.

(c) Since responder's two club response denoted an interest in
spades and/or hearts; and since the three no-trump rebid
denied an interest in spades, responder is known to have a
positive interest in hearts.

As a part of the Stayman Convention, the direct response of two
spades, two hearts, or two diamonds over the opening one no-trump
bid is a natural bid, and indicates a hand that is too weak to play
at any other contract. Each of these responses commands opener
to pass. The hands with which two hearts, two spades or two diamonds would be bid over one no-trump are these:

(1)	(2)	(3)
♠ J 8 2	♠ K J 10 5 3	♠ Q 4
♡ Q 9 7 6 4 2	♡ 3	♡ 6
◇ 6 5 2	◇ 9 6 5 3	◇ J 10 8 4 3 2
♣ 4	♣ 7 6 2	♣ 8 7 5 3

A bid of three clubs or three diamonds over a one no-trump
opening bid is also a natural bid, showing the suit bid, but indicat-

ing a pretty bad hand. Each of these jump responses (in the minor suits) is a pre-emptive bid, and commands partner to pass. These are the types of hands with which a jump to three clubs or three diamonds is made:

(1)	(2)
♠ 4 2	♠ 5 3
♡ 5 3	♡ 8
◇ 10 7 6 5 4 3 2	◇ J 7 6 4
♣ 7 5	♣ Q J 6 5 3 2

The Stayman Convention is also used to good advantage over an opening two no-trump bid, the three club response being artificial and demanding that opener name his major suit of four or more cards. If the major suit is not possessed, opener rebids three diamonds. Here are the types of hands with which responder should bid three clubs over the original two no-trump opening bid:

(1)	(2)	(3)
♠ Q x x x	♠ x x x x	♠ K J x x
♡ Q x x x	♡ x x x	♡ x x
◇ x x x x	◇ A J x x	◇ x x
♣ x	♣ x x	♣ Q x x x x

With Hand (1), if opener rebids three hearts or three spades, responder will bid a game in opener's suit.

With Hand (2), if opener rebids three spades, responder will raise to four spades.

With Hand (3), if opener rebids three spades, responder will raise to four spades; if, instead, opener rebids three hearts or three diamonds, responder will rebid three no-trump.

G. The Drury Convention

This convention has particular application to duplicate bridge. Its purpose is to define whether third- or fourth-hand opening bids in a major suit are normal or subnormal.

In response to a third- or fourth-hand opening bid of one in a major suit (the opposition passing, the bid of *two clubs* is artificial and asks partner to show the value of that opening bid. With a minimum or subminimum hand, the opener must rebid *two diamonds;* any other bid denotes a sound opening bid.

To illustrate:

South (Opener—4th position)	North (Responder)
♠ A 2	♠ 8 6 4 3
♡ A Q 10 8 4	♡ K 7 5
◇ A 9 3	◇ Q J 7
♣ 6 4	♣ A Q 5
1 ♡	2 ♣ (a)
2 ♡ (b)	4 ♡ (c)

  (a) "Define your bid, partner."
  (b) "I have a sound opening bid."
  (c) "Then we have a game."

South (Opener—3rd position)	North (Responder)
♠ A Q 9 4	♠ K J 7
♡ Q 6 2	♡ A J 8 3
◇ 7 4	◇ Q 8 6 3
♣ K J 8 7	♣ 5 2
1 ♠	2 ♣ (a)
2 ◇ (b)	2 ♠ (c)

  (a) "Define your bid, partner."
  (b) "Subminimum, partner."
  (c) "Sorry, but we have no game."

H. JACOBY TRANSFER BIDS

Used by responder over an opening one no-trump bid. The originator is Oswald Jacoby.

Over an opening bid of one no-trump, a response of two diamonds is an artificial bid which demands that opener rebid two hearts regardless as to the latter's heart holding. Similarly, a response of two hearts over an opening one no-trump bid demands that opener rebid two spades. The purpose is to get the opener (the strong hand) to become the declarer, so that the opening lead will come up to him (as fourth hand) rather than through him (as the second-hand dummy).

To illustrate:

(1)	(2)
♠ 8	♠ Q 10 7 5 4 2
♡ A J 7 5 3	♡ 6 3
◇ 6 4 3	◇ 5 4
♣ 9 6 4 3	♣ 8 6 3

On (1) responder bids two diamonds, over which opener automatically bids two hearts.

On (2) responder bids two hearts, over which opener automatically bids two spades.

The Jacoby Transfer Convention also facilitates the handling of responding hands of intermediate strength. For example, partner opens with one no-trump (16–18 points), and you hold:

> ♠ Q 10 8 6 5 2
> ♡ 8 3
> ◇ 7 4
> ♣ K 6 2

In "Standard American" bidding, a response of two spades would ask opener to pass—and a game might be missed; whereas a response of three spades instead, which is a forcing bid, might well lead to an unmakable game.

Employing the Jacoby Transfer Convention, responder would bid two hearts with the above hand, and opener would make the conventional rebid of two spades. Now responder would raise to three spades, thereby showing an unbalanced hand of 7–8 points (including distributional points). Opener would then be in a position to know whether to go on to game or to pass.

I. THE TEXAS TRANSFER CONVENTION

This convention was devised in you know where and is used after an opening bid of one no-trump. Its purpose is to make the stronger hand (the opening no-trumper) the declarer, so as to have the advantage of the opening lead made up to it instead of through it. The reasoning is that the opening no-trump bidder usually has suits containing tenace combinations such as A Q, K J x, K x, etc. If his hand is put down as dummy, the opening lead *through* these combinations will usually give the defenders a trick; whereas declarer, possessing any of these combinations, will usually gain a trick if the opening lead rides around to him in fourth position.

In the Texas Transfer Convention, when partner opens the bidding with one no-trump (16–18) and responder's hand lends itself to a game contract in a major suit, responder bids four of the suit that *ranks immediately below* his true suit. That is, a four diamond response over one no-trump *demands* that opener rebid four hearts;

and a four heart response *demands* that opener rebid four spades.

On the following hands, you would respond *four diamonds* over partner's one no-trump opening bid and he must rebid *four hearts*.

(1)	(2)
♠ K 7 5	♠ 6 4
♡ A J 9 7 4 3	♡ Q J 10 8 6 4 3
◇ 4 2	◇ K 10 9
♣ 8 3	♣ 2

J. THE FLINT CONVENTION

This convention, which was invented by Jeremy Flint of England, has become quite popular in expert circles during the past few years. We, also, have incorporated it into our system of bidding.

The convention is a method whereby one can stop at a part-score contract after an opening bid of two no-trump. In response to two no-trump, three diamonds is an artificial bid which *demands* that opener rebid *three hearts* regardless of his heart holding. If the responder wishes to play at three hearts, he can pass. Over the three heart bid, if responder elects to bid either three spades, four clubs, or four diamonds, opener is expected to pass. Here is an example:

North		South	
♠ K 8 4		♠ 9	
♡ A Q		♡ 10 8 7 5 4 3	
◇ A J 7 3		◇ 6 5 2	
♣ A K J 3		♣ 8 4 2	

North	East	South	West
2 NT	Pass	3 ◇	Pass
3 ♡	Pass	Pass	Pass

Should responder, after bidding three diamonds and obtaining the forced rebid of three hearts from opener, now bid three no-trump, it shows a good diamond suit and a mild interest in a slam. For example:

South holds:

♠ Q 10 4
♡ 10 3
◇ A Q 10 8 3
♣ 7 5 2

North	East	South	West
2 NT	Pass	3 ◊	Pass
3 ♡	Pass	3 NT	

K. The Weak No-trump

The weak no-trump opening bid denotes a hand containing 12–14 high-card points and may contain a worthless doubleton. Here are some illustrations:

(1)	(2)	(3)
♠ K 7 5	♠ A J 4	♠ Q 6 3
♡ Q J 6	♡ 7 6	♡ K J 2
◊ A Q 5 3	◊ Q 7 5 3	◊ 8 5
♣ 5 3 2	♣ A J 8 6	♣ A K 7 5 2

The weak no-trump is actually an offensive convention. In effect, however, it also functions as a defensive convention in that it acts like a pre-emptive bid by depriving the opponents of one-level bids and forcing them to step into the auction at the two-level (which is not as easy as stepping in at the one-level).

A raise to two no-trump requires 11–12 points, and a raise to three no-trump 13 or more points.

Using the weak no-trump, opener's rebid of one no-trump, after having opened the bidding with one of a suit, indicates at least 15 points. That is, if he had 12–14, he would have opened with one no-trump. Hence, a sequence such as 1 D by opener, 1 H by responder, and a rebid of one no-trump by opener shows a minimum of 15 points.

The inexperienced player who is not familiar with the workings of the weak no-trump opener is often trapped by the one no-trump rebid, since in standard practice this bid shows a minimum opening bid of one in a suit. But in the "weak no-trump system," remember that the bid shows 15 or more points. So don't reopen the bidding with a poor hand if one no-trump is passed out to you.

II. Defensive Conventions

A. The Landy Convention

This bid was originated by Alvin Landy, who was the Executive Secretary of the American Contract Bridge League.

The bid consists of a direct, artificial *two club overcall* over an opening bid of one no trump. The two club bid is in lieu of a light take-out double and asks partner to name his longest suit. When the bid was devised, it was intended to be used only over a weak no-trump opening bid (12–14), but is now used against all types of one no-trump openings (16–18; 15–17). Over the weak no-trump opening, the artificial two club overcall shows in the area of 13–14 points and commands partner to name his longest suit; over a strong no-trump opening bid, in the area of 15 points, with the command to partner to name his longest suit. By inference, a double of one no-trump shows a strong hand and is to be construed as a penalty double, with partner being permitted to take out only if he has a very poor hand (less than 6 points).

With the following hands possessed by you, the opponent on your right opens the bidding with one no-trump (16–18). You bid *two clubs* (Landy), asking partner to name his longest suit.

(1)	(2)	(3)
♠ A Q 8 2	♠ J 6 5 3	♠ K Q 10 7 5
♡ K J 6 2	♡ Q 9 8 4	♡ A Q J 4
◇ K 10 8 7	◇ A K Q 9	◇ Q 10 2
♣ 5	♣ 7	♣ 4

The Landy two club bid is also employed by fourth hand in the pass-out position, and has the same meaning as when used directly over the one no-trump opening bid. That is:

North	East	South	West
1 NT	Pass	Pass	2 ♣

West's two club overcall is for takeout.

B. The Ripstra Convention

This convention, like the Landy Convention, is designed for use against an opening one no-trump bid. When your right-hand opponent opens the bidding with one no-trump and you are interested in both major suits, you overcall *with two in whichever minor suit you have the better holding*. Partner must respond with a major suit if he has one. He shows contentment with the minor suit which you have bid—either by passing it or raising it to the three-level, depending on the texture of his hand. The two club or two diamond bid shows a light take-out double type of hand.

If your right-hand opponent has opened one no-trump, you over-call (artificially) with *two clubs* on:

(1)	(2)	(3)
♠ A J 8 4	♠ K Q J 7	♠ K Q 9 5
♡ K Q 7 3	♡ Q 10 9 4	♡ K J 8 2
◇ 8	◇ 6 4	◇ —
♣ Q J 9 2	♣ A K 4	♣ K J 10 9 4

In each case, responder will bid either (1) two spades, (2) two hearts, (3) three clubs, or (4) pass.

If your right-hand opponent has opened with one no-trump, you overcall (artificially) with *two diamonds* on:

(4)	(5)
♠ A 9 4 2	♠ Q J 8 6
♡ A 10 5 3	♡ K J 10 5
◇ K J 7 4	◇ A Q 8
♣ 5	♣ 6 3

The above hands are all minimum-type holdings, with which a *vulnerable* two club or two diamond bid is not recommended. Not vulnerable, the Ripstra Convention—on the above hands—figures to bring a good result. If vulnerable, another queen should be added to (4) and (5).

As with the Landy Convention, the Ripstra Convention is also employed in the pass-out position. That is:

North	East	South	West
1 NT	Pass	Pass	2 ♣ or 2 ◇

West's minor suit bid is for takeout.

C. The Michaels Cue Bid Convention

This convention is initiated by a cue bid in a minor suit that has been opened by the right-hand opener. That is, a cue bid by South of two clubs over East's one club opening bid or a cue bid by South of two diamonds over East's opening one diamond bid denotes a light take-out double favoring the major suits.

For example, over an opening bid of *one club*, the next opponent, if not vulnerable, would bid two clubs on:

(1)	(2)
♠ A J 10 8 4	♠ K J 10 6
♡ Q 10 8 6 3	♡ Q J 6 4 2
◇ 7 4	◇ K 5 3
♣ 3	♣ 2

If vulnerable, the requirements are, of course, stepped up:

(3)	(4)
♠ A J 10 8 4	♠ A J 10 9 6
♡ K J 10 6 3	♡ A J 6 4 2
◇ 7 5	◇ Q 4
♣ 3	♣ 6

This convention is primarily for duplicate bridge since it is highly risky, necessitating sticking out your neck to obtain, at best, a part-score. The bid is reserved for those types of hands where an overcall is impractical, either because no overcalling suit is possessed or because the potential overcaller has two respectable major suits and he doesn't know which one to bid. In these situations, by cue-bidding the opponent's minor suit, he enables partner to pick the latter's best major suit.

The Michaels Cue Bid is not used by fourth hand if the responder has passed out the opening bid. That is:

North	East	South	West
1 ♣	Pass	Pass	2 ♣

West's two club bid shows a tremendous hand. In this position, West would double for a takeout with a lighter-than-normal hand if he were interested in a major suit game. In so doing, he would be giving his partner the opportunity of playing at no-trump.

CHAPTER 23

The Safety Play in Duplicate Bridge

In a broad sense, a "safety play" is one in which the declarer attempts to reduce to a minimum the risk of losing his contract. More specifically, the term "safety play" refers to *the play of a suit,* as opposed to the play of the entire hand. What the safety play usually involves is the deliberate giving away of a trick which might not have to be given away in order to (1) either protect against a bad distribution of that suit or (2) to avoid losing too many tricks in that suit. Where, for example, declarer can afford to lose one trick in a suit, but he cannot afford to lose two tricks (which would mean the defeat of his contract), he will seek the safety play to restrict his losers to but one trick. On occasion declarer cannot afford to lose any tricks in a suit, and he will then search for the safety play which will enable him to avoid losing a trick. In most of these safety-play situations, declarer sacrifices a possible overtrick to obtain his objective. When this is done, declarer is, in effect, taking out insurance against a bad break that would defeat his contract. The cost of the insurance is the payment of a possible overtrick.

All of the above relates to *rubber-bridge play,* in which the motive behind the quest for the safety play is the recognition of one fact: *The fulfillment of the contract is the· sole consideration,* and the contract is never jeopardized for the sake of an overtrick.

Where the safety of the contract is the prime consideration—in rubber bridge—the loss of a possible overtrick is a small premium to pay. But in duplicate bridge, the overtrick can be worth as much as the contract itself—even an "insignificant" overtrick at a small slam contract—*and the deliberate concession of a trick to guarantee the fulfillment of a game or slam contract is a luxury that no one can afford* (with an occasional exception, which will be introduced later on in this chapter).

In brief, at match-point play, one cannot afford to adopt as his guiding philosophy the approach of playing for "safety." If one does, he is wasting his talents and must inevitably be a loser.

Let us examine various safety-play situations, in the light of how the hands should be played in a rubber-bridge game and how they should be played in a duplicate game. It may take you a few pages to adjust yourself to the realization that a bad play at rubber bridge can be a good play at duplicate bridge; and that a good play at rubber bridge can be a bad play at duplicate bridge.

DEAL 1.

        ♠ A 9 8 2
        ♡ A 6 5
        ◇ 8 3
        ♣ K Q J 4

        ♠ K 10 7 6 4
        ♡ K Q 8 2
        ◇ A K
        ♣ A 2

Sitting South, you become the declarer at a *six no-trump* contract. West opens the queen of diamonds, which you capture with your king.

At rubber bridge, there is just one correct line of play: you lead the four of spades at trick two, and when West follows with the three-spot, you insert dummy's eight. Your contract is now absolutely guaranteed. If East captures the eight with the jack or queen, your ace and king of spades will pick up the two outstanding spades, and you will have your contracted-for twelve tricks.

The "finesse" of the eight-spot was, of course, the safety play designed to guard against West holding the Q J 5 3 of spades. Admittedly, this was a most unlikely possibility, but the cost of the safety play was an insignificant 30 points to safeguard the slam.

But at match-point play, this safety play would not be given even a passing thought. Surely the four missing spades figure to be divided 2-2 much more often than 4-0. And by playing the ace and king of spades and catching the four missing spades 2-2, you would now make all 13 tricks. And certainly, on the combined holdings, everybody in the room figures to be in six spades or six notrump, making all thirteen tricks if the spades are divided 2-2. To take the safety play on the outside chance that spades are divided 4-0 would be the height of folly.

The theme here is, of course, that the important consideration at match-point play is *how often* you expect a play to work and not how much (in total points) it could gain or lose. Mathematically, a 4-0 division would occur 10 percent of the time (West would have all four spades 5 percent of the time, and East the other 5 percent). A 2-2 division would occur 40 percent of the time. Is there any doubt as to the proper play at duplicate bridge? Or, for that matter, is there any doubt about the correctness of the safety play at rubber bridge?

Deal 2.

        ♠ 7 5 4
        ♡ Q 9 6 4
        ◇ A 8 4
        ♣ A K 3

        ♠ A K 2
        ♡ A J 10 5 2
        ◇ K 3
        ♣ 6 5 2

With no adverse bidding, you, sitting South, have arrived at a *four heart* contract. West leads the jack of clubs, you put up dummy's king—and East drops the *queen!*

In rubber bridge, there would be no problem. You would spurn the trump finesse in the interests of safety. You would bang down the ace of hearts and then lead another heart, making haste to get rid of the adverse trumps as quickly as possible. West would win the second trump lead with the king, East following suit. You would now chalk up a game bid and made.

Had you taken the heart finesse at trick two, as fate would have it, West would have won with the king and would have returned the ten of clubs, and East would have trumped away dummy's ace. You would now have gone down a trick—and it would have served you right, for you were forewarned that East had been dealt a singleton club and that, if the trump finesse lost, West would return a club for East to trump.

But at duplicate, the play of this hand is not quite as simple. Assuredly every pair figures to be in the four heart contract. Some will not get the club lead from a six-card suit headed by the J 10. A few West defenders undoubtedly will choose to lead from a doubleton, in which case the various South declarers can take the trump finesse "on the house." Can you afford not to take the trump finesse and settle for ten tricks, when other declarers might well be making eleven tricks?

As to the answer, there really is none that we can give with any conviction. All we can say is that if you try for eleven tricks by taking the trump finesse, half the time you'll make eleven tricks— and half the time you'll make nine. You pay your money and you take your chances at duplicate. At rubber bridge, the proper play is clear: *no finesse.*

DEAL 3.

♠ K 6 5
♡ A 8 4
◇ Q J 10 9 3
♣ 8 3

♠ A Q 4
♡ K 7 2
◇ A 7 5 4
♣ A 6 2

You are playing rubber bridge, and have arrived at a *three no-trump* contract. West opens the king of clubs, and you employ the holdup play, declining to take your ace. The queen of clubs is then continued, and again you decline to win the trick. West then leads the jack of clubs, which you win as East discards a low spade.

It becomes quickly apparent that in order to fulfill your contract, you must develop two more diamond tricks. It is equally apparent that if West gets the lead, you will go down. Hence, in rubber bridge, you must try to do everything in your power to prevent West from obtaining the lead with the king of diamonds.

The correct play is to play the ace of diamonds and not finesse. (We are discussing rubber bridge.) If you have the good fortune to catch the singleton king, you're home. If you don't catch it, you lead another diamond. If *East* has the king, he has no club to return, and you have fulfilled your contract. If *West* takes the second diamond lead, you were predestined to defeat whether you finessed for the king or didn't. The safety play of the diamond ace, in rubber bridge, is made to prevent West from cashing a singleton king of diamonds. You are perfectly willing to give a diamond trick away to East, but you must do everything you can to minimize (or eliminate) the possibility of West obtaining the lead.

In duplicate bridge, on the other hand, you have a 50-50 chance of making eleven tricks by entering dummy and finessing East for the king of diamonds. If he has it, you will bring in five diamond tricks by repeated finesses. To bang down the ace of diamonds on the 6 or 7 percent chance of catching West with a singleton king, thereby giving up on the 50 percent chance that East has the diamond king, is bad mathematics—and bad duplicate play. Incidentally, if you bang down the ace and *don't* catch the king in the West hand, you will be either bottom or tie-for-bottom on the board, for when you next lead another diamond, if East has the king, you'll make ten tricks—and everybody else who took the finesse will make eleven tricks; and if West has the king, all of you, at three no-trump, just went down two tricks.

So at duplicate bridge you forget about the safety play (of playing the diamond ace to catch the king instead of finessing for the king) and play to win the maximum number of tricks.

DEAL 4.

```
            ♠ K 7 6 4
            ♡ 7 6
            ◇ 6 3 2
            ♣ K Q 3 2

            ♠ A J 5 3 2
            ♡ A K
            ◇ K 8 4
            ♣ A J 7
```

Both sides vulnerable. South dealer.

The bidding:

South	West	North	East
1 ♠	Pass	2 ♠	Pass
4 ♠	Pass	Pass	Pass

Against the four spade contract, West opens the queen of hearts, South's ace winning. Potentially, South has four losers, three in diamonds and one in spades. But if East can be kept out of the lead, declarer can discard one of his losing diamonds on dummy's fourth club after trumps are drawn.

The normal play of a nine-card suit headed by the A K J in the combined hands is to play the ace and king in the hope of catching the queen, as opposed to finessing the jack. But, on this deal, if the ace and king fail to drop the queen and East has the latter card, a diamond shift by East may defeat declarer's four spade contract.

In rubber bridge, the safety play in the trump suit is automatic: You lead a spade to the king, both opponents following suit. Then a spade is returned from the dummy. East plays the ten and South inserts the jack. Whether the jack wins or loses, South has just fulfilled his contract. If it wins, the ace then fells East's queen and South makes at least eleven tricks by discarding one of his diamonds on the board's high club. If the finesse of the jack loses, there is nothing West can return that will prevent declarer from again discarding one of his three diamonds on dummy's fourth club.

In rubber bridge, the above safety play involved giving up a trump trick *to West*—if the latter held the queen—in order to safeguard the game contract. In a sense, the proper play of the trump suit was dispensed with in the interests of the proper play of the entire hand. The trick that had been given away to West would always be regained by being able to discard a losing diamond on dummy's fourth club.

Now let's look at the play of this hand in a duplicate game. Certainly every pair will arrive at the four spade contract and will probably get the same lead of the queen of hearts. Should one play the hand to make sure of making his contract? Or should one seek an alternative play in his quest for a possible overtrick?

First of all, in match-point play one cannot adopt an attitude of extreme pessimism. After all, if *East* has the diamond ace, which

he will have 50 percent of the time, South will always make 11
tricks even if he loses a trump trick. And further, with East possessing the diamond ace, if declarer catches the queen of trumps
in the West hand, he will make 12 tricks. If *West* has the diamond
ace and declarer catches the trump queen, he will also make 11
tricks, losing only two diamonds. But, of course, if *East* has the
Q 10 x of trumps and *West* has the diamond ace, then by playing
the king and ace of trumps, declarer may very well go down.

Certainly, in duplicate bridge, there is no clear-out answer about
how to play the hand, for the safety of the contract is not the
prime consideration. As to the best way to play for an overtrick
(or two) is a moot question.

DEAL 5.

♠ A J 10 8 4
♡ 5 3 2
◇ 9 5
♣ 9 7 2

♠ 6
♡ A K Q
◇ A K Q 10 3
♣ A 8 4 3

Both sides vulnerable. South dealer.
The bidding:

South	West	North	East
1 ◇	Pass	1 ♠	Pass
3 ♣	Pass	3 ♠	Pass
3 NT	Pass	Pass	Pass

West opens the jack of hearts, which you capture with the queen.
At rubber bridge, proper play is to cash the ace of diamonds and
then lead a low diamond toward the board's nine-spot. This guarantees nine tricks: four diamonds, three hearts, one spade and one
club.

At duplicate bridge, however, the rubber-bridge safety play
would be wrong, for by using it you will fail to make an overtrick
whenever either opponent holds the J x or the J x x of diamonds, a
most likely possibility. At duplicate, correct play is to cash the ace,
king, and queen of diamonds.

When this deal arose in a rubber-bridge game some years ago, our declarer failed to make his contract because he didn't employ the safety play. Had he been playing duplicate, he would have been in good company. As it was, however, he got H--- from his partner for not taking the safety play. Here are the four hands:

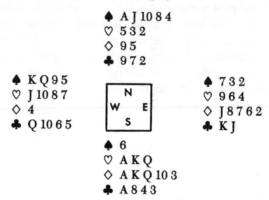

It is appreciated, of course, that the safety play of leading a low diamond toward the board's nine-spot is designed to protect against either hand holding the J 8 x x x of diamonds. Admittedly, this distribution is not likely to exist—but, then, safety plays at rubber bridge are employed to take care of improbable distributions.

DEAL 6.

A virtually-identical type of situation is the following, in which a safety play at rubber bridge is a "must," whereas at match-point play the safety play will lose an overtrick more often than not.

```
    ♠ 9 7 2
    ♡ 8 4
    ◇ A K Q 10 9
    ♣ 6 3 2

    ♠ A K 3
    ♡ A K 6 2
    ◇ 3 2
    ♣ A 8 7 5
```

Against South's *three no-trump* contract West leads the queen of hearts. At rubber bridge, the simple, automatic safety play is to lead a low diamond at trick two and insert dummy's nine or ten. Whether this trick wins or loses, you have just fulfilled your contract.

Mathematically, in the above diamond situation, by cashing the ace, king, and queen of diamonds, you figure to drop the jack, thereby making an overtrick. Of course, if you don't drop the jack, you will go down. Nevertheless, in duplicate, you play the ace, king and queen, for in so doing you'll make ten tricks more often than you'll make just eight (by failing to drop the jack).

Putting it another way, in a duplicate game, if you finesse the nine or ten, you'll make nine tricks 50 percent of the time (whenever East has the diamond jack). By cashing the ace, king, and queen of diamonds instead, you'll make 10 tricks more than 50 percent of the time.

DEAL 7.

♠ A K 5
♡ Q J 6 2
◇ A 9 8 3
♣ K 4

♠ Q 6 3
♡ A K 5
◇ K J 7 4 2
♣ A 6

The contract is *six no-trump*. West opens the queen of clubs, which you win with the king. How would you play the diamond suit, needing three diamond tricks to guarantee the slam contract?

In rubber bridge, you can underwrite your slam by leading the diamond king. This will assure three diamond tricks no matter how the four adverse diamonds are divided. If *West* fails to follow to the lead of the diamond king, you then lead a diamond to dummy's ace, after which a third diamond will be led off the board—and all East can make out of his original holding of the Q 10 x x will be the queen. And, of course, if *East* fails to follow to the first lead of the diamond king, then your safety play of the diamond king will have restricted your losses to but one trick since by now leading another diamond—through West's remaining Q 10 6—West will make only the queen of diamonds.

In duplicate bridge, the proper play will depend on how you intend to play the diamond suit, for safety or for the maximum number of tricks. If it is your intention to play the king and ace—in the hope that the four adverse diamonds are divided 2-2—then the play of the king first, as in rubber bridge, is acceptable. If West has all four diamonds, you will have made your contract, whereas an original diamond lead to dummy's ace will have cost you your contract; but, conversely, if East has the four outstanding diamonds, then the play of the king first will cost you an overtrick, whereas the lead to the diamond ace first (revealing the void in the West hand) would have enabled you to pick up East's Q 10 6 5 (by finessing twice) without the loss of a trick.

Since it is a pure guess as to which opponent—if any—has the Q 10 6 5 of diamonds, it is equally a pure guess—in duplicate play—whether to play the diamond king first (to guarantee the contract); or, instead, to lead a diamond to the ace. In duplicate, on this deal, every pair figures to get to six no-trump (point-count addition)—and the failure to make the extra trick might be just as costly as the failure to fulfill the contract.

DEAL 8.

This deal bears a great deal of similarity to the preceding one. The difference is that the combined hands contain *eight* diamonds instead of nine.

♠ A K 5
♡ Q J 6 2
◇ A 9 8 3
♣ K 4

♠ Q 6 3
♡ A K 5
◇ K J 4 2
♣ A 6 2

Against South's *six no-trump* contract West opens the queen of clubs, declarer's ace winning. Three diamond tricks are needed to fulfill the contract. By employing a safety play, they are absolutely guaranteed.

At trick two, the king of diamonds is laid down, both opponents following suit. Then comes a low diamond, West following low, and the nine-spot is put up from dummy. Either the nine-spot will win, in which case it becomes declarer's third diamond trick, or the nine-spot will be captured by declarer's ten or queen, in which case diamonds will have broken 3-2 and dummy's ace will later pick up the opponents' last diamond, making the fourth diamond a winner. The safety play of the king is designed to protect against West having the Q 10 x x or the Q 10 x x x of diamonds, in which case an original play of the ace from dummy will lose two tricks.

There is no question about the correctness of the safety play in a rubber-bridge game. But at match-point play, the safety play *must be* wrong, for here is a deal where every pair in the room will arrive at a six no-trump contract (1 NT by South, 6 NT by North). And the best play to make four diamond tricks (an overtrick) is to lead a low diamond to dummy's ace and then return a low diamond, South's jack being finessed. Whenever East was dealt the Q x x of diamonds (or the Q x), declarer will make an overtrick by the above line of play. And the likelihood of East having the Q x x or Q x of diamonds is greater than the chances of West having the Q 10 x x or Q 10 x x x or the 10 x x x (in the latter case, the play of the king first will fell East's singleton queen, and declarer, by finessing *West* for the marked ten of diamonds, will bring home four diamond tricks).

DEAL 9.

The safety play in this deal is identical to that in the preceding deal—though in a slightly different form—and is a recurring type of situation in both rubber and duplicate bridge.

> ♠ A 8 4
> ♡ K Q 6
> ◇ 7 5 3 2
> ♣ A Q 7
>
> ♠ K J 9 7 5
> ♡ A J 2
> ◇ A K
> ♣ K 8 2

South arrives at a *six spade* contract, against which West opens the jack of diamonds, declarer's king winning. In rubber bridge, the

winning play is to lay down the king of spades, everybody following suit; then a low spade would be led and dummy's eight-spot
inserted. The eight would win if West started with the Q 10 x x, or
it would be captured by East's ten or queen. In the latter case, the
opponents would have but one spade remaining, which dummy's
ace would pick up.

The above is the proper play at rubber bridge to guarantee the
contract. But again, at match-point play, it would be wrong. In
duplicate, the correct play is to lead a spade to the ace, and then a
spade off dummy, South's jack being finessed. This line of play
will bring in an overtrick more often than the initial play of the
spade king will guarantee an otherwise unmakable contract.

DEAL 10.

A similar-type situation is the following, in which the safety play
at rubber bridge is automatic; and in duplicate, the safety play is
"anti-percentage."

♠ 9 7 6
♡ 7 5 3 2
◇ A 4 2
♣ 8 6 5

♠ A K Q
♡ A K 6
◇ K J 7 5
♣ A 10 3

Against South's *three no-trump* contract, West opens the four of
hearts, and East's ten is taken by declarer's king. To make his contract, declarer must develop a diamond trick. (The thought of establishing dummy's fourth heart should be eliminated, for West almost
surely has led from a four-card, or longer, suit.)

At rubber bridge, correct technique is to lead the king of diamonds first, then a diamond to the ace, and a third diamond off the
board. Whenever East has the diamond queen—any number of
times—declarer's jack will become promoted into his ninth trick.

The safety play—in rubber bridge, as above—is to prevent West
from making a trick out of a doubleton queen of diamonds. At
duplicate bridge, however, while the safety play gains a trick whenever West was dealt the Q x of diamonds, it loses a trick whenever

East was dealt the Q x x of diamonds. And the latter combination is more likely to exist—mathematically—than the former. Therefore, the correct match-point play is to insert dummy's ace of diamonds first and then lead a low diamond back, finessing the jack on the second round of diamonds.

Deal 11.

As was mentioned, there are occasional situations at match-point play where a safety play should be employed. One of these would be where you are in a doubled contract which, if fulfilled, will almost invariably yield you a good score. In this circumstance, to play for an overtrick is absurd, since the fulfillment of the doubled contract will give you a top—and there is no such thing as a "top top." Another situation where a safety play might profitably be employed arises where you have reached a really good contract which few, if any, other pairs figure to reach. Here is an example of the latter type of situation. The deal arose in a New York City tournament some years ago.

> ♠ K 10 7 3 2
> ♡ K 8 5 3
> ◇ A 6
> ♣ 7 5
>
> ♠ A 9
> ♡ A 4
> ◇ K 10 9 8 7 5 3
> ♣ A K

South reached a *six no-trump* contract, against which West opened the jack of clubs, taken by South's king. This was unquestionably a superior contract, with the combined hands containing but 28 high-card points. Even if a slam were reached by other North–South pairs, it was quite likely that they would tend to bid *six diamonds* rather than six no-trump. And the trick score for six no-trump would be 190, while the trick score for six diamonds, making an extra trick, would be but 140. Thus if South could make 12 tricks at six no-trump, he figured to get a top on the board.

At trick two, the three of diamonds was led, West played the deuce, the six-spot was put up from the North hand—and it captured the trick when East showed out! From here in it was smooth sailing, declarer losing a diamond trick to West. Here is the deal:

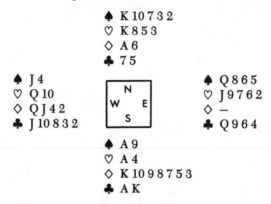

                    ♠ K 10 7 3 2
                    ♡ K 8 5 3
                    ◇ A 6
                    ♣ 7 5

    ♠ J 4   ♠ Q 8 6 5
    ♡ Q 10   N   ♡ J 9 7 6 2
    ◇ Q J 4 2   W   E   ◇ —
    ♣ J 10 8 3 2   S   ♣ Q 9 6 4

                    ♠ A 9
                    ♡ A 4
                    ◇ K 10 9 8 7 5 3
                    ♣ A K

In putting up dummy's six of diamonds, declarer was taking out insurance against the four missing diamonds being in the West hand. He really did not expect the six-spot to win the trick, feeling certain that East figured to have either the queen or the jack. And if East won the trick, then declarer would still have the ace and king to pick up the two remaining cards in that suit.

At rubber bridge, the safety play of the six of diamonds would have been the only proper play. At duplicate, it was not concern with the safety of the contract that brought the safety play into use. It was the realization that 12 tricks at no-trump would pay more than 13 tricks at a six diamond contract.

DEAL 12.

Another example of using the safety play if you have reason to believe that you are in a game or slam contract that probably will not be reached by most pairs is contained in the following deal.

                    ♠ J
                    ♡ 7 4 2
                    ◇ A K Q 6 3 2
                    ♣ 8 7 3

                    ♠ A K 3
                    ♡ A 8 5 3
                    ◇ 7 4
                    ♣ J 10 9 2

West	North	East	South
1 ♠	2 ◇	Pass	2 NT
Pass	3 NT	Pass	Pass
Pass			

West opened the five of spades, and dummy's jack won the trick. Game was now assured if declarer could make only five diamond tricks. At trick two, South led a low diamond off dummy, and permitted East to win the trick when the latter played the diamond jack, West following with the eight-spot. This safety play—the concession of a trick which might not have to be given away—was designed to guard against a 4-1 division of the adverse diamonds. The reasons for the safety play were these:

It looked as if bidding and making three no-trump would be a fine match-point result. The combined hands totaled only 22 high-card points; there had been an opening bid to contend with, and it is usually most difficult to get to a makable game against an opening bid. And the lead had given declarer a present of a trick which he could not have obtained on his own power. Had hearts been opened initially, declarer would have had no choice but to hope that the five adverse diamonds were divided 3-2 (and if they were so divided, then against a heart opening declarer would make just nine tricks).

DEAL 13.

As illustrated in the preceding deal, if the opening lead is more favorable than others are likely to receive, you can risk the loss of a trick to make certain of your contract. Here is another example.

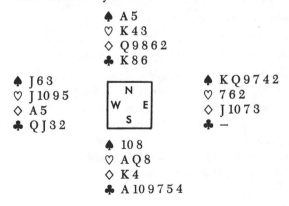

```
                    ♠ A 5
                    ♡ K 4 3
                    ◇ Q 9 8 6 2
                    ♣ K 8 6
    ♠ J 6 3                          ♠ K Q 9 7 4 2
    ♡ J 10 9 5      ┌─────────┐      ♡ 7 6 2
    ◇ A 5           │    N    │      ◇ J 10 7 3
    ♣ Q J 3 2       │ W    E  │      ♣ —
                    │    S    │
                    └─────────┘
                    ♠ 10 8
                    ♡ A Q 8
                    ◇ K 4
                    ♣ A 10 9 7 5 4
```

With both sides vulnerable, South, playing the weak one no-trump (12–14), opened with one no-trump and North raised to three. West led the jack of hearts. South won in his hand and played a low club and, when West followed with the club two, made the safety play of inserting dummy's eight of clubs. This play guaranteed five tricks in the suit and avoided the risk of laying down the ace or king and finding a void on the wrong side. The precaution was justified partly because the opening lead left declarer with all suits under control but also because:

1. The opponents held nine spades between them, and other declarers would surely get a spade lead.
2. The length in spades is probably with East, who would have had the lead in the more likely event of North playing the hand.
3. With a spade opening, if either defender held the Q J x of clubs, then the three no-trump contract would go down.

Assuming "Standard American" bidding by South, it was quite likely that, at other tables, the bidding would have gone:

	South	North		South	North
	1 ♣	2 NT		1 ♣	1 ◇
	3 NT		or	2 ♣	2 NT
				3 NT	

With a spade lead the contract is doomed unless the clubs fall together; so there is good reason (plus the operation of the laws of probability) to hope they will not.

DEAL 14.

As was observed in the two previous deals, the deliberate giving away of a trick that might not have to be given away can be the proper play even in a duplicate game. But the reason is not because it is a safety play, but rather because it is the "percentage" play. A percentage play is, of course, nothing more than the selection from a choice of two (or three) different and optional lines of play of the one that offers the greatest chance of success. As an example, witness the following deal, which should be played the identical way in both rubber bridge and match-point play.

♠ A J 10 6 2
♡ 8 3 2
◇ 7 5
♣ 6 4 3

♠ Q 5
♡ A K 5
◇ A K 4
♣ A 9 8 5 2

Against South's *three no-trump* contract, West opens the jack of diamonds, South's king winning. Upon examination, South perceives that he needs four spade tricks to fulfill his contract.

At trick two, he leads the queen of spades, West puts up the king—and a low spade is played from dummy, permitting the king to win. The contract is now fulfilled, unless one of the opponents started with five spades, in which case the contract was unmakable. Had West's king been taken by dummy's ace, the contract would have been defeated. Here is the complete deal:

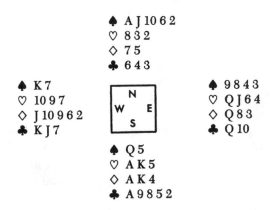

♠ A J 10 6 2
♡ 8 3 2
◇ 7 5
♣ 6 4 3

♠ K 7
♡ 10 9 7
◇ J 10 9 6 2
♣ K J 7

♠ 9 8 4 3
♡ Q J 6 4
◇ Q 8 3
♣ Q 10

♠ Q 5
♡ A K 5
◇ A K 4
♣ A 9 8 5 2

If dummy's ace of spades were to take West's king, then South could make but three spade tricks. By conceding a trick to the king, the contract is fulfilled whether the adverse spades break 3-3 or

4-2. By capturing the king with the ace, the success of the contract *depends on spades breaking 3-3*, which they do not.

The mathematics of the situation are these: when six of a suit are outstanding, they will break 3-3 only 36 percent of the time; a 4-2 division will occur 48 percent of the time.

In rubber bridge, there can be no arguing with the fact that the *only* proper play is to allow West's king of spades to win the first spade lead, for in so doing the contract will be made if it is at all makable. At match-point play, it is proper to allow the king of spades to win the first spade lead because if you take the king with your ace, *you will go down 64 percent of the time* and you will make an extra trick (five spade tricks) *only 36 percent of the time*. In other words, by taking the king with the ace, you will get a top board about one time out of three; and a bottom board two times out of three.

Deal 15.

The following is a simple rubber-bridge deal which, in duplicate, would create problems:

♠ 7 5 3
♡ 6 4
♢ K 7 5 4 3 2
♣ 8 4

♠ A K 4 2
♡ A K 2
♢ A J 6
♣ A J 5

South arrived at a *three no-trump* contract, against which West leads the heart queen, declarer winning with the king. South then cashes his diamond ace, both opponents following suit. Then comes the diamond jack, West covers with the queen—and the question is whether to take the queen with the king.

At this point, the only outstanding diamond is the ten-spot. In rubber bridge, there is no problem; you concede the trick to West's queen of diamonds. Whatever West returns, you now have ten tricks: two spades, two hearts, five diamonds, and one club.

But in duplicate bridge, if you concede the jack of diamonds to West's queen, you will make ten tricks; but if the queen is taken by the king and *East follows with the ten-spot, you will make 11* tricks. However, if you take the queen with the king *and don't drop the ten-spot,* you will make just seven tricks, since you will, in this case, never be able to bring in any more diamond tricks, there being no entry to dummy.

The issue, as always at match points, is whether to play for the safety of the contract or to try for an overtrick or two. Every pair in the room is going to be in three no-trump on this deal. How will *they* play it? If you knew, you could play as they would; or play as they wouldn't, if you desire to gamble. But you don't know how they will play it unless you assume that their rubber-bridge instincts will militate against their taking the jack with the queen. If the adverse diamonds are divided 2-2, then by taking the jack with the queen (catching the ten-spot), you have a top or tie-for-top. If you don't catch the ten-spot, you have a bottom or tie-for-bottom.

Our advice is this: Where in your opinion it is a pure guess, play safely for your contract, thus getting a plus score. Some team may not bid a game; some team may get to five or six diamonds. By making your sure ten tricks, you will beat all of the aforementioned teams. And if diamonds divide 3-1, you have a tie-for-top.

Deal 16.

```
        ♠ A 10 8 7 3
        ♡ 8 5 3
        ◇ K 2
        ♣ 7 5 2

        ♠ K Q
        ♡ A 10 7 4
        ◇ A 7 5
        ♣ A K 6 3
```

South arrives at a *three no-trump* contract, against which West opens the queen of diamonds, declarer's ace winning the trick. Declarer counts that he has eight top tricks.

At trick two, he leads the king of spades, and then plays the queen. On the second spade lead, West follows with the *nine-spot.*

South, needing four spade tricks to fulfill his contract, promptly overtakes his own queen with dummy's ace. He then gives away the ten of spades to whoever has the jack. The eight and seven of spades are now both winners, ·with the diamond king as an entry to cash them. This was the actual layout:

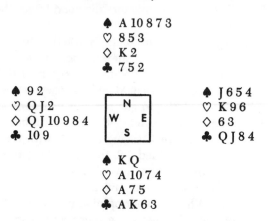

♠ A 10 8 7 3
♡ 8 5 3
◇ K 2
♣ 7 5 2

♠ 9 2
♡ Q J 2
◇ Q J 10 9 8 4
♣ 10 9

♠ J 6 5 4
♡ K 9 6
◇ 6 3
♣ Q J 8 4

♠ K Q
♡ A 10 7 4
◇ A 7 5
♣ A K 6 3

The proper play, as presented above, applies to rubber bridge. When West drops the spade nine, the game contract is assured by overtaking the queen with the ace (if declarer does not overtake, he goes down).

But in match-point play, the overtaking can cost an extra trick, which would have been the case had West been dealt the J 9 2 of spades instead of the doubleton 9 2. In this latter situation, had declarer not overtaken, he could then have entered dummy via the king of diamonds, and the ace of spades would then have caught the jack, giving declarer five spade tricks. Actually, at match-point play, declarer might even try for 11 tricks by this line of play:

He leads the king of spades and then the queen. He next plays a low club, conceding the trick to the opposition, which returns a diamond to dummy's king. The ace of spades is then led, in the fond hope of catching the jack. If "yes," then five spade tricks are made, after which a club is led to declarer's A K. If the six missing clubs are divided 3-3, then three club tricks will be brought home. If the jack of spades is not caught, however, then a 3-3 division of the six outstanding clubs becomes necessary for the fulfillment of the contract. And if the jack of spades is not caught, and the clubs do not divide 3-3, then declarer goes down. Of course, as was illustrated, he can settle for nine tricks by overtaking the queen of spades with the board's ace (when the nine of spades falls), but . . . hope springs eternal, and declarer has the option of going all out to play for the maximum number of tricks.

DEAL 17.

The next deal contains a standard-type safety play that arises quite frequently.

```
            ♠ 7 4 2
            ♡ K 9
            ◇ 6 5 3
            ♣ A Q 10 7 6

            ♠ A K Q 3
            ♡ A 5
            ◇ A J 8
            ♣ 9 8 5 3
```

Against South's *three no-trump* contract West opens the seven of hearts, East's jack being taken by South's ace. South then leads a club, West follows with a low club—and declarer deliberates: Should he finesse the queen or the ten? Let us say he finesses the queen, which loses to East's king, and a heart is then returned, dummy's king winning. Again a problem for declarer arises: Shall he lay down the ace of clubs, to drop the jack? Or shall he return to his own hand, and lead a low club, finessing dummy's ten-spot? If he guesses right, he will fulfill his contract; if he guesses wrong, the opponents will obtain the lead to run their established hearts.

The correct play in rubber bridge—to give declarer his *maximum chance of obtaining four club tricks*—is to first lay down the ace of clubs in the hope of catching the king or jack in the East hand. If you catch an honor, four club tricks—and the contract—are assured. If the king or jack is not caught, declarer returns to his own hand, and leads a low club toward the board's queen. The only time declarer will not make four club tricks in the suit is when

East started with the K J x or K J x x of clubs, in which case four club tricks could never have been made. The actual deal was:

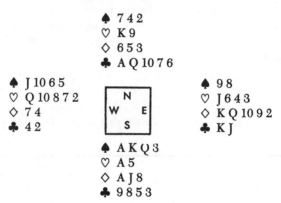

```
              ♠ 7 4 2
              ♡ K 9
              ◇ 6 5 3
              ♣ A Q 10 7 6
♠ J 10 6 5                      ♠ 9 8
♡ Q 10 8 7 2      N             ♡ J 6 4 3
◇ 7 4         W       E         ◇ K Q 10 9 2
♣ 4 2            S              ♣ K J
              ♠ A K Q 3
              ♡ A 5
              ◇ A J 8
              ♣ 9 8 5 3
```

In duplicate bridge, as in rubber bridge, probably the best play is to lay down the club ace first. In so doing you give up your (slim) chance of making five club tricks (which you could make if West held specifically the K x, the K J, the K J x, or the K J x x, *and* you correctly guessed how to play the club suit). However, since your chances of making five club tricks are slight, you should play the hand for the best chance of making four club tricks, and your contract. The initial play of the club ace is unquestionably your best bet.

DEAL 18.

Here is a deal on which the expert rubber-bridge player and the expert duplicate player would probably part company at trick one.

```
              ♠ A K J
              ♡ 7 5 2
              ◇ A J 10 8 4
              ♣ 9 5

              ♠ Q 10 5
              ♡ K 9 3
              ◇ K 9 7
              ♣ A K 10 4
```

South dealer. Neither side vulnerable.

The bidding:

South	West	North	East
1 ♣	1 ♡	2 ◇	Pass
2 NT	Pass	3 NT	Pass
Pass	Pass		

West opens the queen of hearts, dummy plays the deuce, and East the four-spot. What should South play?

In rubber bridge, South should decline to win the trick. Should West now continue with the ace and another heart, East will fail to follow suit to the third heart lead, as South captures the trick with his king. The king of diamonds will then be led, after which the nine of diamonds will follow, the finesse being taken. If it loses, East has no heart to return and declarer makes ten tricks.

If, upon being permitted to win the first heart, West now leads the jack of hearts, declarer will take it with his king. He will again now lead the king of diamonds, and then the nine-spot. If the nine loses to East's queen, either East will have no heart to return (if the hearts were divided 5-2 originally) or, if he has a third heart to return, then the adverse hearts were divided 4-3 and declarer could not have lost more than three hearts and a diamond no matter how he played the hand.

As a final possibility, if, after his queen of hearts wins the opening lead, West decides to shift to another suit, let's say spades, the trick will be won by dummy's king. Declarer would then lead the jack of diamonds from dummy, and finesse *East* for the diamond queen. Even if this finesse lost, *West* would again have the lead, and he would be back in the same position as at the completion of trick one, except that in the interim declarer would have established his diamond suit.

All the above was with reference to rubber bridge, where the safety of the contract was the sole consideration and the play was geared to this safety factor. But in duplicate bridge, only the result can determine which was the losing play and which was the winning play. At match-point play, if declarer wins the opening lead with his king of hearts, he has a 50–50 chance of getting a top on the board. All he has to do is guess which way to finesse for the diamond queen. If he can pick up the diamond suit without the loss of a trick, he will have 11 top tricks. In duplicate bridge, the 50–50 gamble, if successful, will pay handsome dividends. The 50–50 gamble, however, if unsuccessful, will give you a bottom on the board. As to what is right or wrong, there is no answer. The hands were:

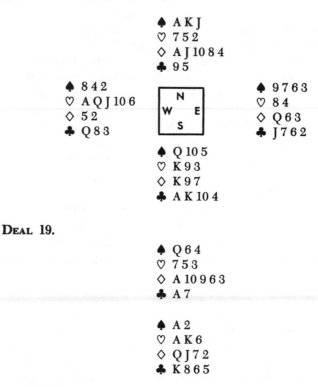

♠ A K J
♡ 7 5 2
◇ A J 10 8 4
♣ 9 5

♠ 8 4 2
♡ A Q J 10 6
◇ 5 2
♣ Q 8 3

N
W E
S

♠ 9 7 6 3
♡ 8 4
◇ Q 6 3
♣ J 7 6 2

♠ Q 10 5
♡ K 9 3
◇ K 9 7
♣ A K 10 4

DEAL 19.

♠ Q 6 4
♡ 7 5 3
◇ A 10 9 6 3
♣ A 7

♠ A 2
♡ A K 6
◇ Q J 7 2
♣ K 8 6 5

South has arrived at a *three no-trump* contract, against which West leads the five of spades. At rubber bridge, there is just one right play: the four of spades from dummy, and win the trick with the ace. Now lead the diamond queen and finesse. If the finesse loses, there is nothing East can return which will prevent declarer from making nine tricks, for the dummy's remaining Q 6 of spades will effectively prevent the defenders from cashing the spade suit.

At match-point play, however, declarer has at least a 50–50 chance to make a trick more than the rest of the field by putting up the queen of spades on the opening lead. If the queen wins, declarer will have a top on the board regardless of whether the diamond finesse wins or loses. However, if the queen of spades is covered by the king, declarer may well lose his contract—which was the case when the deal was actually played. Here are the hands:

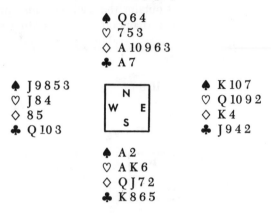

<pre>
              ♠ Q 6 4
              ♡ 7 5 3
              ◇ A 10 9 6 3
              ♣ A 7
♠ J 9 8 5 3   ♠ K 10 7
♡ J 8 4   N   ♡ Q 10 9 2
◇ 8 5   W   E   ◇ K 4
♣ Q 10 3   S   ♣ J 9 4 2
              ♠ A 2
              ♡ A K 6
              ◇ Q J 7 2
              ♣ K 8 6 5
</pre>

Thus, in duplicate, there is always the conflict about whether to play safe in a normal contract or to play for an overtrick.

DEAL 20.

<pre>
              ♠ 10 9 7 6
              ♡ K 10
              ◇ J 5
              ♣ A Q 9 6 2

              ♠ A K Q J 5
              ♡ 7 4 3
              ◇ A 10
              ♣ J 10 4
</pre>

With no adverse bidding, South arrives at a *four spade* contract. West opens the deuce of diamonds, the five is played from dummy, East puts up the queen, and South ... ?

In rubber bridge, East's queen should be permitted to win! If it is, declarer's contract is guaranteed. Let's say East then returns a diamond, South taking his ace. Trumps are then drawn and the club finesse taken, losing to East's (presumed) king. It now becomes a routine matter for declarer to get rid of two of his hearts on dummy's established clubs. His only losers are a diamond, a club, and a heart.

But if, in rubber bridge, declarer takes the opening diamond lead with his ace, then when East obtains the lead with his (presumed) king of clubs, he will return a diamond to West's king; and West will automatically shift to a heart, enabling East to take two heart tricks. The actual hands were:

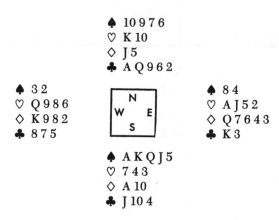

```
              ♠ 10 9 7 6
              ♡ K 10
              ◇ J 5
              ♣ A Q 9 6 2
♠ 3 2                          ♠ 8 4
♡ Q 9 8 6        N             ♡ A J 5 2
◇ K 9 8 2     W     E          ◇ Q 7 6 4 3
♣ 8 7 5          S             ♣ K 3
              ♠ A K Q J 5
              ♡ 7 4 3
              ◇ A 10
              ♣ J 10 4
```

In rubber bridge, the safety play—of not capturing the opening diamond lead—is designed to make sure that West will be unable to regain the lead to play a heart through dummy's K 10. And this can be accomplished only by not capturing East's queen of diamonds at trick one.

But at match-point play it is not an open-and-shut situation, for if the club finesse is successful and West has the heart ace, declarer can make 12 tricks. By conceding the first diamond lead, declarer leaves himself in the position where the opponents might take the first two tricks (a diamond and a heart), thus restricting declarer to but 11 tricks, and possibly a bad match-point score.

When this deal arose in the National Championships of 1955, bidding and making four hearts was worth 10 out of 12 match points. But then, probably the opening lead by West was often a heart, dooming declarer to defeat. (Assuming, of course, that after East cashed two heart tricks he shifted to a diamond.)

DEAL 21.

♠ 10 3 2
♡ 8 5
◇ Q 6 2
♣ J 8 6 5 3

♠ A K Q J 9 8
♡ A K 10 3
◇ A
♣ A K

With no adverse bidding, sitting South, you have reached a *six spade* contract. West opens the four of hearts, and East's queen of hearts is taken by your ace.

At *rubber bridge,* proper safety-play technique is to return the three of hearts! When you regain the lead on the next trick, you trump your ten of hearts with dummy's ten of spades. After that you draw trumps and claim the balance of the tricks. The hands were:

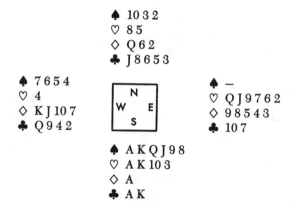

♠ 10 3 2
♡ 8 5
◇ Q 6 2
♣ J 8 6 5 3

♠ 7 6 5 4   ♠ —
♡ 4   ♡ Q J 9 7 6 2
◇ K J 10 7   ◇ 9 8 5 4 3
♣ Q 9 4 2   ♣ 10 7

♠ A K Q J 9 8
♡ A K 10 3
◇ A
♣ A K

If you try to cash your ace of hearts at trick two, West will ruff. Later, when South tries to ruff a low heart in dummy, West will ruff again, forcing dummy's ten-spot to overruff. Now declarer will have a losing heart which he will be unable to ruff out since West's remaining trumps will be higher than dummy's.

But to suggest this safety play at match-point play would be wrong, for declarer has an excellent chance of making a most vital overtrick by cashing the two top hearts (assuming a normal distribution of the adverse hearts), ruffing a third heart with a low trump and then ruffing his fourth heart with the board's ten of trumps. To abandon the possibility of making an overtrick in duplicate bridge must be a losing play. At rubber bridge, it is equally wrong to play for an overtrick when in so doing one jeopardizes a slam contract.

DEAL 22.

```
        ♠ A 6
        ♡ K 10 8 3
        ◇ 6
        ♣ A Q 10 9 6 2

        ♠ Q 10 8 4 3
        ♡ A 5 2
        ◇ A J 2
        ♣ K 8
```

South arrives at a *three no-trump* contract, against which West opens the diamond five, East puts up the king, and South captures the trick with his ace. It is apparent that if East ever gets the lead and returns a diamond through South's remaining J 2, South will be in sad shape.

In rubber bridge, the resolution is not too difficult. Declarer gets to dummy via the king of hearts and leads a low club, putting up the *eight-spot* from his own hand. If the eight-spot wins, with both opponents following suit, the contract is now guaranteed (one spade, two hearts, one diamond, and six clubs). If West captures the eight with the jack, whatever he returns cannot hurt declarer since South's J 2 of diamonds constitutes protection against West. If West returns, say, a spade, dummy's ace wins and the ace of clubs is then played, felling South's king, after which North takes the remainder of the clubs.

So much for the play at rubber bridge. But at match-point play, can South abandon the excellent chance that the five adversely held clubs are divided 3-2 (which they will be over two-thirds of the time)? In this latter case, South has ten tricks by cashing his six clubs. The "safety-play" concession of a club figures to give South a bottom on the board (except if East does happen to have the

Jxxx or the Jxxxx of clubs). At match-point play, a declarer cannot afford to concede a *probable* overtrick to safeguard a normal contract.

DEAL 23.

The extremes to which one goes in rubber bridge to guarantee a game contract can be observed in the following deal.

```
              ♠ 7 4
              ♡ 9 3
              ◇ 6 5
              ♣ A K J 8 5 4 2

              ♠ J 10 9 3 2
              ♡ A K 7
              ◇ A J 2
              ♣ 7 6
```

Both sides vulnerable. South dealer.
The bidding:

South	West	North	East
1 ♠	Pass	2 ♣	Pass
2 NT	Pass	3 NT	Pass
Pass	Pass		

West leads a low heart, and East's queen is taken by South's king. South then plays the six of clubs and when West follows with the three-spot, dummy's deuce is played! Regardless of what happens on this trick, South has just fulfilled his contract.

This safety play is designed as protection against West's holding the outstanding Q 10 9 3 of clubs. Frankly, this is a most unlikely distribution but the sacrifice of a possible overtrick is a small premium to pay in order to insure the game and rubber.

In duplicate bridge, this safety play would actually be given some consideration, although probably it would not be taken. The reason why it would be given some thought is that South has arrived at an excellent game contract with but 21 points in the combined hands. It seems to be a deal on which possibly half the field will not reach a game. Hence, the making of a game—with or without an overtrick—figures to yield a good result. In addition, a favorable (to declarer) heart opening was made. Had a diamond been led instead, declarer would have the worry that East might obtain the lead, to return a diamond through declarer's remaining J 2.

Nevertheless, even with the favorable lead, dummy's deuce of clubs would not be played to the first trick, for it would be the winning play only if West started with the Q 10 9 3 of clubs; and the play of the deuce would lose an overtrick whenever East started with a singleton nine or ten, or the doubleton 10 9. With the heart opening, declarer should probably finesse the jack of clubs at trick two, thus making an overtrick whenever West started with the Q x or the Q x x of clubs and guaranteeing the contract in case East started with the Q x x of clubs.

It would be wrong, percentage-wise, to play the ace and king of clubs immediately, hoping to catch either of the opponents with the Q x of clubs, for if the queen were not caught, declarer's excellent three no-trump contract would go down the drain.

The only justification for banging down the ace and king of clubs would be if one were truly desperate—and wanted to make sure of obtaining either a top or a bottom on the board.

DEAL 24.

♠ A Q
♥ Q 7 5 2
♦ 6 4
♣ A J 10 7 6

♠ 10
♥ A K J 10 9 6
♦ A 9
♣ Q 9 8 2

South is playing a *six heart* contract, against which West opens the diamond king, declarer's ace winning. The ace and king of trumps are then played, picking up the adverse pieces. Which finesse to take, the spade or the club?

If whichever finesse you take loses, the opponents will then cash a diamond. Is it strictly a 50–50 proposition? The answer is "no"—in a rubber bridge game.

The safety (or percentage) play is to cash the ace of clubs first, with the outside hope that one of the opponents was dealt the singleton king of clubs. This is a possibility, since there are but four clubs outstanding. Should you have the good fortune to drop the king, you will now make all 13 tricks. If you fail to drop the king, you then return to your hand via a trump and take the spade finesse. If it wins, then on the ace of spades you will discard your losing diamond. A concession of a trick to the club king will then give you your contract.

But duplicate bridge, again, presents a different situation. If the club king does not fall and the spade finesse is unsuccessful, then declarer will be down two tricks instead of one. This will give him a sure bottom on the board since those South players who took the club finesse will be down only one. And further, if the club finesse is successful, declarer will make an extra trick; whereas, by playing rubber-bridge "percentages" and abandoning the club finesse by playing the ace you will make 12 tricks at most if you don't drop the singleton king.

In duplicate bridge, the 50–50 chance for 13 tricks simply cannot be sacrificed. The club finesse, therefore, should be taken. This line of play will be the losing line only if the club finesse is unsuccessful *and* the spade finesse is successful.

DEAL 25.

This deal was played in a National Championship many years ago, and two friends of ours got a bottom on the board because declarer decided to gamble for a top or a bottom.

$$\spadesuit \; 7\,3$$
$$\heartsuit \; 9\,6\,4$$
$$\diamondsuit \; A\,K\,J\,6\,5$$
$$\clubsuit \; 10\,7\,5$$

$$\spadesuit \; A\,6$$
$$\heartsuit \; A\,K\,Q\,10\,8\,3$$
$$\diamondsuit \; 9\,8$$
$$\clubsuit \; Q\,J\,3$$

Both sides vulnerable. South dealer.
The bidding:

South	West	North	East
1 ♡	Pass	1 NT	Pass
3 ♡	Pass	4 ♡	Pass
Pass	Pass		

West opened the queen of spades, South taking the trick with his ace. Three rounds of trumps were then taken (West having started with the J 7 2), after which declarer finessed dummy's jack of diamonds successfully. The ace and king of diamonds were then cashed, revealing that the six adverse diamonds were divided nicely and evenly, 3-3. He now chalked up three overtricks, making six hearts, five diamonds, and the spade ace.

Of course, if the diamond finesse had lost, declarer would have gone down since the defenders could then have cashed a top spade, the ace and king of clubs.

In rubber bridge, after declarer had drawn trumps, the correct play to assure the contracts absolutely, would have been to cash the ace and king of diamonds (if the queen happened to fall, declarer's losing spade could be discarded on the board's jack of diamonds). But regardless of whether the diamond queen fell or didn't, declarer would then switch to clubs and establish a sure winner out of his Q J 10 of clubs. He would then make one spade, six hearts, two diamond tricks, and a club trick, for a total of ten tricks. In duplicate, who can say what's right? And who can criticize a declarer for playing "unsafe" when he has just made two overtricks for an undisputed top on the board?

CHAPTER 24

How Will the Other Declarers Play This Deal?

In rubber bridge, one's primary concern is the fulfillment of the contract and not whether he obtains the optimum theoretical result. Nor does it matter to him whether he is in a good or bad contract; nor does he speculate as to what the rest of the field will do on any particular deal, since no one else will ever play it. In rubber bridge, one lives in his own little world, and there is just one enemy, at his left flank and at his right.

But in duplicate bridge, the prime consideration is always the quest for supremacy over one's competitors, those who will be holding the same cards as he holds; and the thought of obtaining the optimum theoretical result is always uppermost in his mind. And the issue of whether one is in a good or a bad contract always influences one's play of a hand. Also, at match-point play, what the other declarers in the room figure to do on the same hand has a profound effect on how one will play it. In a broad sense, in duplicate bridge, the prime advantage of knowing what would be right in rubber bridge is that one can then knowingly deviate, rather than conform, if circumstances indicate that abnormal play is called for. In duplicate bridge, one cannot afford to be an "isolationist"; that is, he cannot live his life "far from the madding crowd's ignoble strife."

This chapter concerns itself with the above: the illustration of the various factors which must be taken into consideration when playing out a deal in duplicate bridge.

At match-point play, one must continually strive to guess what others will do on the deal that he is playing. Admittedly he will often misguess. Nevertheless, one must always attempt to evaluate his contract, for such evaluation is necessary if best results are to be obtained. For example, when just making one's contract figures to yield an excellent result, it would be foolhardy to jeopardize that contract for the sake of an overtrick unless one's chances of making that overtrick are magnificent. On the other hand, if the contract is a poor one and a bad result seems certain if the deal is played in normal, straightforward fashion, one must go to any length to equal or surpass the standard result.

Without any doubt, the best spot for "shooting" or "swinging" (gambling to receive a top in the full knowledge that the gamble may result in a bottom) lies in the play of the hand when you are the declarer. In the bidding, one cannot know or predict with any assurance the result that an unusual bid will yield, for his partner's action may negate any plan he might have formulated. "Shooting" in the bidding is a unilateral action which partner might easily misinterpret. In the play of the hand, however, you, as declarer, are in complete control. You can calculate the risks involved and develop your course of action secure in the knowledge that your partner cannot interfere. In the play, many opportunities are presented to adopt a line of play that is different from the normal line and that is almost as good—if not as good—as the standard line.

Let us now observe, via examples, how the attempt to determine what other declarers figure to be doing on a particular hand will affect your course of action.

DEAL 1.

Apart from the topflight experts, most bridge players are rubber-bridge players at heart and they will generally not jeopardize a game or slam contract (in duplicate) for the sake of an overtrick.

The appreciation of this point will usually bring you an excellent result on hands like this one, on which you should realize that the other declarers will probably not gamble for the overtrick since in so doing they might go down at a guaranteed game contract. Yet, from the viewpoint of proper play (as determined by mathematics), the overtrick can be brought home about 75 percent of the time. To those who are not mathematically inclined, *three times out of four* by playing for the overtrick, you will get a top on the board; one time out of four, a bottom. And three tops out of every four will win virtually any tournament you will ever play in.

```
            ♠ J 9 5 4 3
            ♡ K 5 2
            ◇ 6 2
            ♣ A J 10

            ♠ A K Q 10 2
            ♡ A 8 3
            ◇ A 5 4
            ♣ 5 3
```

Both sides vulnerable. South dealer.
The bidding:

South	West	North	East
1 ♠	Pass	2 ♠	Pass
3 ♠	Pass	4 ♠	Pass
Pass	Pass		

West opens the queen of hearts, which you capture with your ace. The ace and king of trumps are then cashed, picking up the adverse trumps. And at this point the rubber-bridge player and the expert duplicate player part company.

In rubber bridge, there is no problem. You have a guaranteed contract, with one heart loser, one diamond loser and one club loser.

But at duplicate bridge, the safety of the contract is not necessarily the sole consideration. On this hand you have about a 75 percent chance of making an extra trick and by trying for the extra trick, about a 25 percent chance of going down at the four spade contract. In these circumstances, it must be right (in duplicate) to risk going down one time out of four and getting a top three times out of four.

Therefore, after drawing trumps, a club is led, and dummy's ten-spot is inserted. East wins with the queen, and returns a heart, which is taken by the board's king. The closed hand is then re-entered via a trump, and a second club finesse is tried, dummy's jack being played. It wins. On the ace of clubs declarer discards his losing heart. His only losers are a club and a diamond.

Of course, if the second club finesse had lost, declarer would have gone down (if East had another heart), losing two clubs, a heart and a diamond. But the odds were 3–1 that West held either the king or queen of clubs. The complete deal was:

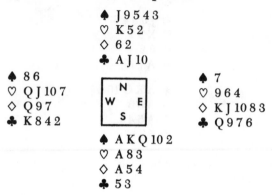

♠ J 9 5 4 3
♡ K 5 2
◇ 6 2
♣ A J 10

♠ 8 6
♡ Q J 10 7
◇ Q 9 7
♣ K 8 4 2

♠ 7
♡ 9 6 4
◇ K J 10 8 3
♣ Q 9 7 6

♠ A K Q 10 2
♡ A 8 3
◇ A 5 4
♣ 5 3

DEAL 2.

The concession of a possible overtrick is certainly justified when, in making the concession, you gain a sure overtrick. This point is the theme of the next deal.

♠ A 2
♡ J 9 6 3
◇ 7 5 4
♣ Q J 10 2

♠ Q 6
♡ A Q 10 7 5 4
◇ A 8 2
♣ K 7

East–West vulnerable. South dealer.
The bidding:

South	West	North	East
1 ♡	Pass	2 ♡	Pass
4 ♡	Pass	Pass	Pass

The opening lead by West is a low spade. You play the deuce from dummy, East puts up the ten, and you win the trick with your queen. What now?

It is obvious that you received a very favorable opening lead, a lead which gave you a present of a trick. True, that lead might also be made at other tables against the perfectly normal four heart contract. But then, there are many players who refuse to lead away from kings. If they had led a diamond, you couldn't possibly make more than 10 tricks, losing two diamonds and a club. With the spade lead, 11 tricks are almost surely in the bag since your two losing diamonds can be discarded on dummy's to-be-established clubs. The club ace and and the trump king should be your only losers. Should you take the trump finesse? The answer is No!

Normally, with ten trumps headed by the A Q J, the proper play is to finesse since the finesse will be successful more often than the play of the ace to catch a singleton king. But on this deal you have not only gained a trick on the opening lead, you have also received the timing to establish the club suit upon which you can discard your two losing diamonds. Why jeopardize your excellent result on the board by risking a trump finesse for the king?

So, at trick two, you bang down the ace of trumps (in case a singleton king happens to be floating around). Each opponent follows with a low trump, leaving only the king outstanding. You then play the king of clubs, East taking his ace. Belatedly, East shifts to a diamond, which you take with your ace.

A club to dummy's queen is next played, after which your two losing diamonds are discarded on the board's jack and ten of clubs. Whether East trumps the ten of clubs is immaterial. You have made 11 tricks, with the club ace and the trump king being your only losers. The complete deal was:

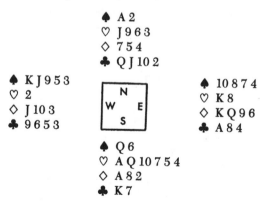

```
                    ♠ A 2
                    ♡ J 9 6 3
                    ◊ 7 5 4
                    ♣ Q J 10 2
♠ K J 9 5 3                          ♠ 10 8 7 4
♡ 2              ┌─────────┐         ♡ K 8
◊ J 10 3        │    N    │          ◊ K Q 9 6
♣ 9 6 5 3       │ W     E │          ♣ A 8 4
                 │    S    │
                 └─────────┘
                    ♠ Q 6
                    ♡ A Q 10 7 5 4
                    ◊ A 8 2
                    ♣ K 7
```

It will be noted that with the normal jack of diamonds lead—which was made at every table but one—declarer can make only ten tricks even with the successful trump finesse. With the diamond lead, declarer wins the first diamond and lays down the king of clubs, East winning with his ace. The defenders then cash two diamonds. When declarer regains the lead, he enters dummy and takes the successful trump finesse. His losing spade is discarded on one of the board's high clubs.

It should be appreciated that with the diamond opening, if the trump finesse had lost, declarer would have been down at his four heart contract.

To repeat, when you receive an opening which gives you a trick which you could not have made on your own power, don't jeopardize your good result by trying to get a better result. If you do, you might lose everything—and gain nothing even if the better result is achieved.

For the record, making 11 tricks at the four heart contract (for a score of 450) was worth 11 match points out of a possible 12. Had the heart finesse been taken—successfully—12 tricks would have been made and the same 11 match points would have been obtained! (One East–West pair played the contract at four spades, doubled, and went down two tricks, giving their North–South opponents a plus score of 500 points.)

DEAL 3.

It should be apparent to all readers that an overtrick is all-important. It should be equally apparent that there will be occasions when going down only one trick—rather than two or three which the rest of the field might be doing—can be equally important. Here is a case in point.

```
            ♠ 6 3
            ♡ J 4
            ◇ A K J
            ♣ K J 9 8 7 3

            ♠ Q J 4
            ♡ A K 10 9
            ◇ 10 7 3 2
            ♣ Q 10
```

South is playing a three no-trump contract, against which West opens the five of spades, East's ace winning. East returns the nine of spades, South puts up the jack, which *wins* as West drops the deuce. West is now marked with a five-card spade suit, and East still has a spade remaining.

At rubber bridge, South would take both the diamond finesse and the heart finesse, hoping to bring in four diamond tricks and four heart tricks. Admittedly his chances are not too good, but if either finesse loses, he will go down merely an extra fifty points, an insignificant loss when a game is at stake.

But at duplicate bridge that extra 50-point loss may give him a bottom on the board. Surely every pair in the room figures to be in three no-trump, and going down one (losing four spades and the club ace) should yield an average result, if not above average. That both the heart and diamond finesses will be successful *and* that the diamond queen will be singleton, doubleton or tripleton in the West hand (in order to make four diamond tricks) will occur possibly one time out of every four or five. Playing to make the contract, then, will give you a top one time out of every four or five. The other times you will get a bottom. And nobody can win a duplicate game with a 20–25 percent score!

So you lead the queen of clubs, which West wins with the ace. West then cashes three spade tricks, and you are down one. Had you taken either the heart or the diamond finesse, you would have gone down two or three. The actual deal was:

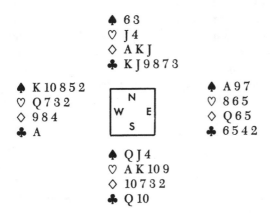

For the record, going down one trick at the three no-trump contract would have yielded you 8½ match points out of 12!

DEAL 4.

Here is another illustration of where making sure of not going down more than one trick is the proper match-point play (and improper in rubber bridge).

```
              ♠ Q J 9 7
              ♡ K 9 5
              ◇ J 6 2
              ♣ A Q 9

              ♠ A K 10 8 5 2
              ♡ Q J 10
              ◇ A K 3
              ♣ 3
```

Neither side vulnerable. South dealer.

South	West	North	East
1 ♠	Pass	3 ♠	Pass
4 NT	Pass	5 ◇	Pass
6 ♠	Pass	Pass	Pass

West's opening lead of the heart two is taken by East's ace, after which East returns a heart, declarer's jack winning.

At rubber bridge, there is one proper line of play. Trumps are drawn, the king of hearts is cashed, and then the ace and king of diamonds are taken, on the outside chance of dropping the doubleton queen. If the queen falls, the contract has just been fulfilled. If it does not drop, the club finesse is taken. If it wins, declarer discards his losing diamond on the club ace. If it loses, declarer is down two, losing a heart, a club, and a diamond.

But duplicate bridge is a horse of another color. This is a slam everybody figures to get to. And if you go down two tricks, you have a bottom on the board. In duplicate, you simply can't afford to cash the ace *and* king of diamonds on the remote possibility of dropping the queen. You cash the ace of diamonds—and then take the club finesse. If it wins, you have a tie-for-top. If it loses, you are down one (discarding your losing diamond on the club ace) for very close to an average score since everybody in the slam contract will also go down one, unless they had the good fortune to drop the Q x of diamonds. If the club finesse loses, your score will beat that of all the other pairs who cashed the ace and king of diamonds and failed to drop the queen.

The complete deal was:

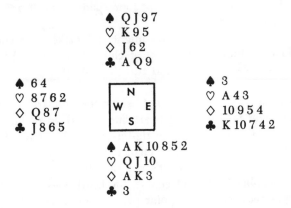

```
                  ♠ Q J 9 7
                  ♡ K 9 5
                  ◇ J 6 2
                  ♣ A Q 9
   ♠ 6 4                          ♠ 3
   ♡ 8 7 6 2          N           ♡ A 4 3
   ◇ Q 8 7        W       E       ◇ 10 9 5 4
   ♣ J 8 6 5          S           ♣ K 10 7 4 2
                  ♠ A K 10 8 5 2
                  ♡ Q J 10
                  ◇ A K 3
                  ♣ 3
```

DEAL 5.

Here is another deal which illustrates that settling for down one trick can easily be one's best bet, even at a game contract reached voluntarily.

```
                  ♠ 5
                  ♡ A J
                  ◇ A K 10 9 6 4
                  ♣ J 10 9 3


                  ♠ A 7 6 4 3 2
                  ♡ Q 10 9
                  ◇ Q J
                  ♣ Q 5
```

East–West vulnerable. North dealer.

North	East	South	West
1 ◇	Pass	1 ♠	Pass
2 ◇	Pass	2 NT	Pass
3 NT	Pass	Pass	Pass

Despite South's spade bid, West opens the king of spades, South holding up as East follows with the eight-spot. West continues with the queen of spades, which you win as East discards the four of hearts. West is known to have started with the K Q J 10 9 of spades. You have eight sure tricks. If you take the heart finesse and it wins, you will have fulfilled your contract. If the heart finesse loses, you may go down three tricks, losing four spades, one heart, and the ace and king of clubs.

If the heart finesse loses, you might still make your contract if East held both the ace and king of clubs. What to do? Settle for down one, or play to make and run the risk of going down three tricks.

If you want to "swing" or "shoot," settle for eight tricks—and hope that others will take a losing heart finesse and go down three. In this case, you will have a top or tie-for-top on the board. However, you do have at least a 50–50 chance to make your contract by taking the heart finesse—and it's not easy to give up such a good chance. In rubber bridge, of course, the heart finesse would be the only proper play. At match-point play, there is no right play and no wrong play; there is just a winning play and a losing play.

DEAL 6.

To give consideration to what other pairs in the field will be doing on the same hand is a must at duplicate. Here is a good example.

> ♠ A K Q 10 6 4
> ♡ J 2
> ◇ 5
> ♣ A 10 9 3
>
> ♠ J 3
> ♡ A K 7 4
> ◇ K J 7
> ♣ J 8 7 5

Neither side vulnerable. North dealer.

North	East	South	West
1 ♠	Pass	2 NT	Pass
3 ♠	Pass	3 NT	Pass
Pass	Pass		

West leads the diamond four, East puts up the queen, and you win the trick with the king.

In rubber bridge, the play would be routine; you have ten cashable tricks and any line of play is correct provided you wind up with at least nine tricks. But in duplicate, it is a very tough hand to play, for consideration must be given to what the rest of the field figures to do when they play the board.

In evaluating your contract, it would seem that most pairs would be playing at four spades rather than three no-trump. At the four spade contract, 11 tricks will be made unless East has *both* the king and queen of clubs (which he will have but 25 percent of the time). So what good are 10 tricks at three no-trump (plus 430) if most pairs will make 11 tricks at four spades (plus 450)? You've got to play for 11 tricks even at the risk of jeopardizing your contract.

The best play is to lead a low heart at trick two toward dummy's jack. If West has the queen, the board's jack will become your eleventh trick. If East has the heart queen, however, back will come a diamond—and down you go for *no* match points. But bidding three no-trump and making four would have given you very few (if any) match points anyway. This was the actual deal:

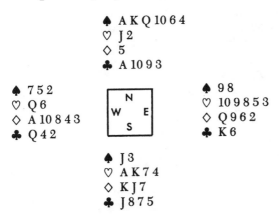

```
              ♠ A K Q 10 6 4
              ♡ J 2
              ◇ 5
              ♣ A 10 9 3
  ♠ 7 5 2                        ♠ 9 8
  ♡ Q 6          N               ♡ 10 9 8 5 3
  ◇ A 10 8 4 3  W   E            ◇ Q 9 6 2
  ♣ Q 4 2          S             ♣ K 6
              ♠ J 3
              ♡ A K 7 4
              ◇ K J 7
              ♣ J 8 7 5
```

When this deal was played, bidding three no-trump and making four would have netted you 1½ match points, with 12 as top! Bidding three no-trump and making five would have yielded you 11½ match points! And bidding four spades and making five would have been worth 8 match points.

DEAL 7.

There will be days when you get to a horrible contract, and yet you may emerge with a gorgeous match-point score. Here is an example.

```
                    ♠ 7 5
                    ♡ 10 2
                    ◇ A K 7 5 3 2
                    ♣ Q 10 4

                    ♠ A Q 9
                    ♡ A J 9 8 3
                    ◇ 8 4
                    ♣ A J 5
```

Neither side vulnerable. South dealer.

South	West	North	East
1 ♡	Pass	2 ◇	Pass
2 NT	Pass	Pass (!)	Pass

West leads the four of spades, East puts up the king and you, sitting South, win the king with your ace.

As you examine the combined hands, you don't like what you see. Every team in the room figures to be in three no-trump. With the normal 3-2 division of the five outstanding diamonds, at least nine tricks will be there for the taking (by conceding the first diamond trick). So whether you make nine, ten, eleven, twelve, or thirteen tricks, you figure to get a near-bottom on the board since you will lose to every team that is in three no-trump. How should you play the hand?

First of all, you must assume (hope) that the five outstanding diamonds are divided 4-1 or 5-0. So you do not give away the first diamond trick. Instead, you lead a diamond to the ace, after which you lay down the ten of hearts. East covers with the queen, and you take the trick with your ace. You return the jack of hearts, West's king winning. West plays back the jack of spades, which you win with your queen. When it's all over, you have nine tricks—but everybody who was in three no-trump went down, for they all attacked the diamond suit (and correctly so). The setup was this:

```
              ♠ 7 5
              ♡ 10 2
              ◊ A K 7 5 3 2
              ♣ Q 10 4
♠ J 10 6 4 3 2    ┌─────────┐    ♠ K 8
♡ K 6 5           │    N    │    ♡ Q 7 4
◊ 6               │ W     E │    ◊ Q J 10 9
♣ K 7 2           │    S    │    ♣ 9 8 6 3
                  └─────────┘
              ♠ A Q 9
              ♡ A J 9 8 3
              ◊ 8 4
              ♣ A J 5
```

Admittedly, you were quite lucky that the adverse diamonds were divided abnormally. But that was your sole hope, for without the bad division you were lost.

DEAL 8.

As has been mentioned, to jeopardize a slam contract in rubber bridge for the sake of an overtrick is absurd. But in duplicate bridge, the risking of one's slam contract for the overtrick can be a winning gamble, especially if the contract figures to be reached by every-body and you want (or need) better than an average score. Here is an illustration:

```
              ♠ Q J 8 5 2
              ♡ A Q 4
              ◊ A 10 6
              ♣ 7 5


              ♠ A K 9 6 3
              ♡ K 8 2
              ◊ K J 4
              ♣ A Q
```

Both sides vulnerable. South dealer.

South	West	North	East
1 ♠	Pass	3 ♠	Pass
4 NT	Pass	5 ♡	Pass
5 NT	Pass	6 ♣	Pass
6 ♠	Pass	Pass	Pass

West opens the five of hearts, which you win with dummy's queen. In rubber bridge, you have an absolutely guaranteed vulnerable small slam contract. You draw trumps, cash the ace and king of hearts, and then play the ace of clubs, followed by the queen of clubs. It matters not which opponent wins the last trick with the king of clubs, for that opponent has just become the victim of an end play:

```
              ♠ Q J 8
              ♡ —
              ◇ A 10 6
              ♣ —

              ♠ 9 6 3
              ♡ —
              ◇ K J 4
              ♣ —
```

If the opponent who wins the trick with the king of clubs leads either a heart or a club, you will trump it in dummy and discard your four of diamonds; if, instead, he leads a diamond, you will get a "free" finesse since the lead will ride around to your K J 4 if *West* won the club king, or around to dummy's A 10 6 of diamonds if *East* won the club king.

By playing it safely, you can guarantee 12 tricks. But if you play it "unsafely" in duplicate bridge, you might well make 13 tricks, which would be the case if East had the club king *and* you guess which way to finesse for the diamond queen. Of course, if you play it unsafely and West has the club king and you misguess the diamond finesse, you will go down in a guaranteed slam.

Part of the justification for playing wide open (to make 13 tricks) is that it might be that at some tables West opened either a club or a diamond, either of which would have given declarer 12 tricks with a 50–50 finesse to make 13 tricks. However, against this is our feeling that it is perhaps best to play safely for 12 tricks because the odds are against one taking *two* finesses successfully.

DEAL 9.

```
              ♠ K J 9 6
              ♡ 3
              ◇ 5 4
              ♣ A K J 10 6 2
```

♠ A Q 10 8 5
♡ A 4
♢ J 10 6 3
♣ 5 3

Both sides vulnerable. North dealer.

North	East	South	West
1 ♣	Pass	1 ♠	Pass
2 ♠	Pass	4 ♠	Pass
Pass	Pass		

West leads the queen of hearts, South's ace winning. The king and ace of trumps are then cashed, both opponents following suit. And now the burning issue: how to play the club suit?

In duplicate, the normal play is probably to cash the ace and king of clubs, and then ruff a club in the closed hand. If the adverse clubs divide 3-2, dummy's three remaining clubs will now be high. Declarer then ruffs his remaining heart, and on the board's high clubs he discards three of his diamonds. His only loser in these circumstances is the jack of diamonds, and he makes two overtricks.

An alternative line of play for those who are inclined to gamble to make the maximum number of tricks is to finesse the jack of clubs immediately after drawing trumps. If the finesse loses, declarer will make just 10 tricks, for the defenders will cash the king and ace of diamonds. North–South will now have a bottom on the board.

However, if the initial club finesse wins, declarer returns to his own hand via a trump and finesses again. He will then bring in six club tricks and will be able to discard all four of his diamonds on dummy's clubs. It will now be routine for South to make all 13 tricks by ruffing his heart with dummy's last trump. This line of play, if successful, will give North–South a top on the board.

This latter line of play—an immediate club finesse—will yield a bottom 50 percent of the time: whenever East holds the queen of clubs. The play is not recommended unless South is desperate and feels that he needs a top board to be in the running. In this case, the gamble has justification.

In rubber bridge, it doesn't matter much how you play it since it is simply a question of whether you make 10, 12, or 13 tricks at the four spade contract. But at match-point play, overtricks are worth their weight in uranium (remember how once upon a time it was gold?)—and it sometimes becomes a pure guess to separate the right line of play from the wrong line.

DEAL 10.

```
              ♠ 6 3 2
              ♡ 8 7 5
              ◇ K J
              ♣ A Q 10 6 5

              ♠ A K
              ♡ A 4 3
              ◇ A Q 10 6 4
              ♣ J 9 7
```

Neither side vulnerable. South dealer.
The bidding:

South	West	North	East
1 NT	Pass	3 NT	Pass
Pass	Pass		

West opens the king of hearts. How should you play this hand?

In rubber bridge, there would be no problem. You would hold up your ace for one round and win the second round. You would then take the club finesse. If it lost and East had a third heart to return, the hearts would have been divided 3-3-3-4 all around the table and you would lose at most three hearts and a club. Or, for that matter, if you wish to guard against a short suit lead in hearts by West (East having, let us say, five hearts), you could win the opening or second heart lead and cash nine top tricks. In duplicate bridge, however, you have a choice of several different and logical actions.

First of all, everybody in the room figures to arrive at the three no-trump contract. In all probability, West's king of hearts lead is the normal opening lead which will be made at every table.

If you want to play for a top or a bottom, win the opening heart lead and take the club finesse. If it's successful, you will make all 13 tricks. If it loses and West started with six hearts, you will make 12 tricks since East, in this case, will not have a heart to return. But if West started with five hearts, you will go down if the club finesse loses since the defenders will now take four heart tricks.

And if the hearts were divided 4-3, you will make 9 tricks, losing three hearts and a club.

If, instead, you win the second heart lead and the club finesse is successful, you will make 12 tricks. If you win the second heart lead and the club finesse is unsuccessful, you will make 11 tricks if the five adversely held hearts were divided 5-2 and nine tricks if the adverse hearts were divided 4-3.

If you hold up the heart ace until the third round (everybody following), you will make 11 tricks if the club finesse is successful and 10 tricks if it is unsuccessful.

So much for the statistics—which are of little help in determining whether to take the heart ace on the first, the second or the third round. If we knew what the other South declarers were going to do, we would at least have a guide to direct us in our action. But we don't know, unfortunately. Our own preference is to win the opening lead, for in so doing we have a 50–50 chance for a top score (making all 13 tricks); and we will get a bottom score only if the club finesse loses *and* the hearts were divided 5-2 originally. Also in our favor is the situation where the club finesse loses and West started with six hearts, for we will then make 12 tricks. If the club finesse loses and the hearts were divided 4-3, everybody in the room who took the first or second heart lead will make nine tricks while those who declined to take the ace until the third round will make 10 tricks. By taking the first heart, we feel that we will get better than an average score most of the time.

DEAL 11.

```
        ♠ 8 5 4
        ♡ A J 9 2
        ◇ K 5 2
        ♣ 7 3 2

        ♠ A 2
        ♡ Q 10 8
        ◇ A J 10 9 3
        ♣ A K 4
```

South arrives at a *three no-trump* contract, against which West opens a low spade and East plays the queen, which is permitted to win the trick. A spade is then played back, South's ace winning.

Declarer has six sure winners. The possibility of obtaining the three additional tricks exists in either of two places: (1) the heart suit if the king of hearts is in the West hand or (2) the diamond suit if declarer can guess where the queen is. Which finesse to take?

In rubber bridge there is just one proper line of play. You first lead the king and ace of diamonds on the outside chance of dropping the queen of diamonds (a little more than 25 percent). If the queen does not drop, you take the heart finesse. Played in this fashion, you don't restrict yourself to a choice of one or the other finesse. In effect, you get two chances for the price of one.

At match-point play, it is touch and go how you should play the hand. By taking the rubber-bridge play, you might easily go down two tricks by failing to drop the diamond queen *and* by losing the heart finesse. Going down two tricks when everybody else went down one will give you the same zero that you would get if you made any game contract while everybody else made an extra trick at the same contract.

To repeat, the safest way to play the hand to make the contract is to cash the king and ace of diamonds first, hoping to drop the queen; if you fail to catch the queen, you take the heart finesse. Accepting this, whatever else you do will be with your eyes open and the willingness to gamble.

DEAL 12.

As has been stated and illustrated, the best spot to gamble is in the play of the hand where you have full control of the situation and don't have to worry about your partner's interfering. Here is another example.

```
        ♠ K 7 5
        ♡ A 6
        ◇ A K
        ♣ A Q J 10 4 2

        ♠ 10 6 2
        ♡ J 8 7 4
        ◇ 5 4 2
        ♣ K 9 7
```

Both sides vulnerable. North dealer.

North	East	South	West
2 ♣	Pass	2 NT	Pass
3 NT	Pass	Pass	Pass

The above bidding is not recommended, but that's the way it did occur in a Philadelphia duplicate game some years ago. (We would open the North hand with two no-trump, and South would raise to three no-trump.)

West opens the nine of hearts (probably a "top-of-nothing" lead), the six is played from dummy, and East wins with the queen. East returns a low heart, dummy's ace winning.

We have nine top tricks and in rubber bridge we would promptly take them without fooling around. But, in duplicate bridge, if you want to gamble, lead a club to South's nine-spot and then play the deuce of spades with the intent of putting up dummy's king if West follows with a low spade. If West has the spade ace and takes it, the best he can do is to lead a heart to East's king. Whenever West has the spade ace, you will make 10 tricks.

Of course, if East has the spade ace, you figure to go down since the opponents will, in this case, be able to cash three or four spade tricks and two hearts. But even if you adopt the gambling play of leading a spade toward the board's king, you won't necessarily go down since the spade suit may be blocked. (East may have, for example, the A J x x x of spades, with West holding the Q x, in which case the opponents will be able to take only two spade tricks.)

Everything considered, probably the gamble for the extra trick is the preferable line of play in duplicate, even though it does jeopardize the game contract. *At least* 50 percent of the time you will succeed in making an overtrick. Also, if East happens to have the ace of spades, there is no assurance that he will play back a spade. After all, from his position, he may well assume that since you went after spades you are trying to establish that suit. He may, for example, make the neutral return of a diamond—and you will have your nine tricks back again.

In this chapter, the subject has been the consideration of how the other declarers will play the hand which is currently confronting you and the effect of their presumed play upon your play of the hand. An extension of this theme would be the consideration of how a particular deal will be *bid* at other tables, what the normal contract figures to be, and what the normal result figures to be.

The above paragraph is by way of an introduction to how one should play a sacrificial contract. In rubber bridge, when you sacrifice against a game contract, your approach is always to hold your losses to a minimum; that is, to go down as few tricks as possible (you have been doubled, of course). But in duplicate play, the question of *how much* you go down is often a secondary consideration, for your result will be evaluated on a relative basis and not on an absolute basis. For example, if the opponents get to a non-vulnerable game of four hearts which they figure to make for a score of 420 or possibly even 450 or 480 and if you have sacrificed at four spades, it will usually make no difference whether you go down 500, 800, 1100, 1400, or 1700. Once you go down more than 480 points, you figure to get about zero match points, for each team that will be playing your cards will be losing 420, 450, or 480. But if you can manage to go down only 300, your match-point score will be an excellent one since you will outscore all the pairs in your direction against whom a game was bid and made.

The three final deals in this chapter illustrate the line of reasoning that should be applied when one is playing a sacrifice contract.

DEAL 13.

In determining how to play a hand at which you have taken a sacrifice bid, the first thing to do is to attempt to figure out whether the opponents would have fulfilled their contract. This deal arose in the 1954 Middlesex (England) Pair Championships.

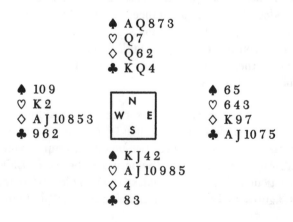

```
                    ♠ A Q 8 7 3
                    ♡ Q 7
                    ◇ Q 6 2
                    ♣ K Q 4
     ♠ 10 9                          ♠ 6 5
     ♡ K 2              N            ♡ 6 4 3
     ◇ A J 10 8 5 3   W   E          ◇ K 9 7
     ♣ 9 6 2              S          ♣ A J 10 7 5
                    ♠ K J 4 2
                    ♡ A J 10 9 8 5
                    ◇ 4
                    ♣ 8 3
```

Neither side vulnerable. South dealer.

South	West	North	East
1 ♡	2 ◇	2 ♠	3 ◇
3 ♠	Pass	4 ♠	Pass
Pass	5 ◇	Double	Pass
Pass	Pass		

North opened the ace of spades and then led a low spade, South's king winning. South then cashed the ace of hearts, after which he led another heart, West taking the trick with his king.

West realized that against the four spade contract the defenders could take for sure a heart and a club trick. If the four adverse diamonds were divided 2-2, the defenders could also take two diamond tricks, thus defeating the four spade contract. Therefore it was correct to play the hand on the assumption that the diamonds were divided 3-1, for otherwise the sacrifice would have been in vain.

On the bidding, South appeared to hold mostly spades and hearts. Thus it was more likely that North held three diamonds if anyone did. So West led the ace of diamonds and then the jack, finessing successfully when North played low. North's queen of trumps was then picked up by dummy's king, after which West re-entered his hand by ruffing a heart. Eventually West lost a club trick, thereby going down two for an excellent match-point result.

Deal 14.

This sacrifice deal is similar in type to the preceding one.

```
        ♠ J 10 6 4
        ♡ 6
        ◇ 8 5 4
        ♣ K 8 7 3 2

        ♠ A K 9 7 3
        ♡ A J 10
        ◇ 9 7 2
        ♣ 5 4
```

East-West vulnerable. East dealer.
The bidding:

East	South	West	North
1 ♡	1 ♠	4 ♡	4 ♠
Double	Pass	Pass	Pass

West opens the king of diamonds, which wins the trick. He then leads the ace of diamonds, upon which East plays the queen. West now cashes the jack of diamonds, East discarding the four of hearts. West then shifts to the nine of hearts, East puts up the queen, and South captures the trick with his ace. What now? First, the analysis.

You know (as declarer) that you would have won two heart tricks against the four heart contract. If the adversely held spades are divided 2-2, then the four heart contract would have been defeated. Even if the adverse spades were divided 3-1, the four heart contract would still have been defeated if the club king is a winner defensively. Thus, even a two-trick set (300 points) against an unmakable four heart contract will give you a very bad matchpoint score.

Consequently, you must proceed on the assumption that the four heart contract is makable, and that, first, the four adverse spades *must be* (you hope!) divided 3-1. If such is actually the case, you must then hope that North's king of clubs would not have won a trick on defense.

After winning the fourth trick with your ace of hearts, you lay down the ace of trumps, both opponents following suit. You then lead the jack of hearts and trump it in dummy with the jack of spades. Next you lead a low trump off dummy and finesse your nine-spot—successfully! Your remaining heart is then ruffed with the board's last trump. Subsequently, you lose two club tricks.

All in all, your losers were three diamonds and two clubs, for an excellent score (minus 300) against East–West's makable four heart contract. The complete deal was:

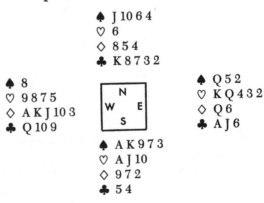

```
              ♠ J 10 6 4
              ♡ 6
              ◇ 8 5 4
              ♣ K 8 7 3 2
   ♠ 8                         ♠ Q 5 2
   ♡ 9 8 7 5      N            ♡ K Q 4 3 2
   ◇ A K J 10 3  W   E         ◇ Q 6
   ♣ Q 10 9         S          ♣ A J 6
              ♠ A K 9 7 3
              ♡ A J 10
              ◇ 9 7 2
              ♣ 5 4
```

Deal 15.

This final deal does not technically belong in this chapter since it deals with *defensive* play rather than with declarer's play. However, we have included it here because it does demonstrate—as in the two preceding deals—the functioning of the expert duplicate mind when playing a sacrificial contract. Defensively, when playing against a sacrifice bid that the opponents have made against your sure game contract, it is not the amount by which you beat them that is important but rather whether you beat them *more* than your game contract was worth, or *less*. If less, you have a bad score. If more, you have an excellent score, whether you beat them 800 or 2900.

This deal was played many years ago in a tournament, and the West defender was the late Ely Culbertson.

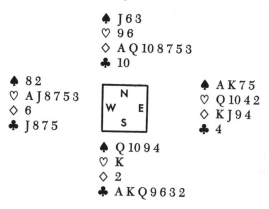

```
                    ♠ J 6 3
                    ♡ 9 6
                    ◇ A Q 10 8 7 5 3
                    ♣ 10
       ♠ 8 2                          ♠ A K 7 5
       ♡ A J 8 7 5 3      N           ♡ Q 10 4 2
       ◇ 6            W       E        ◇ K J 9 4
       ♣ J 8 7 5          S           ♣ 4
                    ♠ Q 10 9 4
                    ♡ K
                    ◇ 2
                    ♣ A K Q 9 6 3 2
```

North–South vulnerable. East dealer.
The bidding:

East	South	West	North
1 ♠	2 ♣	2 ♡	Pass
4 ♡	5 ♣	Double	Pass
Pass	Pass		

West led the eight of spades, which was taken by East's king. East then cashed the ace of spades, after which he led a third round of spades, West trumping. From the bidding, East certainly *figured* to have the king of hearts. If this were the case, then West could now underlead his ace of hearts and East would then return another spade, thus making a winner out of West's jack of clubs. This would give the defenders 800 points.

But, from West's point of view, it was unnecessary to underlead the ace of hearts, for by cashing the ace West would be certain to defeat North–South 500 points, more than the value of the non-vulnerable game East–West could have made at four hearts. And, since a plus score of 500 points figured to be a top on the board, why try for 800, which would be the same top?

Had Culbertson underled his ace of hearts, declarer would have won it with his singleton king and would have escaped the 500-point set, losing only 200 for going down one. North–South would then have had a near-top on the board.

In rubber bridge, it would have been a toss of a coin for West to have underled his ace of hearts since he had North–South beaten for 200 points at the completion of trick three and it was a justifiable gamble to try for 800 rather than 500. But at match-point play, there was no problem: 500 figured to be just as good as 800.

CHAPTER 25

Declarer's Play: The Play at Competitive Part-Score Contracts

At match-point play, one lands in precarious contracts much more often than he does in a rubber-bridge game. Without a doubt, the majority of these dangerous contracts arise at the part-score level in the highly competitive struggle for the part-score. The reason behind these struggles is that one has learned that he must be much more aggressive in duplicate play, especially in the frequent situations when the opening side has stopped bidding at a low level, and the defensive side has the option of sticking its neck out by reopening the bidding or selling out.

Since it has been amply demonstrated in experience that when the opening side purchases the contract at the one or two level without any competition, the defensive side usually obtains a poor match-point score, the reason for the necessity of more aggressive action becomes apparent. In match-point play, each deal is equal in importance to each other; and, therefore, success is measured not by the amount of gain, but by *frequency* of gain. That is, if one sticks his neck out three times (by either reopening the bidding or by making a subminimum overcall), and steals a part-score twice in a row, for a top on the board, and the third time he gets doubled and goes down 1400 points, he has just won two boards out of three, for a 66.67 percent score, which is usually enough to win any tournament or duplicate game. In rubber bridge, such tactics would quickly bankrupt the defensive bidder, for the two stolen part-scores will not compensate for the 1400-point loss incurred on the third deal.

Thus, in match-point play where, again, each board is the exact equivalent of each other in terms of worth, one is called upon to make many more crucial decisions than in rubber bridge. And, in these circumstances, it is only natural that one will, on numerous occasions, find himself out on a shaky limb, with the issue becoming whether the limb will snap or not.

Let us now view the play at competitive part-score contracts and examine the mental processes of declarers who find themselves in tenuous situations with which there can be no compromise; either they survive as heroes or perish ignominiously.

DEAL 1.

♠ A K
♡ 8 4 3
◇ 7 5 2
♣ Q J 9 6 3

♠ J 9 8 7 2
♡ 7 5
◇ 9 6 4
♣ A K 10

Neither side vulnerable. West dealer.

West	North	East	South
1 ♡	Pass	1 NT	Pass
2 ♡	Pass	Pass	2 ♠
Double	Pass	Pass	Pass

West opens the heart king, after which he cashes the ace and leads a third heart, South ruffing as East follows with the queen.

A trump is then led to dummy's king, and the trump ace is taken next, both opponents following suit with low cards to each trump lead. A club is now led to declarer's king—after which comes the pause for inventory.

You are down to your last two trumps, and the opponents have the queen and ten of trumps. If you lead another trump and West happens to have both the queen and ten, he will pick up your last trump. In all probability, you will take no more tricks since the opponents will cash their hearts and diamonds. You will, in this case, be down four tricks, for a loss of 800 points.

If, on the other hand, you lead another trump and it turns out that one opponent has the queen and the other opponent has the ten, you will be in good shape, for you will still have a trump left. You will be down only one (losing two hearts, three diamonds, and a trump). It was noted earlier—or should have been—that the opponents were a cinch to fulfill their two heart contract with perhaps one overtrick, losing just two spades and two clubs. If the defense (against two hearts) managed to get a spade ruff in, then the two heart contract would just be made without the overtrick.

If, however, when you have entered your hand via the club king —at trick six—you decide not to lead any more trumps and, instead, to play your clubs, the opponents will make their two trumps separately whether they are split 1-1 or are both in the same hand. You will now lose two trump tricks, two hearts, and three diamonds to incur a 300-point penalty. This 300-point loss, against their part-score contract of two hearts, figures to give you the exact same zero you would have obtained had you gone down 800 points.

And so, with a hope and a prayer, you lead a trump at trick seven—and West takes his queen as East follows suit with the ten-spot! This was the complete setup:

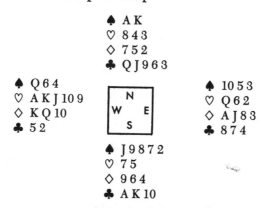

```
              ♠ A K
              ♡ 8 4 3
              ◊ 7 5 2
              ♣ Q J 9 6 3
♠ Q 6 4                        ♠ 10 5 3
♡ A K J 10 9      N            ♡ Q 6 2
◊ K Q 10      W       E        ◊ A J 8 3
♣ 5 2             S            ♣ 8 7 4
              ♠ J 9 8 7 2
              ♡ 7 5
              ◊ 9 6 4
              ♣ A K 10
```

If, when West takes his queen of spades, he leads the king of diamonds, the defenders will cash three diamond tricks to beat you one trick. But you can get lucky on this hand!

Earlier, when you led a club off dummy to your king, you might have created the impression in *West's* mind that his partner, East, held the club ace. Should West now lead another heart—to force you to trump with your last trump—you will make your doubled contract with an overtrick! With a heart lead, you will trump with your last trump, cash the club ace, and then lead the club ten, overtaking it with dummy's jack. On dummy's two high clubs, you will then discard two of your losing diamonds. Thus, with the defensive slip, your only losers will be two hearts, one trump and one diamond.

Deal 2.

As will be observed, North–South did not bid this hand well but the play by South was perfection itself—as it had to be to avoid a disaster (down 200 against a part-score contract).

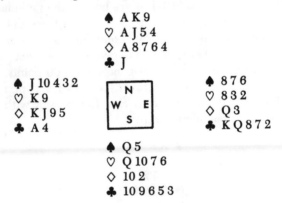

```
              ♠ A K 9
              ♡ A J 5 4
              ◇ A 8 7 6 4
              ♣ J
  ♠ J 10 4 3 2                    ♠ 8 7 6
  ♡ K 9          N               ♡ 8 3 2
  ◇ K J 9 5   W     E             ◇ Q 3
  ♣ A 4           S               ♣ K Q 8 7 2
              ♠ Q 5
              ♡ Q 10 7 6
              ◇ 10 2
              ♣ 10 9 6 5 3
```

Both sides vulnerable. North dealer.

North	East	South	West
1 ◇	Pass	Pass	1 NT
Pass	Pass	2 ♣	2 ♠
3 ♣	Double	Pass	Pass
Pass			

South, having passed his partner's opening bid, chose to re-enter the auction with a speculative two club bid rather than sell out to West's one no-trump call. When West then bid his spades, North, assuming that South had a six-card suit, raised the clubs on a singleton jack. East doubled with alacrity.

West opened a spade, and declarer cashed three spade tricks, discarding a diamond from the South hand on the third spade lead. Then came the ace of diamonds, followed by a diamond ruff. A heart was now led and the jack finessed successfully. Another diamond was then played, East discarding a heart (it would not have changed the result if East had ruffed high) and South again ruffing. Declarer next led a heart to the ace, after which a fourth round of diamonds was played. Regardless of what East did, South could not be prevented from winning his ninth trick with a trump. The doubled three club contract was thus fulfilled for a score of 670 and an undisputed top on the board: 12 match points out of a possible 12.

As can be observed, four hearts is easily makable and the few North–South pairs who managed to reach this contract scored either 620 or 650.

DEAL 3.

This deal arose in the Life Masters Pairs Championships of 1964. It illustrates quite vividly what has been emphasized and re-emphasized throughout this text: In rubber bridge one does not venture forth to contest a partial as often as he does in match-point play. Thus, more risks are undertaken at match-point play, not because one enjoys taking them but rather because, with each deal being the exact equivalent of every other, self-preservation demands that one does so.

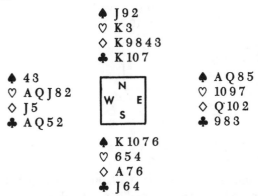

♠ J 9 2
♡ K 3
◇ K 9 8 4 3
♣ K 10 7

♠ 4 3
♡ A Q J 8 2
◇ J 5
♣ A Q 5 2

♠ A Q 8 5
♡ 10 9 7
◇ Q 10 2
♣ 9 8 3

♠ K 10 7 6
♡ 6 5 4
◇ A 7 6
♣ J 6 4

East–West vulnerable. South dealer.

The bidding:

South	West	North	East
Pass	1 ♡	Pass	2 ♡
Pass	Pass	Double	Pass
2 ♠	Pass	Pass	Double
Pass	Pass	Pass	

South was Bobby Reynolds, of Miami Beach, Florida, and his partner was Paul Trent of New York City. Mr. Reynolds was the 1959 winner of the Life Masters Individual Championship.

North's reopening double was strictly a match-point bid. He would not have dreamed of making it in a rubber-bridge game.

West opened the four of spades, the deuce was played from dummy, East put up the eight, and South's ten captured the trick. The six of diamonds was now led, West and dummy played low, and East won with the ten-spot. East returned the heart ten, South and West followed with low hearts, and the board's king captured the trick. The board's remaining heart was then played back, East's nine-spot winning.

East now laid down the ace of spades, after which he exited with his remaining heart, dummy ruffing. Declarer next led a diamond to his ace, and then a diamond to the board's king, West discarding the club deuce. This position had now been reached:

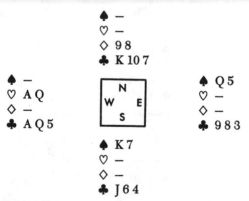

To trick nine, dummy's nine of diamonds was led, East ruffing with the five and declarer overruffing with the seven.

If, at this point, declarer had cashed his king of trumps to pick up East's queen, he would have gone down, for when he next led a club, West (who would have discarded the five and queen of clubs on the two preceding tricks) would have taken his now-singleton ace of clubs and would have cashed his high hearts.

But after overruffing with the seven-spot, Bobby led a club, West rising with his ace. West now played the ace of hearts, which declarer ruffed with the king as East discarded a club. When South now led a club to dummy's king, he had just made his eighth, and contract-fulfilling trick. Trick thirteen was taken by East's queen of trumps.

DEAL 4.

This deal typifies the thin hair by which many close penalty doubles hang at match-point play. The hand came up in the National Mixed Pair Championships of 1950.

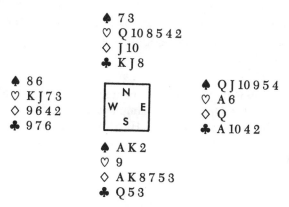

```
                        ♠ 7 3
                        ♡ Q 10 8 5 4 2
                        ◇ J 10
                        ♣ K J 8
      ♠ 8 6                              ♠ Q J 10 9 5 4
      ♡ K J 7 3          ┌─────┐         ♡ A 6
      ◇ 9 6 4 2          │  N  │         ◇ Q
      ♣ 9 7 6          W │     │ E       ♣ A 10 4 2
                         │  S  │
                        └─────┘
                        ♠ A K 2
                        ♡ 9
                        ◇ A K 8 7 5 3
                        ♣ Q 5 3
```

East dealer. East–West vulnerable.
The bidding:

East	South	West	North
1 ♠	1 NT	Pass	2 ♡
2 ♠	Double	Pass	Pass
Pass			

Had South elected to open his singleton heart, declarer would have fulfilled his contract since, in this case, he would have obtained the timing to establish a club trick.

But South chose to open the king of diamonds and to continue with a low diamond, East ruffing. East now made the deceptive lead of the spade nine,, but South promptly climbed up with the king to return another low diamond, North ruffing with the seven and East overruffing with the ten. The jack of trumps then forced out South's ace, after which South led the diamond king, East ruffing.

East now had just the queen of trumps remaining, while South still possessed the deuce of trumps. If declarer picked up South's remaining trump, then when declarer ultimately attacked the club suit, South would obtain the lead to cash his two remaining diamonds. If, instead, declarer elected not to pick up South's deuce of trumps, South would obtain the lead with the queen when declarer went after the clubs. He would then play still another diamond, forcing declarer to ruff with the latter's last trump—and South's deuce of trumps would become promoted into a winner, as the sole surviving trump.

Thus, a gambling double had paid dividends to the extent of 200 points and 11 match points out of 12.

Deal 5.

An inspirational vulnerable reopening bid by Alvin Roth of New York City in the Open Pair Championships of 1950 brought Roth and his partner, John Kunkel of Harrisburg, Pennsylvania, a top on the board. Mr. Roth's bid is recommended only for those who are capable of them.

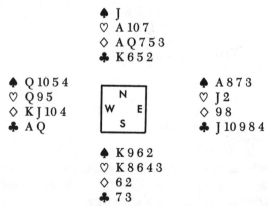

$$
\begin{array}{c}
\spadesuit \text{ J} \\
\heartsuit \text{ A 10 7} \\
\diamondsuit \text{ A Q 7 5 3} \\
\clubsuit \text{ K 6 5 2}
\end{array}
$$

West:
♠ Q 10 5 4
♡ Q 9 5
◇ K J 10 4
♣ A Q

East:
♠ A 8 7 3
♡ J 2
◇ 9 8
♣ J 10 9 8 4

South:
♠ K 9 6 2
♡ K 8 6 4 3
◇ 6 2
♣ 7 3

West dealer. North–South vulnerable.

The bidding:

West	North	East	South
1 ◇	Pass	1 ♠	Pass
2 ♠	Pass	Pass	3 ♡ (!)
Pass	Pass	Pass	

The play was top-notch. West opened his fourth-highest spade and East took his ace. East returned the jack of clubs, which West won with the ace before returning the queen, dummy's king winning.

Roth now led a club from dummy and ruffed it low. He simply played to find three trumps on his left and two on his right, in which case an overruff could not cost him a trick. West did overtrump, but by subsequently winning the diamond finesse, trumping a spade in dummy and dropping the opposing trumps in two leads, Roth made his contract. (His only losers were two spades, a trump, and the club ace.) Between those North–South pairs who did not reach a heart contract and those who did but went down, plus 140 was an excellent score: 10½ match points out of 12.

DEAL 6.

Here is a deal where highly competitive part-score bidding ended up in a three heart North–South contract that was doubled by East. Even if South had gone down a trick (100 points), he would have secured a good score since East–West could have fulfilled their three-level contract. However, by virtue of excellent play, South fulfilled his doubled contract and received 12 match points out of a possible 12.

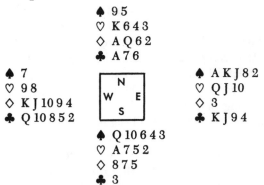

```
              ♠ 9 5
              ♡ K 6 4 3
              ◇ A Q 6 2
              ♣ A 7 6
♠ 7                         ♠ A K J 8 2
♡ 9 8          N            ♡ Q J 10
◇ K J 10 9 4  W   E         ◇ 3
♣ Q 10 8 5 2      S         ♣ K J 9 4
              ♠ Q 10 6 4 3
              ♡ A 7 5 2
              ◇ 8 7 5
              ♣ 3
```

East dealer. East–West vulnerable.

The bidding:

East	South	West	North
1 ♠	Pass	1 NT	Double
2 ♣	2 ♡	3 ♣	3 ♡
Double	Pass	Pass	Pass

West opened the seven of spades, East won with the king, then played the ace—West discarding a low club—after which East led the eight of spades, South inserting the ten-spot. West ruffed this trick with the eight of hearts.

Had declarer overruffed with dummy's king, he would have gone down, since there would be no way of averting the loss of two trump tricks and a diamond. But on this trick South calmly discarded a diamond from dummy.

West now shifted to a club, dummy's ace winning. The king of trumps was then laid down, and this was followed by a trump to South's ace, leaving the queen outstanding. The queen of spades was now cashed, the board's six of diamonds being discarded. Next came a successful diamond finesse, after which the diamond ace was cashed, East discarding a club. A club was then trumped in the closed hand, and then a spade was ruffed in dummy. Another club was now ruffed by declarer, and then a diamond ruffed in dummy. No matter what East had played anywhere along the line, all he could ever make was his high queen of trumps. Declarer's only losers were two trump tricks and two spades.

Deal 7.

It may be that the reader has not as yet been plagued by the psychic bidding of his opponents. If such *is* the case, then those unhappy days are still ahead and are unavoidable. In experience, one learns that complete faith should never be put in the bidding of the opponents. That is, one doesn't say automatically, "*He* bid, therefore *he* has." Of course, when no better clues are available, then the bidding of the opponents must serve as a guide. But, as was stated, one shouldn't put all his eggs in one basket, except as a last resort.

Here is an example of a declarer who assumed that the opening bidder had all the outstanding high cards. As a result of this assumption, he lost a contract that should have been fulfilled.

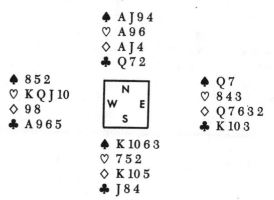

♠ A J 9 4
♡ A 9 6
◇ A J 4
♣ Q 7 2

♠ 8 5 2
♡ K Q J 10
◇ 9 8
♣ A 9 6 5

♠ Q 7
♡ 8 4 3
◇ Q 7 6 3 2
♣ K 10 3

♠ K 10 6 3
♡ 7 5 2
◇ K 10 5
♣ J 8 4

Neither side vulnerable. West dealer.
The bidding:

West	North	East	South
1 ♡	Double	Pass	1 ♠
Pass	2 ♠	Pass	Pass
Pass			

West opened the king of hearts, dummy's ace winning. A spade was then led to the king, after which a spade was returned and dummy's jack finessed.

East, of course, won this trick with his queen, and played back a heart, West taking his queen and jack. West then exited with a trump, declarer winning with his ten-spot. South now led a diamond, and finessed dummy's jack, which lost to East's queen. East returned a diamond, declarer's king winning. Since South was now compelled to break the club suit, the defenders made three club tricks to hand declarer a two-trick set.

Admittedly, West did "figure to have" the queen of spades and the queen of diamonds more often than East figured to have those cards since East had remained silent throughout the auction. But there was no law which said that West was certain to have them. It was completely unnecessary—from the viewpoint of correct play —for declarer to have assumed that West had all the missing high cards. Actually, declarer could have made his contract relying only on his own technique.

After winning the opening heart lead with dummy's ace, declarer should immediately have returned a heart. Presumably, West would now cash two heart tricks—and West would be end-played! If he returned either a trump or a diamond, he would trap his partner's queen in whatever suit he led. And, if he returned a club instead, he would establish a trick in that suit for declarer.

Let's say that West, after cashing two hearts, returned a trump, East's queen falling to declarer's king. The adverse trumps would then be picked up by South, after which the ace, king, and jack of diamonds would be played, eliminating diamonds from the North–South hands (hearts were eliminated earlier). East would win the third diamond with the queen (or, if West had the queen, he would win the third diamond lead). The defender who won the diamond queen would now have no choice but to lead a club. In so doing, he would establish a club trick for declarer.

Played in this manner—properly, that is—declarer's only losers would have been two hearts, a diamond, and two clubs.

As a last word, West *did not* have an opening bid. But West had paid a card fee, as had everybody else, and if he wanted to open the bidding, who except his partner had a right to criticize?

DEAL 8.

This deal arose in the Phoenix Trials of 1963. The "Trials" is an invitational contest amongst our nation's top-ranking pairs to determine which three pairs will represent the United States in International competition during the following year. This hand serves as a representative sample of the functioning of our expert minds.

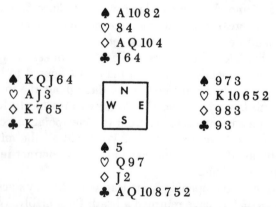

```
                    ♠ A 10 8 2
                    ♡ 8 4
                    ◇ A Q 10 4
                    ♣ J 6 4
  ♠ K Q J 6 4          N          ♠ 9 7 3
  ♡ A J 3        W         E       ♡ K 10 6 5 2
  ◇ K 7 6 5           S          ◇ 9 8 3
  ♣ K                              ♣ 9 3
                    ♠ 5
                    ♡ Q 9 7
                    ◇ J 2
                    ♣ A Q 10 8 7 5 2
```

North–South vulnerable. South dealer.

The bidding:

South	West	North	East
Pass	1 ♠	Pass	Pass
2 ♣	2 ◇	3 ♣	3 ♠
4 ♣	Pass	Pass	Pass

West opened the king of spades, dummy's ace winning. As declarer viewed the situation, West did not have both the ace and king of hearts. If he did, he would have opened the king in order to inspect the dummy and judge the best play at trick two. Hence, East was known to have either the ace or king of hearts.

Had East also held the king of clubs, he surely would not have passed West's opening bid of one spade. Therefore West possessed the king of clubs, and it just had to be wrong to finesse for that card.

So at trick two declarer led a low club from dummy and put up his ace. He was rewarded for his analysis by the fall of West's king. East's remaining trump was then picked up, after which declarer finessed successfully for the diamond king. An overtrick was thus scored for an excellent match-point result.

DEAL 9.

At rubber bridge, this deal would have passed by unnoticed, for nothing more was at stake than the making of an overtrick at a part-score contract. However, it arose in the National Open Pair Championships of 1963, in which event there is never anything insignificant about an overtrick.

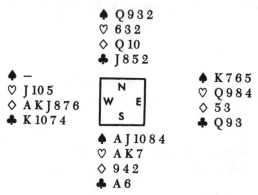

```
              ♠ Q 9 3 2
              ♡ 6 3 2
              ◇ Q 10
              ♣ J 8 5 2
  ♠ —                      ♠ K 7 6 5
  ♡ J 10 5     N           ♡ Q 9 8 4
  ◇ A K J 8 7 6 W   E      ◇ 5 3
  ♣ K 10 7 4     S         ♣ Q 9 3
              ♠ A J 10 8 4
              ♡ A K 7
              ◇ 9 4 2
              ♣ A 6
```

Both sides vulnerable. West dealer.

The bidding:

West	North	East	South
1 ◇	Pass	1 ♡	Double
2 ♡	Pass	Pass	2 ♠
Pass *	Pass	Pass	

West opened the king of diamonds, and then cashed the ace of diamonds, felling dummy's queen. East had played "high-low" on the first two diamond leads, so West now led the jack of diamonds.

In rubber bridge, declarer would create no problems for himself. He would ruff with the board's nine or queen of spades and East would overruff. Eventually the defenders would take a heart and a club, and declarer would make his two spade contract.

But match-point technique is a horse of another color, for one doesn't win tournaments by settling for his contract and ignoring overtricks.

When West led the jack of diamonds at trick three, declarer did not trump in dummy. Instead, he discarded a sure ultimate loser, a little heart (losing nothing in so doing).

West then shifted to the jack of hearts, declarer taking it with the ace. The king of hearts now followed, after which declarer ruffed his remaining heart. Now came the nine of spades, and the finesse was taken successfully. The queen of spades came next, and that also won the trick. Then the board's last spade was led, which declarer won with his jack. The ace of spades now dropped East's king. A club trick was later won by the defenders, and that was that. Declarer thus made an overtrick, losing but three diamonds and a club.

DEAL 10.

One of the quirks of match-point scoring is that it is sometimes possible to get as many match points for being set as for making your contract. The reason is that you score a point for every pair whose score you better. If *everyone* in your direction is minus and if you have the smallest minus score, it will be worth exactly as much as any plus score.

---

* Rather conservative, we think.

Here is a good example:

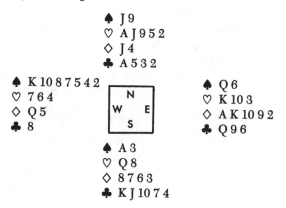

```
                    ♠ J 9
                    ♡ A J 9 5 2
                    ◇ J 4
                    ♣ A 5 3 2
♠ K 10 8 7 5 4 2                      ♠ Q 6
♡ 7 6 4          ┌─────────┐        ♡ K 10 3
◇ Q 5           │    N    │         ◇ A K 10 9 2
♣ 8             │ W     E │         ♣ Q 9 6
                │    S    │
                └─────────┘
                    ♠ A 3
                    ♡ Q 8
                    ◇ 8 7 6 3
                    ♣ K J 10 7 4
```

Both sides vulnerable. North dealer.
The bidding:

North	East	South	West
1 ♡	2 ◇	3 ♣	3 ♠
4 ♣	Pass	Pass	Pass

The deal was played in a tournament some years ago, and North–South were playing ACOL, a system that encourages light opening bids and lighter free raises and responses than most American players use. As a result, North–South were able to buy the contract away from the superior East–West spade suit.

West opened the diamond queen which East overtook with the king. The ace of diamonds was then cashed, and this was followed by the ten of diamonds, West ruffing with the eight-spot. Declarer declined to overruff this with the board's ace, feeling that if he did and subsequently misguessed the club situation (losing a trick to the queen), he might well go down two tricks for a loss of 200 points (going down 200 is known as "the kiss of death," for it usually means no match points).

When West ruffed the third diamond lead, declarer discarded a spade from dummy, in effect exchanging a trick for a trick and, in reality, conceding down one (assuming that the heart finesse would lose).

At trick four, West returned a spade, East's queen falling to declarer's ace. A trump lead to the ace revealed that East possessed the queen, and it became routine for declarer to finesse that card. The queen of hearts was then finessed, losing to East's king, and that was that. Declarer was able to ruff his fourth diamond and then discard his losing spade on the dummy's jack of hearts.

As the cards lay, declarer could have made his contract by over-ruffing at trick three, taking a finesse against the club queen (if it lost, however, West would shift to a spade and declarer would go down 200 points), returning to dummy with a fourth-round dia-mond ruff, and repeating the trump finesse. After picking up East's queen, South would give up the queen of hearts to East's king and would discard his losing spade on the high jack of hearts.

But South correctly judged that with the field playing "American Style," most East–West pairs would be plus 140 or 170 for playing three spades since North's free raise to four clubs did not figure to be made. As a matter of fact, *all* the East–West pairs did arrive at a three spade contract. Half of them made nine tricks, and the other half made ten tricks when the North player did not find the winning defense for holding West to nine tricks by leading a low heart after cashing the ace of clubs.

Thus, since all the other East–West pairs were plus either 140 or 170, our South player received the identical match-point score (10 out of 10) for being minus 100 as he would have received for being plus 130 (four clubs bid and made). Nice work, if you can find it.

CHAPTER 26

Declarer's Play: The Functioning of the Expert Mind

The deals that are presented in this chapter were all played by our topflight experts in topflight competition. The primary purpose for the introduction of these deals is to give the reader an insight into the functioning of the expert mind in match-point situations. Our objective—and hope—is that the experts' approach will rub off on the reader and become ingrained for future application.

DEAL 1.

```
        ♠ A K
        ♡ Q 10 6 5 3
        ◇ K 5 3 2
        ♣ 8 4

        ♠ 8 7
        ♡ A 4
        ◇ A J 8 6 4
        ♣ A J 9 2
```

With no adverse bidding, you, sitting South, have contrived to get to a *six diamond* contract. West opens the king of clubs. What are your reactions as you gaze at the North–South cards? What are you going to do?

The "average" reaction probably would be: "How did I ever get to this hopeless contract?" And, in this frame of mind, the average declarer would now proceed to go down two tricks in average fashion, losing a diamond, a club, and a heart. The result—in match points—would be a tie-for-bottom on the board: one-half match point out of a possible twelve.

Our actual South declarer won the opening lead of the king of clubs with his ace, after which he plunked down the ace of hearts. (There are days when singleton kings are floating around—but this was not one of them.) Now came a diamond to dummy's king, then a finesse of the diamond jack was taken successfully. South now laid down the ace of diamonds, felling East's queen. He next led his remaining heart, West's king winning. West then cashed the queen of clubs for the setting trick.

It is appreciated by all that if you develop the habit of going down at voluntarily arrived-at slam contracts, you will win no duplicate games. However, in this case, after South had gone down at his six diamond contract, he examined the East–West cards and remarked: "Not too bad. Probably at least an average board."

Now, gentle reader, may we ask for your opinion? Why should being down one at an overbid slam contract, which the rest of the field certainly didn't figure to reach, become "at least an average board" and how did our declarer sense that it was? For the record, North–South received 7½ match points out of 12 for being down one!

Let's take a look at all four hands:

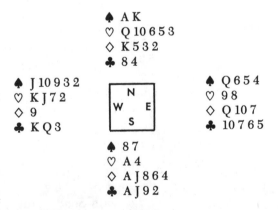

```
                    ♠ A K
                    ♡ Q 10 6 5 3
                    ◇ K 5 3 2
                    ♣ 8 4
   ♠ J 10 9 3 2              ♠ Q 6 5 4
   ♡ K J 7 2      ┌─────┐    ♡ 9 8
   ◇ 9            │  N  │    ◇ Q 10 7
   ♣ K Q 3      W │     │ E  ♣ 10 7 6 5
                  │  S  │
                  └─────┘
                    ♠ 8 7
                    ♡ A 4
                    ◇ A J 8 6 4
                    ♣ A J 9 2
```

When our South declarer originally surveyed the North–South hands, he came to the conclusion that three no-trump figured to be the normal contract. Against the probable spade opening—from either side, since spades had not been bid and the opponents had more spades than any other suit—declarer would have to bring in *five* diamond tricks (or, instead, if he were really lucky, *four* heart tricks) to fulfill his contract. Knowing from past experience that the field would play the king and ace of diamonds to drop the queen— as opposed to finessing the jack—our declarer realized that if the queen didn't drop, three no-trump figured to go down a trick, or more. Consequently, he finessed for the queen of diamonds, hoping that the adverse diamonds were divided 3-1. Only if they were so divided could he hope to tie with those who would be going down at three no-trump. If the diamonds were divided 2-2, then the entire North–South field would be making at least three no-trump —and no matter how the adverse diamonds happened to be divided, he would always be defeated at his slam contract.

Our South declarer appreciated fully, when the king of hearts failed to drop, that he was in a doomed contract. But uppermost in his thoughts was how he could best extricate himself with the minimum loss. And, as the reader has witnessed, 7½ match points out of 12 was a pretty good salvage job.

Deal 2.

This deal arose in the National Team-of-Four Championships of 1957. For the benefit of those readers who might not be familiar with team-of-four play, here is a brief description of how it works.*

Two teams are playing each other. In one room, two members of, say, Team A, sit North–South. In the other room, the other two members of Team A sit East–West. The identical boards are played in each room. Thus, if the North–South pair of Team A makes a small slam on Deal 1, worth, let us say, 980 points, and when the board is replayed, the North–South members of Team B (playing against the East–West members of Team A) bid only a game which they make with two overtricks for a score of 480 points, Team A has won 500 points. Usually 20 to 32 deals are played and which- ever team has the highest *total* score is the winner.

With the above paragraph as a background, when the following deal arose, one team was 2000 points behind at the end of the third

---

* The subject of the various types of events is presented in Chapter 33.

quarter. But they picked up 2510 points on this deal, and eventually won the match by 180 points! The method by which they picked up these points is, we believe, most instructive, for the same psychology was employed that is frequently employed at match-point play.

♠ A Q J 10 8
♡ K 7 4
◇ 4 3
♣ Q 6 4

♠ K 6 5
♡ A J 10
◇ A K 10 5
♣ A K 7

When the North–South pair which was leading by 2000 points sat North–South, their bidding went:

North	South
Pass	2 NT
4 ♣	4 NT
5 ♣	5 NT
7 NT	

The four club bid was the Gerber Convention for aces; ditto the five club bid for kings. Thus, North found that his side had every ace and king.

South, seeing 12 top tricks, played to get a count on the East–West distribution. He found out that West had started with four hearts originally, and East with three. So he took the percentage play of finessing West for the queen of hearts. It lost and he went down two tricks, vulnerable, for a loss of 200 points.

When the board was replayed, the North–South team arrived at a *seven spade* contract. This declarer also discovered that West had started with four hearts, and East with three. But he decided to play the *short* hand for the heart queen. This shrewd decision to try for the only sort of swing that could save his team met with startling success. He made his grand slam for a score of 2310 (honors are counted in total-point team-of-four play), while his teammates in the other room had defeated the seven no-trump contract for a plus score of 200. Thus, the net profit on the board was 2510 points.

The play of the seven spade contract should be of interest.

East opened the jack of clubs, South's king winning. Three rounds of trumps were then cashed, it being noted that East had started with three trumps. The ace of clubs was now cashed, West discarding a diamond. Thus East was known to have had six clubs originally. Next came the ace and king of diamonds, East discarding a club on the second diamond lead. The "count" was now complete: East had had dealt to him six clubs, three spades, and one diamond. His remaining three cards had to be three hearts—and West, therefore, had four hearts. In this situation, the "percentage" was to finesse West for the queen of hearts, since whenever a key card is outstanding, it figures to be in the hand of the defender who has the greater number of cards in that suit. But our declarer elected to make the "anti-percentage" play of finessing East for the heart queen—and luck decreed that he should have it.

For the benefit of readers who may not be too experienced at total-point team-of-four play, further explanation of the "psychology" involved may be advisable.

When one side is far behind—as in the actual deal—and presumably can get back into contention only via a sizable "swing," it is usually wise to make plays that are against (if not too much against) percentage. The assumption is that the other declarer will play as technically correctly as possible, hence the swing can be created only if his (say) 60 percent play fails and a 40 percent play succeeds. The vagaries of chance being what they are, this "desperation" technique of adopting an anti-percentage play has salvaged many a cause that presumably was lost. As evidence, witness the above deal.

As an aside, the same type of reasoning applies to bidding. The team which is *far ahead* must bid dubious slams on the assumption that its opposite number will do just that in an effort to catch up. If the slam is made at both tables or fails at both, that's all right for the team that is leading, since it will have lost no ground. The point is to negate a large swing in favor of the team that's behind. Of course, there are wheels-within-wheels in this business—deliberate double-crosses by the trailing team which may *underbid* in the hope that bad distribution will foul up the declarer who lands at the proper contract. However, the foregoing gives the general guide as to how good teams operate.

DEAL 3.

This is a simple deal—and yet we doubt that one out of 20 players would have played it correctly in a duplicate game. Our South declarer was the one out of 20, and he came out with a top-on-the-board instead of the absolute bottom toward which he was heading.

♠ A J 10 9 5
♡ K 7 2
◇ 6 3
♣ K J 7

♠ Q 8 2
♡ A J 5
◇ 8 4
♣ A Q 10 9 3

Both sides vulnerable. South dealer.
The bidding:

South	West	North	East
1 ♣	Pass	1 ♠	Pass
2 ♣	Pass	5 ♣	Pass
Pass	Pass		

North's bidding left much to be desired, but there was South in a five club contract instead of the four spade contract that figured to be the normal contract for the entire room.

West's opening lead was a low trump, declarer's ten-spot winning. It was quite obvious to our declarer that at the four spade contract every declarer would make at least 11 tricks if the spade finesse were successful (plus 650) and 10 tricks if the spade finesse lost (plus 620). So even if South somehow succeeded in fulfilling his five club contract (plus 600), he figured to get a bottom, or near-bottom, on the board. Hence, abnormal play was called for.

Having won the opening trump lead (thank goodness a diamond had not been opened!), declarer then cashed the king and ace of trumps, picking up the adverse pieces. He then led a spade to dummy's ace—and he caught East with a singleton king! Four more spade leads then followed, declarer discarding his two losing diamonds. Then came the king of hearts, after which the jack of hearts was finessed. When it won, declarer was the happy possessor of all 13 tricks for a plus score of 640. Even if the heart finesse had lost, declarer would have scored 620 points for five clubs bid and made with an overtrick, thus tying all the teams who made exactly four spades.

Of course, if the spade ace did not luckily drop East's singleton king, declarer would have gone down at his five club contract— but it would have cost him no match points, for every other North–South team had bid and made exactly four spades! Of course, none of them made the anti-percentage play of laying down the spade ace. They all took the spade finesse, losing to East's singleton king, after which East cashed the king and queen of diamonds. The actual deal was:

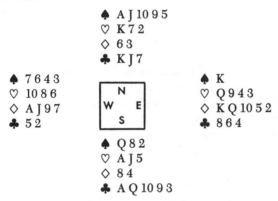

```
                    ♠ A J 10 9 5
                    ♡ K 7 2
                    ◇ 6 3
                    ♣ K J 7
  ♠ 7 6 4 3                         ♠ K
  ♡ 10 8 6         ┌─────────┐      ♡ Q 9 4 3
  ◇ A J 9 7        │    N    │      ◇ K Q 10 5 2
  ♣ 5 2            │ W     E │      ♣ 8 6 4
                   │    S    │
                   └─────────┘
                    ♠ Q 8 2
                    ♡ A J 5
                    ◇ 8 4
                    ♣ A Q 10 9 3
```

To sum up, at the five club contract South's only hope was that East had the singleton king of spades. And as luck (which often comes to the skillful) would have it, South's hope materialized.

DEAL 4.

This deal is introduced as a sort of change of pace, in order to remind the reader that duplicate bridge and rubber bridge can be quite different. The hand serves to demonstrate both the approach of the expert *rubber-bridge* player to the bidding of slams and the presentation of excellent technique, both match-point and rubber-bridge, in the handling of a delicate grand slam contract. We think the reader will find the story both entertaining and instructive.*

* The story is taken, verbatim, from *The Bridge World*, February 1946, pp. 33–34.

"A Duplicate Boomerang"

Ben Allen was the cardroom bore. He was a fanatic on the subject of duplicate bridge. He could talk of nothing but duplicate, and his reserve stock of chatter seemed inexhaustible. Ordinary bridge, the rubber variety, he held in contempt. He not only never played it himself; he would not even stoop to watch a rubber-bridge game.

Yet one afternoon, after his last unwilling victim had edged his way into the corridor, Ben Allen flung himself down in an easy chair near a table where a rubber-bridge game was in progress. A quick survey of the room had disclosed no other vacant easy chair, and he was a bit fagged. He settled back comfortably, closed his eyes, and yawned.

The usual group of onlookers was gathered around the players, but the hands were colorless for some time. Then one of the players jumped to four no-trump, using the Blackwood Convention.

With this bid, the gallery came to life. One of them, in an effort to see the cards, trod on Ben Allen's extended foot and rudely wakened him. Ben was about to protest violently when he noticed the tension around the table.

He heard the crisp response of five spades and pulled himself forward to watch. The hand he saw and the bidding he heard were as follows:

> ♠ A K Q J 9 6 4 2
> ♡ 6 4
> ◊ K
> ♣ 7 2

Opener	Responder
1 ♡	1 ♠
2 ♣	4 NT
5 ♠	5 NT
6 ◊	7 ♠

It was at this point in the proceedings that Ben Allen went violently into action and hurled his boomerang.

"Seven no-trump, you dern fool!" he shrieked. "Seven no-trump! Can't you see that you've got a grand slam in no-trump?"

"What of it?" replied the declarer, shrugging the pest off his neck. "What about the hundred honors in spades?"

"What's honors got to do with it? A sure grand slam in no-trump ruined!"

At this point the jack of clubs was led, and both our kibitzer and declarer found themselves gazing at:

> North
> ♠ 10 8
> ♡ A K 10 8 5
> ◇ A
> ♣ A Q 9 6 5
>
> South
> ♠ A K Q J 9 6 4 2
> ♡ 6 4
> ◇ K
> ♣ 7 2

Declarer noted that he could not get the expected discard on the diamond ace and that he would therefore have to work for his thirteenth trick. He turned to Ben and asked derisively, "Where's your grand slam in no-trump?"

Then he set about his task in masterly fashion. Playing the club ace, he took one round of trumps as a precautionary measure, and then led the ace and king of hearts, both oponents following suit. The third heart he trumped with the ace of spades, and, as one declarer showed out of hearts, he entered dummy via the ten of trumps and ruffed a fourth heart. He then spread his hand, the fifth heart having become promoted into a winner.

When the defenders tossed their remaining cards on the table, Ben Allen reached over and picked up the club king from the opening leader's exposed hand. With a triumphant leer, he slammed it back on the table and addressed the declarer:

"You see! If you had had the guts to finesse the club queen on the first trick, you could have made a grand slam at *no-trump!*"

He hurried from the room, and the players shook their heads

dolefully. "Finesses have no business working for a guy like that," said declarer sadly. "Now we'll *never* be able to shut him up."

DEAL 5.

It has been stated and illustrated that at match-point play the safety of the contract often becomes a secondary consideration. This philosophy also extends to slam contracts, especially to slams which one figures will be bid by virtually every other pair in the room. In the latter situations, one can never ignore the possibility of trying for an overtrick. Even if a *slight* risk exists—in that the slam contract might be jeopardized for the sake of the overtrick—one should try for the overtrick.

Conversely, when one finds himself in a grossly overbid slam contract, which just about no other pair figures to arrive at, one should dismiss any thought of an overtrick and concentrate exclusively on the fulfillment of the contract. If it is fulfilled, an excellent match-point score will result; if it goes down, a zero or near-zero will be obtained. Here is a good illustration. The deal arose in the National Pair Championships of 1954.

♠ A K
♡ 5
◇ A K Q 10 6 2
♣ J 10 8 3

♠ Q 8 6
♡ 10 8 4 3
◇ J 9
♣ A Q 9 4

How the bidding developed so that South found himself in a *six club* contract would not be believed if it were presented. We therefore are not introducing it. Against this contract, West opened the ten of spades.

It was apparent to our declarer that he was in a slightly optimistic contract. It was equally apparent that if he won the opening lead with dummy's king of spades and took the trump finesse immediately he would make either 11 tricks or all 13, depending on the outcome of the finesse. Of course, our declarer was not interested in either 11 or 13 as his objective. His attention was focused on finding the best line of play to make 12 tricks, even if it involved forsaking the conceivable overtrick.

After winning the opening lead with the king of spades, South cashed the ace of spades. He now led a trump to his ace—spurning the finesse—and then played the queen of spades, discarding dummy's singleton heart. He next led a trump, which West took with the king as East followed suit. Declarer had just "wrapped up" his six club contract for 12 match points out of a possible 12!

The complete deal was:

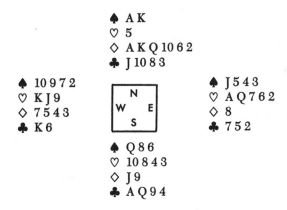

♠ A K
♡ 5
◇ A K Q 10 6 2
♣ J 10 8 3

♠ 10 9 7 2
♡ K J 9
◇ 7 5 4 3
♣ K 6

♠ J 5 4 3
♡ A Q 7 6 2
◇ 8
♣ 7 5 2

♠ Q 8 6
♡ 10 8 4 3
◇ J 9
♣ A Q 9 4

It is obvious that if West had opened a heart the six club contract would have been defeated automatically. Similarly, if declarer had taken the trump finesse at trick two, he would have been down at trick three, with West surely switching to a heart after taking the trump king. And further if, after winning the opening lead with the spade king and then cashing the spade ace, declarer had chosen to enter his own hand via the diamond jack (instead of via the trump ace) West would subsequently have had it within his power to return a diamond for East to trump. Thus, declarer's ultra-safe play was essential on this deal.

Incidentally, the reader may point out that his line of play wasn't *absolutely* safe. Quite true. By cashing the ace and king of spades and then the queen *before* drawing trumps, he ran the risk that one of the opponents might trump in. However, it is a fact that *absolute* safety is not found too often at the bridge table. On the above deal, the trump finesse at trick two would have given declarer a 50–50 chance for survival. The cashing of the king, ace, and queen of spades offered him a much finer chance. And so, realistically and winningly, he accepted the better of what was available.

DEAL 6.

Here is a "problem" which, in retrospect, is a simple one. Yet we wonder how many of our duplicate players, had they been confronted with the problem in actual play, would have found the winning solution.

♠ K Q 10 3 2
♡ Q J 9 8
◇ 8
♣ A 7 2

♠ —
♡ A 5
◇ K J 9 7 6 5 4 3 2
♣ K 3

You are sitting South, and have arrived at a *six diamond* contract. West opens the four of spades, you put up the king—and it wins the trick, enabling you to discard the heart five. You then lead the eight of trumps, East follows with the ten and you play . . . the jack or the king?

When this deal arose in the National Championships of 1964, Oswald Jacoby, sitting South, came up with the right answer at once. He put up his king of diamonds—and felled West's queen. His only loser was a trick to the trump ace.

How come Jacoby put up the king of trumps and not the jack? Well, it was rather obvious that West had led away from the ace of spades. Surely if West had held both the ace of spades *and* the ace of diamonds, he would not have underled his spade ace at trick one. Hence, Jacoby knew that East held the trump ace.

As to why West underled the spade ace, it should be mentioned that Jacoby had bid most confidently to six diamonds and West was convinced that orthodox defense didn't figure to be the winning defense. Therefore he gambled on an unorthodox lead.

The complete deal was:

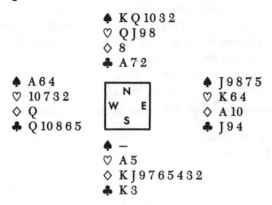

```
              ♠ K Q 10 3 2
              ♡ Q J 9 8
              ◇ 8
              ♣ A 7 2
♠ A 6 4                        ♠ J 9 8 7 5
♡ 10 7 3 2                     ♡ K 6 4
◇ Q                           ◇ A 10
♣ Q 10 8 6 5                   ♣ J 9 4
              ♠ —
              ♡ A 5
              ◇ K J 9 7 6 5 4 3 2
              ♣ K 3
```

DEAL 7.

One of the major recurring problems at match-point play is whether one should play to guarantee a game contract that every pair in the room figures to arrive at or whether he should, instead, accept a 50–50 chance for an overtrick which, if made, will give him a top on the board and, if not made, will mean a defeated contract and a bottom. Here is an example of precisely such a situation in a rather unusual setting.

```
              ♠ 9 8 2
              ♡ J 10
              ◇ 7 5 4
              ♣ Q J 8 6 3

              ♠ A Q
              ♡ A Q 9
              ◇ A 8 3 2
              ♣ A K 7 5
```

Both sides vulnerable. South dealer.
The bidding:

South	West	North	East
2 NT	Pass	3 NT	Pass
Pass	Pass		

West opened the king of diamonds, East followed with the nine-spot, and declarer permitted West's king to win. The queen of diamonds was then continued, East discarded the deuce of hearts, and South took the trick with his ace.

Before presenting the thoughts that ran through declarer's mind prior to his play of the hand, let us tell the circumstances under which the deal was being played.

The hand arose in the last of four sessions of the Masters' Individual Championships of 1959. It was the 23rd of 26 boards. The South declarer was Bobby Reynolds of Miami, the ultimate winner of this grueling event. Going into the final session, Bobby was in second place, 18 points behind the leader (12 top on each board). In this final session, Bobby had had an excellent game up to this point and it was his feeling that he was currently leading the field by a nice margin. Thus, his prime concern was not to increase his lead but to maintain it. In other words, he was not interested in gaining ground but in doing everything in his power *to avoid losing ground*. Frankly, as he put it to us later, he would have been perfectly happy to get an average score on the four boards remaining to be played. If he could only do that, he was sure he would win the championship.

And so, upon winning the second diamond lead with the ace, Bobby perceived that he had eight top tricks: five clubs, one spade, one heart, and one diamond. The ninth trick could come from one of two places, either the spade finesse or the heart finesse. If whichever finesse he took lost, it would lose to West, who would then cash the remainder of his established diamonds to hand South a one-trick set—and bottom or tie-for-bottom on the board.

If somebody had put a gun at Bobby's head and *forced* him to take one finesse or the other, he would of course have taken the heart finesse. After all, if the spade finesse worked, declarer would make just nine tricks; whereas, if the heart finesse worked, declarer could then take another heart finesse and make 10 tricks. Certainly, then, if Bobby were forced to stake his existence on a 50–50 finesse, the heart finesse would offer a more prosperous future if he survived.

Permit us to break off briefly, and ask a question: Would you, in Bobby's position (and frame of mind), have settled for an *absolutely guaranteed nine tricks?* They are there for the taking, if you are willing to forget about making an overtrick. Bobby was willing to settle for his contract, and he did. For his play, he was rewarded with 8 match points out of 12.

After taking the second diamond lead (trick two), Bobby cashed the ace and king of clubs, both opponents following suit. The opponents now *had no more clubs.* He then led a *diamond,* thrusting West into the lead, and West cashed the remainder of his diamonds (all in all, four diamond tricks). West now had to lead either a spade or a heart into this position:

```
              ♠ 9
              ♡ J 10
              ◇ —
              ♣ Q J 8

              ♠ A Q
              ♡ A Q 9
              ◇ —
              ♣ 7
```

Whether he led a spade or a heart, South would get a "free finesse" and his ninth trick in whatever suit West chose to lead. Actually, West led a spade and Bobby chalked up a game bid and made. This was the complete deal:

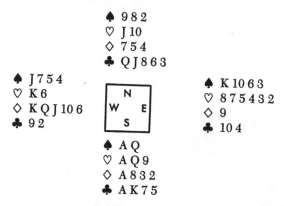

```
                      ♠ 9 8 2
                      ♡ J 10
                      ◇ 7 5 4
                      ♣ Q J 8 6 3

    ♠ J 7 5 4                          ♠ K 10 6 3
    ♡ K 6            ┌─────────┐        ♡ 8 7 5 4 3 2
    ◇ K Q J 10 6     │   N     │        ◇ 9
    ♣ 9 2            │ W     E │        ♣ 10 4
                     │   S     │
                     └─────────┘
                      ♠ A Q
                      ♡ A Q 9
                      ◇ A 8 3 2
                      ♣ A K 7 5
```

To conclude, if Bobby had "guessed" to take the spade finesse, he would have made the same nine tricks that he made via the end play (with no 50–50 guess). But if he had misguessed by taking the heart finesse, he would have gone down one and would have secured 2 match points out of 12, instead of the 8 he actually obtained. And if you think the difference wasn't important, Bobby won the Championship by *one-half a match point* over Art Robinson of Philadelphia!

DEAL 8.

One of the greatest players the world has ever known is Helen Sobel. An example of her ability can be seen from this deal, which arose in the National Open Pair Championships of 1949. One cannot help but admire the brilliance of her analysis.

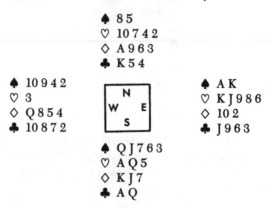

```
                    ♠ 8 5
                    ♡ 10 7 4 2
                    ◇ A 9 6 3
                    ♣ K 5 4
    ♠ 10 9 4 2                      ♠ A K
    ♡ 3                             ♡ K J 9 8 6
    ◇ Q 8 5 4                       ◇ 10 2
    ♣ 10 8 7 2                      ♣ J 9 6 3
                    ♠ Q J 7 6 3
                    ♡ A Q 5
                    ◇ K J 7
                    ♣ A Q
```

Both sides vulnerable. East dealer.

East	South	West	North
1 ♡	Double	Pass	2 ◇
Pass	2 NT	Pass	3 NT
Pass	Pass	Pass	

West opened the deuce of clubs which Helen Sobel, sitting South, took with her ace. She promptly led the three of spades, playing East for the doubleton A K of spades! How could anybody be that clairvoyant, you might ask? Well, let us follow her trend of thought.

West's lead of the deuce of clubs, as the fourth best, showed exactly four cards in that suit. Helen assumed that if West had held two hearts (her partner's bid suit), he would have opened that suit in preference to leading from a broken-down four-card suit. East, for his opening bid, just about had to have the A K of spades and the king of hearts since only 14 high-card points were outstanding. That West had *exactly* a singleton heart was apparent to Mrs. Sobel, for if West were void of hearts, he would certainly have led from the five-card suit which he then would have possessed. So West was "marked" with three four-card suits and a singleton heart. Ergo, East had exactly two spades—the ace and king.

It is, in a sense, anticlimactic to present the play of this deal, but here it is. When East took South's three of spades with his king at trick two, he returned a club, declarer's queen winning. Another low spade lead then forced East's ace, and East played back another club, dummy's king winning as Helen discarded the five of hearts from her own hand. The queen of hearts was then finessed successfully, after which Helen cashed the ace of hearts, West discarding a spade. Now came South's three high spades, arriving at this position prior to the lead of the last spade:

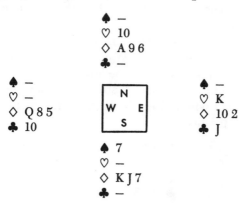

```
              ♠ —
              ♡ 10
              ◇ A 9 6
              ♣ —
♠ —                        ♠ —
♡ —         ┌─────┐        ♡ K
◇ Q 8 5     │  N  │        ◇ 10 2
♣ 10        │W   E│        ♣ J
            │  S  │
            └─────┘
              ♠ 7
              ♡ —
              ◇ K J 7
              ♣ —
```

When Helen led the seven of spades, West discarded the ten of clubs, dummy the ten of hearts, and East the jack of clubs. Knowing (from the outset) that *East* had started with two spades, five hearts, two diamonds, and four clubs, Helen now led the king of diamonds, after which she played the jack of diamonds, which, obligingly, West covered with the queen, dummy's ace winning. With East's ten-spot falling on this trick, the board's nine-spot was now a winner, and declarer made 11 tricks for an undisputed top score on the board.

Just what Helen would have done if West had not covered the jack of diamonds with the queen, we don't know with absolute certainty. But we are quite certain that she would have diagnosed the situation correctly and would have let the jack ride. After all, if she had had the feeling that East's doubleton diamond was the Q x originally, she would have led a low diamond on the second diamond lead to drop the queen, instead of leading the jack. Probably her "intuition"—or something—whispered to her that East had started with the doubleton 10 x, and she played accordingly.

DEAL 9.

No discussion of the "functioning of the expert mind" would be complete without the presentation of a deal devoted to "deception." This final deal is actually an elementary one, and the proper play would be identical in both rubber bridge and duplicate bridge. Nevertheless, we'd be willing to wager that at least half of our nation's bridge players (rubber and duplicate) would not come up with a natural "psychological" play which stands to gain everything and to lose nothing.

When the deal arose in a tournament some years ago, our South declarer was a full-fledged expert. At no cost whatsoever he made a deceptive discard and, in so doing, he lured a defender into giving declarer a present of a trick that the latter would have been unable to make on his own power. Here is the deal. Let us put you into the South seat as the declarer.

```
              ♠ 8 7 3
              ♡ A 9 4
              ◇ A 6 4 3
              ♣ 9 6 5

              ♠ A Q 2
              ♡ K Q J 10 7 3
              ◇ K 5
              ♣ Q 10
```

Both sides vulnerable. South dealer.
The bidding:

South	West	North	East
1 ♡	Pass	2 ♡	Pass
4 ♡	Pass	Pass	Pass

West opens the king of clubs and then leads the ace of clubs, felling your queen. He next plays the jack of clubs. What do you play from the South hand?

The only proper play is to discard the deuce of spades! Why this discard, rather than trumping the club jack?

First, the loss of one spade trick is inevitable so nothing is lost. But second, and more important, is that this discard may create an impression of spade weakness and thus perhaps may induce West into shifting to a spade. Admittedly, if West has the king of spades, he *probably* won't lead away from it. However, this discard will certainly cause West to give at least a passing thought to leading a spade, and who knows what West may do after he thinks about what to lead next?

In the actual play, West did fall victim to declarer's deuce of spades discard—and his spade lead enabled declarer to fulfill an otherwise unmakable contract. This was the complete deal:

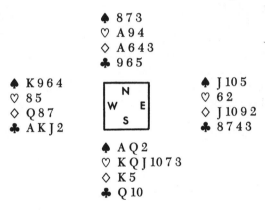

```
                    ♠ 8 7 3
                    ♡ A 9 4
                    ◇ A 6 4 3
                    ♣ 9 6 5
  ♠ K 9 6 4                        ♠ J 10 5
  ♡ 8 5            N               ♡ 6 2
  ◇ Q 8 7       W     E            ◇ J 10 9 2
  ♣ A K J 2        S               ♣ 8 7 4 3
                    ♠ A Q 2
                    ♡ K Q J 10 7 3
                    ◇ K 5
                    ♣ Q 10
```

Actually, West did have a problem as to what to lead to trick four. A club lead was out of the question since that lead would enable declarer to trump in dummy while discarding a loser from his own hand. A diamond lead was dangerous and would have cost a trick if declarer had the K J of diamonds instead of the K 5. A spade lead was obviously dangerous since (from West's viewpoint) declarer might well have the A Q of spades. And a trump lead might also cost a trick if, for example, East held the Q x x of trumps.

Thus, by discarding the deuce of spades on the lead of the club jack at trick three, declarer gave West an opportunity to go wrong. And West seized the bait, giving declarer 11½ out of 12 match points. Had West led either a heart or a diamond at trick four, South would have gone down and would have received 5 match points out of 12. Of course, had the spade king been favorably located (in East's hand), declarer would always have made his contract. As was stated, however, since declarer always had at least one spade loser, he stood to lose nothing by discarding it at trick three, hoping to seduce West into leading a spade.

Frankly, we disapprove of West's lead. But, then, if declarer had ruffed the jack of clubs, West would have had no chance to go wrong. These are the "little things" that win big tournaments.

CHAPTER 27

Well-Played Hands at National Tournaments

The deals in this chapter were all played in national tournaments during the past 25 years. We salute the various South declarers on each of these deals with a "Well done!" for their fine play.

DEAL 1.

♠ A K Q J 6 3
♡ 10 6 3 2
◇ —
♣ 8 7 3

♠ —
♡ A K Q J 9 8 7
◇ K
♣ K J 6 5 4

South is playing a *six heart* contract. West opens the ace of diamonds, dummy ruffing. What do you play at trick two?

If you lead a trump to the South hand, you cannot make more than 12 tricks. The proper play is to lead a low spade at trick two and ruff it. Now trumps are drawn, ending up in the dummy, and on the board's five spades declarer discards his five clubs. And that all-important overtrick gives you a tie-for-top on the board. This was the deal:

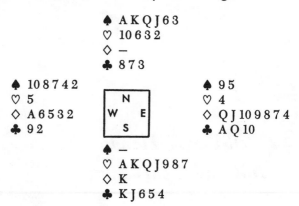

Alvin Landy, the Executive Secretary of the A.C.B.L., came up with the right play at trick two when this deal arose in the National Championships of 1950.

The reader will note that if a trump is led from the dummy at trick two, there is no re-entry for establishing *and* cashing the fifth spade. Declarer will be able to discard only four of his five clubs on dummy's top spades. He will, of course, still make his 12-trick contract—but he will fail to get that oh-so-important overtrick.

DEAL 2.

This deal arose in the National Open Pair Championships of 1951. Sitting South was Oswald Jacoby.

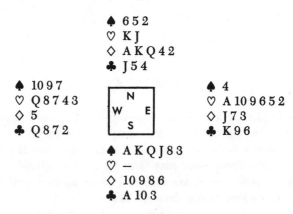

North–South vulnerable. North dealer.

North	East	South	West
1 ◇	1 ♡	1 ♠	4 ♡
Pass	Pass	6 ♠	Pass
Pass	Pass		

Had West opened a low heart in response to his partner's overcall, declarer, by inserting the jack, would have made all 13 tricks. But Jacoby received the opening lead of the ten of spades instead—and he had his work cut out for him to make 12 tricks.

The opening trump lead was won with the jack, after which West's remaining two trumps were picked up. A diamond was next led to the ace, followed by the king of diamonds. When the diamond jack failed to drop, the diamond suit was blocked. If the queen of diamonds were now cashed, South's fourth diamond would be high and there would be no way of cashing dummy's fifth diamond.

Jacoby solved this problem in neat fashion. After cashing the king of diamonds, he led the board's king of hearts, upon which he discarded a diamond as East won the trick. East now shifted to a club, South winning with his ace. South then led his remaining diamond to dummy's queen and on the deuce and four of diamonds, Jacoby discarded his two losing clubs.

The interesting (not to Jacoby) aspect of this deal is that Jacoby received a below-average match-point score; for at most tables a heart was opened, the various declarers all guessed right by putting up the jack and eventually made all 13 tricks by getting rid of a diamond on the king of hearts and discarding South's two losing clubs on the board's two low diamonds.

Deal 3.

As has been seen throughout this text, the element of safety, which is so vital at rubber bridge, is frequently just an academic concept devoid of practical implications at match-point play. The deal that follows illustrates this point in rather vivid fashion. It arose in the 1961 Life Masters Pairs Championships, and the South declarer was Peter Leventritt.

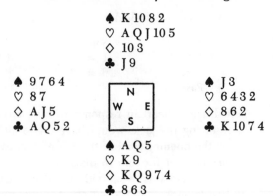

Neither side vulnerable. South dealer.
The bidding:

South	West	North	East
1 ◇	Pass	1 ♡	Pass
1 NT	Pass	2 NT	Pass
3 NT	Pass	Pass	Pass

West opened the four of spades, and East's jack was taken by Leventritt's ace. Declarer then paused for reflection and analysis.

It soon became obvious that three no-trump was there for the taking; and it was equally apparent that three no-trump could have been defeated had a club been opened. So the question became: to run home with nine tricks or not?

But another factor had to be taken into consideration: probably the majority of the field would get to a four heart contract (so it seemed to Leventritt). With the jack of spades falling, the making of 10 tricks would be a routine affair. Hence, assuming that the spade lead was the normal opening against three no-trump, three no-trump bid and made figured to yield a below-average score. So Leventritt had to play for an overtrick (he had not come to the Nationals to get below-average scores).

At trick two, he led the nine of hearts to dummy's queen, after which he led the ten of diamonds and put up his king when East followed with the deuce. West won with the ace—and returned a spade! (If West had seen all four hands, he, as we, would of course have returned a club.)

Leventritt now felt better about the whole thing. He won the spade return with the queen, cashed the king of hearts, crossed to dummy with a spade, and ran the board's remaining hearts and the king of spades. West discarded badly and left himself with the blank ace of clubs and the J 5 of diamonds. Leventritt diagnosed the end-play situation and led a club off the board, West's ace winning. West was now compelled to lead a diamond into declarer's Q 9. Leventritt thus wound up making 11 tricks. In rubber bridge, he would have settled for nine.

DEAL 4.

This deal was played in the National Championships of 1957.

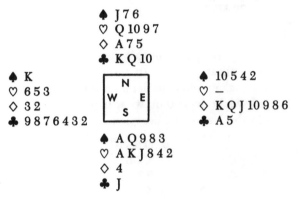

Both sides vulnerable. North dealer.

North	East	South	West
Pass	4 ◇	4 ♡	Pass
5 ◇	Pass	5 ♠	Pass
6 ♡	Pass	Pass	Pass

The South declarer was Ivar Stakgold.

The three of diamonds was opened, North's ace winning, East dropping the king. A diamond was then ruffed high in the closed hand, after which the king of trumps was cashed, East showing out. Then came the jack of hearts, followed by a heart to dummy's ten-spot. West's trumps had now been removed.

Dummy's remaining diamond was now ruffed, West discarding a club. Hence, East was known to have started with seven diamonds originally. The jack of clubs was led next, taken by East's ace. East returned a club and declarer cashed the board's queen and king, discarding two spades from his own hand as East discarded a diamond on the last club lead.

East's distribution was now an open book: he had started with exactly seven diamonds, two clubs, and four spades (he had failed to follow suit to the first round of hearts).

Stakgold knew that East could not have the king of spades, for no East player in his right mind would have opened the bidding with four diamonds had he held four spades headed by the king, seven solid diamonds missing the ace, and the ace and one club. So Stakgold did not finesse for the king of spades. Instead, he played his ace of spades, with the certainty that he would catch West's singleton king.

DEAL 5.

Actually, the correct play of this deal would be identical in both rubber and duplicate bridge. In both games, the use of a safety play would be taken into consideration but whether or not it would be employed would depend on what happened in another suit. The deal arose in the National Championships of 1937.

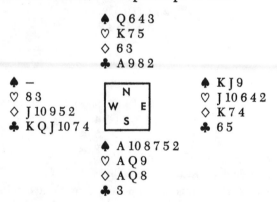

```
              ♠ Q 6 4 3
              ♡ K 7 5
              ◇ 6 3
              ♣ A 9 8 2
   ♠ —                        ♠ K J 9
   ♡ 8 3          N           ♡ J 10 6 4 2
   ◇ J 10 9 5 2  W   E        ◇ K 7 4
   ♣ K Q J 10 7 4   S         ♣ 6 5
              ♠ A 10 8 7 5 2
              ♡ A Q 9
              ◇ A Q 8
              ♣ 3
```

Neither side vulnerable. North dealer.
The bidding:

North	East	South	West
Pass	Pass	1 ♠	3 ♣ *
4 ♠	Pass	6 ♠	Pass
Pass	Pass		

* The weak jump overcall.

West opened the king of clubs, dummy's ace winning. As declarer surveyed and appraised his contract, he realized that this was a slam contract very few (if any) pairs would get to and that if he went down he figured to get no match points. Hence, the quest for the best play to fulfill the contract became the order of the day. There was not even a passing thought about the possibility of making an overtrick.

After winning the opening club lead, declarer promptly took the diamond finesse, successfully. A low trump was then led to dummy's queen, East taking the queen with the king as West failed to follow suit. It now became routine—upon regaining the lead—for declarer to enter dummy via the heart king and to trap East's remaining J 9 of trumps.

This is a deal where most players would go wrong. We imagine that, after winning the opening club lead, they would lead a trump to the ace—and go down then and there, for East would now have two trump tricks.

Our declarer realized that the key to fulfillment rested on what happened in the diamond suit. If the finesse worked, then a safety play could (and *would*) be taken in the trump suit; if the finesse lost, then desperation measures, in the form of playing the trump ace to catch the king, would be necessary. Hence, the diamond finesse had to be taken first; and on its outcome would come the knowledge of how to play the trump suit.

When the diamond finesse proved successful, declarer led a low trump out of his hand, with the intention of putting up dummy's queen if West played low. No matter which opponent (if any) held the three outstanding spades, declarer would be absolutely sure of restricting his trump losses to exactly one spade trick, thus guaranteeing his contract.

Deal 6.

This deal arose in the National Championships of 1961 and features a nice stroke of technique by Alfred Sheinwold. Without the application of "table judgment," however, his technical execution—to make an overtrick—would not have been given the opportunity of coming into play.

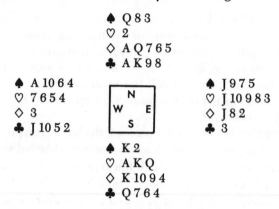

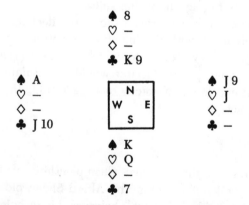

Sheinwold, sitting South, arrived at a *six no-trump* contract.

It took West a long time to make his opening lead, from which Sheinwold deduced (at his own risk!) that West held the ace of spades and had decided not to lead it. West finally opened the seven of hearts, which declarer took with his ace. The deuce of spades was promptly returned, West followed with a low spade, and dummy's queen won the trick. The five diamonds were then taken, declarer discarding a club from his own hand. Then came the ace of clubs, followed by a club to the queen.

Now Sheinwold cashed his two remaining hearts, and this was the position prior to his lead of the last heart:

On the lead of the queen of hearts, West found it impossible both to protect the clubs and hold the ace of spades. He actually tossed away the ten of clubs, and dummy's nine-spot became that all-important overtrick.

DEAL 7.

One of the hands in the Men's Pairs Championships of 1953 was the following. It serves as proof that, in the field of bridge, nature imitates art. Probably every serious student of the game has seen this type of play in textbooks or in newspaper columns, but surprisingly few recognized and applied it in the tournament. One of those who did was Bill Root, our South declarer.

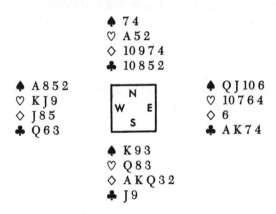

```
              ♠ 7 4
              ♡ A 5 2
              ◇ 10 9 7 4
              ♣ 10 8 5 2
♠ A 8 5 2                      ♠ Q J 10 6
♡ K J 9          N             ♡ 10 7 6 4
◇ J 8 5      W       E         ◇ 6
♣ Q 6 3          S             ♣ A K 7 4
              ♠ K 9 3
              ♡ Q 8 3
              ◇ A K Q 3 2
              ♣ J 9
```

East–West vulnerable. South dealer.
The bidding:

South	West	North	East
1 NT	Pass	Pass	Pass

West opened the deuce of spades, and Bill won it with the king. He cashed the ace and king of diamonds, but East discarded a low heart on the second diamond lead. The diamond suit was "blocked": South couldn't cash five diamond tricks. What next?

The opponents could obviously take three spades and three top clubs as soon as they obtained the lead, so Bill couldn't afford to try any developmental plays in hearts or clubs. It looked as though the block in diamonds would limit him to four diamonds, a spade, and a heart.

Fortunately for him, Bill knew the books. He simply led a spade, and dared the opponents to beat him. At double-dummy, East would have won and returned a heart immediately. In the actual play, the opponents gratefully took their spades and Bill gratefully discarded a diamond from dummy on the third round of spades.

Now Bill was in a position to take five diamonds, a spade, and a heart as soon as the opponents stopped taking tricks in the black suits. Plus 90 on the North–South cards was an excellent match-point score. As a matter of fact, even if Bill had gone down a couple of tricks on the hand, he would still have received a good score since the opponents could make at least nine tricks at a spade contract. Bill's opening one no-trump bid had made it most difficult for the vulnerable opponents to enter into the auction. In effect, he had "stolen" the entire board, lock, stock, and barrel.

DEAL 8.

This deal arose in the Life Masters Individual Championships of 1952. The South declarer was Miss Louise Durham of Mississippi.

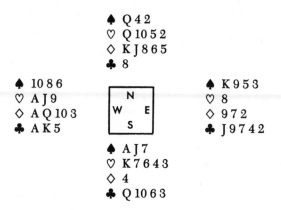

```
                    ♠ Q 4 2
                    ♡ Q 10 5 2
                    ◇ K J 8 6 5
                    ♣ 8
      ♠ 10 8 6          N          ♠ K 9 5 3
      ♡ A J 9       W       E      ♡ 8
      ◇ A Q 10 3        S          ◇ 9 7 2
      ♣ A K 5                      ♣ J 9 7 4 2
                    ♠ A J 7
                    ♡ K 7 6 4 3
                    ◇ 4
                    ♣ Q 10 6 3
```

Neither side vulnerable. North dealer.
The bidding:

North	East	South	West
Pass	Pass	1 ♡	Double
Redouble	1 ♠	Pass	1 NT
2 ♡	Pass	Pass	2 ♠
3 ♡	Pass	Pass	Double
Pass	Pass	Pass	

At rubber bridge, West (a good player) would have sold out to three hearts without a double. At match points, however, he felt compelled to double. If he could set three hearts two tricks, he had to make sure of collecting 300 points instead of only 100 for—as West figured it—all the other East–West pairs were being allowed to score 110 points at spades.

He opened the king of clubs, and Miss Durham made her contract —and then some!

After winning the opening club lead, West shifted to the ten of spades and South won with the jack. She led a diamond, and West took his ace to lead another spade. Miss Durham took the ace of spades and ruffed a club to discard a spade on the diamond king.

Now declarer ruffed a spade in her hand and another club in dummy. It was pleasant to see West's ace of clubs fall on this trick.

Miss Durham next ruffed a diamond for re-entry, and then led a trump toward dummy. West could have held her to nine tricks (her contract) by putting up the ace of hearts and returning a heart. No matter which hand won, West would eventually get his jack of hearts.

However, West properly saw no virtue in giving up completely when there was still the remote chance that his partner had the king of hearts. So he played the nine of hearts, and dummy won a finesse with the ten. Now Miss Durham ruffed a diamond, and then led the queen of clubs through West's A J of trumps toward dummy's blank queen! And, of course, the queen could not be prevented from winning a trick, which became the overtrick at the doubled three heart contract.

Actually, even if Miss Durham had not made an overtrick, she would have scored a top on the board.

Deal 9.

The deal which follows was played in the National Open Pair Championships of 1947. The South declarer was the late Phil Abramsohn. The primary point of this hand is to emphasize the issue of not doubling a slam contract merely because you have a "feeling" that you can defeat it. By doubling in this case, you tip off declarer that you possess the outstanding key cards; and, in so doing, you frequently enable him to fulfill a contract which, without the telltale double, would have gone down to defeat.

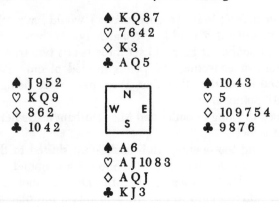

♠ K Q 8 7
♡ 7 6 4 2
◇ K 3
♣ A Q 5

♠ J 9 5 2
♡ K Q 9
◇ 8 6 2
♣ 10 4 2

♠ 10 4 3
♡ 5
◇ 10 9 7 5 4
♣ 9 8 7 6

♠ A 6
♡ A J 10 8 3
◇ A Q J
♣ K J 3

North–South vulnerable. South dealer.
The bidding:

South	West	North	East
1 ♡	Pass	1 ♠	Pass
2 NT	Pass	3 ♡	Pass
4 ♡	Pass	6 ♡	Pass
Pass	Double	Pass	Pass
Pass			

West opened the two of spades and when the dummy came into view, it was perfectly obvious to Mr. Abramsohn that West's double was based on the king and queen of hearts since, in addition to the jack of spades, these were the only picture cards outstanding. Without West's double, South would have double-finessed in trumps on the theory that East held either the king or queen of trumps. With the double, this latter line of play was out of the question.

Declarer captured West's spade lead with his ace, after which a spade was led to dummy's queen. This was followed by a third round of spades, which declarer ruffed. Then came three rounds of clubs, ending up in dummy. Dummy's high queen of spades was now led, East trumped with the three-spot, and declarer overtrumped it. Then followed the king, queen, and ace of diamonds, the latter card being ruffed in dummy. At this point, with the lead being in dummy, declarer had remaining the A J 10 of trumps, and West held the K Q 9. A low heart was now led, declarer put up his ten-spot, which was taken by West's queen—and West was end-played, being forced to lead away from his K 9 of hearts into South's A J of hearts.

DEAL 10.

One of the recurring types of guesses in bridge is which way to finesse when you have eight of a suit between you and partner, with the A J in one hand and the K 10 in the other. Sometimes it's a guess, and sometimes it shouldn't be. The latter situation is demonstrated on this deal, which came up in the 1946 National Championships. The South declarer was B. J. Becker.

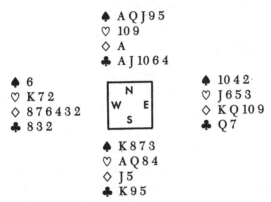

```
                    ♠ A Q J 9 5
                    ♡ 10 9
                    ◇ A
                    ♣ A J 10 6 4
    ♠ 6                              ♠ 10 4 2
    ♡ K 7 2          N              ♡ J 6 5 3
    ◇ 8 7 6 4 3 2  W   E            ◇ K Q 10 9
    ♣ 8 3 2          S              ♣ Q 7
                    ♠ K 8 7 3
                    ♡ A Q 8 4
                    ◇ J 5
                    ♣ K 9 5
```

Against South's *six spade* contract, West opened a diamond, dummy's ace winning. Three rounds of trumps were then taken, ending up in the South hand, after which declarer's remaining diamond was ruffed. Now came the king and ace of clubs. When East's queen fell, there was no further problem. Subsequently, West obtained a heart trick.

Had Becker not caught the queen of clubs, he would then have led a third round of that suit. *If West had the queen* (Q x x originally), he would become end-played. If he returned a heart, declarer would obtain a free finesse; and if, instead, West returned a diamond, declarer would discard one of dummy's two hearts, while simultaneously trumping the trick in his own hand.

If it turned out (theoretically) that *East* won the third club lead with the queen (Q x x originally), then, as a last resort, declarer would take the 50–50 heart finesse. But he wasn't going to take it unless he were forced to—and he wasn't.

DEAL 11.

On the preceding deal, the major theme was the avoidance of a finesse. On the deal which follows, the finesse was the only proper play, for whether it won or lost, declarer was sure to fulfill his contract. The hand came up in the 1950 National Open Pair Championships.

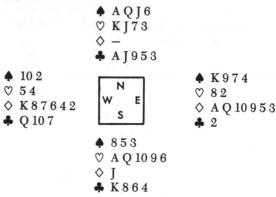

```
                    ♠ A Q J 6
                    ♡ K J 7 3
                    ◇ —
                    ♣ A J 9 5 3
  ♠ 10 2                              ♠ K 9 7 4
  ♡ 5 4              N               ♡ 8 2
  ◇ K 8 7 6 4 2    W   E             ◇ A Q 10 9 5 3
  ♣ Q 10 7           S               ♣ 2
                    ♠ 8 5 3
                    ♡ A Q 10 9 6
                    ◇ J
                    ♣ K 8 6 4
```

Against South's *six heart* contract, West led the six of diamonds, which dummy ruffed. Two rounds of trumps came next, picking up the adverse pieces. The king of clubs was then cashed, after which a low club was led from the closed hand. When West followed suit with the ten-spot, dummy's jack was inserted. It won, and the slam became assured.

But what if the finesse had lost? In this case, East would be winning the trick with the defenders' sole remaining club, the queen. If East now returned a diamond, declarer would discard a spade from his own hand, while ruffing the trick in dummy. Declarer's other losing spade would then be discarded on the board's fifth club.

If East chose to return a spade (upon winning with his hypothetical queen of clubs), declarer would now have no losers in that suit, since his remaining losing spade would be tossed on the board's fifth club.

As can be observed, had declarer elected to play the ace and king of clubs in the hope of catching the queen (instead of finessing), he would have lost both a club trick and a spade trick.

DEAL 12.

This deal, taken from the National Men's Pair Championships of 1953, provided our South declarer, John Moran, with an excellent opportunity for a swindle.

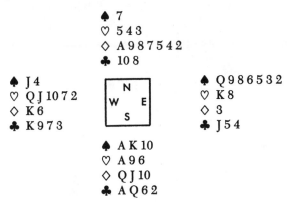

♠ 7
♡ 5 4 3
◊ A 9 8 7 5 4 2
♣ 10 8

♠ J 4
♡ Q J 10 7 2
◊ K 6
♣ K 9 7 3

♠ Q 9 8 6 5 3 2
♡ K 8
◊ 3
♣ J 5 4

♠ A K 10
♡ A 9 6
◊ Q J 10
♣ A Q 6 2

Neither side vulnerable. South dealer.
The bidding:

South	West	North	East
1 ♣	1 ♡	Pass	1 ♠
Double	Pass	3 ◊	Pass
3 NT	Pass	Pass	Pass

West's opening lead of the heart queen was overtaken by East's king, declarer ducking. On winning East's heart return, Moran led the jack of diamonds, and passed it when West followed with the six-spot. Declarer, naturally, hoped the finesse would lose, as the diamond block would then be wiped out. When the jack held the trick, desperation measures became necessary. Moran played the nine of hearts next! On lead with the heart, West carelessly cashed his remaining tricks in that suit, allowing South to jettison a diamond and free that suit. When South regained the lead, his remaining diamond to dummy's ace picked up West's king, and enabled South to bring home the diamond suit.

Obviously, West should have been more skeptical about declarer's "Greek Gift." A moment's reflection would have made the diamond situation obvious. The return of the diamond king became mandatory at the fifth trick, thus effectively preventing the cashing of the board's diamond suit.

DEAL 13.

This final deal is, in retrospect, a simple one. Yet when the hand arose in the National Championships of 1955, not many declarers made 11 tricks at their heart contract. Most of them made only nine. Our South declarer, Jerome Scheur of Boston, was one of those who made the maximum 11 tricks.

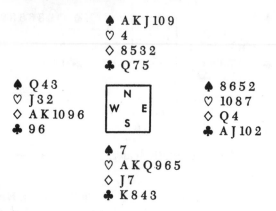

```
                    ♠ A K J 10 9
                    ♡ 4
                    ◊ 8 5 3 2
                    ♣ Q 7 5
  ♠ Q 4 3                              ♠ 8 6 5 2
  ♡ J 3 2          ┌─────────┐        ♡ 10 8 7
  ◊ A K 10 9 6     │   N     │        ◊ Q 4
  ♣ 9 6            │ W   E   │        ♣ A J 10 2
                   │   S     │
                   └─────────┘
                    ♠ 7
                    ♡ A K Q 9 6 5
                    ◊ J 7
                    ♣ K 8 4 3
```

Both sides vulnerable. West dealer.
The bidding:

West	North	East	South
Pass	Pass	Pass	1 ♡
Pass	1 ♠	Pass	2 ♡
Pass	2 ♠	Pass	3 ♡
Pass	Pass	Pass	

West cashed his top diamonds and then led the high ten of diamonds. East discarded a low spade, and declarer ruffed.

Mr. Scheur cashed the top trumps, throwing off dummy's last diamond and a club. He then led his singleton spade and finessed dummy's nine-spot! When it won, the ace and king of spades were played, the latter felling West's queen. Declarer was now able to discard his four clubs on the board's spades and claim the balance of the tricks.

It is most unusual to finesse in a situation where dummy has no sure entry, but declarer's play was perfectly proper. The only chance for loss was that East originally held the Q x or Q x x of spades, which was out of the question (logically speaking) in view of East's spade discard on the third diamond lead. True, East probably had the club ace, in view of West's original pass with the A K 10 9 6 of diamonds and the J x x of hearts; and so the club queen would not be an entry.

But—and this is the key to the finesse—even if the spade finesse lost, South would still make his contract because East would *have to* put dummy in the lead by returning either a spade or a club. (East was known to have no red cards remaining.) In short, South might (perhaps one time out of 100) surrender a spade trick unnecessarily, but he would always get that trick back with interest by losing only one club trick. And if the spade finesse worked, South would make at least 10 tricks.

It was a neat play, and simple enough if you saw it. Did you?

CHAPTER 28

The Approach to Defense at Match-Point Play

I. Defense at Rubber Bridge

Every bridge player, from the topflight expert down through the rankest neophyte, will agree that of the three departments of bridge—bidding, declarer's play, and defenders' play—the most difficult to master is defensive play. Going further, there is unanimous concurrence in the oft-repeated assertion that more mistakes are made in defense than in either of the other departments of bridge. There are two major reasons accounting for this deficiency in the techniques of defense.

First, when the declarer is playing out a hand, he sees the 26 cards that belong to him and his partner, the dummy. He knows exactly how many cards of each suit his side possesses, what the quality of the cards is, and what his specific problems are. In brief, he knows his *precise* strength and weakness and is thereby enabled to deploy his resources in an intelligent manner while waging his campaign *to fulfill his contract*. The defenders, on the other hand, do not see their 26 cards, but only the 13 that each of them holds. Thus the defenders' task—the objective being *the defeat of declarer's contract*—is automatically much more difficult since each must try to figure out, or deduce, or imagine (or guess) what his partner is holding.

Second, it is an established fact that "scientific development" in the field of defense has lagged far behind the scientific development of bidding methods and techniques of declarer's play. There are relatively few guiding principles to point the way to winning defense. As a consequence, a defender is frequently on his own because the pattern of correct defense varies greatly from deal to deal. Many diverse defensive situations arise where there exists no precedent to take a defender by the hand and lead him to the desired objective: the defeat of declarer's contract. In these situations, judgment and/or imagination must operate independently of any established governing law.

From the defenders' point of view, in order to attack and counterattack successfully, they must rely on the few "scientific" principles that are available to them. These consist of a system of "conventional leads" and a system of "signals." With the application of these principles of standard leads and standard signals, the defenders are better able to convey to each other the route that must be traversed to attain the best result. While this partnership rapport will not eliminate guesswork, it will narrow the areas where guesswork will otherwise exist, thereby resulting in fewer mistakes. But the defenders' use of signals—their most potent weapon—can often turn out to be more useful to the declarer than to the defensive recipient of the signals.

At match-point play, proper defense is even more difficult than at rubber bridge. In rubber bridge, the objective is a permanent one: to defeat declarer's contract. The prevention of overtricks is of no importance. At match-point play, there is no fixed objective since the scoring is on a relative basis. The prevention of declarer from making an overtrick can bring the optimum defensive result (in match points) even if declarer is permitted to fulfill a vulnerable small slam contract. Thus, in duplicate, one cannot set his sights, as an objective, on the defeat of declarer's contract. A defender must gauge each specific adverse contract and try to deduce whether his aim should be to defeat the contract or to concentrate exclusively on preventing declarer from getting an overtrick. The choice is not always easy.

Let us then examine a little more closely the philosophy and approach of the match-point defender, who is operating from a different foundation than his rubber-bridge counterpart.

II. Defense at Match-Point Play

Just as, from the viewpoint of the *declarer,* the safety of his contract is not necessarily the prime consideration at match-point play, similarly, from the viewpoint of the *defenders,* the defeat of declarer's contract is not necessarily their prime consideration.

It is obviously true that the leads, signals, and plays that are available to the duplicate bridge player are identical to those available to the rubber-bridge player. But, as was stated, the *objectives* of the match-point player may be quite different. Permit us to reintroduce and re-emphasize this most vital point.

In rubber bridge, the defenders' permanent approach is to defeat every contract, whether it be a part-score, a game, or a slam. And if an overtrick or two is given to declarer as a consequence of the all-out effort to defeat him, it is a small premium to pay, especially when one considers that the effort *will,* on many occasions, defeat a game or a slam worth 400–1500 points. But in match-point play, in most cases, you must play to prevent overtricks rather than take gambling, desperation measures to defeat the contract which, if they fail, will give declarer an overtrick or two—and will result in your getting a bottom on the board.

Let us now look at a few hands which point out the differences in the defenders' approach at rubber bridge and duplicate bridge. Let us begin with the subject of the opening lead.

III. The Opening Lead

Generally speaking, it is the conservative rubber-bridge player who usually does best on the opening lead at match-point play. He makes a "normal" lead, from his longest suit or a neutral lead against no-trump contracts; and from a safe sequence of high cards against suit contracts. He doesn't get fancy, having learned that it doesn't pay to get fancy before the dummy has been put down. During this past decade, this conservatism has been adopted by all the better match-point players.

One of the most important things the rubber-bridge player must learn at match-point play is that there are many situations where he must give up gracefully. If, for example, the opponents get to a game after vigorous, constructive, noncompetitive bidding, one doesn't make a desperation lead to beat their contract by hoping that a miracle might occur.

The characteristic of the "against percentage," "gambling," "desperation" opening lead is that in rubber bridge one risks an insignificant overtrick or two on the outside chance of defeating the contract, while in duplicate bridge the overtrick can be worth more than the contract. Here is an example.

The bidding, with North–South vulnerable, has been:

South	West	North	East
1 ♠	Pass	2 NT	Pass
3 ♡	Pass	3 NT	Pass
Pass	Pass		

You, East, hold:

> ♠ J 7 5
> ♡ J 10 4 2
> ◇ 10 8 6 3
> ♣ K 2

The three of diamonds is a normal, safe lead—and it offers very little hope of defeating the contract. In rubber bridge, the king of clubs may turn out to be the winning lead: partner *may* have the Q J x x x of clubs and an outside entry. But the king of clubs lead will, more often than not, enable declarer to make an overtrick and at match-point play this may well result in your getting a bottom on the board.

Incidentally, for those who might be inclined to lead a heart (from your best suit), this is a bad lead. North, for his jump to two no-trump, showed a stopper in the heart suit. And South, for his subsequent three heart bid, indicated that he possessed a heart suit. For East to lead a heart in the face of the obviously strong North–South heart holding must be a losing choice.

By making the safe lead of the three of diamonds, East is not trying to gain anything. He is simply trying not to lose anything. And, by not losing where the more aggressive leaders have lost, East will, on a relative basis, be gaining.

Here is an example of where the apparently normal opening lead should be avoided, for the opponents' bidding indicates that the normal lead figures to be the losing lead.

You are sitting West, holding:

♠ Q 7 5 3 2
♡ A K 4
◇ 7 5
♣ 8 4 3

The bidding by vulnerable opponents has proceeded:

South	West	North	East
1 ◇	Pass	3 ♣ °	Pass
3 NT	Pass	4 NT	Pass
Pass	Pass		

The "normal" opening lead is the three of spades, and probably this would be the correct lead in a rubber-bridge game despite the apparently slim chances of defeating the four no-trump contract.

But at match-point play, the spade lead might well give declarer an overtrick or two. So, with the aim of not giving anything away, the king of hearts should be opened—and when the dummy comes into view, the ace of hearts is promptly cashed. Here is the actual deal:

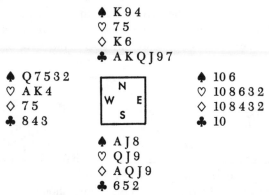

♠ K 9 4
♡ 7 5
◇ K 6
♣ A K Q J 9 7

♠ Q 7 5 3 2   ♠ 10 6
♡ A K 4   ♡ 10 8 6 3 2
◇ 7 5   ◇ 10 8 4 3 2
♣ 8 4 3   ♣ 10

♠ A J 8
♡ Q J 9
◇ A Q J 9
♣ 6 5 2

With the spade opening by West, declarer will make all 13 tricks. With the king of hearts lead, followed by the ace, declarer makes only 11 tricks—and East–West get an excellent match-point score.

The above is actually a fine illustrative hand, from the viewpoint

° A strong, jump-shift response, denoting slam aspirations.

of highlighting the recurring types of situations where one is confronted with the decision of whether to attempt to defeat a game contract or not. This is one of the most difficult aspects of defensive play at match points, primarily because it is foreign to the nature of most players to tamely give up the ghost. Hard-and-fast rules are quite impossible to present, and an "ear to the bidding" of the specific deal at hand becomes the sole guiding factor.

If, for example, you (West) had held the same hand:

♠ Q 7 5 3 2
♥ A K 4
♦ 7 5
♣ 8 4 3

and the bidding had proceeded:

South	West	North	East
1 ♣	Pass	1 ♦	Pass
1 NT	Pass	2 NT	Pass
3 NT	Pass	Pass	Pass

the correct opening lead *would be* the three of spades, as the normal opening which offers the best hope of defeating the contract (and, incidentally, a lead that everybody figures to make as the proper lead). This *might* have been the setup:

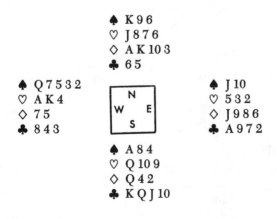

With a spade lead by West, South goes down at his three no-trump contract. With the opening lead of the king of hearts, followed by a shift to spades, declarer can make his contract.

An interesting illustration of the opening lead based on an ear to the bidding arose in the National Team-of-Four Championships of 1958. This deal illustrates the point that was made a few pages back, that when the opponents have displayed that they possess an overwhelming preponderance of high cards one is usually reluctant to make an aggressive lead for fear of giving declarer a present of a trick or two which he could not obtain under his own power. In these situations, the expert will make what he considers to be a neutral, safe lead. On occasion, however, the "safe" lead turns out to be the most disastrous one, whereas the aggressive, presumably dangerous lead would have been the winning one.

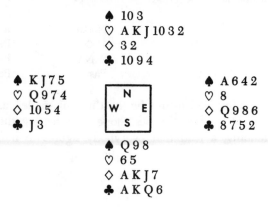

```
                    ♠ 10 3
                    ♡ A K J 10 3 2
                    ◇ 3 2
                    ♣ 10 9 4
    ♠ K J 7 5                         ♠ A 6 4 2
    ♡ Q 9 7 4         N               ♡ 8
    ◇ 10 5 4       W     E            ◇ Q 9 8 6
    ♣ J 3            S                ♣ 8 7 5 2
                    ♠ Q 9 8
                    ♡ 6 5
                    ◇ A K J 7
                    ♣ A K Q 6
```

Both sides vulnerable. South dealer.

South	West	North	East
1 ◇	Pass	1 ♡	Pass
2 NT	Pass	4 NT	Pass
6 NT	Pass	Pass	Pass

West didn't think it advisable to lead a spade away from the king against the slam contract for fear of leading into an A Q combination that he figured was possessed by North–South. So he elected to lead a diamond and declarer, by taking two heart finesses, fulfilled his contract. (Actually, he made an overtrick by catching the jack of clubs.)

When the deal was subsequently replayed, the bidding proceeded as follows:

South	West	North	East
1 ◇	Pass	1 ♡	Pass
2 NT	Pass	4 NT	Pass
Pass	Pass		

The West defender, in this situation, had a "feeling" that an aggressive lead was called for, so he led his fourth highest spade. After the first four tricks had been played, declarer was down one.

As was mentioned, "fancy" opening leads are losing leads more often than not at match-point play. For example, the blind opening lead of a king from a K J 10 9 x x or K J 10 9 x combination on the outside chance of catching the singleton queen in dummy has merit in a rubber-bridge or total-point game. Such a lead is a bold stroke which, on rare occasions, turns out to be successful. And, when unsuccessful, the cost is nothing more than the payment of an overtrick or two. But the duplicate player cannot afford to gamble away the overtrick on the slight possibility of dropping the singleton queen in dummy. For example, if West holds:

♠ J 10 9
♡ 6 4
◇ 8 3
♣ K J 10 9 6 2

and the bidding has proceeded:

North	East	South	West
1 ◇	Pass	2 NT	Pass
3 NT	Pass	Pass	Pass

for West to open the king of clubs in the hope of catching a single-ton queen in dummy is such a long-shot possibility that it isn't even worth considering. More often than not, the lead of the king will give declarer a present of his probable queen of clubs. Frankly, on the given bidding, to lead *any* club figures to be a losing lead, for even if West eventually establishes the suit, he has no entry to cash it.

With the above hand, the safe, passive lead of the jack of spades is recommended. The lead may well gain and, more important, it figures not to be a losing lead.

Yet there can be situations in match-point play where the lead of the king from a K J 10 x x or K J 10 x x x combination figures to be the winning lead—or, at least, does not figure to be a losing lead. Here is such a situation. The deal arose in a New York City duplicate game in 1947.

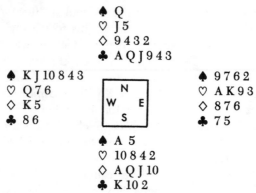

```
                    ♠ Q
                    ♡ J 5
                    ◇ 9 4 3 2
                    ♣ A Q J 9 4 3
  ♠ K J 10 8 4 3                      ♠ 9 7 6 2
  ♡ Q 7 6            ┌─────────┐      ♡ A K 9 3
  ◇ K 5             │    N    │      ◇ 8 7 6
  ♣ 8 6            W│         │E     ♣ 7 5
                    │    S    │
                    └─────────┘
                    ♠ A 5
                    ♡ 10 8 4 2
                    ◇ A Q J 10
                    ♣ K 10 2
```

East–West vulnerable. North dealer.
The bidding:

North	East	South	West
Pass	Pass	1 ◇	1 ♠
2 ♣	2 ♠	3 NT	Pass
Pass	Pass		

Looking at the South hand, we all agree that his jump to three no-trump was overly aggressive. And we think that all of us will concur that, if we were holding the West hand, we would be absolutely certain that South possessed the *ace of spades*.

Further, we think we would all lead a spade against the three no-trump contract, what with partner having supported our spades. And now, we imagine, would come a parting of the ways, for most of us would lead either the eight of spades (our fourth best) or the jack of spades, the top of our inner sequence. If either of these leads is made, declarer breezes in with his contract: two spades, one diamond, and six clubs.

Since we have made up our minds *to lead a spade,* is not the lead of the king of spades proper? If declarer happens to have both the ace and queen of spades, what difference which spade you lead since in this case he will make two spade tricks? If dummy has, let us say, the Q x or the Q x x of spades (facing declarer's A x or A x x), again will not declarer make two spade tricks regardless of whether you open the eight or the jack of spades? But if dummy happens to have the singleton queen of spades, will not your lead of the king limit declarer to but one spade winner while simultaneously establishing your spade suit? Surely the lead of the spade king puts you in the position of standing to gain everything while standing to lose nothing.

In the actual play, West opened the king of spades and the appearance of the singleton queen in dummy was a joy to behold. When the play had been completed, declarer was a most unhappy fellow, having secured, as he knew, a bad result (actually 2 match points out of 12).

If you are in doubt as to what to lead (and this happens quite often to everybody), try to lead what you think the others sitting in your position will lead. That is, if you have an awkward choice of leads, "play with the room."

For example, if the bidding has gone:

North	South
1 ♣	1 ♡
2 ♣	3 NT

and you are West, holding:

♠ K 2
♡ K J 9 3 2
♦ Q 5
♣ J 8 6 4

you are in a most uneasy position. A club lead cannot be right, and hearts have been bid on your right. A desperation lead from either the Q x of diamonds or the K x of spades will cost you a trick (or more) most of the time. As a lesser of evils, it is better to attack in hearts. For one thing, South's heart bid might have been a psychic, or it might have been made on a broken-down four-card suit like 10 x x x or Q x x x. Also, it is quite conceivable that the bidding at other tables went:

North	South
1 ♣	2 NT
3 NT	

in which case every West defender will make the normal lead of a heart with your hand. This was the actual deal:

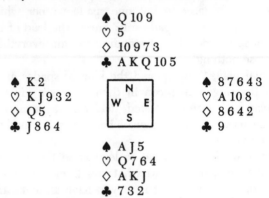

```
                    ♠ Q 10 9
                    ♡ 5
                    ◊ 10 9 7 3
                    ♣ A K Q 10 5
    ♠ K 2                              ♠ 8 7 6 4 3
    ♡ K J 9 3 2         N             ♡ A 10 8
    ◊ Q 5          W         E        ◊ 8 6 4 2
    ♣ J 8 6 4          S             ♣ 9
                    ♠ A J 5
                    ♡ Q 7 6 4
                    ◊ A K J
                    ♣ 7 3 2
```

With the heart lead, East–West will cash five heart tricks. With a diamond or spade lead by West, South will make at least nine tricks.

This chapter on "the approach to defense at match-point play" has dealt almost exclusively with the subject of the blind opening lead and the reasoning that motivated various types of leads. The chapter which follows concerns itself with match-point defense subsequent to trick one.

CHAPTER 29

Defensive Play: The Middle Game

It is a fact that the opening lead is frequently nothing more than a wishful-thinking shot-in-the-dark, based on hearsay evidence: the bidding of the opponents. Thus, the first blow struck by the defenders is an action that does not generally fall into the realm of scientific selection.

But *after* the opening lead has been made, "science" comes to the fore and begins to take over. The defenders come into possession of much meaningful knowledge when the dummy is put down. First, the proper interpretation of partner's opening lead conveys significant information to the leader's partner about the leader's holding in that suit (the top of a sequence lead, the fourth highest, etc.). Second, dummy's strong points and weak points become visible. Third, declarer's bidding, reappraised in terms of the dummy, presents clues about which are his strong suits and which are presumably his vulnerable spots. All of these data can become meaningful with the application of reason.

It is at this point—after the exposure of the dummy—that the defenders can really start coordinating their attack and resolving the problems that are confronting them.

Let us then examine the mental processes of the match-point defenders after the opening lead has been made and the dummy has been put down. As we view the illustrative deals that follow, it must always be remembered that the objective of the defenders is not necessarily the defeat of declarer's contract but, quite frequently simply the prevention of an overtrick.

DEAL 1.

You are sitting West, and the bidding has proceeded:

South	West	North	East
1 ♡	Pass	2 ♡	Pass
4 ♡	Pass	Pass	Pass

You open the trump six, and the dummy is put down:

```
              ♠ K J 10 9 2
              ♡ Q J 7 3
              ◇ 5 3
              ♣ 6 2
  ♠ A 7 6 3
  ♡ 6 5
  ◇ Q 7 4 2
  ♣ A Q 3
```

Your opening trump lead is taken by declarer's nine as your partner follows suit. South next cashes the trump ace, your partner playing the eight.

Declarer then leads the queen of spades, which you win with your ace. And now you are confronted with the decision, the outcome of which will determine whether you get a good score or a poor one.

At rubber bridge, there would be just one proper play—you would lead a low diamond. The reason would be a simple and logical one: you need four tricks to defeat the contract. In spades and hearts, all you can ever make has been made: one trick with your spade ace. Hence, three tricks must be made in diamonds and clubs. When you lead a diamond, it is with the realization that if your partner doesn't have the ace the four heart contract is unbeatable. (Dummy's solid spades are staring you in the face.) And if partner has the ace of diamonds, upon winning it, he will automatically return a club since from *his* point of view he will appreciate the fact that declarer's contract is beatable only if you have the diamond king *and* the club ace, or the A Q of clubs instead. From his vantage seat, the club return will be a mandatory one since without the club ace in your hand the defense is lost.

But at match-point play, it's quite a complicated matter to determine what to lead after you've taken your spade ace at trick three. First, suppose your partner has the king of clubs rather than the ace of diamonds. In this case—if you only knew—you would cash the ace of clubs and then lead another club, thus preventing declarer from making an overtrick. If, instead, you lead a low diamond and declarer happens to have the A K of diamonds, he will probably make two overtricks by discarding all of his clubs on the board's established spades. So, if you cash your club ace at trick four, there will be no possibility that declarer will make two overtricks.

But suppose you decide to try to defeat the contract and you risk a low diamond lead at trick four, hoping to find your partner with the ace. And it turns out to be a good day—he has the ace! What is he going to return?

You realize, of course, that he is just as worried as you are about declarer making an overtrick. When he takes the diamond ace, he might well decide to return a diamond in the hope that you possess the king. You could aid him, of course, by leading the queen of diamonds (instead of a low one), thus denying possession of the king and "forcing" him to return a club. If, then, you have made up your mind to lead a diamond at trick four, certainly the lead of the diamond queen is the superior play.

The point we are making is that at match-point play defense is infinitely more difficult than at rubber bridge since you can't ever really be sure whether your efforts should be geared to defeating declarer's contract or preventing him from making a most vital overtrick. In rubber bridge, there is usually one winning line of defense; at match-point play, there can be two, three, or even four lines—and it often becomes a pure guess as to which will yield the optimum result.

The North–South hands might have been:

North
♠ K J 10 9 2
♡ Q J 7 3
◊ 5 3
♣ 6 2

South (1)	South (2)	South (3)
♠ Q 4	♠ Q 4	♠ Q 4
♡ A K 10 6 4	♡ A K 10 6 4	♡ A K 10 6 4
◊ K J 10	◊ A K 6	◊ A K J
♣ K J 10	♣ K 8 3	♣ J 10 9

If South holds Hand (1) and West shifts to a low diamond at trick four, East will take the ace and return a club to defeat the four heart contract.

If South holds Hand (2) and West shifts to a low diamond at trick four, declarer will make 12 tricks by trumping his third diamond and discarding his three clubs on dummy's high spades. If, instead, West cashes the club ace at trick four, he will hold declarer to just 11 tricks.

If South holds Hand (3) and West shifts to a diamond at trick four, once again declarer will make 12 tricks. But if, instead, West cashes the club ace and then plays another club to East's king, declarer will make just 10 tricks.

Which of the three hands should West assume South possesses? Is it not an outright guess?

DEAL 2.

Here is a deal in which a one-trick set of a voluntarily arrived-at game contract gave the defenders just an average match-point score. The top defensive score was attained by one pair of defenders who defeated the contract two tricks. The deal arose in the National Championships of 1946.

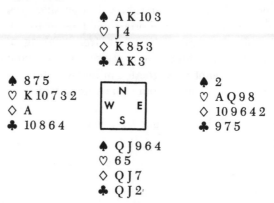

```
              ♠ A K 10 3
              ♡ J 4
              ◇ K 8 5 3
              ♣ A K 3
  ♠ 8 7 5                       ♠ 2
  ♡ K 10 7 3 2    ┌──────┐      ♡ A Q 9 8
  ◇ A             │  N   │      ◇ 10 9 6 4 2
  ♣ 10 8 6 4   W  │      │  E   ♣ 9 7 5
                  │  S   │
                  └──────┘
              ♠ Q J 9 6 4
              ♡ 6 5
              ◇ Q J 7
              ♣ Q J 2
```

Both sides vulnerable. North dealer.
The bidding:

North	East	South	West
1 ◇	Pass	1 ♠	Pass
3 ♠	Pass	4 ♠	Pass
Pass	Pass		

Against the four spade contract, most West defenders opened the diamond ace, declarer dropping the seven-spot. It was readily apparent to the East defenders that the ace was a singleton since West surely would not have opened the ace (especially in the face of North's having opened the bidding in that suit) if he had held the A Q, the A J, or the A Q J. To trick two, West led the three of hearts, East's ace winning, after which East returned a diamond, West ruffing. West now cashed the heart king, for the setting trick. Nice winning defense—at rubber bridge only.

At one table, when West shifted to the three of hearts at trick two, East appreciated that West possessed the king of hearts. If he hadn't, then assuredly he would have led his top heart (the ten, or the seven, etc., as the case might be) to make sure that no ambiguity would arise.

So, at trick two, this particular East defender put up the *queen* of hearts, not the ace. He then returned a diamond for West to ruff. West now played back another low heart to East's ace and East led another diamond, West ruffing. Thus, the defenders took the first five tricks and secured a well-earned top for their maximum effort.

Deal 3.

Here is another example of the agonizing problem of whether one should play to defeat a game contract or whether, instead, one should attempt to prevent declarer from making an overtrick.

You are sitting East.

♠ Q 10 3
♡ Q 9 5
◇ 7 4
♣ A Q J 10 8

♠ K J 9 2
♡ 10 4
◇ Q 10 8 3
♣ K 5 2

The bidding has proceeded:

South	West	North	East
1 ♡	Pass	2 ♣	Pass
3 ♡	Pass	4 ♡	Pass
Pass	Pass		

Your partner opens the eight of spades, the ten is played from dummy, you cover with the jack, and declarer wins the trick with the ace. Declarer now cashes the ace and jack of trumps, after which he leads a low club and finesses dummy's queen. You win the trick with your king—and take time out to analyze the situation.

If your partner has the ace of diamonds, you figure to defeat the contract by leading a diamond to partner's ace. He will then play back a spade, and your K J should both be winners. In rubber bridge, the diamond return would be the only correct play.

But, on South's strong bidding, your partner does not figure to have the diamond ace. If declarer has that card, he may well take the rest of the tricks (by discarding his spade and diamond losers on dummy's established clubs).

On percentage—and an ear to the bidding—your best play is to cash the king of spades, thus preventing declarer from making two overtricks. Admittedly, there will be occasions when this will give declarer an otherwise unmakable contract but much more often it will give you an excellent match-point score. The complete deal was:

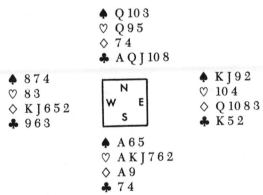

```
                    ♠ Q 10 3
                    ♡ Q 9 5
                    ◇ 7 4
                    ♣ A Q J 10 8
    ♠ 8 7 4                        ♠ K J 9 2
    ♡ 8 3            N             ♡ 10 4
    ◇ K J 6 5 2   W   E           ◇ Q 10 8 3
    ♣ 9 6 3           S           ♣ K 5 2
                    ♠ A 6 5
                    ♡ A K J 7 6 2
                    ◇ A 9
                    ♣ 7 4
```

DEAL 4.

In the two preceding illustrations, it was observed that when the opponents are in a contract that they figure to make, you should not take desperation measures to beat them if your unsuccessful effort results in their making an overtrick. But, conversely, when the opponents appear to be in a fine contract that the rest of the field does not figure to reach, you must make an all-out effort to beat them. If, in this circumstance, they succeed in making an overtrick, your additional match-point loss will be very little, if any. Here is such a situation. You are the East defender.

♠ A K Q 3 2
♡ 10 7 4
◇ A 10 3
♣ 6 5

♠ J
♡ A K 5
◇ 6 4 2
♣ A Q J 10 9 3

Neither side vulnerable. East declarer.
The bidding:

East	South	West	North
1 ♣	1 ♡	Pass	4 ♡
Pass	Pass	Pass	

Your partner opens the eight of clubs, and you pause to take inventory. Certainly your chances of defeating the four heart contract appear to be most remote. On the bidding, your partner might not have even one jack. There are just 12 high-card points outstanding, and declarer probably has all of them. Four hearts bid and made looks like a bad match-point score for you.

There is one ray of hope that the expert mind would grasp: that partner possesses the seven of clubs. If such is the case, then you play the nine of clubs on his opening lead, permitting declarer to take the trick with his king. Then when declarer leads a trump, you win it with your king and shift to the singleton jack of spades. When another trump is next led, you hop up with your ace and lead the three of clubs to partner's hoped-for seven-spot. He will then return a spade for you to trump for the setting trick.

Of course, if declarer has the seven of clubs, he will make an overtrick, but we doubt that it will cost you much in the way of match points. Actually, four hearts bid and made would have given you, as defenders, only two match points out of 12. Four hearts, making an overtrick, would have given you 1½ match points. Had you defeated four hearts, you would have earned 12 match points. The full deal was:

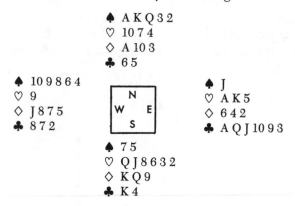

♠ A K Q 3 2
♡ 10 7 4
◇ A 10 3
♣ 6 5

♠ 10 9 8 6 4
♡ 9
◇ J 8 7 5
♣ 8 7 2

♠ J
♡ A K 5
◇ 6 4 2
♣ A Q J 10 9 3

♠ 7 5
♡ Q J 8 6 3 2
◇ K Q 9
♣ K 4

From declarer's point of view, he could have foiled you by playing back a club at trick two. In this case, you could never have put your partner back into the lead to give you a spade ruff but you would have lost nothing.

DEAL 5.

One of the more important attributes possessed by the expert defender is his ability to recognize when he must become aggressive and when he must adopt a passive waiting role. The non-expert defender too often gets frantic for fear that if he doesn't do something positive, tricks will run away from him. Here is a simple illustration of this theme, in double-dummy * fashion.

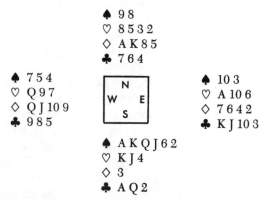

♠ 9 8
♡ 8 5 3 2
◇ A K 8 5
♣ 7 6 4

♠ 7 5 4
♡ Q 9 7
◇ Q J 10 9
♣ 9 8 5

♠ 10 3
♡ A 10 6
◇ 7 6 4 2
♣ K J 10 3

♠ A K Q J 6 2
♡ K J 4
◇ 3
♣ A Q 2

* "Double dummy" is a standard bridge expression. It means playing out a hand (as a problem) while looking at all 52 cards.

Neither side vulnerable. South dealer.

South	West	North	East
1 ♠	Pass	1 NT	Pass
4 ♠	Pass	Pass	Pass

West opens the queen of diamonds, dummy's king winning. The ace of diamonds is then cashed, upon which South's deuce of clubs is discarded.

A heart is then led off the board, East plays low and declarer inserts his jack, West's queen winning.

If West now returns either a spade, a heart, or a club, declarer will fulfill his contract. A heart or a club return will create a trick for declarer which he could not make on his own power; while a spade (trump) return will give declarer an entry to dummy to lead either a heart or a club.

When West takes the heart queen at trick three, he should make the safe, neutral, passive lead of the diamond jack, which he knows declarer will trump. The defenders can now relax, sit back, and wait for declarer to lead hearts or clubs to them.

DEAL 6.

When a defender has a pure guess about which suit he should lead, his choice should be determined by viewing the dummy, and leading that suit which—*if his guess is correct*—will yield the most tricks. This is a normal, everyday, simple situation and is included here merely for the sake of completeness.

You are sitting West, and the bidding has proceeded:

South	West	North	East
1 ♡	Pass	2 ♡	Pass
4 ♡	Pass	Pass	Pass

```
                    ♠ Q J 10 6
                    ♡ Q J 10 8
                    ◇ 4 3
                    ♣ 6 4 2
        ♠ A 7 5
        ♡ 5 3
        ◇ Q 9 7 5
        ♣ Q 9 7 5
```

You open the five of trumps, dummy's ten-spot winning. A second round of trumps is taken by the board's jack. Your partner follows suit each time. To trick three, declarer leads the six of spades and plays the king from his own hand, which you capture with your ace. What should you lead now?

Obviously, it must be a diamond or a club, for in these suits lies your sole hope of getting any more tricks. The proper play must be a club (the five-spot) since the club suit offers the better hope of gaining more tricks. That is, if your partner has, let's say, the A K of clubs, you might get three club tricks if you lead a club. If, instead, your partner has the A K of diamonds, all your side can ever make are two diamond tricks if you lead a diamond.

DEAL 7.

The reluctance to lead away from a king has become ingrained in many players, primarily because such a lead has, in the past, lost more than it has gained. Nevertheless, there are many perfectly normal situations where necessity demands that this aggressive lead be made. Here is such a situation.

You are sitting East, and the bidding has proceeded:

North	East	South	West
1 ◇	2 ♣	2 ♠	Pass
3 ♠	Pass	4 ♡	Pass
4 ♠	Pass	Pass	Pass

Your partner opens the five of clubs and the dummy comes into view:

♠ A K J 4
♡ 3
◇ Q J 10 9 5
♣ J 10 9

            ♠ 7
            ♡ J 10 8
            ◇ K 8 6
            ♣ A Q 8 7 6 3

You win the club opening with the ace, on which South drops the king, an obvious singleton.

On reflection, it becomes apparent that declarer will be able to develop a club trick later by leading dummy's jack of clubs, forcing your queen, which he will trump, and establishing the nine of clubs as a winner (this is known as a "ruffing finesse"). On the bidding, a heart discard on the club nine doesn't figure to do declarer much good, but a diamond discard—if declarer doesn't have the ace—will enable the latter to get rid of a sure loser.

So, upon taking the club ace, you should shift to a diamond, either a low one or, preferably, the king in the hope that your partner has the ace of diamonds. If declarer happens to have that card, you haven't lost a thing, since in this case declarer would always have finessed you out of the king of diamonds.

When this deal arose in a tournament some years ago, the play of the king of diamonds, followed by another diamond, would have given the defenders 9 match points out of 12. Any other lead would have given them just two match points. The complete setup was:

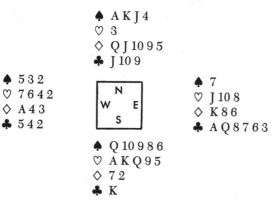

```
                    ♠ A K J 4
                    ♡ 3
                    ◇ Q J 10 9 5
                    ♣ J 10 9
  ♠ 5 3 2                              ♠ 7
  ♡ 7 6 4 2          N                ♡ J 10 8
  ◇ A 4 3        W        E           ◇ K 8 6
  ♣ 5 4 2            S                ♣ A Q 8 7 6 3
                    ♠ Q 10 9 8 6
                    ♡ A K Q 9 5
                    ◇ 7 2
                    ♣ K
```

DEAL 8.

The ability to count out the distribution of the opponents' cards is, of course, a most valuable asset to possess, whether the game is rubber bridge or match-point play. At match points, this ability pays off much more frequently than at rubber bridge. The reason is that the attempt to count out a hand must be undertaken on every deal, whether it be a slam, a game, or a part-score contract. Putting it another way, at match-point play one must put forth an all-out maximum effort on every deal. One cannot ever afford to relax, for if he does, that all-important overtrick may be his downfall.

In textbooks, most of the counting hands are presented from the viewpoint of the declarer. But this "right" also belongs to the defenders. Here is an example of defensive "counting out."

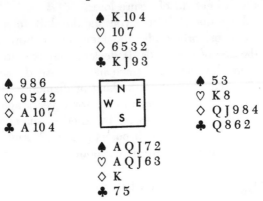

```
                      ♠ K 10 4
                      ♡ 10 7
                      ◇ 6 5 3 2
                      ♣ K J 9 3
    ♠ 9 8 6          ┌─────────┐      ♠ 5 3
    ♡ 9 5 4 2        │    N    │      ♡ K 8
    ◇ A 10 7         │ W     E │      ◇ Q J 9 8 4
    ♣ A 10 4         │    S    │      ♣ Q 8 6 2
                     └─────────┘
                      ♠ A Q J 7 2
                      ♡ A Q J 6 3
                      ◇ K
                      ♣ 7 5
```

The bidding:

South	West	North	East
1 ♠	Pass	2 ♠	Pass
4 ♠	Pass	Pass	Pass

You, sitting West, open the nine of spades, declarer winning with the jack. A trump is then led to dummy's king. The ten of hearts is played next, East covers with the king, and South captures the trick with his ace. Then follows the queen of hearts, and a low heart, dummy trumping the latter with the ten-spot. On this trick East discards the four of diamonds.

A low diamond is next led off the board, East puts up the jack, declarer the king, and you win the trick with your ace. You return a diamond, East's queen being trumped by declarer. The ace of trumps is now led, picking up your last trump.

At this point you know the exact distribution of the South hand: five spades, five hearts, one diamond (all by observation), and, therefore, two clubs.

And so, when South next leads a low club, you automatically play low, forcing declarer to guess whether to put up the board's jack or king. If he puts up the jack, you will hold him to four; if, instead, he makes a good guess by putting up the king, he will make an overtrick—and there wasn't anything you could have done about it.

The point here is not to climb up with the club ace when South leads a low club. To do so will give South the present of an overtrick.

If, when you captured South's king of diamonds with your ace and then played another diamond, South had followed to the second diamond and trumped the third, you would have known that he had started with but one club. And, in this case (hypothetical), when South led a club, you would promptly hop up with your ace.

CHAPTER 30

Defensive Play: The Play at Competitive Part-Score Contracts

As has been stated, defense at match-point play is much more difficult than at rubber bridge, for in the latter, the objective is constant and clear-cut: to defeat declarer's contract. If declarer happens to make an overtrick, it is of no consequence in rubber bridge. But in duplicate, the overtrick, more often than not, spells the difference between victory and defeat; and the defenders are always confronted with the conflicting objectives of whether to try to defeat declarer's contract or, instead, to concede the contract and attempt to prevent declarer from making an overtrick. The resolution of which objective is the specific order of the day is frequently most difficult to determine.

Match-point defense at part-score contracts is even more difficult than at game and slam contracts. In the latter, especially at voluntarily arrived-at games and slams, declarer's side is known to possess the preponderance of high cards and the defenders consequently have fewer variables to worry about. That is, each defender can usually prove that his partner's assets are limited and within a narrow range. But at part-score contracts, where the high-card strength is more or less evenly divided between the two opposing sides, each defender has greater difficulties in determining precisely how much strength and which specific cards his partner might possess; and, as a result, he is forced to guess the winning line of defense much more often than at game and slam contracts.

Let us view some deals in which the competitive struggle for the part-score created problems for the defenders about the proper line of defense, and observe simultaneously the logical thinking that resulted in the successful resolution of these problems.

DEAL 1.

Had this deal arisen in a rubber-bridge game, it would have "wasted its sweetness on the desert air," for nothing more was involved than whether declarer fulfilled a "measly" two heart contract or whether he went down one trick. But , fortunately for posterity, the deal arose in the National Open Pairs Championship of 1951, in which, of course, each deal was equally important. This deal is also presented as evidence of why Charles Goren and Helen Sobel were considered to be two of the world's finest players. Their defense against South's contract was magnificent.

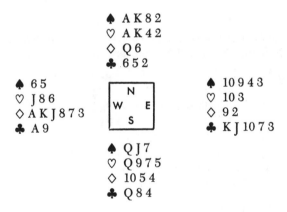

```
              ♠ A K 8 2
              ♡ A K 4 2
              ◇ Q 6
              ♣ 6 5 2
♠ 6 5                            ♠ 10 9 4 3
♡ J 8 6          N               ♡ 10 3
◇ A K J 8 7 3  W   E             ◇ 9 2
♣ A 9             S              ♣ K J 10 7 3
              ♠ Q J 7
              ♡ Q 9 7 5
              ◇ 10 5 4
              ♣ Q 8 4
```

Both sides vulnerable. West dealer.

West	North	East	South
1 ◇	Double	Pass	1 ♡
2 ◇	2 ♡	Pass	Pass
Pass			

Sitting West was Helen Sobel, and the East defender was Charles Goren.

Mrs. Sobel opened the king of diamonds, Goren playing the nine-spot, after which the ace of diamonds was cashed, Goren completing the echo by following with the deuce. The jack of diamonds was then led, a small club being discarded from dummy, with Goren discarding the seven of clubs.

Had Mrs. Sobel now cashed the ace of clubs, followed by a club to Goren's king, declarer would have made the rest of the tricks. But Mrs. Sobel perceived that if her partner held as good as the ten of trumps she would defeat the contract (provided that Goren held the king of clubs, which his discard seemed to indicate he had). So, instead of playing the ace of clubs, she led the nine-spot, Goren's king winning. Goren now returned a club to Mrs. Sobel's ace. Mrs. Sobel then switched to a diamond, Goren "uppercutting" with the ten of trumps, declarer overtrumping with the queen. Mrs. Sobel now had a sure trump trick, and declarer suffered a one-trick set.

DEAL 2.

This deal, which arose in a Philadelphia tournament in 1958, depicts a simple, recurring, defensive judgment situation.

You are sitting West, and the bidding has proceeded as follows:

West	North	East	South
1 ♠	Pass	2 ♠	Pass
Pass	Double	Pass	3 ♡
Pass	Pass	Pass	

```
                      ♠ K 7 3 2
                      ♡ A K 10
                      ◇ A 4 3
                      ♣ 8 5 2
          ♠ A Q 10 6 5
          ♡ 8 4
          ◇ K 10 7
          ♣ K J 6
```

You open the ace of spades, everybody following suit. It is rather obvious that declarer has no more spades, your partner having raised originally on, quite apparently, J x x. It is equally evident that dummy's king of spades will afford declarer a discard. To lead a diamond cannot accomplish anything since you cannot now prevent declarer from discarding a losing diamond on the board's king of spades. On the other hand, if you had club tricks coming to you, they are still available.

Thus, at trick two, a club shift is called for. Actually, your partner figures to have something in clubs, surely either the queen or the ace. After all, he did bid. A low club is led at trick two—and everything turns out for the best. Here is the deal:

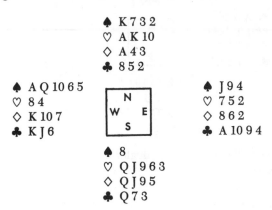

```
                    ♠ K 7 3 2
                    ♡ A K 10
                    ◇ A 4 3
                    ♣ 8 5 2
♠ A Q 10 6 5                        ♠ J 9 4
♡ 8 4            ┌─────────┐        ♡ 7 5 2
◇ K 10 7        W │ N       │ E      ◇ 8 6 2
♣ K J 6          │    S     │        ♣ A 10 9 4
                └─────────┘
                    ♠ 8
                    ♡ Q J 9 6 3
                    ◇ Q J 9 5
                    ♣ Q 7 3
```

Your lead of the six of clubs at trick two is taken by partner's ace, after which partner returns the ten of clubs and you cash two more club tricks. Now you make the safe exit of the queen of spades. Eventually, you obtain a diamond trick, to hand declarer a one-trick set.

Had you made any other lead at trick two except a low club, declarer would have fulfilled his contract.

DEAL 3.

In the preceding deal, there was presented an example of what is called "active" defense. This type of defense is one in which the defenders cannot afford to sit back and wait for the declarer to make the first move. If they do, the declarer will gain the advantage. And so they attack.

Just as often, however, the defense must employ a "passive" defense; that is, they must sit back and wait for declarer to attack and hope that declarer misguesses the true situation.

On this deal, the defense started out with an active defense, after which they withdrew and employed a passive defense. As a consequence, declarer suffered a two-trick set.

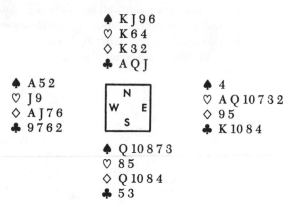

```
                    ♠ K J 9 6
                    ♡ K 6 4
                    ◇ K 3 2
                    ♣ A Q J
  ♠ A 5 2                              ♠ 4
  ♡ J 9            ┌─────────┐        ♡ A Q 10 7 3 2
  ◇ A J 7 6        │    N    │        ◇ 9 5
  ♣ 9 7 6 2        │ W     E │        ♣ K 10 8 4
                   │    S    │
                   └─────────┘
                    ♠ Q 10 8 7 3
                    ♡ 8 5
                    ◇ Q 10 8 4
                    ♣ 5 3
```

Both sides vulnerable. North dealer.
The bidding:

North	East	South	West
1 NT	2 ♡	2 ♠	3 ♡
3 ♠	Pass	Pass	Pass

West opened the jack of hearts, which won the trick when everybody played low. The nine of hearts was then played, dummy followed with the six-spot, and East overtook with the ten. East next laid down the ace of hearts, declarer ruffing with the queen and West overruffing with the ace.

West now exited with a trump, declarer winning with dummy's king. The nine of trumps was then led and overtaken by declarer's ten, felling the adversely held trumps. The club finesse was now tried, losing to East's king. And, at this point, the question in East's mind was whether he should attack in diamonds or whether he should play a passive role and wait for declarer to attack the diamond suit.

Had East now led a diamond, say the nine-spot, declarer would have held his losses in that suit to just one trick; he would have covered the nine with the ten and no matter what West played, the latter would make only his diamond ace. But East realized that whatever West had in diamonds wouldn't run away since declarer had obviously started with six cards in diamonds and clubs (declarer was known to have possessed five spades and two hearts originally). So upon winning the club king, East made the passive return of a club into the board's high A Q. Declarer won the trick with the ace and then cashed the queen, upon which he discarded a diamond.

He next led the king of diamonds and West, who was alert, permitted the king to win. Another diamond was then played, and the ten inserted with the hope that East possessed the jack. West now won two diamond tricks, and declarer incurred a two-trick set, vulnerable, for minus 200 points. East–West secured 10½ match points out of 12 for their efforts.

It should be noted that if West had taken the diamond king with the ace he would have been end-played: A heart or a club return would have enabled declarer to trump the trick in dummy, while simultaneously discarding the ten of diamonds from his own hand. And a diamond return, instead, would have been into declarer's Q 10, giving him a free finesse and two diamond tricks.

But West was on his toes, and he knew that it couldn't be a losing play to permit the board's king of diamonds to win the trick. After all, West did know, by observation, that declarer had started with five spades, two hearts, two clubs—and, hence, four diamonds. The only (theoretical) danger of not taking the diamond king was that East held the queen of diamonds, a virtual impossibility in view of declarer's failure to lead a diamond toward the king (which, actually, he would have done had he not held the queen).

And so, while a "passive" role was played by the defenders in the middle game, their thinking was of the "active" type.

Deal 4.

There comes a time in every match-point player's life when he feels constrained to bid abnormally in an effort to obtain a top score on the board. Here is such a case.

It should be pointed out, before getting to the bidding and the play, that East and West, by prearrangement, were not opening four-card major suits in first or second position *unless* the opener held either four spades and four hearts or four hearts and four diamonds, in which case the higher-ranking (major) suit would be opened. The East–West players were Said Haddad, sitting West, and Mrs. Terry Michaels, sitting East.

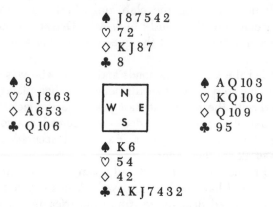

```
                    ♠ J 8 7 5 4 2
                    ♡ 7 2
                    ◇ K J 8 7
                    ♣ 8
    ♠ 9                                  ♠ A Q 10 3
    ♡ A J 8 6 3        N                 ♡ K Q 10 9
    ◇ A 6 5 3      W       E             ◇ Q 10 9
    ♣ Q 10 6           S                 ♣ 9 5
                    ♠ K 6
                    ♡ 5 4
                    ◇ 4 2
                    ♣ A K J 7 4 3 2
```

North–South vulnerable. East dealer.
The bidding:

East	South	West	North
1 ♠	2 ♣	Double	Pass
Pass	Pass		

West's double of South's two club overcall was strictly a gambling double and was based on the hope that the defenders could beat a vulnerable South two tricks. If this could be accomplished, then they would score 500 points, which would be more than the value of a non-vulnerable game which East–West might be able to make.

West opened the nine of spades, which was taken by East's ace. East returned the three of spades, South played the king, and West trumped. At this point, West was able to reconstruct almost precisely the East and South hands, suit by suit and card by card.

Since East was known to have possessed exactly four spades, she therefore also had four hearts (or else she would not have opened with one spade on a four-card suit). Since South figured to have either six or seven clubs (including the A K) for his vulnerable two club overcall, East figured to have either three diamonds and two clubs, or two diamonds and three clubs. And surely East possessed the queen of diamonds, for without that card she would not have had an opening bid. (East was known to have, in high cards, the A Q of spades and, almost surely, the K Q of hearts. With the queen of diamonds, she would have just 13 points; and, of course, a 4-4-3-2 distribution.)

From West's point of view, he realized that East–West were probably ice-cold for four hearts,[*] a contract which the other East–West pairs figured to reach. Hence it became imperative, if a bottom were to be averted, that North–South must be set 500 points and not just 200.

So, after ruffing South's king of spades at trick two, West calmly underled his ace of diamonds, putting declarer to a guess. Had declarer diagnosed the situation and put up the king, he would have fulfilled the contract (seven clubs and the king of diamonds). However, not being clairvoyant, he put up the jack of diamonds, East's queen winning.

East now cashed the king of hearts, after which she led a diamond to West's known ace. West next underled his ace of hearts, East's queen winning. East then played the queen of spades, and declarer was a dead duck, for he could not now prevent West's queen of trumps from winning a trick.

All in all, the defenders made two heart tricks, two diamonds, the ace of spades, and two trump tricks. West thus attained the 500 points for which he was striving—and it was worth 12 match points out of a possible 12.

From this deal, one can see the thin thread by which one's destiny hangs at match-point play. Had declarer inserted dummy's king of diamonds at trick three (instead of the jack), he would have fulfilled his doubled two club contract for a score of 180 points. In this case, North–South would have secured 12 match points out of 12 instead of East–West securing those points. At rubber bridge, in terms of total points, it would not have mattered too much whether South fulfilled his contract or whether he went down one trick (a swing of 380 points).

Deal 5.

Here is another example of a hand where a horrible gambling match-point double paid handsome dividends. The deal arose in the Regional Open Pair Championships held in Memphis in 1961.

---

[*] Only if East held three small clubs would the four heart contract be defeated. In this case, North would ruff the third round of clubs and eventually make his king of diamonds.

```
                        ♠ K J 6 5 2
                        ♡ 7 4 3
                        ◇ A K 5
                        ♣ 3 2
        ♠ 10 9 8 7                          ♠ A Q 3
        ♡ Q J 5          ┌─────────┐        ♡ A 10 2
        ◇ 10 4           │    N    │        ◇ Q 9 2
        ♣ Q 9 8 5        │ W     E │        ♣ A 10 6 4
                         │    S    │
                         └─────────┘
                        ♠ 4
                        ♡ K 9 8 6
                        ◇ J 8 7 6 3
                        ♣ K J 7
```

Both sides vulnerable. North dealer.
The bidding:

North	East	South	West
1 ♠	Double	1 NT	Double
Pass	Pass	Pass	

West's double was awfully close, but of such stuff are winners
(and losers) made. We do not recommend such doubles, despite
the excellent result achieved on this deal.

The opening lead by West was the spade ten, which was covered
by North's jack, East's queen winning. East shifted to the club
four, South inserted the jack, and West took the trick with his
queen. West returned a club, East taking his ace and continuing
the suit, South winning with the king. The ace and king of diamonds were now cashed, and a third diamond led, East winning
with the queen.

On this third diamond lead West signaled violently by discarding
the queen of hearts, which led South to believe that West possessed
the ace of hearts. East first cashed his high ten of clubs, and then
led a low heart, on which declarer played low, West's jack capturing the trick. West now returned the nine of spades, which won
the trick when everybody followed with low spades. Another spade
lead was captured by East's ace, after which East cashed his ace
of hearts. All told, the defenders took three spades, two hearts, one
diamond, and three clubs, thereby inflicting an 800-point set on
declarer.

This result was worth 25 match points, with 25 being top on the board. You couldn't ask for—nor get, if you did—anything better.

We would be remiss in our duty if we failed to extend our sympathies to South. He was one of many who purchased the contract at one no-trump. But he was the only one who was doubled.

DEAL 6.

When one examines all four hands in this deal, the winning defense is easy to find. Yet the fact remains that when this hand was encountered in the National Championships of 1954 only one defender (out of six who defended against the identical contract), found the winning line of play.

Before presenting the four hands, let us pose the situation as a problem. You are sitting West, and the bidding has proceeded:

East	South	West	North
Pass	1 ♡	2 ♣	2 ♡
Pass	Pass	3 ♣	Pass
Pass	3 ♡	Pass	Pass
Pass			

You open the king of clubs, East plays the six-spot, and declarer the seven-spot. You find yourself gazing at:

♠ A 5 4
♡ 6 4 3 2
◇ K 6 2
♣ 8 5 3

♠ K 8 7
♡ Q J
◇ J 10
♣ A K J 10 9 4

To trick two, you lead the ace of clubs, your partner follows with the deuce, and declarer drops the queen. What do you lead to trick three?

All the defenders (except one) now switched to the jack of diamonds—and the contract was fulfilled.

Here are the four hands:

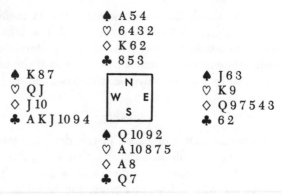

To trick three, "our" West defender led the four of clubs, dummy's eight was played, and East uppercut with the king of trumps, declarer overruffing with the ace. It was now impossible for declarer to avoid the loss of two trump tricks and a spade. Simple but neat defense, wasn't it?

DEAL 7.

This lowly part-score hand gave Cliff Russell of Miami Beach the opportunity of making a highly spectacular defensive play in the National Open Pair Championships of 1963.

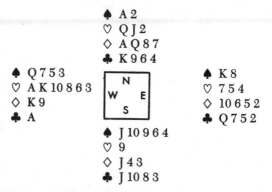

Both sides vulnerable. West dealer.
The bidding:

West	North	East	South
1 ♡	1 NT	Pass	2 ♠
Pass	Pass	Pass	

Harry Harkavy of Miami Beach, sitting West, opened the king of hearts and continued with the ace, which South ruffed. A club was then led, West taking his ace and leading a third round of hearts, dummy's queen winning as South discarded a diamond. The spade ace was now played and Russell, sitting East, rose to the occasion brilliantly by unblocking with his spade king. He realized that this would give West a better chance to regain the lead and control the hand by continuing hearts.

If Russell had made the "normal" play of the spade eight on the ace, he would have been given the lead via the trump king and would have been compelled to help South by leading a minor suit.

But with the king being tossed on the ace, Harkavy obtained the lead with his queen when declarer led a second spade. Harkavy now had two trumps remaining, as did declarer. The ten of hearts was then led, declarer ruffing, leaving himself with one trump, with West having two trumps.

No matter what declarer did from here in, he was unable to take more than four trump tricks, two diamonds, and one heart. Actually, he led a club, which Harkavy ruffed. Harkavy then continued with a fifth round of hearts, forcing declarer to expend his last trump. Declarer made just two more tricks, in diamonds, and went down one.

DEAL 8.

This is a cute deal, featuring an unusual opening bid by East and perfect defense by North–South. The deal arose in the District 11 Regional Championships of 1963 at Columbus, Ohio.

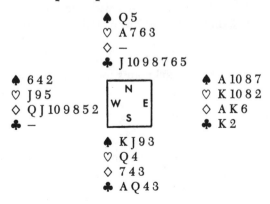

```
                  ♠ Q 5
                  ♡ A 7 6 3
                  ◇ —
                  ♣ J 10 9 8 7 6 5
 ♠ 6 4 2                              ♠ A 10 8 7
 ♡ J 9 5          ┌─────────┐         ♡ K 10 8 2
 ◇ Q J 10 9 8 5 2 │    N    │         ◇ A K 6
 ♣ —             │ W     E │         ♣ K 2
                  │    S    │
                  └─────────┘
                  ♠ K J 9 3
                  ♡ Q 4
                  ◇ 7 4 3
                  ♣ A Q 4 3
```

Neither side vulnerable. East dealer.
The bidding:

East	South	West	North
1 ♣ (!)	Pass	Pass	Pass

By way of explanation for East's opening one club bid: (1) East–West were employing weak no-trumps (12–14 points), so East couldn't open with one no-trump; (2) East–West were not opening four-card major suits, so East couldn't open with one spade or one heart; (3) so he bid one club, for he had heard that no expert player would ever permit his opponent to play a hand at one club, especially in a Regional Open Pair Championship. That he was quite wrong on the latter point is rather obvious. One club was passed out—and declarer very nearly did likewise.

South got off to an inspired diamond lead, which was trumped by North. The return of the queen of spades was ducked by East because he didn't want South in the lead later to give North another diamond ruff. Now North underled his ace of hearts, which East ducked around to dummy's jack, figuring that North was leading away from the queen. South won with the queen and led another diamond. North trumped, laid down the ace of hearts, after which he played another heart, South ruffing.

The third diamond lead from South was trumped by North, and a small spade was led. East knew there were no more diamonds in the South hand, and he also believed that North held the queen, jack, and nine of spades. To salvage a possible trick, he inserted the eight of spades, which South won with the nine. A third spade lead by South was then ruffed by North, and the jack of trumps was led.

The reader can guess the outcome: North–South wound up taking all 13 tricks and scored 350 points for defeating East's one club contract seven tricks!

DEAL 9.

This deal presents a problem in defense at trick two. When it arose in a Philadelphia duplicate game some years ago, our East defender, Charles J. Solomon, came up with the right answer. Let's see if you can do likewise.

♠ Q 8 7 4
♡ J 8 6 5 2
◇ 9 8
♣ Q 5

          ♠ 9 3 2
          ♡ A 9 7 3
          ◇ A 7 3
          ♣ A J 6

North–South vulnerable. East dealer.

East	South	West	North
1 ♣	2 ◇ *	Pass	Pass
Pass			

You are sitting East. Your partner opens the deuce of clubs, the
five is played from dummy, and you put up the jack, which wins
the trick as declarer follows with the four-spot. What do you lead
to trick two?

Actually, you have a blueprint of the club situation. Your partner
held four clubs (he led the deuce as his fourth highest), headed by
the king. Hence, declarer also held four clubs originally. You want
to get a club ruff without permitting a club ruff in dummy. (If a
club is ruffed in dummy, you will be forced to overruff with the ace,
gaining nothing thereby.)

Here are the four hands:

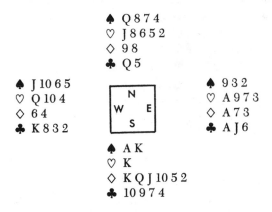

♠ Q 8 7 4
♡ J 8 6 5 2
◇ 9 8
♣ Q 5

♠ J 10 6 5   ♠ 9 3 2
♡ Q 10 4   ♡ A 9 7 3
◇ 6 4   ◇ A 7 3
♣ K 8 3 2   ♣ A J 6

♠ A K
♡ K
◇ K Q J 10 5 2
♣ 10 9 7 4

---

* South's jump overcall of two diamonds is a strong bid, denoting about
seven-plus winning tricks (South was vulnerable).

At trick two, East's proper play is to lead a low trump. Dummy will win this trick and will probably lead the jack of hearts (deceptively) which you will take with your ace. You will now cash your ace of diamonds, removing dummy's last trump, after which you will lead your ace of clubs. Then will come a club to partner's king. When partner now leads a fourth club, you will ruff for the setting trick.

DEAL 10.

To the rubber-bridge kibitzer, it presents a thrill when he sees a defender defeat a small slam contract by a brilliant defensive lead or play. To the duplicate kibitzer, it presents just as much of a thrill when he perceives a brilliant defense which defeats a lowly two club contract. (Or, as in the preceding deal, a two diamond contract.) Here is an illustration of the latter. The defenders were George Rapee and Howard Schenken, sitting East and West respectively.

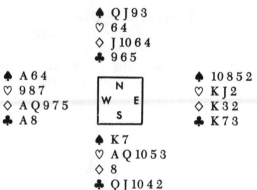

```
              ♠ Q J 9 3
              ♡ 6 4
              ◇ J 10 6 4
              ♣ 9 6 5
♠ A 6 4                      ♠ 10 8 5 2
♡ 9 8 7          N           ♡ K J 2
◇ A Q 9 7 5   W   E          ◇ K 3 2
♣ A 8            S           ♣ K 7 3
              ♠ K 7
              ♡ A Q 10 5 3
              ◇ 8
              ♣ Q J 10 4 2
```

Neither side vulnerable. North dealer.
The bidding:

North	East	South	West
Pass	Pass	1 ♡	Double
Pass	1 ♠	2 ♣	Pass
Pass	Double	Pass	Pass
Pass			

After winning the ace of trumps at trick one, Schenken continued by playing the eight of trumps. Dummy played low, and

Rapee made the first brilliant ducking play. He withheld the king and forced declarer to win the trick in his own hand. (Had Rapee taken his king, South would have tossed the ten-spot and later would have reached the dummy, via the nine-spot, to take a successful heart finesse.)

To trick three, declarer led the king of spades, and now it was Schenken's turn to make the essential holdup play. When he withheld the ace, declarer had no hope of reaching dummy. He next led the ace of hearts, and then continued hearts. East won with the jack of hearts, cashed the king of clubs, and now led a low diamond.

When it was all over, South had lost two clubs, two hearts, one spade, and one diamond, going down one trick, doubled, for a 100-point loss.

CHAPTER **31**

Defenders' Play: The Functioning of the Expert Mind

As Chapter 26 considered "the functioning of the expert mind" from declarer's point of view, this chapter embodies the same theme, but from the viewpoint of the defensive side.

DEAL 1.

This deal arose a long time ago, in the National Mixed Pair Championships of 1939. Its moral was expressed by the South declarer, Lee Hazen of New York City, when he stated: "What a pleasure it was to be able to trust a defender to do the right thing. I had arrived in fast company."

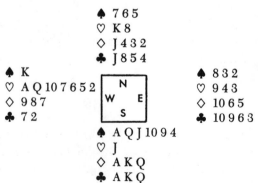

```
                    ♠ 7 6 5
                    ♡ K 8
                    ◇ J 4 3 2
                    ♣ J 8 5 4
♠ K                                    ♠ 8 3 2
♡ A Q 10 7 6 5 2      N               ♡ 9 4 3
◇ 9 8 7           W       E           ◇ 10 6 5
♣ 7 2                    S            ♣ 10 9 6 3
                    ♠ A Q J 10 9 4
                    ♡ J
                    ◇ A K Q
                    ♣ A K Q
```

Both sides vulnerable. West dealer.

466

The bidding:

West	North	East	South
3 ♡	Pass	Pass	4 ♡
Pass	4 NT	Pass	6 ♠
Pass	Pass	Pass	

West, incidentally, was Oswald Jacoby, the world's top-ranking player.

Regarding the bidding, Mr. Hazen stated frankly that his six spade bid was just a shot in the dark, because he could not figure out any way of discovering scientifically whether North had the vital king of spades.

The ace of hearts was opened, followed by another heart, dummy's king winning, with South discarding a diamond. A trump was then led, with declarer having the intention of finessing for the king, when suddenly a thought struck him: Why was Jacoby leading a second round of hearts when he knew darned well that Hazen had but one heart? (Hazen would not have bid a small slam all by himself with two low hearts.)

The only reason, Hazen concluded, could be that Jacoby wanted him to take the trump finesse. So Hazen went up with his ace of trumps, spurning the finesse, and dropped Jacoby's singleton king.

From the defensive viewpoint, Jacoby's lead of the second heart was a brilliant lead. Unfortunately for him, he was playing against Lee Hazen.

This deal, incidentally, is used by many teachers for the testing of the proficiency of would-be students who are registering for an advanced course in bridge. If any one declines to take the trump finesse for the reason given by Mr. Hazen, he is deemed to be "too good" to be taking bridge lessons, and he is not accepted into the class.

DEAL 2.

This deal, which arose in the Pacific Pair Championships of 1952, presents a highly imaginative play by the East defender, Albert Okuneff. We imagine that virtually every player in the world, sitting in the South seat, would have misguessed the actual situation.

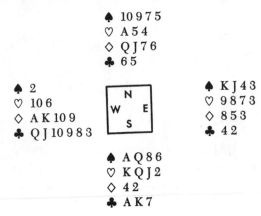

♠ 10 9 7 5
♡ A 5 4
◇ Q J 7 6
♣ 6 5

♠ 2
♡ 10 6
◇ A K 10 9
♣ Q J 10 9 8 3

♠ K J 4 3
♡ 9 8 7 3
◇ 8 5 3
♣ 4 2

♠ A Q 8 6
♡ K Q J 2
◇ 4 2
♣ A K 7

Neither side vulnerable. South dealer.
The bidding:

South	West	North	East
1 ♣	Pass	1 ◇	Pass
1 ♠	Pass	2 ♠	Pass
3 NT	Pass	4 ♠	Pass
Pass	Pass		

The opening lead of the queen of clubs was captured by declarer's ace, after which he played the king of clubs and then another club, which was ruffed in dummy with the ten-spot. Albert Okuneff, East, overruffed this trick with his *king!*

This play firmly established in declarer's mind the fact that West held the jack of trumps, for surely East otherwise would have overruffed with the jack instead of the king.

East returned a diamond, West cashing his ace and king of that suit. He then played another diamond, dummy winning. "Knowing" that West possessed the jack of trumps, declarer then took his ace and queen of trumps, hoping to drop West's (hypothetical) jack. When West showed out on the lead of the queen, declarer belatedly realized that he had been duped.

Had East overtrumped the third club lead with the jack, declarer would have subsequently made the normal play of finessing East for the king.

DEAL 3.

The situation presented in this deal probably would not have developed in a rubber-bridge game, where the safety of the contract is one's prime consideration. But the hand came up in a duplicate game which, as the reader realizes by now, can be a different world.

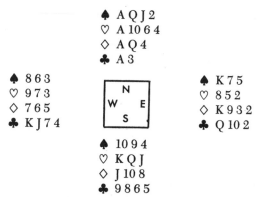

```
              ♠ A Q J 2
              ♡ A 10 6 4
              ◊ A Q 4
              ♣ A 3
♠ 8 6 3                          ♠ K 7 5
♡ 9 7 3          N              ♡ 8 5 2
◊ 7 6 5       W     E           ◊ K 9 3 2
♣ K J 7 4        S              ♣ Q 10 2
              ♠ 10 9 4
              ♡ K Q J
              ◊ J 10 8
              ♣ 9 8 6 5
```

Against South's *three no-trump* contract, West opened the club four, which was captured by East's queen when dummy played low. The ten of clubs was returned and won by dummy's ace.

Declarer came to his own hand via the heart king, after which he tried the spade finesse, losing to East's king. From his partner's opening lead of the four of clubs, East knew that West had started with exactly four clubs ° (the three-spot was in dummy and the deuce in East's hand). Prospects for defeating three no-trump seemed rather slim. So East did not return his deuce of clubs, his purpose being to give declarer the impression that East was out of clubs in order to get declarer to attempt the diamond finesse. East therefore played back a low spade, a "safe" return.

And declarer fell for the bait, reasoning that since East did not return a club he had no more clubs. Declarer won East's spade return with dummy's jack, re-entered his own hand via the heart

° The normal lead against no-trump contracts is the fourth from the highest in one's longest suit. Therefore, since West had led the four-spot, and the two and the three were in evidence, West had to have started with exactly four clubs, since he could have none lower than the four-spot.

queen, and tried the diamond finesse, East's king winning. East *now* returned his "concealed" deuce of clubs, and West cashed two club tricks to defeat declarer.

As is evident, declarer had nine tricks all along but he was led to believe that the try for the overtrick involved no risk. How wrong he was!

DEAL 4.

Here is another deal which might be entitled, "Succumbing to the Lure of a Finesse for the Sake of an Overtrick." For the declarer the ending was a most unhappy one; for the defenders, unbounded joy.

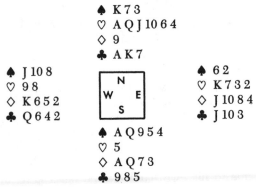

♠ K 7 3
♡ A Q J 10 6 4
◇ 9
♣ A K 7

♠ J 10 8
♡ 9 8
◇ K 6 5 2
♣ Q 6 4 2

♠ 6 2
♡ K 7 3 2
◇ J 10 8 4
♣ J 10 3

♠ A Q 9 5 4
♡ 5
◇ A Q 7 3
♣ 9 8 5

South reached a *six spade* contract, against which West led the club deuce, North's king winning. The king, queen, and ace of trumps were then cashed, after which the five of hearts was led and dummy's queen finessed. East nonchalantly followed with the deuce of hearts!

The ace of hearts was then played, declarer discarding a diamond. On this trick West played the nine of hearts, having played the eight-spot on the previous heart lead.

Declarer was now absolutely convinced that West had started with the K 9 8 of hearts; and, hence, that the king would fall on the next lead of the suit. He confidently led a third heart, East followed with the seven, and declarer ruffed—and West failed to follow suit.

Eventually declarer lost two diamonds and a club, for a two-trick set—and zero match points, which was what he deserved.

To make the contract, all declarer had to do was to lead the jack of hearts at trick seven and "give it away," discarding a club or a diamond. Actually, it would have won the trick, after which it would have been routine to establish the heart suit for discards of declarer's remaining losers.

DEAL 5.

We can't prove it, but we're quite certain that the majority of our nation's experts, had they been sitting South, would have fallen for West's play at trick three and would have lost their contract.

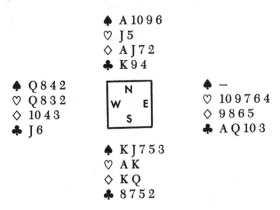

```
                    ♠ A 10 9 6
                    ♡ J 5
                    ◇ A J 7 2
                    ♣ K 9 4
  ♠ Q 8 4 2          ┌─────────┐          ♠ —
  ♡ Q 8 3 2          │   N     │          ♡ 10 9 7 6 4
  ◇ 10 4 3           │ W   E   │          ◇ 9 8 6 5
  ♣ J 6              │   S     │          ♣ A Q 10 3
                     └─────────┘
                    ♠ K J 7 5 3
                    ♡ A K
                    ◇ K Q
                    ♣ 8 7 5 2
```

Both sides vulnerable. South dealer.
The bidding:

South	West	North	East
1 ♠	Pass	3 ♠	Pass
4 ♠	Pass	Pass	Pass

West made an inspired opening lead of the jack of clubs, which was covered by dummy's king and East's ace. Then came the queen of clubs, which won the trick, followed by the ten of clubs. West trumped this trick (although the ten-spot was high) and shifted to a low heart, declarer's king winning.

From declarer's point of view, West's voluntary trumping of East's high ten of clubs seemed to indicate a disinterest in spades—and presumably he would not have trumped if he were concerned with the protection of the spade queen. Hence, it looked as though

West had no interest in spades and that, consequently, he did not have the queen.

And so, when declarer captured West's heart return with the king, he led a low trump to the board's ace—and West now had himself another trump trick.

Of course, South might still have gone down if left to his own resources, by leading a spade to the ace. Nevertheless, a big assist must be given to West for creating the impression that his trump holding was worthless, thereby leading South to conclude that East was the possessor of the spade queen.

Actually, we imagine that if East had discarded a heart or a diamond on the ten of clubs declarer, upon obtaining the lead, would have chosen to lay down the king of trumps on the assumption that since West had only a doubleton club he was more likely to have the queen of spades than was East. And, had this been done, the spade situation would have been revealed (East failing to follow suit), and West would never have made his queen of spades.

DEAL 6.

Permit us to introduce this deal, which is a defensive problem, from the point of view of the South declarer. And, further, let us put you into the South seat for a moment. The bidding has proceeded:

South	West	North	East
1 ♠	2 ♡	3 ◇	Pass
3 ♠	Pass	4 ♠	Pass
Pass	Pass		

West opens the king of hearts, and the dummy is put down:

> ♠ Q 5
> ♡ Q 3
> ◇ Q J 8 7 5 4
> ♣ A J 9
>
> ♠ A J 10 8 7 3 2
> ♡ J 2
> ◇ A 2
> ♣ K 5

After the king of hearts wins, West cashes the ace of hearts. He then leads the nine of spades, and you put up dummy's queen, which wins as East follows with the four-spot. You then lead the board's remaining spade, East plays the six, you finesse the jack—and West wins with the king!

West then returns a heart, which you trump. To make your contract, either you will finesse West for the queen of clubs or get to dummy via the ace of clubs and finesse East for the king of diamonds. You decide to finesse West for the queen of clubs. You lead the king of clubs first, then you play your remaining club and insert dummy's jack. East takes the jack with the queen, plays back a heart, and you eventually go down two tricks since you must still lose a diamond. If it's any consolation, had you taken the diamond finesse instead of the club finesse, that also would have lost and you would be down one trick.

Now let's go back and take it from West's point of view.

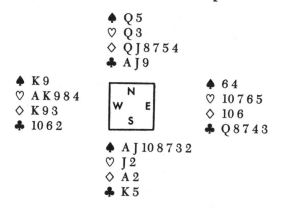

```
              ♠ Q 5
              ♡ Q 3
              ◇ Q J 8 7 5 4
              ♣ A J 9
♠ K 9                          ♠ 6 4
♡ A K 9 8 4      N             ♡ 10 7 6 5
◇ K 9 3        W   E           ◇ 10 6
♣ 10 6 2         S             ♣ Q 8 7 4 3
              ♠ A J 10 8 7 3 2
              ♡ J 2
              ◇ A 2
              ♣ K 5
```

You will note that after West cashed the ace and king of hearts he was end-played. Whether he returned a heart, a diamond, a spade or a club, you would (or could) gain a trick.

But West found a way out by pulling the wool over your eyes. He led the nine of spades! And no one is blaming you for assuming that East had the king of spades and for finessing East for that card. And when West won the second spade lead with his then-singleton king, he was out of the end play. You had been "taken"—and there could be no recovery.

DEAL 7.

This deal came up in the National Men's Pairs Championship of 1955. It depicts some razzle-dazzle defense which had declarer coming and going—and he finally went the way of all flesh.

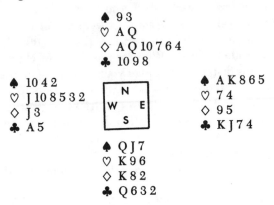

```
                    ♠ 9 3
                    ♡ A Q
                    ◇ A Q 10 7 6 4
                    ♣ 10 9 8
  ♠ 10 4 2                            ♠ A K 8 6 5
  ♡ J 10 8 5 3 2        N            ♡ 7 4
  ◇ J 3            W         E        ◇ 9 5
  ♣ A 5                S             ♣ K J 7 4
                    ♠ Q J 7
                    ♡ K 9 6
                    ◇ K 8 2
                    ♣ Q 6 3 2
```

Neither side vulnerable. North dealer.
The bidding:

North	East	South	West
1 ◇	1 ♠	1 NT	2 ♡
3 ◇	Pass	3 NT	Pass
Pass	Pass		

Sitting East was Edgar Kaplan, and West was Ivan Erdos.

West opened the deuce of spades, which East captured with the *ace* (not the king). He then led the king of clubs and continued with the four of clubs.

Our poor declarer was now in a quandary. It certainly looked as though Kaplan had the ace of clubs, judging by his lead of the king. So South put up the queen of clubs, which was taken by West's ace. West now played another spade, East won with the king and cashed the jack and seven of clubs to hand declarer a two-trick set.

What motivated Kaplan to defend as he did? Well, on the bidding South was marked with the king of hearts. (South had bid three no-trump in the face of West's two heart bid, without knowing that

North held the A Q of hearts. So Kaplan assumed (hoped) that Erdos had the ace of clubs for his free two heart bid. Hence the play of the king of clubs at trick two, which "convinced" declarer that East possessed the ace of clubs.

Deal 8.

That the experts live in a different world can be seen from this deal, which arose in the National Championships of 1953. The West defender was Harry Harkavy and after the play had ended, he stated that he had made a "mistake" in his defense. We are reasonably certain that 99 out of every 100 of our nation's bridge players, if they were asked to find the play that Harkavy called a "mistake," would be unable to do so.

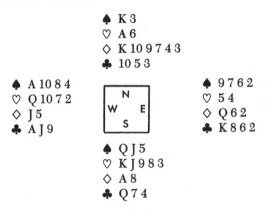

```
                    ♠ K 3
                    ♡ A 6
                    ◇ K 10 9 7 4 3
                    ♣ 10 5 3
    ♠ A 10 8 4                      ♠ 9 7 6 2
    ♡ Q 10 7 2          N           ♡ 5 4
    ◇ J 5            W     E         ◇ Q 6 2
    ♣ A J 9            S            ♣ K 8 6 2
                    ♠ Q J 5
                    ♡ K J 9 8 3
                    ◇ A 8
                    ♣ Q 7 4
```

Both sides vulnerable. South dealer.
The bidding:

South	West	North	East
1 ♡	Pass	2 ◇	Pass
2 ♡	Pass	3 ♡	Pass
3 NT	Pass	Pass	Pass

Harkavy opened the four of spades, which was taken by dummy's king. A low diamond was then led, declarer "finessing" his eight-spot, which lost to West's jack. West now switched to the nine of clubs, taken by East's king, and East returned a spade, West's ace winning. All the defenders could now take was the ace of clubs, and the three no-trump contract was fulfilled. Had East returned a club instead of a spade (when he took the club king), declarer would have gone down.

Harkavy later pointed out that his "mistake" was in not cashing the ace of spades *before* leading the nine of clubs. Had he done so, his partner would have known not to play back a spade but to play back a club. In other words, by cashing the spade ace, he would have eliminated East's guess about which black suit to play back.

DEAL 9.

Here is a deal where the West defender felt that desperation measures were necessary to defeat a slam contract. Having the courage of his convictions, he made a daring opening lead which, as luck would have it, brought about the desired result.

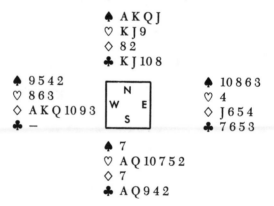

```
            ♠ A K Q J
            ♡ K J 9
            ◇ 8 2
            ♣ K J 10 8
♠ 9 5 4 2                    ♠ 10 8 6 3
♡ 8 6 3          N          ♡ 4
◇ A K Q 10 9 3  W   E       ◇ J 6 5 4
♣ —                S        ♣ 7 6 5 3
            ♠ 7
            ♡ A Q 10 7 5 2
            ◇ 7
            ♣ A Q 9 4 2
```

Both sides vulnerable. West dealer.

West	North	East	South
3 ◇	Double	Pass	4 NT *
Pass	5 ◇	Pass	6 ♡
Pass	Pass	Pass	

Against South's *six heart* contract, Alfred Sheinwold, sitting West, opened the three of diamonds, with the fervent hope that East held the jack of diamonds! East was most amazed when his jack of diamonds won the trick.

* The Blackwood Slam Convention.

Fully realizing that West had made the very risky underlead of the A K Q of diamonds *only for a purpose*, East quickly came upon the reason: West had a void in some side suit—either clubs or spades —and wanted a ruff. Reverting back to the bidding, East found the correct solution.

South had bid the small slam virtually by himself, holding no high cards in either spades or diamonds, and no more than the A Q of hearts. So East deduced that South had to have quality in clubs, and probably also length. East therefore returned a club, which West ruffed for the setting trick.

DEAL 10.

This deal presents a neat deceptive play by a defender. The play stood to gain everything and to lose nothing if the declarer happened to diagnose the situation. The hand arose in the National Championships of 1946.

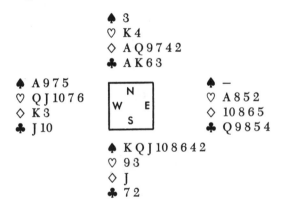

```
              ♠ 3
              ♡ K 4
              ◇ A Q 9 7 4 2
              ♣ A K 6 3
 ♠ A 9 7 5                      ♠ —
 ♡ Q J 10 7 6         N         ♡ A 8 5 2
 ◇ K 3            W       E     ◇ 10 8 6 5
 ♣ J 10              S          ♣ Q 9 8 5 4
              ♠ K Q J 10 8 6 4 2
              ♡ 9 3
              ◇ J
              ♣ 7 2
```

Neither side vulnerable. South dealer.
The bidding:

South	West	North	East
4 ♠	Pass	Pass	Pass

The queen of hearts was opened, covered with the king, and taken by East's ace. A heart was then returned and won by West's ten. Now the jack of clubs was played and captured by dummy's ace, after which the board's singleton spade was led, South's king being taken by West's ace. West then played the ten of clubs, which was won by dummy's king.

Declarer's only problem now was how to get back to his own hand to draw West's remaining trumps. He led the ace of diamonds —and on it West dropped the king! After study, declarer decided to ruff a club. West, of course, overruffed, and declarer was down one.

We are not criticizing declarer for his line of play. He had a 50-50 guess, and he happened to guess wrong. And, after all, the diamond king might well have been a singleton. But if a small diamond had been played instead of the king, declarer would probably have elected to enter his hand by ruffing a diamond.

From West's point of view, the deceptive false card could lose nothing. After East had failed to follow to the first round of trumps, West *knew* that declarer now had nothing left but trumps. That is, West knew that when declarer followed to the ace of diamonds he had started with eight spades, two hearts, two clubs, and one diamond.

CHAPTER 32

Types of Duplicate Games and International Match-Point Scoring

Duplicate bridge is the basis of all forms of competitive bridge play—that is, the identical deals are played by a minimum of four pairs (two tables), thus giving a comparison of results for each pair sitting North–South and each pair sitting East–West.

In this book we have featured that form of duplicate bridge involving a field of permanent North–South pairs playing against a field of permanent East–West pairs. That is, each player had the same partner during the entire game, and each partnership played against pairs sitting in the opposite direction. The specific movement that was used was described in the earlier chapters and is known as the Mitchell movement. In this movement, the North–South pairs sit at their original tables during the entire game, while the East–West players move to the next higher-numbered table at the completion of each round (the boards moving to the next lower-numbered table).

There are other types of movements which are standard, such as the Howell movement, in which each pair moves to a designated position and table at the completion of each round, and each pair plays each of the other pairs. There are no permanent North–South pairs and no permanent East–West pairs. In this type of game there is just one winning pair—the one who scores the greatest number of match points—as contrasted to the Mitchell type of game, where there is a winning North–South pair and a winning East–West pair. For those who might be interested in the technical details of the various types of movements, they are spelled out in detail in *Duplicate Bridge Direction.*

Another highly popular type of duplicate game is the "individual." In this game you change partners at the end of each round, and during the game you play once with each of the other players as your partner, and twice against each of the other players. That is, the perfect individual movement brings you Mr. Smith as your partner one time and as an opponent twice, once on your left and once on your right.

The scoring of an individual game is the same as the scoring of a regular duplicate game: on each board played, you obtain one match point for each pair you and your partner outscore, and one-half match point for each pair you tie. At the conclusion of the game there is just one winner—he who scores the most match points. The precise technical details of the individual game, for those who are interested, are also given in the *Bridge Director's Manual.*

I. The Team-of-Four Game

A reference to this type of game was made in Chapter 26, p. 391. The trend toward team-of-four play has grown stronger during the years, which can be attributed in part to the fact that only eight players are required.

Each participating team plays both sides of the board at some time during the match, one half of the team sitting North–South and, on the replay, the other half of the team sitting East–West. To illustrate how this works, the North–South half of Team A plays against the East–West half of Team B. When the board is replayed, the East–West half of Team A plays the same board against the North–South half of Team B. Thus, the team against team comparison is for the full board, instead of any given direction, as in a duplicate pairs contest. For example, if on Board 7 the North–South half of Team A bids two spades and fulfills that contract with an overtrick for a score of 140 (60 + 30 + 50), while the North–South half of Team B also bids two spades on the same board but makes the contract without the overtrick, for a score of 110, Team A has secured the better result and wins one match. Had the results been identical, say each team made 110, then each team would have secured one-half a match.

During the progress of the game, Team A will play against Team B, Team C, Team D, Team E, etc., while Team B will play against Team A, as well as against Team C, Team D, Team E, etc., the result of each team versus team play being determined in exactly the same manner as when Team A played against Team B. Whichever team wins the greatest number of matches during the game is the winner.

The team-of-four game creates a test of skill superior to any other in duplicate. There can be few complaints of tough breaks and no alibis, since the contesting teams hold exactly the same hands, and the manner in which they are bid and/or played earns a team a win, a loss, or a tie.

There are two forms of team-of-four competition. One is known as *board-a-match* (as discussed in the preceding paragraphs) and the other as *knockout*. In the latter, *two* teams engage in head-to-head competition, and the scoring is either on a cumulative (total point) basis, as in rubber bridge, or by IMPs (International Match Points).

II. Knockout Team-of-Four Play

All knockout team-of-four play involves just two teams at a time, one team playing a specified number of boards against the other. The loser of the match is eliminated. Each winning team plays another winning team, the loser again being eliminated. At the end, there is just one winning team, all the others having been "knocked out."

Up until about 25 years ago, all knockout team-of-four play in the United States used cumulative or total points to determine the winner (as in rubber bridge). That is, if on say Board 4, the North-South half of Team A made a vulnerable small slam in spades against the East-West half of Team B, it scored 1430 points. If, on the replay, the North-South half of Team B also bid the vulnerable small slam in spades, but went down a trick for a loss of 100 points, then Team A gained 1530 points on the deal. If, let us say, 16 boards are played between Team A and Team B, whichever team has scored the greater number of total points on these deals is the winner.

has scored the greater number of total points on these deals is the winner.

This method of total point scoring conforms to the spirit of rubber bridge, but the defect for tournament play is that a big swing on *one* board can nullify good results on *many* other boards. For example, one team can outscore its opposing team by a small margin on *each of 15 boards,* and on the sixteenth and final board it can lose so many points that it loses the entire match.

A glaring example of this defect of total point scoring in knockout team-of-four play can be observed in the following deal, which arose in the Reisinger Knockout Team-of-Four championships of 1963. The Reisinger Championships, by the way, is the only remaining major knockout team-of-four championship which is still decided by total points. All other major knockout team-of-four championships use IMP scoring to determine the winner. This IMP scoring (International Match Points) is a European importation. It is discussed in detail immediately after the presentation of this deal.

East–West vulnerable.
South dealer.

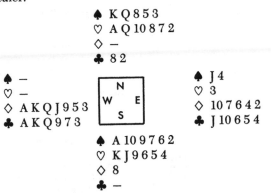

```
                    ♠ K Q 8 5 3
                    ♡ A Q 10 8 7 2
                    ◇ —
                    ♣ 8 2
    ♠ —                             ♠ J 4
    ♡ —                             ♡ 3
    ◇ A K Q J 9 5 3                 ◇ 10 7 6 4 2
    ♣ A K Q 9 7 3                   ♣ J 10 6 5 4
                    ♠ A 10 9 7 6 2
                    ♡ K J 9 6 5 4
                    ◇ 8
                    ♣ —
```

The bidding:

	Table 1.				Table 2.		
S	W	N	E	S	W	N	E
2 ◇ *	7 ◇	P	P	P	2 ◇	2 ♠	3 ◇
7 ♡	Dble	P	P	4 ♣	7 ◇	Dble	P
P				P	P		

* An artificial bid showing spades and hearts.

At Table 1, the North–South team scored 1770 points for fulfilling their doubled seven heart contract. At Table 2, their East–West teammates scored 2330 points for fulfilling their (vulnerable) seven diamond contract. Thus, the winning team gained 4100 points on one deal.

The above deal occurred in the first half of the match. The team which was on the "wrong end" of the deal resigned before the second half of the match was to begin, feeling that they no longer had a chance to win.

It was because of recurring situations such as the above that a new method of scoring knockout matches was developed and is now widely utilized. In a sense, the new method—International Match Point scoring—is a compromise between the total point scoring of rubber bridge and the match-point scoring of duplicate bridge. By IMP scoring, in knockout team-of-four matches, the *difference* in cumulative points on each deal by which one quartet beats another is converted into IMPs by the arbitrary scale given below:

New International Match Point Scale
(Effective September 1, 1962)

Difference in Points	IMP	Difference in Points	IMP
0–10	0		
20–40	1	750–890	13
50–80	2	900–1090	14
90–120	3	1100–1290	15
130–160	4	1300–1490	16
170–210	5	1500–1740	17
220–260	6	1750–1990	18
270–310	7	2000–2240	19
320–360	8	2250–2490	20
370–420	9	2500–2990	21
430–490	10	3000–3490	22
500–590	11	3500–3990	23
600–740	12	4000 and upward	24

To illustrate how this IMP scoring works, suppose that on a given deal Smith and Jones bid and make a nonvulnerable game at three no-trump, scoring 400 points. At the other table, their teammates defeat the three no-trump contract one trick, scoring 50 points. The quartet thus gains 400 points plus 50 points, or 450 points. Employing the above scale, they score 10 IMPs.

What the IMP scale does is to reduce the size of a swing on any one board. This, in turn, can offset a "tragedy" that might have occurred on one board to a team which had played consistently well otherwise, and outplayed its opponents on the majority of boards. In the Reisinger Championships given earlier, for example, where a team lost 4100 points on one deal, they would have lost 24 IMPs had the IMP scale been used. If, on any two succeeding boards, they gained 600–740 points on each of them, they would now be even with their opponents, for they would have recovered 12 IMPs on each of these two boards.

While IMP scoring does not negate completely the element of luck, it does reduce its impact on the final result. That is why it has grown in favor, for it tends to pay greater dividends for *consistently skillful* play.

III. The Approach to IMP Bidding and Play

In Chapter 5, there was discussed the strategy of duplicate (match-point) bidding as compared to rubber-bridge bidding. It was pointed out that all games at duplicate should be bid if one feels that a 50–50 chance of making them exists; whereas in rubber bridge a nonvulnerable game should be bid on a 40 percent chance and a vulnerable game on a 35 percent chance. It was also noted that small slams should be bid on a 50 percent chance of fulfillment in both rubber and duplicate bridge. With regard to grand slams, it was stated that they should be bid more frequently in duplicate bridge than in rubber bridge; in rubber bridge, a 2–1 chance was necessary, while in duplicate a 55–60 percent chance was deemed to be good enough odds.

In part-score bidding, it was emphasized that it was much more vigorous and frequent in duplicate bridge than in rubber bridge, the primary reason being that each deal was equal in importance to each other, in terms of the reward (match points).

With respect to play, it was observed that the fundamental difference between rubber and duplicate bridge was that in rubber bridge the safety of the contract was the sole consideration, while in duplicate play the safety of the contract was often subordinated to the quest for an overtrick.

There is no question in our minds that virtually all match-point players in the United States are completely unfamiliar with the proper techniques of bidding and play when IMP scoring is used. When to stretch for a game, what odds are required to bid small slams and grand slams, whether to take a safety play, how vigorously one should compete for a part score, etc., are subjects which, in our opinion, are unknown areas to even our better match-point players. In general; one might say that the match-point player, playing IMPs, behaves as though he were still playing duplicate bridge. Actually, there is quite a difference between bidding and play at IMP scoring, as compared with bidding and play at match-point scoring.

It is the intent of this chapter to illustrate the differences, and thereby to acquaint the match-point player with the full implications of IMP scoring. He will then be enabled to alter his normal match-point techniques when playing IMPs.

Before getting to the specifics of match-point versus IMP strategy and tactics, one fundamental point must be emphasized: Against whom are you competing in each type of game?

At match points, you are always trying to outscore *each* of the other pairs who will be playing the same deal, for your score is based on how many of the other teams you beat. At IMPs, you are trying to beat just *one team* (at a time).

In duplicate bridge, one usually needs a 60–65 percent game to win. That is, if 10 is top on a board, one needs to average 6–6½ match points on each board. In an IMP team-of-four match, on the other hand, all you have to do to win is to outscore your *one* opponent on each deal, by any margin whatsoever. A 51 percent game to their 49 percent is quite sufficient (if it were possible, a 50.1 percent game to their 49.9 percent would be quite sufficient). Thus, at IMP scoring, since your result is determined by what you do against just one opponent (and what your partners did against their partners), all you have to do to win is to outscore your specific opponent. The necessity for gambling, as in duplicate, becomes unnecessary, unless you happen to be playing against a distinctly superior team. Steady play, plus making fewer mistakes than your opposing team, is all that is required. Generally speaking, conservative, down-the-middle bidding and play yield much higher returns at IMPs than at duplicate (match-point) play.

Let's now get to the specifics.

IV. The Odds on Game and Slam Contracts in IMP Bidding

NOTE WELL: For a full understanding of this section, it is necessary for the reader to refer to the IMP scale presented on p. 483 of this chapter.

A. GAME CONTRACTS

As was stated in Chapter 5, at match-point play one should bid a game if he feels that he has a 50–50 chance of making it. At IMPs, one should bid a *nonvulnerable* game if he feels that he has *almost* a 50 percent chance of fulfillment. A *vulnerable* game, on the other hand, should be bid when one feels that he has approximately a 37 percent chance of making it. Let us see why.

Suppose you are *not vulnerable*, and the bidding has proceeded:

You	Opponent	Partner	Opponent
1 ◇	Pass	1 ♠	Pass
1 NT	Pass	2 NT	Pass
?			

If, on a borderline hand, you choose to bid three no-trump, and you make it, you score 400 points. If you go down a trick, you lose 50 points. If you stop at two no-trump and make just eight tricks, you score 120 points. If you stop at two no-trump and make nine tricks, you score 150 points.

Thus if you bid the game and make it, you gain 250 points (if you had stopped at two no-trump and made three you would have scored 150 points. The difference between 400 and 150 is, of course, 250 points). 250 points are worth 6 IMPs.

However, if you bid three no-trump and go down a trick, you will be losing 170 points (120 which you could have made by passing two no-trump and making it, plus the 50 which the opponents get for defeating you one trick). 170 points are worth 5 IMPs.

So, actually, the odds appear to be approximately 6–5 (57 percent) in your favor for the bidding of close nonvulnerable games. However, on a badly split hand you will get doubled, and in these circumstances you will go down much more often than not. Allowing for this, the long-run odds in your favor are probably nearer to even money than 6–5.

The bidding of close *vulnerable* games brings you much better odds. Referring to the above bidding sequence again, if you bid three no-trump and make it, you will score 600 points. If you go down a trick, you will lose 100 points. If you pass two no-trump and make it, you will score 120 points. If you pass two no-trump and make an extra trick, you will score 150 points.

Thus, if you bid the vulnerable game and make it, you will gain 450 points. (If you had stopped at two no-trump and made three, you would have scored 150 points. The difference between 600 and 150 is 450.) 450 points are worth 10 IMPs.

However, if you bid three no-trump and go down a trick, you will be losing 220 points. (120 which you could have scored by passing two no-trump plus 100 which the opponents would have obtained by defeating you one trick.) 220 points are worth 6 IMPs.

Assuming that close vulnerable games will be made about half the time when you bid them, every time you make a game you win 10 IMPs; every time you go down a trick, you lose 6 IMPs. Hence, if you make these close games 3 times out of 8 (winning 3 and losing 5), you break even in IMPs. Arithmetically, 3 out of 8 is 37½ percent.

With regard to the bidding of close (even-money) small slams, the odds are just about the same at IMP scoring, duplicate bridge, and rubber bridge: a 50 percent chance is good enough odds at each game.

For example, at IMP scoring, if a *nonvulnerable* small slam in spades is bid, one scores 980 points. If, however, the small slam goes down a trick, the loss is 50 points plus the 450 points that would have been scored had we stopped at four or five spades. Thus, the difference between making the slam and going down is 480 points, or 10 IMPs. Putting it another way, if we bid a nonvulnerable small slam in spades and make it, while our opposing team bids only a game in spades and makes two overtricks, we gain 500 points (980 minus 480). 500 points are worth 11 IMPs. But if we had gone down at our small slam contract, our opposing team would have gained 500 points (450 plus 50). They would then have scored 11 IMPs. And so, the bidding of close, nonvulnerable small slams is essentially a 50–50 proposition.

With regard to the bidding of close *vulnerable* small slams, this is the situation:

If one bids a vulnerable small slam in no-trump and makes it, he scores 1440 points. If his opposing team bids only a game in no-trump and makes three overtricks, they score 690 points. The difference is 750 points, or 13 IMPs.

If one bids the vulnerable small slam in no-trump and goes down a trick, he loses 100 points. If his opposing team bids three no-trump and makes two overtricks, they score 660 points. In this case, the "game-bidding" team has gained 760 points, or 13 IMPs. Thus, again, it boils down to a 50–50 proposition; one gains as much as he loses in bidding a close vulnerable slam.

Concerning the bidding of grand slams, the mathematical odds are the same as at match points: about a 55–60 percent chance is considered good enough.

If one bids a nonvulnerable grand slam in diamonds, and makes it, he scores 1440 points. If his opposing team bids only a small slam in diamonds, and makes an overtrick, they score 940 points. The grand slam bidders thus gain 500 points, or 11 IMPs. But if the grand slam bidders go down a trick, the small slam bidders gain 990 points, or 14 IMPs. Thus a team stands to gain 11 IMPs or lose 14 by bidding a 50–50 grand slam, making the odds 14–11 against bidding a nonvulnerable grand slam. 14–11 is about 56 percent against you. Hence, if one chooses to bid a grand slam, he should feel that he has at least a 56 percent chance *in his favor,* to offset the mathematical odds against his bidding of the grand slam.

If vulnerable, a grand slam bid and made in diamonds will net you 2140 points. If your opposing team bids only a small slam in diamonds, and makes an overtrick, they will score 1390 points. In this case you gain 750 points, or 13 IMPs. But if you go down a trick at your grand slam contract, you lose 100 points. Your opposing team, in this situation, gains 1490 points (1390 plus 100), scoring 16 IMPs. If the defeated grand slam had been in spades or no-trump, they would have gained 17 IMPs (1430 or 1460 plus 100, for a score of 1530 or 1560 respectively). Thus the odds against the grand slam bidder are approximately 16.6 * to 13, or 57 percent. Hence, if one elects to contract for a vulnerable grand slam, he should feel that he has at least a 57 percent chance in his favor to offset the mathematical odds against his bidding of the grand slam.

---

* There are five suits, of which three are a major or no-trump. 3 out of 5 is 60 percent or .6.

However, it must be pointed out that in grand slam situations the mathematics presented above can be very misleading in a practical sense. It is quite conceivable that on a deal where you have visions of a grand slam, your opposing team may not even have thoughts of a small slam! It has happened time and again that a team bids a grand slam and goes down, while on the replay the opposing team arrives at a mere game. In this case, the loss incurred in bidding the grand slam can be staggering. To illustrate:

Suppose you bid a vulnerable grand slam in hearts and go down a trick, while your opponents stop at a game on the replay. Your team has just lost 780 points (680 + 100), or 13 IMPs. If you had stopped at a small slam and fulfilled it, you would have scored 1430 points, thereby gaining 750 points. Your team would now have won 13 IMPs. Thus a "swing" of 26 IMPs is involved. Had you fulfilled your grand slam contract, you would have scored 2210 points, defeating your opponents by 1530 points. In this latter case, your team would have scored 17 IMPs (instead of 13 which would have been scored by fulfilling a six heart contract). Thus by making the grand slam you gain but 4 additional IMPs if you make it when they bid only a game. And if you happen to go down, your loss is 26 IMPs (13 which you could have made by stopping at a small slam, and 13 which they will get for being plus 780 points on the board).

V. Competing for Part-Scores

At IMP scoring, competitive part-score bidding is much more akin to match-point than to rubber bridge. That is, one must compete for a partial much more vigorously at IMPs than at rubber bridge but perhaps not quite as vigorously as at match-point play. If maximum results are to be obtained at IMPs, one must do a lot of "protective" bidding or "balancing." One must go out of his way to prevent an opponent from purchasing a contract at the one or two level. For example, if you allow an opponent to purchase the contract at two hearts when you can make two spades, a swing of 6 IMPs is involved: 3 IMPs which you could have scored at two spades (plus 110) as contrasted to the 3 IMPs which they will secure at two hearts (plus 110). And if it turns out that in bidding two spades you push them to three hearts, which goes down a trick (not vulnerable), you will be gaining 5 IMPs: they lose the 3 IMPS which they would have secured for making two hearts; and you win 2 IMPs for being plus 50. Three or four swings like the above more often than not will be the difference between winning or losing the match.

Generally speaking, duplicate bridge players have learned not to sell out at the one or two level when the opening side has passed out at these levels. Certainly the readers of this book realize that few match points are secured by permitting the opening side to purchase one or two level contracts without opposition. But where the "unknowing" match-point players will tend to go wrong is in competing up at the three-level. At this level there is a major difference in strategy and tactics between match-point bidding and IMP bidding.

The key to IMP bidding is to think about obtaining *any* plus score on part-score hands at the three-level, as opposed to concentrating on how big a plus score or how small a minus score one can secure. Let us see why.

Suppose the bidding has gone, with the opponents being vulnerable:

Opponent	Partner	Opponent	You
1 ♡	1 ♠	2 ♡	2 ♠
3 ♡	Pass	Pass	?

You hold:

♠ K x x x
♡ A x x
◇ Q 10 x
♣ x x x

Frankly, it is a pure guess as to whether you can make three spades. And it is just as much of a guess as to whether they can make three hearts.

At match points, you might well consider bidding three spades, on the perhaps 50–50 chance that it will make, for an excellent score. Even if you happen to go down a trick, doubled or undoubled, you will still get a good score for being minus 100 or 50, *if* they could have made three hearts. But at IMP scoring you should *pass* for the following reasons.

If you can make three spades, the probability with your flat hand is that they can't make three hearts. So whether you're plus 140 or plus 100 is a matter of only 1 IMP: plus 140 gives you 4 IMPs; plus 100 (for their going down) gives you 3 IMPs.

If they can make three hearts and are permitted to play it there, they will get 4 IMPs (plus 140). If they can make their contract you probably can't make yours, so if you bid three spades and go down a trick, doubled, they will get 100 points, worth 3 IMPs. So again, whether you're minus 140 or 100, the difference is only 1 IMP.

But if both three spades and three hearts are doomed to go down —not at all unlikely in view of your flat hand and the fact that each side figures to hold about half the deck in high cards, the swing can be 5 or 6 IMPs. That is, if you bid three spades and go down 100 points, they get 3 IMPs; if you go down 50, they get 2 IMPs. But if they play the hand at three hearts and go down, you get 3 IMPs (plus 100 points).

Had you held an unbalanced type of hand, it could easily be that both three spades and three hearts would be makable contracts, in which case it would pay you to bid, for you might then gain 8 IMPs: 4 IMPs for being plus 140 at three spades instead of 4 IMPs which they would get for being plus 140 at three hearts. But, again, with your flat hand and a partnership holding of half the high cards possessed by each side, there is no valid reason for assuming both contracts are makable.

Thus, in borderline part-score situations, when uncertainty exists as to which side figures to make its contract, don't swing for the maximum score if there appears to be a decent chance of beating them at their contract. Orient yourself to thinking in terms of "What's my best chance of getting *any* plus score?" Being more specific, fight vigorously for the maximum plus score through the two-level—and then readjust your sights to *any* plus score at the three-level.

VI. Sacrifice Bidding

As was stated in Chapter 5, our position on sacrifice bidding at match points is that it is always a hazardous venture, since its successful employment depends on one's accurate diagnosis as to whether the opponents can surely fulfill their game or slam. Since one seldom can be sure, sacrifice bidding is usually a pure gamble. Nevertheless, sacrificing can be very rewarding at match-point play —and a major victory is attained if your sacrifice costs 300 points instead of allowing the opponents to score 400 points for three no-trump bid and made; or if your sacrifice loses 500 points when the opponents could have scored 620 for four hearts bid and made.

But at IMPs the approach to sacrifice bidding has risk versus gain aspects which require some explanation. At IMPs, a successful nonvulnerable sacrifice costing 300 points to prevent the nonvulnerable opponents from making 400 (three no-trump) nets you a profit of 100 points, which are worth 3 IMPs. Thus, if your partners are permitted to play at three no-trump, and make that contract, your team has gained 3 IMPs.

But if three no-trump is unmakable, your partners will now be minus 50, while you will be minus 300. The opponents therefore gain 350 points, worth 8 IMPs. In this case, had you not sacrificed, your adversaries would be down one trick, and the board would be a standoff. Certainly, in this case, if the issue of whether or not to take a sacrifice was a moot question, it was a bad investment in terms of profit and loss.

When both sides are vulnerable, a close sacrifice is even a poorer investment. For example, if you go down 500 points to prevent the opponents from making a four heart contract worth 620 points, while your partners are permitted to play four hearts, your team has gained 120 points, worth 3 IMPs. But if four hearts is unmakable, you lose 500 points and your partners lose 100, giving the opponents a score of 600 points, or 12 IMPs. So your sacrifice gains 3 IMPs if the four heart contract is makable, and it loses 12 IMPs if it is unmakable. Therefore, as a business proposition, before you make a sacrifice bid, you had better be pretty certain that the opponents can make their contract.

When sacrificing against slam contracts, the IMP situation is just about the same as at match points: it *appears* to be more promising than sacrificing against game contracts. But the rub is that the slam may not be bid by your partners, or they may bid it and go down, in which case you lose a staggering amount of points. To illustrate:

Suppose the opponents get to a vulnerable small slam in spades (worth 1430 points) and you decide to sacrifice at seven clubs, going down 5 tricks for a loss of 1100 points. Should your partners bid and make six spades, your team has gained 330 points, or 8 IMPs.

But what if your partners bid only a game, scoring 680 points. In this case your side has lost 420 points (1100 minus 680), for a loss of 9 IMPs. Or suppose your partners bid the small slam in spades and go down! Now the opponents are plus 1200 (1100 plus 100) and they score 15 IMPs.

If the opponents bid the slam, which is makable, and you do not sacrifice, they will score 1430 points. If your partners bid only a game, scoring 680, your team will lose 750 points, worth 13 IMPs. If, in this situation, you had sacrificed losing 1100 points, the opponents would have gained 420 points, (1100 minus 680), worth 9 IMPs. You gain, therefore, only 4 IMPs by your sacrifice.

VII. Penalty Doubles

In match-point play, you do not double the opponents unless you consider your cards are worth a plus score on their own merit— that is, you do not double unless you feel that your side possesses the better cards and the opponents are trying to deprive you of your rightful heritage. If, on the other hand, the opponents seem to be overbidding with better cards, there is no need to double, for if they go down at an overambitious contract, you will obtain a good result without doubling.

At IMPs, the position is just about the same as at match-point play: you don't double unless you feel that the opponents are trying to "steal" with inferior cards. For example, suppose the nonvulnerable opponents have wended their way up to four spades on a shaky auction. You are reasonably certain that they will go down a trick. You do not double, as you might very well do in rubber bridge in the hope of beating them two tricks. You just pass at IMPs. Let us see why.

If you double and beat them a trick, you score 100 points instead of 50. If the contract was a bad one, presumably your partners stopped at two or three spades, scoring 140. So you score, by your double, 240 points instead of the 190 you would have received without the double. This is a matter of 1 IMP—the difference between scoring 5 IMPs (190) or 6 IMPs (240).

But suppose the opponents have not overbid. Now your double gives them a score of 590 for making four spades. Assuming that your partners arrived at the same contract (they bid it confidently), undoubled, scoring 420 points. Thus the opponents gain 170 points, or 5 IMPs. What price double?

And what could be most costly would be if your double guides them to the proper way of playing the hand. Now they fulfill an otherwise unmakable contract, at which your partners go down because of no "helpful" double. Your opponents score 590 points, while your partners are minus 50, a swing of 640 points or 12 IMPs.

Generally speaking, in virtually all doubling situations, it is the conservative player rather than the aggressive doubler who comes out ahead, due to the fact that the odds favor the coward and not the "brave" hero. So don't try to get rich in a hurry—in all borderline situations go for the *surest, not the greatest,* plus score.

VIII. The Play at IMPs

Probably the most important difference between *play* at match points and at IMPs is the relative insignificance of small swings, like an overtrick, or playing a hand in no-trump rather than in spades, hearts, diamonds, or clubs. For example, if you play a hand at two diamonds in match-point play when you could have made two spades, you figure to get a poor result for scoring 90 rather than 110. But at IMPs, if you make two diamonds, scoring 90 points, while the opposing team, holding your cards, bids two spades, scoring 110 points, the difference of 20 points results in the loss of only one IMP. Similarly, if you score 110 points by making two hearts while your opposing team scores 120 points for making two no-trump, you have lost nothing, since a 10-point swing is zero IMPs.

Further, if you make a vulnerable game in a spade contract, scoring 620 points, while the opposing team makes a game in no-trump on the same cards, scoring 600 points, your side has gained 20 points, or one IMP, again an insignificant amount. And if they happen to make an overtrick, giving them 630 points to your 620, the result would be a tie. As is apparent, playing in a "superior" match-point contract is of little significance at IMP play, and if the "superior" match-point contract is a slight gamble and happens to go down, the loss, if vulnerable, will be 12 IMPs if the opposing side fulfills the safer game contract. So, as at rubber bridge, one looks for the *safest* part-score or game.

In the play, you adopt the rubber-bridge attitude of playing to fulfill your contract. At IMP scoring, safety plays are always sought for, in both game and part-score contracts. If, for example, you are in a two heart contract and go down a trick because you gambled for an overtrick, you will lose 50 points instead of scoring 110. If against your partners the opponents played safe and made two hearts, their team gains 160 points, or 4 IMPs. Had you made the overtrick in your gamble, you would have scored 140 to the opponents' 110, gaining 30 points—and thus winning 1 IMP.

Here is another example of why one doesn't play for overtricks at IMPs if in so playing he jeopardizes his contract:

♠ 9 6 3
♡ A K Q 6 5 2
◇ 7 5
♣ 8 4

♠ Q 10 5 2
♡ 7 4
◇ A K 6
♣ A K 7 2

Against South's vulnerable *three no-trump* contract West opens the club queen, which you win with the king. Although the five adverse hearts figure to be divided 3-2 (68 percent of the time), in which case ten tricks are makable by winning six hearts, two diamonds, and two clubs, this line of playing should not be adopted when playing IMPs. (At match points the maximum play would be adopted, for your aim is to outscore each of the other teams.) If you happen to run into a 4-1 heart break (28 percent of the time), you will go down two tricks, for a loss of 200 points. If, instead of playing for the overtrick, you lead a low heart at trick two and give it away, you will make your contract whether the adverse hearts divide 3-2 or 4-1.

Let's suppose that when the board is replayed against your partners, the opponents employ the safety play of giving away the first heart. They will then score 600 points for three no-trump bid and made. If you, in playing for the overtrick, run into a 4-1 heart break, you will be down two tricks, for a loss of 200 points. The opponents will, in this situation, be gaining 800 points, or 13 IMPs. If, in playing wide open for the overtrick (the presumed 3-2 heart division), you do make it, you will score 630 points to the opponents' 600. You will thereby gain 1 IMP. Surely, to jeopardize 12 IMPs (600 points) to gain 1 IMP on the assumption that the hearts figure to break 3-2 (68 percent) rather than 4-1 (28 percent) is bad mathematics, bad business—and bad IMP judgment.

And so, with the relative unimportance of overtricks, not only the declarer's play but also the defenders' play becomes simpler. At match-point play, as was illustrated in an earlier chapter, one is never absolutely certain as to whether to play to prevent declarer from making his contract, or whether one should concede the contract and prevent declarer from making what might well be an all-important overtrick. At IMP play the objective is *always to defeat the contract* (as in rubber bridge), and never to prevent an overtrick or two. So what if he makes an overtrick—he will gain, at most, 1 IMP. But if you defeat even a lowly two club contract, you have gained the equivalent of 4 IMPs (plus 50 instead of minus 90, a swing of 140 points).

In conclusion with respect to the play, never give even a passing thought to swings of one or two IMPs. Ignore them in your bidding, your play as declarer, and your play as a defender. Of course, if you can make an overtrick without jeopardizing your contract, or can prevent declarer from making an overtrick without giving up your chances of defeating his contract, then by all means do so. It's always preferable for you to have an extra IMP or two rather than the opponents. This is extra interest on a principal. But never forget that your paramount concern is the safeguarding of the principal: the making of your contract or the setting of the opponents' contract.

This, then, has been an introduction to IMP bidding and play in team-of-four matches. It is, admittedly, a new world, but one must learn to adjust or perish by the wayside. We trust our presentation will serve as an aid to a healthy and prosperous survival.

50 OTHER
HIGHLY-RECOMMENDED TITLES

**CALL TOLL FREE 1-800-274-2221
IN THE U.S. & CANADA TO ORDER ANY OF
THEM OR TO REQUEST OUR
FULL-COLOR 64 PAGE CATALOG OF
ALL BRIDGE BOOKS IN PRINT,
SUPPLIES AND GIFTS.**

DEFENSE
#0520 Blackwood-Complete Book of Opening Leads 12.95
#3030 Ewen-Opening Leads 12.95
#0104 Stewart-Baron-The Bridge Book 4 .... 7.95
#5948 Stewart-The Bridge Player's
     Comprehensive Guide to Defense 12.95
#0631 Lawrence-Dynamic Defense 9.95
#1200 Woolsey-Modern Defensive Signalling 4.95

FOR INTERMEDIATE PLAYERS
#2120 Kantar-Complete Defensive Bridge 15.00
#3015 Root-Commonsense Bidding 14.00
#0630 Lawrence-Card Combinations 9.95
#0102 Stewart-Baron-The Bridge Book 2 .... 7.95
#1102 Silverman-Intermediate Bridge Five
     Card Major Student Text 2.95
#0575 Lampert-The Fun Way to Advanced Bridge 8.95
#0633 Lawrence-How to Read Your Opponents' Cards 8.95
#3672 Truscott-Bid Better, Play Better 8.95
#1765 Lawrence-Judgment at Bridge 8.95

PLAY OF THE HAND
#2150 Kantar-Test your Bridge Play, Vol. 1 .... 7.00
#3675 Watson-Watson's Classic Book on
     the Play of the Hand 9.95
#1932 Mollo-Gardener-Card Play Technique 9.95
#3008 Root-How to Play a Bridge Hand 21.95
#1104 Silverman-Play of the Hand as
     Declarer and Defender 2.95
#2175 Truscott-Winning Declarer Play 7.00
#3803 Sydnor-Bridge Made Easy Book 3 .... 5.00

CONVENTIONS
#2115 Kantar-Bridge Conventions 7.00
#0610 Kearse-Bridge Conventions Complete 24.95
#3011 Root-Pavlicek-Modern Bridge Conventions 14.00
#0240 Championship Bridge Series (All 36) 25.95

DUPLICATE STRATEGY
#1600 Klinger-50 Winning Duplicate Tips 11.95
#2260 Sheinwold-Duplicate Bridge 3.95
#1103 Silverman-Advanced and Duplicate
     Bridge Student Text 2.95

DEVYN PRESS, INC.
3600 Chamberlain Lane, Suite 230, Louisville, KY 40241